ISBN 978-0-483-01997-3
PIBN 10254029

GEORGE LAWRENCE DAY

Congressional Medal of Honor

SECRETARY'S SEVENTH REPORT

HARVARD COLLEGE

CLASS OF

1893

348908
5. 4. 3s.

CAMBRIDGE .·. PRINTED FOR THE CLASS
CRIMSON PRINTING COMPANY
1923

Class Organization

President

GEORGE RICHMOND FEARING. JR.

Secretary

SAMUEL FRANCIS BATCHELDER

720 TREMONT BUILDING. BOSTON

Treasurer

HENRY WARE

53 STATE STREET, BOSTON

Class Committee

GEORGE RICHMOND FEARING. JR.

CHARLES KIMBALL CUMMINGS

HENRY WARE

Cambridge, Mass.,

10 May 1923

Dear Mr. Fearing:

I hope the Class of '93 will have a very
enjoyable celebration of their thirtieth anniversary.
The Class contained an unusual number of men who have
become distinguished in science, letters, teaching, and
various kinds of public service.   If those men are
made to stand up and say something, the Class will be
amused at the extraordinary variety of their opinions,
modes of thought, and fields of service.   I hope that
the Class Secretary will avail himself of the opportunity
to complete his records about the number of marriages in
the Class and the number of children resulting from those
marriages.

I regret that I am preparing to leave
Cambridge for Mount Desert before the 17th of June; so
that I shall miss the afternoon tea to which you invite
me.

Sincerely yours

Charles W. Eliot

Table of Contents

Vital Statistics

Total number of names in this report - - -	451
Of whom there are deceased - - - -	110
Names on present mailing list - - - -	341
Total number of unmarried men - - - -	97
Total number of married men - - - -	354
	451
Families with no children - - - -	86
Families with one child - - - - -	65
Families with two children - - - -	77
Families with three children - - - -	57
Families with four children - - -	38
Families with five children - - - -	19
Families with six children - - - . -	5
Families with seven children - - - -	1
Families with eight children - - - -	4
Families with nine children - - - -	0
Families with ten children - - - -	1
Total number of boys - - - - -	391
Total number of girls - - - - -	326
	717
Pairs of twins - - - - - -	6
Number of second marriages - -	30

'93

THE CLASS LIST

This list contains every name (so far as ascertainable) ever associated with the Class, all thrown into one alphabetical order. The names in SMALL CAPITALS are those of men who entered with the class in 1889 and received the A.B. in 1893. In all other cases the relation to the class is given below the name.

Many men who did not receive the A.B. in 1893 have requested that their names be removed from the list, usually because they were already associated with some other class. A few such men, who had never been heard from since leaving college, when finally located by the Secretary have not felt sufficient interest in '93 even to answer a duly received registered letter enclosing a post-card for reply. The Secretary has taken it upon himself to remove these names also from the active list. All names removed are indicated by brackets, and the reasons given.

In the Supplement to the Sixth Report the Secretary promised "a new and improved list;" but after numerous experiments has decided that the present is the only form capable of giving all the facts without the use of confusing symbols and reference-marks.

ERNEST HAMLIN ABBOTT

*Alvin Adams   *1902
    Scientific, 1889-1892.

*Walter Sawyer Adams   *1915
    A.B. 1895, as of 1893.

[Cyrus Adler]
    Special 1889-90. Does not reply to letters.

George Henry Alden
    1 Grad. 1892-93. A.B. 1893.

*JOHN ALDEN   *1914

[Cyrus Willis Alger]
    Withdraws. Special 1889-90. Affiliates with '91. (See their reports).

Class of 1893

FREEMAN ALLEN
WILLIAM HENRY ALLISON
[Lee Earll Emidon]
    Withdraws. (Sophomore year only. A.B. Univ. of Mich. 1892. A.M. Harv. 1898).
*FRED HOWES ANDERSON   *1893
[Cipriano Andrade, Jr.]
    Withdraws. (A.B. 1892. See their reports).
ALBERT STOKES APSEY
PERCY LEE ATHERTON
WALTER AYER
Henry Berthier Bacon
    Special, 1889-90.
WILLIS ADAMS BAILEY
*Morris Baker   *1912
    Special Scientific, 1889-93.
*WALTER FARNSWORTH BAKER   *1907
WILLIAM FRANCIS BAKER
*COLUMBUS CALVERT BALDWIN   *1899
*JOHN DENISON BALDWIN   *1913
SIDNEY MILLER BALLOU
Edgar James Banks
    Special, 1890-91. With '94, 1891-93. A.B. 1893.
Charles Russell Bardeen
    Special, 1889-90. Joined class Sophomore year.
CHARLES LOWELL BARLOW
Edward Mitchell Barney
    Freshman year only.
[Walter Lewis Barrell]
    Senior year only. Does not reply. (See reports of '90).
*Edwin Bartlett Bartlett   *1918
    Left after Sophomore year.
Murray [Augustus] Bartlett
    A.B. 1892.
LEWIS BASS, JR.
SAMUEL FRANCIS BATCHELDER
*Harold Munro Battelle   *1892
[Charles Sidney Baxter]
    Withdraws. Special, 1889-92. Joined '93 Senior year. A.B. 1893, as of 1892. (See reports of '92).
WILLIAM FIELDS BEAL

GORDON KNOX BELL

Francis Gano Benedict
> Special 1889-92.   Joined class Senior year.

Edward Mellen Bennett
> Entered with '94.   Joined '93 Junior year.

Guy Brown Bennett
> Special, 1889-92.   Joined class Senior year.

Ralph Wilhelm [Alexis] Bergengren
> Special, 1889-91.   Joined class Junior year.

HENRY NEWHALL BERRY
[Shaler Berry]
> Special Scientific, 1889-90.   Regular Scientific, 1890-93.
> S.B. 1893.   Affiliates with '92.   (See their reports).

*EDGAR FRANCIS BILLINGS   *1913

Rudolph Michael Binder [*formerly* Michael Binder]
> Freshman, 1891-92. . Senior, 1892-93.   A.B. 1893.

*RALPH BISBEE   *1913

DEXTER BLAGDEN

CHARLES ARTHUR BLAKE

FRANCIS STANTON BLAKE

HENRY FORDYCE BLAKE
[Henry Spring Blake]
> Special, 1889-90   Withdraws.

*David Blaustein   *1912
> Special, 1889-93.

William Miller Booth
> Special, 1890-91.   Scientific, 1892-93.   S.B. 1893.

[Mortimer Simon Borg]
> Freshman year only.   Afterwards ''hopelessly afflicted with
> mental troubles.''

[Lewis Gerard Borgmeyer]
> Special, 1889-90.   Does not reply to letters.

AUGUSTUS JESSE BOWIE, JR.

*ROBERT PENDLETON BOWLER   *1919

*RALPH HARTT BOWLES   *1919

GEORGE HALE BRABROOK

[Francis Burke Brandt]
> Withdraws.   A.B. 1892.   (See their reports).

CALVERT BREWER

*Stewart Meily Brice   *1910
> Freshman year only.   Joined '94.

Class of 1893

Henry Morgan Brookfield
> Entered Sophomore, 1891-92. Senior, 1892-93.

ARTHUR NICHOLSON BROUGHTON

[Albert Frederick Brown]
> Withdraws. (Special Scientific, 1889-90. S.B. 1890).

Philip Turner Brown
> A.B. 1895, as of 1893.

Royal Benton [*formerly* Charles] Brown
> Special, 1889-91.

ARTHUR TABER BROWNE

[George Wright Buckley]
> Withdraws. (Special, 1889-90).

James Abercrombie Burden, Jr.
> Special, 1889-91. With '95, 1891-92. Joined '93 Senior year.

Charles Roland Burger
> 1 Grad. School 1892-93. A.B. 1893.

*GEORGE EBENEZER BURGESS   *1902

[Lewis Alexander Burgess]
> Sophomore year only. Never located since leaving College.

*ERNEST GISBORNE BURKE   *1903

Percy Fletcher Burrows
> Entered Sophomore.

Edward Angus Burt
> Entered Junior.

CHARLES SHOREY BUTLER

Howard Fulton Butler
> A.B. 1892.

*Guy Stevens Callender   *1915
> Grad. School, 1892-1900. A.B. 1894, as of 1893.

PATRICK THOMAS CAMPBELL

[Walter Stanley Campbell]
> Withdraws. Special, 1889-91. With '92, 1891-92. 2 Law,
> 1892-93. (A.B. 1892. See their reports).

*Everett Pascoe Carey   *1923
> Senior year only.

[Andrew Carnegie, 2d.]
> Special, 1889-90. Left College in February of Freshman
> year. Does not reply to letters.

*EDWARD HEMAN CARPENTER   *1915

Frederick Jay Carr
> Special, 1889-90. With '93 Sophomore year only.

*Joseph William Carr   *1909
    Entered with '94· Joined '93 Senior year. (See reports
    of '94).

[*Raymond Wilbur Carr]   *1911
    Left college March 4, 1890.

Lewis Clinton Carson
    1 Grad. School, 1892-93. A.B. 1894, as of 1893.

WALTER CARY

William Ernest Castle
    Entered Senior.

[*George Frederick Cavanagh]   *1892
    Special, 1889-90.

*Charles Samuel Chase   *1919
    Freshman year only.

CLIFFORD HOFFMAN CHASE

*SAMUEL CHEW   *1919
*Donald Churchill   *1909
    A.B. 1894, as of 1893.

Paul Clagstone
    Entered with '91· Joined '93 Sophomore year.

William Anthony Clark
    Entered Junior, 1890-91. Joined '93, 1892-93.

[Winslow Clark]
    Withdraws. (Special, 1889-92. See reports of '92).

ALBERT SIDNEY GREGG CLARKE

Henry Livingston Coar
    Grad. School and Instr., 1892-95. A.B. 1893.

ALEXANDER LYNDE COCHRANE

JOHN IRA COCHRANE

[*Louis Adolph Coerne]   *1922
    Withdraws. Special, 1888-90. Affiliated with '92· · (See
    their reports).

*EDWARD RUSSELL COFFIN   *1907
GILMAN COLLAMORE

Christopher Walter Collier
    Senior year only.

[George Foster Collier]
    Withdraws. S.B. (Ohio Wes.) 1892. Entered Senior.
    Grad. School 1893-95. A.B. 1894. (See reports of '94).

JOHN LAWRENCE SARSFIELD CONNOLLY

ARTHUR CLIFTON CONRO

Class of 1893

FREDERICK SHEPHERD CONVERSE
[William Knapp Converse]
> Special, 1889-90. Does not reply to letters.

CHARLES EMERSON COOK
George Cram Cook
> Senior year only.

HOWARD HAMBLET COOK

*Irving Jabez Cook   *1908
> Freshman year only.

Louis Craig Cornish
> Special, 1889-91 and 1892-93.

James [Ambrose] Coppinger Cotter
> Special, 1889-91. Joined class Junior year.

*William Norman Cottrell   *1916
> Entered Junior.

*Alfred Frazer Coulter   *1903
> Freshman year only. With '94, 1890-91. 1 Law School, 1892-93.

[*Wilfred Wesley Cressy]   *1900
> Entered Sophomore. Joined '92, 1891-92. A.B. 1892. (See their reports).

John Fergus Crosby
> Sophomore year only.

[John Henry Crowley]
> Junior year only. A.B. 1893 as of 1892. (See reports of '92).

Edward Conway [Charles] Cullinan
> Left after Sophomore year.

CHARLES KIMBALL CUMMINGS
FRANK JOSSLYN CURRIER
GEORGE DE CLYVER CURTIS

*WALTER HOWARD CUSHING   *1921
[Frederick Lewis Dabney]
> Withdraws. Freshman 1889-90. A.B. 1891. (See their reports.)

FREDERICK WILLIAM DALLINGER

*Edward Crosby Darling   *1922
> Entered Sophomore.

Bradley Moore Davis
> Grad. School, 1892-95. A.B. 1893.

PHILIP WHITNEY DAVIS

SAMUEL CRAFT DAVIS
William Horace Davis
   Entered Sophomore.
*George Lawrence Day   *1921
   Special, 1889-90. Left college Feb. 27, 1890.
Jasper Newton Deahl
   Special 1891-92. Joined class Senior year.
*AMBROSE COLLYER DEARBORN   *1920
[Luther Marion Defoe]
   Senior year only. Does not reply to letters.
[William] Hartley Dennett
   1 Grad. 1892-93. A.B. 1893.
*Clarence Bigelow Denny   *1920
   With '93 1889-90. With '94, 1890-91.
CHARLES LUNT DeNORMANDIE
Louis Lee Dent
   Entered Junior A.B. 1894, as of 1893.
Louis Eugene Desbecker
   A.B. 1892.
Bradford Colt de Wolf
   Special, 1889-91.
*Arthur Wyman Dexter   *1915
   Special, 1889-90.
ALBERT JAMES DIBBLEE
Joseph Phillips Dimmick
   Entered Sophomore.
*Silas Dinsmoor   *1921
   Senior year only.
[William Brown Dinsmore]
   A.B. 1893. Withdraws for private reasons.
ROBERT GRAY DODGE
Hugh Dodson
   Special 1889-91.
[*Henry Waldo Doe]   *1905
   With '93, 1889-90. With '94, 1890-91. (See Report IV.).
*JOHN JOSEPH DOLAN   *1919
Charles Thurston Dole
   Special, 1889-92.
WALTER CAZENOVE DOUGLAS, JR.
HENRY ABIJAH THOMPSON DOW

Class of 1893

*Charles William Downing   *1908
    Senior year only.

Tracy Dows
    1889-91, Special. 1892, with '95. 1893, with '96. **1894,**
    1 Law. A.B. 1894.

William Duane
    Senior year only

DIVIE BETHUNE DUFFIELD

Morrill Dunn
    Freshman year only. Joined '94.

DANIEL OSBORN EARLE

HORACE AINSWORTH EATON

John Edgar Eaton
    Senior year only.

John Waldo Eichinger
    Entered Junior.

SAMUEL WALKER ELLSWORTH

Samuel Dean Elmore
    Special, 1889-92. Joined class Senior year.

Guy Thorpe Emerson
    Freshman year only. Joined '94.

Robert [Griswold] Emmet
    Special, 1889-91. Joined class Junior year. A.B. 1897,
    as of 1893.

[*James Biddle Eustis, Jr.]   *1915
    Withdraws. Special, 1889-90. Joined '94. (See their re-
    ports).

Maurice Henry Ewer
    A.B. 1892.

[Charles Nelson Fairchild]
    Special, 1889-94. Does not reply to letters.

Clarence Rudolph Falk
    Special, 1889-91. Joined class Junior year.

Frank Edgar Farley
    Special, 1889-90. Joined class Sophomore year.

WILLIAM OLIVER FARNSWORTH

ROBERT DAVID FARQUHAR

SIDNEY EMERSON FARWELL

Alfred Chase Fay
    Joined Junior year, from '92.

HARRISON GILBERT FAY

GEORGE RICHMOND FEARING

James Henry Fennessy
Special, 1889-91. Law School, 1891-94.

Otis Daniell Fisk
1st. year Scientific, 1889-90. Joined '94·

CHARLES HENRY FISKE, JR.

Austin Bradstreet Fletcher
Special, 1889-91. Scientific School, 1891-93. S.B. 1893.

[Edward Francis Flint]
Special, 1889-90. Does not reply to letters.

HERBERT LINCOLN FLINT

*Louis Bertram Flower   *1917
Senior year only.

Elmer Hollinger Frantz
Junior year only.

Lovat Frazer
Special, 1889-92.

Frederick Aaron Freeark
Entered Junior.

[Alfred Julius Freiberg]
Withdraws, 1923. With '94· Took A.B. with '93· (See reports of '94.)

*ROBERT TILLINGHAST FRENCH   *1897

SOLOMON LEWIS FRIDENBERG

[Alfred Friedlander]
Withdraws. A.B. 1892. (See their reports).

LEE MAX FRIEDMAN

Leonard Alden Frink
Special, 1889-92 Law School, 1893.

Arthur Bowes Frizell
Entered Junior year.

LOUIS ADAMS FROTHINGHAM

WILLIAM HARRY FURBER

Frederik Herman [Johan] Gade
A.B. 1892.

[John Shepard Gage]
Withdraws. Special, 1888-89. L.S.S., 1889-90. Affiliates with '92· (See their reports).

[Charles Lucius Gaines]
Special, 1889-91. Does not reply to letters.

[*Frank Bernard Gallivan]   *1919
    A.B. 1894, as of 1893. Withdrew in 1918 for private rea-
    sons.

Howard Schiffer Gans
    A.B. 1892.

*James Albert Garland, Jr.   *1906
    Special, 1889-93.

CHARLES MERRICK GAY

[John White Geary]
    Withdraws. Entered with '91. With '92, 1888-91. (See
    reports of '92).

THOMAS ASHLEY GIFFORD

*LOUIS WHITMORE GILBERT   *1919

[George Ridley Gillette]
    Withdraws. (Special, 1889-91. LL.B. 1896, as of 1895).

James Waterman Glover
    Grad. School, 1892-95. A.B. 1895, as of 1893.

PHILIP BECKER GOETZ

CHARLES CROSS GOODRICH

ARTHUR HALE GORDON

CLIFFORD ALLEN GOULD

Frederick Louis Grant
    Left Junior year.

[George Davis Greenwood]
    Withdraws (with '92). Special, 1889-91.

Harry Edward Grigor
    Special, 1889-91.

*GEORGE [formerly ADDIS McEVERS] GRISWOLD, 2D *1902
    Name changed in 1892.

*MICHAEL HENRY GUERIN   *1919

*Frederick Putnam Gulliver   *1919
    Grad. School, 1892-97. A.B. 1893.

ANDREW HAHN

ALBERT HALE, JR.

[Arthur Leslie Hale]
    Withdraws. (Special, 1889-90).

Joseph Henry Hall
    Special, 1889-92.

SAMUEL PRESCOTT HALL

*THOMAS HALL, JR.   *1911

FRANK WALTON HALLOWELL

[Nathan Chipman Hamblin]
>   Withdraws. With '92 throughout. Repeated Senior year
>   with '93· (See reports of '92).

[Gates Hamburger]
>   Withdraws (Sophomore year only).

*George Daniel Hammond   *1899
>   1891, with '94· Joined class Senior year.

[BILLINGS] LEARNED HAND

JOHN GODDARD HART

JOHN HENRY HARWOOD

*DRAYTON FRANKLIN HASTIE   *1916

Horatio Hathaway, Jr.
>   Special, 1889-91.

*CHARLES SUMNER HAWES   *1921

OSCAR BROWN HAWES

John Heiss
>   Senior year only.

Frederick Grantham Henderson
>   1889-90, Special Sci. 1890-92, with '94· Joined class Senior
>   year.

William Julian Henderson
>   1891-92, II. Sci. Joined class Senior year.

*OLIVER BRIDGES HENSHAW   *1898

[Roy Durand Herrick]
>   Withdraws. Special, 1889-90. With '93, 1890-92. With
>   '94, 1892-93. ''I have always been more associated with
>   '92.''

WILLIAM CARTER HEYWOOD

JAMES HENRY HICKEY

*John Ashley Highlands   *1920
>   Special, 1891-92. 4 Scientific, 1892-93. S.B. 1893.

HENRY ARTHUR HILDRETH

*John Lewis Hildreth, Jr.   *1920
>   1st year Grad., 1892-93. A.B. 1893.

ERNEST OSGOOD HILER

[*Justin Thomas Hill]   *1900 (?)
>   Special, 1889-90.

[Otis Shepard Hill]
>   Junior, 1889-90. Senior, 1890-91. A.B. 1893. (See re-
>   ports of '91).

*David Hoadley   *1892

[Harry Gans Hochstadter]
Withdraws. With '93, 1889-91. With '92, 1891-92. A.B. 1892. (See their reports).

[Claude Hoffman]
Special, 1889. Left college March 21, 1890. Does not reply to letters.

James Edwin Holland
Special, 1889-93.

JOSEPH CLARK HOPPIN

TRACY HOPPIN

Elwin Lincoln House
Senior year only.

*PHILIP·BARTHOLD HOWARD   *1910

[Everett Chase Howe]
Left Junior year. Does not reply to letters.

William De Lancey Howe
Special, 1889-92. Joined class Senior year.

Ira Woods Howerth
Entered Junior.

CHAUNCEY GILES HUBBELL

John Homer Huddilston
Senior year only.

JOHN THOMAS HUGHES

GEORGE EDGAR HUME

John Strother Humphreys
Senior year only.

[William Penn Humphreys]
1st year Grad., 1892-93. A.B. 1893. Does not reply to letters.

EDWARD LIVINGSTON HUNT

*Robert William Hunter   *1908
Special, 1889-90. Joined class Sophomore year.

*CHARLES PRATT HUNTINGTON   *1919

*HAROLD HUTCHINSON   *1906

Lincoln Hutchinson
Grad. School, 1892-94. A.B. 1894, as of 1893.

CHARLES EDWARD HUTCHISON

*Alpheus Hyatt, Jr.   *1911
Left class Junior year. 2 Scientific, 1891-92.

GEORGE HOADLY INGALLS

*William Henry Isely   *1907
    Senior year only.

[*Yutaro Ito]   *1899 (?)
    Special, 1889-90.

FREDERICK GIBBS JACKSON

PATRICK TRACY JACKSON, JR.

THOMAS AUGUSTUS JAGGAR, JR.

[*Edward Christian Jewell]   *1919
    Withdraws. Entered with '89 but left college. Afterwards
    Law School, 1892-94. A.B. 1894, as of 1893.

*Albert Cheney Johnson   *1916
    Special, 1889-90.

*George Fulton Johnson   *1906
    Senior year only.

Philip Van Kuren Johnson
    Scientific, 1889-91. Special, 1891-92. A.B. 1903, as of
    1893.

*EDWARD RENSHAW JONES

James Francis Jones
    Scientific, 1892-93. S.B. 1893.

[Ernest Parlin Jose]
    Left Senior year. 1 Law, 1892-93. Does not reply to
    letters.

[*Edgar Alonzo Kaharl]   *1916
    Withdraws. (Left Sophomore year. A.B. (Bowdoin)
    1899).

George Howard Kelton
    Left Senior year.

JOHN MARTIN KENDRICKEN

Richard Hunter Kennedy
    Joined Sophomore year. A.B. 1896, as of 1893.

William Howland Kenney
    Special, 1889-90.

[Harry Franklin Kent]
    Joined Sophomore year. Does not reply to letters.

William Edward Kent
    Special, 1889-93.

[Stephen Artin Keuleyan]
    Special, 1889-90. Does not reply to letters.

*Charles Walter Keyes   *1921
    Special, 1889-91. Joined class Junior year.

*Frederick Palmer Kidder   *1900
    Left Senior year. A.B. 1898.

DAVID KIMBALL

[Harry Thayer Kingsbury]
    Withdraws. (Special, 1889-91).

[Joseph Kirwen]
    Withdraws. Joined Senior year, from '94. A.B. 1893.
    (See reports of '94).

William Gholson Kittredge
    Left during Sophomore year.

Robert Everett Kline
    3 Scientific, 1892-93. S.B. 1893.

[Arthur Taylor Knapp]
    Special, 1889-91. Special Law, 1891-92. Does not re-
    ply to letters.

Theodore Wesley Koch
    Senior year only.

[Harry Landes]
    Joined Junior year. A.B. 1893, as of 1892. Affiliates with
    '92. (See their reports).

GAILLARD THOMAS LAPSLEY

RALPH CLINTON LARRABEE

GEORGE WARRINGTON LATHAM

Arthur Gordner Leacock
    Grad. School, 1892-94, etc. A.B. 1893.

*WALTER AUGUSTUS LECOMPTE   *1907

[Ernest Hanson Lewis]
    Special, 1889-90. Does not reply to letters.

[Hume Lewis]
    Withdraws. A.B. 1892. (See their reports).

[Joseph Volney Lewis]
    Withdraws. (4 Scientific, 1892-93. S.B. 1893).

CHARLES HENRY LINCOLN

Eric Isidore Lindh
    Special, 1889-90. Joined class Sophomore year.

[George Elmer Littlefield]
    Withdraws. (Special, 1889-90).

[Walter Littlefield]
    Withdraws. Special, 1889-90. Joined class Junior year.
    Left Senior year.

EDWARD LIVINGSTON

HARRY CHAMBERLAIN LOW
*FRANCIS CRUMP LUCAS   *1920
William Luce
    Left Senior year.
Howard Lyon
    Joined Junior year.
Richard MacAllister
    Special, 1889-90. With '94, 1890-92. Joined '93 Senior year.
George Grant MacCurdy [formerly McCurdy]
    Special Sci., 1891-92. Joined class Senior year.
WALTON BROOKS MCDANIEL
[Frank Witten McDonald]
    Withdraws. (Left Sophomore year).
GEORGE LEARY MCELROY
STEPHEN ANDREW MCINTIRE
[Frederick Edward McKay]
    Special, 1889-90. Does not reply to letters.
FREDERICK CHASE MCLAUGHLIN
*Wayne MacVeagh   *1893
    Special, 1889-93.
*GEORGE BUTLER MAGOUN   *1902
Llewellyn John Malone
    Left Senior year.
Percival Manchester
    Left Junior year.
JOSEPH MANLEY
Ernest Lincoln Manning
    Freshman year only.
Samuel Hubbard Mansfield
    Special, 1889-90.
*HENRY ORLANDO MARCY, JR.   *1922
[Arthur Allen Marsters]
    Withdraws. With '94, 1890-93. A.B. 1893. (See reports
    of '94).
*Charles Guy Martin   *1891
FREDERICK ROY MARTIN
SELDEN ERASTUS MARVIN, JR.
WALTER EFFINGHAM [HOLLISTER] MAYNARD
Harold Gregory Meadows
    Scientific, 1889-94. (Transferred to '94).

[Edwin Marcus Mendel]
>   Regular A.B. 1893.   M.D. (Columbia) 1899.   Does not
>   reply to letters.

*Charles Merriam, 2d   *1915

James Andrew Merrill
>   4 Scientific, 1892-93.   S.B. 1893.

Albion Leroy Millan

Ralph Gifford Miller

[William Joseph Miller]
>   A.B. (Trinity) 1892.   Grad. School 1892-95, etc.   A.B.
>   1893.   Does not reply to letters.

[Emmet Leonidas Moffitt]
>   Heretofore included in the class list by error.   1 Grad.,
>   1892-93.   A.M. 1893.

Charles Edward Moody

*William Vaughn [Stoy] Moody   *1910

Fred Wadsworth Moore

William Charles Moore
>   Scientific, 1890-93.   S.B. 1893.

[Justin Neubert Morse]
>   Left college in January, 1890.   Does not reply to letters.

Roland Jessup Mulford

Louis Mullgardt
>   Special, 1889-90.

*Edward Stanton Mullins   *1915

David Saville Muzzey

Howard Pervear Nash

Herbert Vincent Neal
>   Senior year only.

[George Louis Nelson]
>   Withdraws.   Special, 1889-90.   Affiliates with '91.   (See
>   their reports).

Albert Woodard Newlin
>   Senior year only.

*Howard Gardner Nichols   *1896

*Joseph Longworth Nichols   *1918

[Morton Colton Nicholls]
>   Withdraws.   A.B. 1893, as of 1892.   (See their reports).

*Walter Clark Nichols   *1896

[Daniel Benjamin Ninde]
>   Junior year only.   U. S. Naval Acad. 1891.   LL.B. (Univ.
>   of Mich.) 1895.   Does not reply to letters.

Maxwell Norman
   1889-91, with '93. 1891-93, with '95. 1893-94, with '94.
   A.B. 1895, as of 1894. (See their reports).
Allen Alvin North
   Part of Senior year only.
[*Richard Norton]   *1918.
   Withdraws. Freshman and Sophomore years. Joined '92,
   1891-92. A.B. 1892. (See their reports).
HARRISON PICKERING NOWELL
CHARLES REED NUTTER
[Henry Pearson Nye]
   Withdraws. Special, 1889-90.
THOMAS EDWARD OLIVER
*Gilbert Francis Ordway   *1915.
   Joined Senior year, from '94.
Louis Ernest Osborn
   A.B. 1894, as of 1893.
GEORGE ALFRED PAGE
[*Logan Waller Page]   *1918;
   Special, 1889-91. Scientific, 1891-97. (Affiliated with '95).
[Corwin Ford Palmer]
   Withdraws. Special, 1890-91. With '93, 1891-92. A.B.
   1892. (See their reports).
JOHN HARLESTON PARKER
Vernon Louis Parrington
   Entered Junior.
William Edwin Parsons
   1889-90, with '92. 1891-93, with '93.
George Everett Partridge
   Freshman year only.
*Horace Wilbur Patterson   *1911.
   Left Junior year.
*George Eckhardt Paul   *1898.
   Special, 1889-90.
HENRY GREENLEAF PEARSON
Walter Albert Pease
   Left Junior year.
*Charles Cushman Peirce   *1893.
   Special, 1889-90. 1 Medical, 1890-91.
[Arthur Enoch Perkins]
   Withdraws. (Special, 1889-93).

[*Richard Francis Perkins]   *1911
     Withdraws. Left Junior year.

Roland Edward Phillips
     Senior year only.

Carl Horton Pierce
     A.B. 1894, as of 1893.

GEORGE BURGESS PIERCE

CHARLES BURRALL PIKE

J Monro Taylor Pope
     Left Sophomore year.

[James Otis Porter]
     Withdraws. "I entered and left college with '92''. (See
     their reports).

John Reed Post
     Left Sophomore year.

*WARWICK POTTER   *1893

Edward Pearson Pressey
     A.B. 1894, as of 1893.

[Reginald Chapple Pryor]
     Withdraws. Special, 1889-90.

CHESTER WELLS PURINGTON

[Charles Cornell Ramsay]
     Withdraws. Special, 1889-90. With '92, 1890-92. A.B.
     and A.M. 1892. (See their reports).

*Frank Howard Ransom, Jr.   *1919
     Freshman and Sophomore years. With '94, 1892-94. 1
     Med. School, 1894-95. With '96, 1895-96. A.B. 1896.

Chauncey Otis Rawalt
     Senior year only. Grad. Sch. 1894-96.

THOMAS FRANCIS RAY

*Motte Alston Read   *1920
     Special Scientific, 1889-93. S.B. 1902, as of 1893.

William Maxwell Reed
     Left Junior year.

[Neil Edwin Reid]
     Freshman year only. Does not reply to letters.

Harrison Garfield Rhodes
     Entered Sophomore.

John Wolcott Richards
     Special, 1889-92.

[Thresher Ames Rippey]
> Withdraws. A.B. 1892. (See their reports).

NATHANIEL THAYER ROBB

LEWIS NILES ROBERTS

William Henry Robey, Jr.
> Scientific, 1889-91. Medical, 1891-94.

[Charles Henry Rogers]
> Withdraws. (Special, 1889-90).

EDWARD HARTWELL ROGERS

*Thompson Lamar Ross   ●1920
> Senior year only.

*BENJAMIN HILL ROUNSAVILLE   *1894

WALTER LINCOLN SANBORN

LOUIS PECK SANDERS

*Philip Henry Savage   *1899
> Special, 1889-92. Joined class Senior year.

*HUNTINGTON SAVILLE   *1918

Frank Charles Schrader
> Senior year only.

CARL LINCOLN SCHURZ

*Edgar [Thomson] Scott   *1918
> Freshman, 1889-90. Sophomore, 1891-92.

Walter [Judd] Scott
> Special, 1889-90.

*HARRY EDWARD SEARS   *1920
*LANGLEY [BARNAS] SEARS   *1918

HAROLD INGALLS SEWALL

Charles Grant Shaffer
> Senior year only.

Thomas Hall Shastid
> Senior year only.

EDGAR DWIGHT SHAW

Hubert Grover Shaw
> A.B. 1894, as of 1893.

*OLIVER WADSWORTH SHEAD   *1909

George Lawson Sheldon
> 1 Grad., 1892-93. A.B. 1893.

HOWARD COCKS SHERWOOD

Frank Palmer Sibley
> Special, 1889-91.

*GEORGE FREDERICK SIBLEY   ●1896

[Frank St. John Sidway]
> Withdraws. (Freshman year only).

BURNETT NEWELL SIMPSON

Francis Hinckley Sisson
> Senior year only.

CONRAD HENSLER SLADE

[Edmund Botterell Smith]
> Withdraws. Junior year only. A.B. 1892. (See their reports).

Herbert Brush Smith
> Special, 1889-93. 1 Grad., 1893-94.

HOWARD CASWELL SMITH

Robert Keating [*formerly* Gasten] Smith
> Entered Junior.

Wayne Prescott Smith
> 1 Grad., 1892-93. A.B. 1893.

TOWNSEND HODGES SOREN

Frank Enos Soule
> Special, 1888-91. 1 Law, 1891-92.

HORACE CLAFLIN SOUTHWICK

FRED MAURICE SPALDING

Hartwell Ballou Spaulding
> Special, 1889-91.

John Francis Cyril Spencer-Turner
> See John Spencer Turner.

Josiah Edward Spurr
> With '92, 1888-90. Joined class Junior year.

FRANCIS UPHAM STEARNS

[Frederick St. John Stearns]
> Regular A.B. 1893. Does not reply to letters.

Wallace Nelson Stearns
> Senior year only.

J[oseph] Henry Steinhart
> Freshman year only.

FRANK ELLIOT STETSON

RALPH LESLIE STEVENS

[Harry Jessop Stevenson]
> Special, 1889-91. Does not reply to letters.

HENRY HARDING STICKNEY

[George Edgar Stoker]
    Special, 1891-92. Joined class Senior year. Does not re-
    ply to letters.
ARTHUR PARKER STONE
*Philip Deland Stone   *1890
*RICHMOND STONE   *1896
Willis Whittemore Stover
    Special, 1889-90.
JESSE ISIDOR STRAUS
Lionel Alexander Burnet Street
    Special, 1889-90.
[Lawrence Watson Strong]
    Withdraws. Sophomore and Junior years only. A.B. 1892.
    (See their reports).
WILLIAM JAMES HENRY STRONG
FRANK RAYMOND STUBBS
*CHARLES RUSSELL STURGIS   *1909
*Walter Dana Swan   *1907
    Special, 1889-91.
Thomas Henry Sylvester, Jr.
    Joined Junior year.
[*Robert Weems Tansill]   *1896
    Special, 1889-90.
FREDERICK JOSEPH TAUSSIG
John Clarence Taussig
    Special, 1889-90. Joined class Sophomore year.
WILLIAM OSGOOD TAYLOR
HARRY LORENZO TEETZEL
Derrick Anthony Te Paske
    Senior year only.
Louis Bartlett Thacher
    Special, 1889-92. With '95, 1892-93. A.B. 1894, as of
    1893.
[Eben Blanchard Thaxter]
    With '87, 1883-86. With '92, 1890-91. With '93, 1891-92.
    With '94, 1892-93. Does not reply to letters.
Rufus Kemble Thomas
    Freshman year only.
William Leland Thompson
    Special, 1889-90. With '94, 1890-91. Joined '93 Junior
    year.

Frederick Charles Thwaits
> With '95, 1891-92. Joined '93 Senior year.

Archibald Read Tisdale
> Left Sophomore year. L.S., 1891-93.

HOWE TOTTEN

Edward Sands Townsend
> Left Junior year. L.S., 1892-95.

FREDERICK TOWNSEND

Willis Merrick Townsend
> Special, 1889-90.

BERNARD WALTON TRAFFORD

Lyman Tremain
> Left Sophomore year.

Philip Edmund Tripp
> Special, 1889-90. Scientific, 1890-92. Joined class Senior
> year. A.B. 1894, as of 1893.

[George Turner]
> Joined '94, 1892-93. Does not reply to letters.

John Spencer Turner—name changed 1898 to John
Francis Cyril Spencer-Turner
> Freshman year only.

[John Edmund Tweedy]
> Withdraws. (Special, 1889-90).

[Shem Laban Tyson]
> Special, 1889-90. Does not reply to letters.

JOSHUA DAMON UPTON

*DAVIS RIGHTER VAIL   *1906

[Charles Gershom Van Brunt]
> Withdraws. With '92 throughout. Repeated Senior year,
> and A.B. 1893. (See reports of '92).

[Hugh Flournoy Van Deventer]
> S.B. (Univ. Mich.) 1892. A.B. 1893. Does not reply to
> letters.

[Ashley Joseph Vantine]
> Special, 1889-90. Does not reply to letters.

Thomas Wayland Vaughan
> Grad. School, 1892-94, etc. A.B. 1893.

Enoch Howard Vickers
> Senior year only.

OSWALD GARRISON VILLARD

[George Olien Virtue]
> Withdraws. Junior, 1891-92. A.B 1892. See their reports).

Bernard [*formerly* Benno] William Vogel
> Freshman year only.

*[Henry Ingersoll Waite]   *1920
> Freshman year only.

GEORGE WALCOTT

Julian Constantine Walker
> Freshman year only.

Alfred Wallerstein
> A.B. 1893 from '94.

HENRY WARE

Edgar Haga Warner
> Senior year only.

Oscar Leon Watkins
> Senior year only.

Frank Milton Watters
> Special, 1889-91.

Lorenzo Webber
> Left Sophomore year.

JOSEPH ROWE WEBSTER

Kenneth Grant Tremayne Webster
> Senior year only.

EDWARD MOTLEY WELD

*David Dwight Wells   *1900
> Special, 1889-92. Joined class Senior year.

Leonard Abel Wheeler
> Special, 1889-90.

GEORGE ALBERT WHIPPLE

Herbert Hill White
> Special, 1889-90. Joined class Junior year. Left Senior year. A.B. 1913, as of 1893.

Edward Dwight Whitford
> Special Scientific, 1889-91. With '92, 1891-92. A.B. 1892.

James Raynor Whiting, Jr.
> Entered Junior.

Charles Edward Whitmore, Jr.
> Entered Sophomore.

*Oliver Whyte, Jr.   *1893
> Left Junior year. 1 Law, 1892-93.

*Walter Herriman Wickes   *1907
      With '92, 1888-90.   Joined class, 1890-91.   Left Sopho-
      more year. (See reports of '92).

JOSEPH WIGGIN
James Austin Wilder
      A.B. 1894, as of 1893.

*Henry Francis Willard   *1914
      A.B. 1892.

Charles Edwin Williams
      Senior year only.

*Franklin James Williams   *1901
      With '93 four years.   With '96, 1895-96.   A.B. 1896.

[George Anson Williams]
      Withdraws.   (Left Sophomore year).

[Herbert Pelham Williams]
      Withdraws.   Special, 1889-90.   With '92, 1890-92.   A.B.
      1892. (See their reports).

GEORGE PERRY WILSON
[Charles Tudor Wing]
      Special, 1889-90.   Does not reply to letters.

GEORGE PARKER WINSHIP
Charles Gibson Winslow
      Special, 1889-91.   L.S., 1891-95.

FREDERICK WINSOR
Samuel Lee Wolff
      A.B. 1892.

Arthur Mayer Wolfson
      A.B. 1893 from '94.

*Albert Bowman Wood   *1900
      Special Scientific, 1889-93.

ERNEST HENRY WOOD
[Arthur Lawrence Woods]
      Withdraws.   Special, 1889-90.   Affiliated with '91.   (See
      their reports).

Ralph Woodworth
      Joined Senior year from '94.

Arthur Rufus Trego Wylie
      Senior year only.

CHARLES LOWELL YOUNG
Frank Lester Young
      Special, 1889 90.   Joined class Sophomore year.

Recent Deaths

Since publication of the 25th Anniversary Report.

1918

JOSEPH LONGWORTH NICHOLS
June 17, at Saranac Lake, New York

HUNTINGTON SAVILLE
July 27, at Cambridge, Massachusetts

EDGAR THOMSON SCOTT
October 20, at Chaumont, France

EDWIN BARTLETT BARTLETT
November 5, at West Manchester, Massachusetts

LANGLEY BARNAS SEARS
December 2, at Monson, Massachusetts

1919

CHARLES SAMUEL CHASE
January 3, at Westboro, Massachusetts

FREDERICK PUTNAM GULLIVER
February 8, at Philadelphia, Pennsylvania

LOUIS WHITMORE GILBERT
March 30, at Brookline, Massachusetts

FRANK HOWARD RANSOM
April 2, at Buffalo, New York

ROBERT PENDLETON BOWLER
May 28, at New York City

SAMUEL CHEW
July 5, at Philadelphia, Pennsylvania

JOHN JOSEPH DOLAN
July 20, at Wolfboro, New Hampshire

RALPH HARTT BOWLES
August 31, near Caldwell, New Jersey

MICHAEL HENRY GUERIN
September 11, in Lake Michigan
CHARLES PRATT HUNTINGTON
October 15, at Bronxville, New York
FRANK BERNARD GALLIVAN
November 11, at South Boston, Massachusetts

1920

THOMPSON LAMAR ROSS
January 3, at Granada, Mississippi
JOHN ASHLEY HIGHLANDS
April 15, at New York City
FRANCIS CRUMP LUCAS
June 12, at New York City
MOTTE ALSTON READ
July 15, at Charleston, South Carolina
AMBROSE COLLYER DEARBORN
September 19, at New York City
HENRY INGERSOLL WAITE
September 30, at Westboro, Massachusetts
HARRY EDWARD SEARS
October 20, at Beverly, Massachusetts
CLARENCE BIGELOW DENNY
November 23, at Milton, Massachsetts
JOHN LEWIS HILDRETH, JR.
December 3, at Bayonne, New Jersey

1921

GEORGE LAWRENCE DAY
January 6, at Fort Wadsworth, New York
CHARLES SUMNER HAWES
April 22, at Chicago, Illinois
CHARLES WALTER KEYES
August 14, at East Pepperell, Massachusetts

WALTER HOWARD CUSHING
December 6, at Framingham, Massachusetts
SILAS DINSMOOR
September 17, at Pittsburgh, Pennsylvania

1922

HENRY ORLANDO MARCY, JR.
May 29, at Newton, Massachusetts
EDWARD CROSBY DARLING
August 5, at Philadelphia, Pennsylvania

1923

EVERETT PASCOE CAREY
January 20, at Delhi, California

Alphabetical List of Deaths

Name	Date	Place	Cause
Adams, Alvin	Apr. 5, 1902	Pasadena, Cal.	Pneumonia
Adams, Walter Sawyer	Dec. 23, 1915	Salem, Mass.	Pulmonary tuberculosis
Alden, John	Mar. 16, 1914	Portland, Me.	Acute pneumonia
Anderson, Fred Howes	Dec. 20, 1893	Wakefield, Mass.	Tuberculosis
Baker, Morris	Jan. 17, 1912	Philadelphia, Pa.	Cystic kidneys
Baker, Walter Farnsworth	Oct. 27, 1907	Bogota, N. J.	Arsenical poisoning
Baldwin, Columbus Calvert	Oct. 24, 1899	New York City	Typhoid fever
Baldwin, John Denison	Dec. 8, 1913	Worcester, Mass.	Ptomaine poisoning
Bartlett, Edwin Bartlett	Nov. 5, 1918	West Manchester, Mass.	Sarcoma
Battelle, Harold Munro	June 3, 1892	Boston, Mass.	Pulmonary tuberculosis
Billings, Edgar Francis	Jan. 22, 1913	Boston, Mass.	Accidental poisoning
Bisbee, Ralph	July 28, 1913	Briarcliff Manor, N. Y.	Septicaemia
Blaustein, David	Aug. 27, 1912	Cold Spring, N. Y.	Apoplexy
Bowler, Robert Pendleton	May 28, 1919	New York City	Heart disease
Bowles, Ralph Hartt	Aug. 31, 1919	Near Caldwell, N. J.	Drowning
Brice, Stewart Meily	June 10, 1910	Asbury Park, N. J.	Insanity
Burgess, George Ebenezer	Aug. 19, 1902	Prout's Neck, Me.	Heart disease
Burke, Ernest Gisborne	Feb. 18, 1903	Quincy, Mass.	Pulmonary tuberculosis
Callender, Guy Stevens	Aug. 8, 1915	Indian Neck, Conn.	Cerebral hemorrhage
Carpenter, Edward Heman	Oct. 2, 1915	Castine, Me.	Bright's disease
Carr, Joseph William	Mar. 4, 1909	Orono, Me.	Heart disease
Carr, Raymond Wilbur	Aug. 13, 1911	Albany, N. Y.	Pneumonia
Chase, Charles Samuel	Jan. 3, 1919	Westboro, Mass.	Epilepsy

Name	Date	Place	Cause of death
Chew, Samuel	July 5, 1919	Philadelphia, Pa.	Heart disease
Churchill, Donald	Nov. 27, 1909	Providence, R. I.	Septicaemia
Coffin, Edward Russell	Sept. 2, 1907	Omaha, Neb.	Strangulated hernia
Cook, Irving Jabez	Oct. 24, 1908	New York City	Suicide by shooting
Cottrell, William Norman	Dec. 2, 1916	Chicago, Ill.	Gallstones
Coulter, Alfred Frazer	Mar. 25, 1903	Brighton, Mass.	Cerebral tumor
Cushing, Walter Howard	Dec. 6, 1921	Framingham, Mass.	Paralysis agitans
Darling, Edward Crosby	Aug. 5, 1922	Philadelphia, Pa.	Cerebral tumor
Day, George Lawrence	Jan. 6, 1921	Ft. Wadsworth, N. Y.	Heart. disease
Dearborn, Ambrose Collyer	Sept. 19, 1920	New York City	Diabetes
Denny, Clarence Bigelow	Nov. 23, 1920	Milton, Mass.	Results of blow on head
Dexter, Arthur Wyman	Dec. 17, 1914	Dunsmuir, Cal.	Pulmonary tuberculosis
Dinsmoor, Silas	Sept. 17, 1921	Pittsburgh, Pa.	Results of fall.from wagon
Doe, Henry Waldo	Jan. 24, 1905	Newark, N. J.	Pneumonia
Dolan, John Joseph	July 20, 1919	Wolfboro, N. H.	Pulmonary tuberculosis
Downing, Charles William	Mar. 18, 1908	Colorado Springs, Col.	Pulmonary tuberculosis
Flower, Louis Bertram	Feb. 17, 1917	Coronado, Cal.	Cancer of the bladder
French, Robert Tillinghast	Nov. 16, 1897	Toronto, Canada	Typhoid fever
Gallivan, Frank Bernard	Nov. 11, 1919	South Boston, Mass.	Heart disease
Garland, James Albert	Sept. 13, 1906	Hanover, Mass.	Pneumonia
Gilbert, Louis Whitmore	Mar. 30, 1919	Brookline, Mass.	Infantile paralysis.
Griswold, George, 2d	Dec. 23, 1902	Westchester, N. Y.	Melancholia (suicide)
Guerin, Michael Henry	Sept. 11, 1919	Lake Michigan	Drowning
Gulliver, Frederic Putnam	Feb. 8, 1919	Philadelphia, Pa.	Pneumonia
Hall, Thomas, Jr.	Aug. 19, 1911	Baltimore, Md.	Cerebral tumor
Hammond, George Daniel	Jan. 14, 1899	Asheville, N. C,	Pulmonary tuberculosis

Name	Date	Place	Cause
Hastie, Drayton Franklin	Feb. 16, 1916	Charleston, S. C.	Heart disease
Hawes, Charles Sumner	Apr. 22, 1921	Chicago, Ill.	Apoplexy
Henshaw, Oliver Bridges	July 4, 1898	Camp Alger, Va.	Kick by horse
Highlands, John Ashley	Apr. 15, 1920	New York City	Angina pectoris
Hildreth, John Lewis, Jr.	Dec. 3, 1920	Bayonne, N. J.	After-effects of influenza
Hoadley, David	Sept. 7, 1892	Lake Asquam, N. H.	Drowning
Howard, Philip Barthold	Mar. 24, 1910	Boston, Mass.	Ulcerative endocarditis
Hunter, Robert William	May 18, 1908	Roxbury, Mass.	Pulmonary tuberculosis
Huntington, Charles Pratt	Oct. 15, 1919	Bronxville, N. Y.	Miliary tuberculosis
Hutchinson, Harold	July 15, 1906	Newton, Mass.	Intestinal ulcer
Hyatt, Alpheus	Mar. 29, 1911	New York City	Pneumonia
Isely, William Henry	Aug. 14, 1907	Wichita, Kan.	Appendicitis
Johnson, Albert Cheney	May 25, 1916	Staten Island, N. Y.	Pneumonia
Johnson, George Fulton	Sept. 11, 1906	Calgary, Canada	Pulmonary tuberculosis
Jones, Edward Renshaw	Feb. 18, 1896	New York City	Appendicitis
Kaharl, Edgar Alonzo	Aug. 25, 1916	New Bedford, Mass.	Angina Pectoris
Keyes, Charles Walter	Aug. 14, 1921	East Pepperell, Mass.	Angina Pectoris
Kidder, Frederick Palmer	Dec. 5, 1900	Albany, N. Y.	Cerebral tumor
Lecompte, Walter Augustus	Jan. 13, 1907	Boston, Mass.	Appendicitis.
Lucas, Francis Crump	June 12, 1920	New York City	Paralysis
MacVeagh, Wayne	Jan. 1, 1893	Philadelphia, Pa.	Heart disease
Magoun, George Butler	Dec. 15, 1902	Babylon, L. I.	Suicide by shooting
Marcy, Henry Orlando, Jr.	May 29, 1922	Newton, Mass.	After-effects of influenza
Martin, Charles Guy	Jan. 14, 1891	Cambridge, Mass.	Pulmonary tuberculosis
Merriam, Charles	Mar. 28, 1915	Weston, Mass.	Ludwig's Angina
Moody, William Vaughn	Oct. 17, 1910	Colorado Springs, Col.	Cerebral tumor

Name	Date	Place	Cause
Mns, Edrd Stanton	Feb. 20, 1915	Savannah, Ga.	My ; ritis
Nichols, Howard Gardner	June 23, 1896	Atlanta, Ga.	Fall of machinery
M, Joseph Longworth	June 17, 1918	Saranac Lake, N. Y.	Er meningitis
Nichols, Walter Clark	Jan. 10, 1896	Denver, Col.	Heart disease
rdy, Gilbert Francis 7hr	Ag. 19, 1915	Mt. Ranier, Wash.	Fall hile ; nclimbing
Patterson, Horace 7hr	Feb. 5, 1911	Sten Island, N. Y.	Pneumonia
Paul, George Eckhardt	May 18, 1898	Philadelphia, Pa.	Pulmonary bhis
Peirce, Gdes ; rdan	Sept. 1893	Dover, N. H.	Sle (hydrocyanic acid)
Perkins, Richard Francis	Feb. 14, 1911	Washington, D. C.	Byitis
Potter, Warwick	Oct. 11, 1893	Brest, France	Inflammation of t ash
Ransom, Frank H ward	Apr. 2, 1919	Balo, N. Y.	Heart disease
Read, Me Alston	July 12, 1920	Charleston, S. C	Results of acute arthritis
Ross, Thompson ; dr	Jan. 3, 1920	Grenada, Miss.	Accidental pistol wound
Rounsaville, Benjamin Hill	June 20, 1894	Tamworth, N. H.	Tubercular peritonitis
Savage, Flip Henry	June 4, 1899	Boston, Mass.	Apitis
Sde, Huntington	July 27, 1918	Cambridge, Mass.	Ate t xdr paralysis
Scott, Edgar En	Oct. 20, 1918	#4, France	Not (tpd
Sears, Harry Edward	Oct. 20, 1920	Beverly, Mass.	Suicide by stig
Sears, Langley Barnas	Dec. 2, 1918	Monson, Mass.	Pneumonia
Sdd, Oder Wadsworth	Aug. 3, 1909	Waverly, Mass.	Result of gymnasium accident
Sly, George Frederick	Aug. 13, 1896	Salem, Mass.	Uraemia
Sone, Flip Dand	Aug. 22, 1890	alo Springs, Col.	; ary tuberculosis
Stone, Fid	Mar. 27, 1896	Washington, D. C.	Bia
Sturgis, Gdes Russell	Oct. 2, 1909	Boston, Mass.	Results of scarlet efr
Swan, Vlver Dana	Jan. 2, 1907	Belmont, Mass.	Suicide by shooting
Vail, Davis Righter	Dec. 21, 1906	New York City	Typhoid fever

Waite, Henry Ingersoll	Sept. 30, 1920	Westboro, Mass.	Insanity
Wells, David Dwight	June 15, 1900	Norwich, Conn.	Typhoid fever and Bright's disease
Whyte, Oliver, Jr.	May 30, 1893	Medford, Mass.	Pneumonia
Wickes, Walter Herriman	Aug. 28, 1907	Rutland, Mass.	Pulmonary and intestinal tuberculosis
Willard, Henry Francis	Apr. 28, 1914	Athens, Greece	Typhoid fever
Williams, Franklin James	July 7, 1901	Pasadena, Cal.	Pulmonary tuberculosis
Wood, Albert Bowman	Dec. 9, 1900	Worcester, Mass.	Diabetes

Cox., Thomas; Stroke, Fennessy; No. 7, Cummings; No. 6, Vail (capt.); No. 5, Fearing;
No. 4, Davis; No. 3, Newell; No. 2, Johnson; Bow, Burgess.

VARSITY CREW, 1893

Class of 1893

ERNEST HAMLIN ABBOTT

.Born at Cornwall-on-Hudson, New York, 18 April 1870, of Lyman Abbott
[N. Y. Univ.] (clergyman and editor) and Abby Frances Hamlin.
Fitted at the Hill School, Pottstown, Pennsylvania.
Class Status: Regular.
Degrees: A.B. 1893; Grad. Andover Theol. Sem. 1896.
Married May Louise Kleberg at New Rochelle, New York, 28 September
1899. Children:
　　Alexander Lyman, born 26 July 1900.
　　Lawrence Jacob, 9 July 1902.
　　·Theodore Vaughan, 24 September 1908.
　　Ernest Hamlin, Jr., 4 March 1911.
　　John Maunder Kleberg (born, 1 February, 1900) adopted 23
　　　　November 1922.
Now Editor-in-Chief of *The Outlook* at New York City.

In the summer of 1893 I made my first trip abroad with my
father; incidentally hearing Gladstone under dramatic circumstances. For three years I studied at Union and Andover Theological Seminaries. Then for five and one half years I was
minister of the Congregational Church at Fryeburg, Maine.
With the invaluable aid of Pearson and the young people and
others in the community as well as in Boston, I tried an interesting and fairly successful experiment there in developing a
summer community center. During this period I married; the
first home my wife and I had was thus a parsonage. In 1901
I made a trip in the South and West collecting material for
articles which were published in The Outlook and later in a
book on "Religious Life in America." Two other books of
mine have been published. In 1902 I joined the editorial staff
of The Outlook, becoming associated with my father, editor-in-
chief until his death last fall, and with my oldest brother, Lawrence F. Abbott, President of The Outlook Company. In 1904
I made a study of the Negro question in several Southern cities.
My connection with The Outlook brought me into somewhat
close association with Theodore Roosevelt. In 1914 Hiler and
I found ourselves in Paris on the eve of mobilization and in
London when one declaration of war followed another. In the
spring of 1918 I made some speeches in Kentucky under the
State Council of Defense. In October, 1918, I sailed for Europe

expecting to get to the front as a correspondent, but the Armistice intervened. After spending some time in the army area and on the battlefields I remained in Paris during a large part of the Peace Conference. In 1922 I attended as correspondent the Armament Conference at Washington. I have been at one time or another a member of various boards, committees, councils, and commissions. That I am still alive I owe to my younger brother, Dr. Theodore J. Abbott, who pulled me through an attack of pneumonia in 1920.

I have a family of boys. Two of them (one my oldest son, the other my adopted son) are graduates of Harvard in the class of 1922, and one is a junior at Harvard, in the class of 1924. Their education is largely due to my wife's careful management and their own capacity for self help.

Our residence is in the village where I was born and all my children as well—Cornwall-on-Hudson, New York. For a part of the year we—those of us who are at home—live—or exist— in New York City.

On May 23, 1923, I was honored with the election to the post of Editor-in-Chief of the Outlook, thus succeeding my father.

Alvin Adams

See Report VI, Page 2.

Walter Sawyer Adams

See Report VI, Page 3, and Supplement, Page 125.

GEORGE HENRY ALDEN

Born at Tunbridge, Vermont, 30 August 1866, of Edwin Hyde Alden
    [Dartmouth 1859] (clergyman) and Anna Maria Whittemore.
Entered from Carleton College.
Class Status: I. Graduate School, 1892-93.
Degrees: S.B. (Carleton, Minn.), 1891; A.B. 1893; Ph.D. (Univ. of Wis.)
    1896.
Married Dora Hall Page at Anoka, Minnesota, 23 June 1898. Children:
    Rodney Whittemore, born 18 May 1899.
    Margaret Marion, 12 December 1903.
Now Dean of Willamette University, Salem, Oregon.

1893-1895: Fellowship in History, University of Chicago. 1895-1896: Fellowship in History, University of Wisconsin. 1896-1897: Acting Assistant Professor of History, University of Illinois. 1897-1898: Professor of History and Government, Cornell College. 1898-1903: Professor of History and Political Science, Carleton College. 1903-1909: Assistant and Associate Professor of History, University of Washington. 1909-1914: In business, Secretary and President of land companies. 1914-1915: Acting President, Willamette University. 1915 to present: Dean, College of Liberal Arts, Willamette University.

During the past five years have had to be Acting President of Willamette University at times. For over two years have been chairman of the Higher Education Standards Committee of the Oregon State Teachers' Association which has done considerable to uplift Oregon educational standards.

More detailed records in Who's Who in America.

John Alden

See Report VI, Page 4.

FREEMAN ALLEN

Born at Stockbridge, Massachusetts, 27 September 1870, of Henry Freeman Allen [Harvard 1860] (clergyman) and Georgiana May Stowe.
Fitted at G. W. C. Noble's.
Class Status: Regular.
Degrees: A.B. 1893; M.D. 1899.
Married Mary Ethel Gibson at Boston, 20 July 1911. Child: Henry Freeman, born 23 November 1916.
Now practising medicine in Boston.

For the last 20 years I have lived at 200 Beacon Street, and practised the administration of anesthetics as a specialty. As my only recreation I have hunted with the Norfolk Hounds for the past nine autumns and for the last three years have been first whip of the Norfolk Hounds. I am also active in the New Riding Club of Boston of which I am this year secretary. My son, Henry F. Allen, is now six years old and is beginning to attend school.

WILLIAM HENRY ALLISON

Born at Somerville, Massachusetts, 17 August 1870, of George Augus-
    tus Allison (agent) and Julia Lucinda Powers.
Fitted at Cambridge Latin School.
Class Status: Regular.
Degrees: A.B. 1893; B.D. (Newton Theol. Inst.) 1902; Ph.D. (Univ.
    Chicago) 1905.
Married (1) Elizabeth Lincoln Smith at Newton Center, Massachu-
    setts, 6 September 1899 (died 14 July 1900)
Married (2) Mary Emily Mills at Chicago, 31 July 1905. Child:
    Elizabeth Mills, born 28 January 1907.
Now Professor of Church History, Colgate Theological Seminary, Hamil-
    ton, New York.

It was seventeen years after graduation that I entered upon
the position which I now hold. While I was able to render considerable social service during that period, it stands out in the
perspective of the years, as a prolonged preparation for the
educational work I have been doing since 1910. During four of
the years, I was pastor of churches; during six of the years, I
was teaching in college or seminary; six more years, divided between two periods, were devoted to graduate study. Financially, the prolonged preparation meant losses which I never expect
to recover; in every other way, I believe there are assets and
compensations. In the present state of the world, no work is
more attractive than that of training young men for the Christian ministry and to engage in the task from the standpoint of
history is to be close to the crucial development of modern times.
Official connection with the Federal Council of the Churches of
Christ in America has been an added privilege and opportunity
in recent years. Since the summer before entering college, I
have turned for a summer recreation, whenever possible, to
Lovell, Maine, and two years ago I built a camp on the island
where A. P. Stone has had a camp for many years; Dallinger
and H. L. Flint belong to the group and the memory of all of
us teems with the rich associations of the years. The academic
year 1921-22, I was on leave of absence, spending almost nine
months in Cambridge, much of the time at a convenient desk in
the stack of the Harvard Library. I got hardly more than a
start on *the great book* I still hope to write, but it was a good
year in many ways.

Fred Howes Anderson
See Report VI, Page 8.

ALBERT STOKES APSEY

Born at Cambridge, Massachusetts, 27 November 1870, of William Stokes
Apsey [Colby 1861] (Clergyman) and Jennie Heermans.
Fitted at Cambridge Latin.
Class Status: Regular.
Degrees: A.B. 1893; LL.B. 1895.
Married Laura Louise Soule at Cambridge, Massachusetts, 2 May 1896.
Children:
Lawrence Soule, born 14 November 1902.
Suzanne, 8 January 1907.
Now practising law at Boston.

Memorandum: Since the publication of the last Report, I
have done nothing particularly new or startling; have been going along in much the same manner as heretofore, practising
law in Boston and residing in Cambridge. Among other things,
I hold the following positions: Business Men's Coöperative
Bank, President and Director; Harbor Storage Company, Director; Massachusetts Bonding and Insurance Company, Director; Metropolitan Wharf Trust, Trustee; Riverbank Court
Hotel Company, President and Director; Riverbank Court Securities Company, Trustee; Warren H. Manning Offices. Inc.,
Director; W. P. Soule Company, Inc., Treasurer and Director.
I am also a member of numerous clubs and associations here
and in New York.

PERCY LEE ATHERTON

Born at Boston, 25 September 1871, of William Atherton (leather mer-
chant) and Mary Edwards Dwight.
Fitted at Phillips Andover.
Class Status: Regular.
Degree: A.B. 1893.
Now composing music at Boston.

The story of a worker along creative lines may of course,
contain matter of occasional interest to one's friends. Personally, however, I have no such story and, furthermore, a considerable part of my output remains in New York. I may add,
in passing, that I seem to have stressed the lyric side of music
as witnessed by two comic operas, a brief Oriental opera-com-
ique, suite for flute, sonatas, suite and smaller pieces for violin,

miscellaneous pieces for orchestra, for piano, for voices, and about one hundred songs.

My Boston activities outside my work have been the following: Charitable, as director of the Boston North End Mission for nearly twenty years; Educational, as member of Visiting Committee in Music (at Harvard) for nearly twenty-five years and as member of Advisory Committee for Music in the Boston public schools for four years; Dramatic, as Advisory Head of Music in the Toy Theatre in Boston for two years; Musical, as—a decade ago—President of the American Music Society (Boston Chapter) for three years.

In retrospect: I have been fortunate enough to live abroad over four years (chiefly pursuing musical studies) along with several additional summers of travel covering Great Britain, the Continent and the Near East. This, along with a six months' leisurely trip through the entire Far West, a winter (this past season) in the South and four additional trips to the foothills of the Rockies by varied routes, have afforded me a certain perspective: making I am sure, for a better understanding of our country itself and in its relation to and interrelation with the countries of Europe. . . . To ensure helpful breathing spaces in a life overcrowded with detail, I have gone, each winter, for the past twelve years, to the Lake Placid Club (of which, realizing its immense potentialities I at once became a life member) and there have spent several weeks of mixed work and winter sports. On five occasions I have enjoyed a month or more on one or two of several ranches near Sheridan, Wyoming: Eaton's, H. F. Barr, and Tepee Lodge. These have left memories of enduring interest.

Finally I would record that I remain one of the few genuinely consistent bachelors of '93 and in this connection, as my closing thought, I can but re-quote from an early operetta of mine that (still) "I'm as unhappy as happy can be."

WALTER AYER

Born at Chicago, 26 April 1870, of Benjamin Franklin Ayer [Dartmouth
   1846] (lawyer) and Janet Aurelia Hopkins.
Fitted at Browne and Nichols.
Class Status: Regular.
Degrees: A.B. 1893; LL.B. 1896.

Married Phoebe Lord McCormick at New York City, 30 October 1909.
   Children:
      Robert McCormick, born 26 September 1910.
      Janet, 12 November 1912.
Now a manufacturer at Madison, Wisconsin.

For twelve years Ayer practised law in Chicago with an increasing conviction that the legal profession did not interest
him as a life's work. In 1908 he moved to Madison, Wisconsin,
to take over the management of the Fuller Johnson Company,
a concern well known in the West as a manufacturer of farming
implements. Under his direction a pump was developed which
furnishes power for everything on a farm, from the well to the
ice cream freezer, and a gasoline mower which may be seen am-
bling over park lawns and golf club greens. His next concern
was to brighten the life of the farmer with an electric lighting
outfit, which he developed and makes in quantity for the Western Electric Company.

Ayer was for two years President of the Madison Harvard
Club, and is an outstanding Harvard man in the state. During
the war he was closely associated, in managerial positions, with
various forms of war work in his part of the state.

Clubs and societies: University Club of Chicago, Chicago
Club, Madison Club, University Club of Madison.

[Information kindly secured by M. D. F. '92.]

HENRY BERTHIER BACON

Born at Warren, Massachusetts, 23 April 1865, of Theodore Fayette Bacon
   (mechanic) and Augusta Louise Green.
Fitted at New Hampton Literary Institution.
Class Status: Special, 1889-90.
Married Emma Marion Eaton at Wentworth, New Hampshire, 14 July 1892.
   Children:
      Theodore Eaton, born 28 November 1894.
      Marion Augusta, 3 September 1900.
Now Treasurer of Savings Bank at Bristol, New Hampshire.

Teacher in New Hampton Literary Institution, New Hampton,
New Hampshire, until 1917. Took a year off and did a little
farming on the side. Took up banking in 1918 and am still at
it. I married in 1892, Emma M. Eaton of Wentworth, New
Hampshire. We have two children, son and daughter. The
son graduated from Bates in 1917 and is now headmaster, Han-

over High School, Hanover, New Hampshire. He married a
graduate of Smith and I am now a grandfather. The daughter
is a music teacher. How many more teachers I may be responsible for remains to be seen.

Incidentally I might mention that in 1919 I was the member
from New Hampton of that large body, the New Hampshire
Legislature. In December, 1918, the influenza nearly got me
and left me in such a condition physically that I did not take
active part in law making and cannot be accused of doing any
harm during my term.

WILLIS ADAMS BAILEY

Born at Zanesville, Ohio, 15 August 1870, of Willis Bailey (druggist)
    and Caroline Augusta McConnell.
Fitted at Phillips Andover.
Class Status: Regular.
Degree: A.B. 1893.
Now President of the Bailey Drug Company at Zanesville, Ohio.

Since 1894 I have been in the wholesale drug business and
since 1901 I have been president of the Bailey Drug Company
of Zanesville, Ohio.

Morris Baker

See Report VI, Page 11.

Walter Farnsworth Baker

See Report VI, Page 12.

WILLIAM FRANCIS BAKER

Born at Springfield, Massachusetts, 13 December 1868, of Henry Kingsley
    Baker (railroads) and Abbie Martha Bacon.
Fitted at Phillips Exeter.
Class Status: Regular.
Degree: A.B. 1893.
Married Daisy Gertrude Cocroft at Staten Island, New York, 25 June
    1902. Children:
        William Francis, Jr., born 4 July 1904.
        Gertrude Florence, 5 October 1906.
Now with American Telephone and Telegraph Company at New York City.

After graduating I first worked with the Springfield, Massachusetts, Foundry Company, and afterwards with the "Springfield Union," first as a reporter and later as city editor. Late hours required by newspaper work did not particularly agree with me and I had to give it up after two years. I was then appointed assistant secretary of the Springfield Fire Insurance Company, where I stayed a year. In the fall of 1897 I took a position with the New York Telephone Company, where I remained twenty years, holding various positions of increasing importance, as time went on, in the contract and commercial departments. Part of the time I was Division Manager for New Jersey and we lived for several years in Montclair, New Jersey, where our children were born. An opportunity to get into the banking business with the Guaranty Trust Company of New York attracted me in the spring of 1918, but after a year, I decided that was not my line and I went back to telephone work, this time with the American Telephone and Telegraph Company, where I am now. Recently, I have had considerable experience with radio broadcasting development in connection with the Telephone Company's system. We have lived in Kew Gardens, New York, on Long Island, for the past five years.

Columbus Calvert Baldwin

See Report VI. Page 14.

John Denison Baldwin

See Report VI. Page 14.

SIDNEY [MILLER] BALLOU

Born at Providence, Rhode Island, 24 October 1870, of Oren Aldrich Ballou (cotton manufacturer) and Charlotte Hitchcock Miller.
Fitted at English High, Boston.
Class Status: Regular.
Degrees: A.B. 1893; A.M. 1895.
Married (1) Thomie Morgan Duke at Louisville, Kentucky, 21 December 1895 (died 7 March 1905). Children:
    Oren Aldrich, born 25 April 1900 (died 27 April 1900).
    Barbara, 7 March 1905.
Married (2) Lucia Burnett at Los Angeles, California, 27 July 1907.
Now General Counsel, California and Hawaiian Sugar Refining Corporation, San Francisco, Cal.

Upon graduating from college I taught mathematics and English in the University School, Chicago, during the fall of 1893. Decided to study law and went back to Harvard Law School after Christmas. In May, 1895, I left Law School to go to Hawaii, to accept a position with the law firm of Carter and Kinney. Three years afterward, I became a partner in the firm and practised law in Hawaii, with various partners, for the most part under the name of Kinney and Ballou, until 1911, with the exception of the period when I was Associate Justice of the Supreme Court of Hawaii under appointment by President Roosevelt. In 1911 I went to Washington as an attorney for the Hawaiian Sugar Planters Association, where I remained until the close of 1922. During the latter part of the war I succeeded in getting into the Coast Artillery, being commissioned second lieutenant and sent to training camp at Fort Monroe, where further progress was interrupted by the Armistice. Kept my commission as Reserve Officer and do a little work along special lines. On January 1st, 1923, I assumed the position of General Counsel of the California and Hawaii Sugar Refining Corporation of San Francisco, a refinery owned by the Hawaiian plantations. I write on various matters, ranging from economics to military and naval affairs. At the invitation of the Navy I was present at the bombing tests when German warships were sunk by airplanes and have been at battle practice off the Pacific Coast. Am a vice-president of the Navy League. Member of various clubs including Metropolitan Club of Washington, Racquet Club of Washington, Harvard Club, New York. Chevy Chase Club and Bohemian Club of San Francisco.

EDGAR JAMES BANKS

Born at Sunderland, Massachusetts, 23 May 1866, of John Randolph
    Banks and Julia Maria Dunklee.
Fitted at Greenfield (Massachusetts) High.
Class Status: Special, 1890-91. With 1894, 1891-93.
Degrees: A.B. 1893; A.M. 1895. Ph.D. (Breslau) 1897.
Married (1) Emma Lucy Lyford at South Woodbury, Vermont, 16 July
    1893.
Married (2) Minja de Miksich at Zagreb, Austria 19 August 1914.
    Children:
        Edgar de Miksich born 2 July 1915.
        Daphne, 3 January 1919.
Now in motion picture business at Eustis, Florida.

From 1893 to 1895 was a student in the Graduate School, taking the A.M. in the latter year. For the next three years studied Assyrian with Professor Delitzsch at Breslau, and took the Ph.D. there, thesis being "Babylonische Hymnen der Berliner Sammlung." 1898, appointed United States Consul at Bagdad; three years later removed to Constantinople as private secretary to United States Minister to Turkey. In 1903, after long waiting and much diplomatic pressure, obtained permission from the Sultan to excavate the Babylonian ruin Bismya, the oldest known city in the world. Work done under auspices of University of Chicago. After about two years, camp was robbed and Turkish government stopped the work. Returned in 1905 to catalogue and arrange results for Haskell Museum of University of Chicago. After President Harper's death, my connection with the university ceased, and took up writing and lecturing. In 1912-13 made an exploring trip to Arabia; climbed Mt. Ararat, crossed the Arabian Desert by camel, etc. After return published several books and lectured in more than 200 colleges, etc. Since the last report my occupation was lecturing and writing until 1921, when I was unexpectedly called to Hollywood. Cal.. to give some suggestions on archaeological matters. as to costumes and houses in Babylonia 4,000 years ago. Thus I became associated with Sacred Films, Inc.. and soon became the general manager. director and vice-president. At the end of 1922 I resigned and came to Florida. to organize the company known as Seminole Films. Incorporated. of which I am now the president. Whether we sink or swim. the future only can tell.

CHARLES RUSSELL BARDEEN

Born at Kalamazoo. Michigan, 8 February 1871, of Charles William Bardeen [Yale 1869] (publisher) and Ellen Palmer Dickerman.
Fitted at Syracuse (New York) High, and Teichmann School, Leipzig, Germany.
Class Status: Special, 1889-90. Joined class Sophomore year.
Degrees: A.B. 1893; M.D. (Johns Hopkins) 1897.
Married (1) Althea Harmer at Chicago, 5 August 1905. Children:
    William, born 19 April 1906.
    John, 23 May 1908.
    Helen, 13 October 1910.
    Thomas, 10 April 1912.

Married (2) Ruth Hames at Madison, Wisconsin, 5 October 1920. Child:
    Ame, born 17 September 1921.
Now Dean of the Medical School and Professor of Anatomy at the Uni-
    versity of Wisconsin.

The four years following graduation from Harvard I spent.
at the Johns Hopkins Medical School. I graduated in the first
class graduated from that school and received the first diploma
issued at commencement because the class was lined up in alphabetical order. I then studied and taught in the department
of anatomy there until 1904 when I came to Wisconsin to take
charge of the department of anatomy here and to lay the foundation of the medical school which was established in 1907 and
of which I was appointed dean. For the past sixteen years I
have been busy looking after the development of this school and
in teaching and research and bringing up a family. My chief
recreation at home has been smoking a pipe on the golf links
and my chief recreation abroad has been smoking too many
cigars at scientific and educational meetings.

CHARLES LOWELL BARLOW

Born at New York City, 10 October 1871, of Francis Channing Barlow
    [H. C. 1855] (lawyer) and Ellen Shaw.
Fitted at A. H. Cutler's.
Class Status: Regular.
Degrees: A.B. 1893; LL.B. 1896.
Now practising law at Boston.

After graduating from the Law School I spent a winter in
Washington as secretary to Justice Gray of the Supreme Court,
then practised law in New York until the autumn of 1903, when
I moved to Boston. The years 1909, 1910, and 1911 I passed in
the Adirondacks, the Berkshires, and Switzerland, living two
winters with Joe Nichols at Saranac Lake. During the war
I was for some time chairman of the Boston Local (draft)
Boards and served on the Legal Sub-committee of the Massachusetts Committee of Public Safety.

Our secretary asks for a detailed account of the last five
years. But what can happen to an unmarried man over fifty
which is worth the telling? At least in my case I find nothing.

EDWARD MITCHELL BARNEY

Born at Lynn, Massachusetts, 28 February 1871, of William Mitchell
   Barney (book-keeper) and Mary Louise Neal.
Fitted at Lynn High.
Class Status: Freshman year only.
Degree: S.T.B. (Tufts) 1898.
Married Caroline Chalker Clark, at Wethersfield, Connecticut, 19 July 1904.
Now savings bank treasurer at Lynn.

After leaving college taught school for a while, then studied
for the ministry, receiving the degree of S.T.B. from Tufts in
1898.   His pastorates included the Universalist Churches at
Beverly, Massachusetts (1898); Bradford, Pennsylvania (1902);
Pawtucket, Rhode Island (1904); and Medford, Massachusetts
(1913); his wife acting as "assistant minister." Meanwhile, in
1909, he became treasurer of the Lincoln Coöperative Bank, and
in 1918 abandoned the ministry and became treasurer of the
Commonwealth Savings Bank of Lynn, Massachusetts.   He reports "Speaking almost every day before some form of organization, boosting the mutual savings bank idea. I have the same
wife I had originally, but I have a different dog."

Edwin Bartlett Bartlett

Born at Pittsfield, Massachusetts, 26 November 1872, of William Francis
   Bartlett [H. C. 1862] (manufacturer) and Mary Agnes Pomeroy.
Fitted at Groton.
Class Status: Left after Sophomore year.
Married (1) Susan Amory at Boston, 21 November 1904 (died 2 July
   1910). Child:
      Elizabeth Amory, born 5 December 1906.
Married (2) Gertrude Wildes Cramer at Boston, 2 January 1917.
Died of sarcoma 5 November 1918 at West Manchester, Massachusetts.

Bartlett entered Groton with a number of us boys in the autumn of 1886. Before he had been there many days he unconsciously seemed to be singled out from among them as the
boy to whom we were all drawn. As time went on this feeling
grew, and when he graduated in 1889 there was not a boy in
the school but wanted to be his friend. He had gained their
affection through a sort of ingenuous winsomeness which could
not be explained or described but which was none the less
.strong. Perhaps it was because his nature was entirely free
from social guile. He never set out to make friends. He did

it without knowing. A gentle raillery, conceived in entire good nature, and evoking no rancor, was possibly the first approach to intimacy, and then came everyone's appreciation of his generous and whole-hearted affection for his fellows. In this there was nothing sentimental or shallow. He was always sane and virile, but his strength was tempered with a real sympathy with which his inexhaustible sense of humor never interfered. As we look back on those old days we think of him as having made many of them the happiest in our school life.

Bartlett remained in college only two years and left at the end of his sophomore year to go into business. During these two years he roomed with Lyman Tremain. When he left he went to work for the Thompson & Houston Co. at Lynn, Mass., where he worked for one year inside the works. He was then transferred to their Boston office.

He left this company in 1893 to enter the treasurer's office of the Brookline Gas Co. in Boston as assistant to the purchasing agent, Charles L. Crehore, '90· In 1904, after the consolidation of this company with the Boston Gas Co., he went to the Frank Jones Brewing Co. of Portsmouth, N. H., as Treasurer. In 1904 he married Miss Susan Amory of Boston and a daughter, Elizabeth Amory, born of this union survives him. His wife died July 2, 1910. In 1909 Bartlett left the Frank Jones Brewing Co. to become president and treasurer of the Amsdell Brewing Co. at Albany, N. Y. which was afterwards consolidated with the Kirchner Brewing Co. under the name of the Amsdell-Kirchner Brewing Co. The Amsdell-Kirchner Brewing Co. was not a succes and was sold to New York parties in 1914. Bartlett, severing his connection with it, became a salesman for the Indian Refining Co. with offices in New York.

In 1916 he moved to Boston and became the New England agent of The Ludlam Steel Co. of Albany, N. Y. June 2nd 1917, he married Miss Gertrude Wildes Cramer at Boston.

G. K. B. and H. H.

MURRAY [AUGUSTUS] BARTLETT

Born at Poughkeepsie, New York, 29 March 1871, of Stanley Bartlett
(manufacturer) and Lida Carolina Simpson.
Fitted at Riverview Academy, Poughkeepsie.
Class Status: ''Four years in three.''

Degrees:A.B. 1892; A.M. 1893; LL.D. (Trinity) 1922.
Married Blanchard Howard at Buffalo, 15 April 1903. Child:
Blanchard, born 6 August 1907.
Now President of Hobart College, Geneva, N. Y.

1893-96: Student at General Theological Seminary, New York
City. 1896-97: Curate at Grace Church, New York City. 1897-
1908: Rector, St. Paul's Church, Rochester, N. Y. 1908-1911:
Dean of American Cathedral, Manila, P. I. 1911-1915: Presi-
dent, University of the Philippines, Manila, P. I. 1917-1919:
War work with Red Cross, Episcopal War Commission and Y.
M. C. A.. (From February, 1918, to March, 1919, attached to
18th Infantry, 1st Division, A. E. F., as acting chaplain.
Wounded near Soissons, July 22, 1918). 1919— President of
Hobart College, Geneva, N. Y. Shortly after my return from
France in April, 1919, I was elected president of Hobart College
in Geneva, N. Y., and was inaugurated the following June.
Hobart is affiliated with the Episcopal Church and we celebrated our centennial in June, 1922. Five members of our
faculty besides myself are graduates of Harvard and many of
our students complete their studies at the University. Geneva is
on the main highway between New York and Buffalo, and I hope
all '93 men who may be motoring through will stop over and
see me.

Since the last report I have received the Legion of Honor
(grade of Chevalier) for "services as chaplain of the First
Division, A. E. F." and a citation from General Pershing which
reads as follows: "Y. M. C. A. Sec'y Murray Bartlett, Actg.
Asst. Chaplain 18th Infantry. For distinguished and exceptional gallantry at Soissons, France, on 20 July, 1918, in the operations of the American Expeditionary Forces. In testimony
thereof and as an expression of appreciation of his valor, I
award him this citation. (Signed) John J. Pershing, Command-
er-in-Chief. Awarded on 21 March, 1919."

In June, 1922, I received the degree of LL.D. from Trinity
College, Hartford. In December, 1922, I accepted a commis-
sion as Major, Chaplain's Section of the Officers Reserve Corps.
Clubs: Harvard (New York); Genessee Valley (Rochester);
Country, University, Rotary (Geneva).

LEWIS BASS

Born at Quincy, Massachusetts, 27 May 1871, of Lewis Bass (broker)
  and Adelaide Morrison.
Fitted at Adams Academy.
Class Status: Regular.
Degrees: A.B. 1893; LL.B. 1895.
Now practising law at Boston.

In 1895 passed the Suffolk bar examinations. In 1900 admitted to Federal practice. From 1895 to 1915 associated with
the late Honorable Robert M. Morse in the general practice of
law. Member of the city government 1900, 1901, 1902, 1903,
1904, 1905, 1906, 1917, 1918, 1919. Member of the Legal
Advisory Board 1918. Have always mingled actively with
the populace, and know what it means to sleep within
reach of a telephone. The effect of time is plainly visible on our
facial features as portrayed in the Twenty-Fifth Anniversary
Report. The older a man grows the more his independence as-
serts itself; he kicks off the close confinements of a routine life,
and is less inclined to talk about worldly attainments, gained
through his own initiative, or otherwise, and initiative action
on the part of the individual, has always been the backbone of
this country. We have all lived to see the comforts or discomforts of the Income Tax, a product of the "Old World," and
we have witnessed wide departures from the "Admonitions of
Washington," but we still go on in our chosen path, and outside
of certain other business interests, I am still actively engaged in
the settlement of estates, trusts, real estate transactions, and
corporation law.

SAMUEL FRANCIS BATCHELDER

Born at Cambridge, Massachusetts, 10 March 1870, of Samuel Batch-
  elder [Harvard 1851] (conveyancer) and Marianne Giles Washburn.
Fitted at St. Paul's.
Class Status: Regular.
Degrees: A.B. 1893; LL.B. 1898.
Now a lawyer at Boston.

My life has been the very apotheosis of monotony. Ever since
leaving the Law School in 1898 and making the "Mediterranean cruise" (then a great novelty) the next year, I have
slept nearly every night in the same bed in Cambridge and sat

nearly every day at the same desk in the same building in Boston—where I am now almost the oldest tenant. My mother died fourteen months ago, leaving (as was found) a will executed thirty-one years before. The primary provisions of that will could be carried out to the letter, not a single change, birth, death, or marriage, having occurred in our household during all that interval. In this unstable age, I am inclined to think such a record is pretty nearly unequalled.

I find myself more and more engaged in those unremunerative jobs which somebody has to do, and which the more worldly wise have very prudently shovelled off on me. Never having learned the secret of working fast and accurately at the same time, I am as busy as the Irishman who had nothing to do and no time to do it in. My principal interest is in local historical investigation and the writing of small calibre historical stuff— greatly to the disgust of Professor Channing. I have no wife. I don't even own a Ford—need more be said?

Harold Munro Battelle

See Report VI, Page 22.

WILLIAM FIELDS BEAL

Born at Nahant, Massachusetts, 23 July 1870, of James H. Beal. (banker) and Louisa Jane Adams.
Fitted at B. J. Legate's.
Class Status: Regular.
Degree: A.B. 1893.
Married .Lillian Sprague Darrow at New York City, 4 November 1897.
   Children:
      James, born 4 February 1899 (died 12 August 1901).
      Willis, 14 June 1902.
      Holland, 2 June 1904.
Now in real estate at New York City.

For the last five years I have been in the real estate and building business with the Wells Construction Company. Constantly fighting to suppress negatives and avoid the diseases, pessimism and old age; learning each and every day from a past master in New York real estate, W. A. Pease, Jr., '93, the good and bad of the dirt upon which the city stands; but to me the whole metropolis is not worth one clam-shell from the Back Bay of Boston.

GORDON KNOX BELL

Born at New York City, 19 February 1871, of Edward Rogers Bell
    [Columbia, temp.] and Eliza Nicol Soutter.
Fitted at Groton.
Class Status: Regular.
Degrees: A.B. 1893; LL.B. 1896.
Married Marian Mason Crafts at South Salem, New York, 11 May 1899.
    Child:
        Gordon Knox, Jr., born 7 January 1902.
Now practising law in New York City.

After graduation, I spent three years in the Harvard Law
School, taking my degree of LL.B. in 1896. I was admitted to
the New York bar in February, 1897, and entered the law office
of Turner, McClure and Rolston, 22 William Street, New York.
I have been a partner in that firm since 1909. The name is now
Geller, Rolston and Blanc. Since 1893 I have been to Europe
eight times, around the world once, and to Bermuda, Canada,
and Honolulu. (The last in company with Mr. James Austin
Wilder). I was active in local politics from 1904 to 1916. During that period I was (and still am) a member of the Republican County Committee, President of the 29th Assembly District
Republican Club, Vice-Chairman New York State Convention
of 1910, and represented the 17th Senatorial District of New
York in the Constitutional Convention of 1915. In the convention Mr. Root appointed me a member of the committee on Con-
tingent Expenses, the Committee on Prisons, Penitentiaries and
the Prevention and Punishment of Crime, and the Committee on
State Charities.

In the spring of 1918 I became Chief of the Division of Inquiry, War Trade Board, Washington, D. C., and remained in
that position until May, 1919; when, there being no more work
in Washington for me, I closed the Division of Inquiry, and returned to New York practice.

I have made altogether too many speeches but fortunately
none of them have been published. I belong to the Union, Harvard, and Tuxedo Clubs of New York, and the Harvard and
Tavern Clubs of Boston. I am a past master of Holland Lodge,
No. 8, F. and A. M., of New York, and past district deputy of
the 4th Masonic District. For 12 years I have been a manager
of the House of Refuge (Juvenile Reformatory) on Randall's

Island, New York City, and since 1906 I have been vice-presi-
dent of the Society for the Prevention of Cruelty to Animals.
I am also a trustee of the Police Riot Relief Fund of New York
City.

Health—Almost uniformly good. Pastimes—Almost anything that comes along, especially working on our place at
Katonah, N. Y.

FRANCIS GANO BENEDICT

Born at Milwaukee, 3 October 1870, of Washington Gano Benedict
(real estate) and Harriet Emily Barrett.
Fitted at English High (Boston) and Massachusetts College of Phar-
macy.
Class Status: Special, 1889-92. Joined Class Senior year.
Degrees: A.B. 1893; A.M. 1894; Ph.D. (Heidelberg) 1895; S.D. Hon.
(Wesleyan) 1911.
Married Cornelia Golay at Brewer, Maine, 28 July 1897. Child:
Elizabeth Harriet, born 12 March 1902.
Now Director of Carnegie Nutrition Laboratory at Boston.

Went to Heidelberg, Germany, September 1, 1894. Took degree of Ph.D. in August, 1895. Appointed instructor in chemistry at Wesleyan University in fall of 1895. Ultimately promoted to associate professor and full professor. In 1907 was
called by the Carnegie Institute of Washington to act as direct-
or of the Nutrition Laboratory, built upon ground purchased
of the Harvard Medical School. Building designed and construction superintended. Trips to Europe in laboratory interests in 1907, 1910 and 1913. (All trips rather extended, going
into Russia). Elected member National Academy of Sciences
and several foreign scientific societies. Research work chiefly on
the nutrition of man has brought intimate relationship with International Y. M. C. A. college at Springfield, New York
Zoölogical Park, Columbia University, and New Hampshire
State College. All these institutions coöperating in researches.
All of my time is devoted to the laboratory and to experiments
with special apparatus with close affiliation with clinics and
especially Dr. Elliott P. Joslin of Boston, the finest Yale man I
know. Summers usually spent at my home on the Maine coast
at Machiasport. My former chief, Professor W. O. Atwater,
used to say that ''Heaven was a place where you could conduct
scientific research and never make a report.'' I have had to

write about twenty monographs and approximately one hundred and twenty-five scientific papers. I have at last found a man comparing with my revered Professor, Josiah P. Cooke. He is Dr. Robert S. Woodward, the recently retired President of the Carnegie Institute of Washington. All one's life accomplishments can be traced to the stimulus of these two men.

EDWARD MELLEN BENNETT

Born at West Medford, Massachusetts, 5 October 1871, of Theodore Wilbar Bennett (merchant) and Anna Brown Mellen.
Fitted at W. Nichols's.
Class Status: Entered with 1894. Joined Class Junior year.
Degrees: A.B. 1893; LL.B. 1897.
Now practising law at Boston.

After leaving college I entered the Harvard Law School, from which I was graduated in the year 1897. I spent most of the two years after leaving the Law School in travel and study in Europe, and began the practice of law in Boston in the fall of 1899. I have continued in practice since that time, and as I look back it seems to me that my work in my profession has so largely absorbed my time that there is little that I have done to mention outside of this work. I served as a member of the School·Committee in my home town, Wayland, Massachusetts, for six years. Wayland has been my home since I left the Law School and I have been much interested in local affairs there. I have made one short trip to Europe since I began my work in Boston.

GUY BROWN BENNETT

Born at Owatonna, Minnesota, 27 October 1871, of Leonard Loomis Bennett (banker) and Arabella Fidelia Brown.
Fitted at Owatonna High.
Class Status: Special, 1889-92. Joined Class Senior year.
Degree: A.B. 1893.
Married Winifred Fay Niles at Owatonna, Minnesota, 30 June 1900.
    Child:
        Leonard Niles, born 22 July 1909.
Now bank vice-president at Owatonna, Minnesota.

How can a man write something *new* about such *old stuff?* Not a thing has happened new to me since the Sixth Report. I have no more children and no more wives than I had at that

time, and am doing about the same work and living about the
same way that I have been for many years. Some disappointments have crept in. I have never been able to attend a class
reunion and the fact that I cannot accept the fine invitations of
the New York members is a source of considerable regret to me.
I think of my class and its members frequently, however, and
wish them all, all that their hearts desire.

RALPH WILHELM [ALEXIS] BERGENGREN

Born at Gloucester, Massachusetts, 2 March 1871, of Frederic Wilhelm
    Alexis Bergengren [Upsala] (physician) and Caroline Francis Boynton.
Fitted at Lynn High.
Class Status: Special 1889-91. Joined Class Junior year.
Degree: A.B. 1893.
Married Anna Farquhar at Boston, 26 January 1900.
Now Author and journalist at Scituate, Massachusetts.

I went awhile to the Cowles Art School, Boston, not long
enough to become an artist. Opportunity and emolument
tempting, I made comic pictures for Boston Globe. Herbert
Small, of Small, Maynard and Company, suggesting it. I had
published a book of such pictures, "In Case of Need," by said
firm; book long ago vanished. Lacking incessant and consecutive invention, I ceased comic cartoonist: all this prior to 1900,
when I got married, and there's a date for you! I became
connected, as a staff writer, with the Publicity Bureau, one of
the first, perhaps the first, organizations to provide publicity
for miscellaneous clients: it has long ago vanished. I also began writing for the *Boston Transcript*, magazine section, book
department, and editorial page, and still (occasionally) do. I
wrote for magazines (when they were willing) fiction and articles; I wrote some advertising; I wrote a pirate yarn for
Collier's which led to others, there, in *Everybody's,* and other
magazines. A book of them, "Gentlemen All and Merry Companions" has been published by B. J. Brimmer Company, Boston, 1923. There's another date. Incidentally, I wrote essays
for the *Atlantic Monthly*, reprinted in three small volumes by
Atlantic Monthly Press. The penetration of this firm having
discovered in me a certain childishness, I wrote for them two
juvenile books: "Jane, Joseph and John; their Book of Verses,"
and "David the Dreamer." To round out this record, I am

also writing (1923) for the *Christian Science Monitor*, essays,
book notices, and the simple adventures of a dear little child
named "Betsy."

' I lived in Boston in an apartment, and now I live in Scituate
in a house. If I had travelled I would gladly tell you all about
it; but I haven't, so there you are. I inherited (January,
1922: date!) half of an office building in Lynn, and am managing the property for a brother and myself.

HENRY NEWHALL BERRY

Born at Lynn, Massachusetts, 2 September 1870, of Benjamin Jenkins
    Berry (water commissioner) and Sarah Catherine Newhall.
Fitted at Berkeley School, Boston.
Class Status: Regular.
Degrees: A.B. 1893; LL.B. 1896.
Married Mabel Lavinia Breed at Lynn, 24 October 1900. Children:
    Henry Newhall, Jr., born 29 September 1901.
    Katharine, 21 April 1903.
    Joseph Breed, 10 May 1905.
    Mabel Lavinia, 17 November 1906.
Now practising law at Boston.

Upon leaving college I travelled for several months in the
United States and went into Harvard Law School in April,
1894. I was graduated from the School in June, 1896, and
passed the Suffolk County bar examinations in that month. I
commenced the practice of law at Boston, in September, 1896,
and was then connected with the firm of Nichols and Cobb, a
well-known firm engaged in corporation law on Water Street,
Boston. I continued this association until Nichols and Cobb
dissolved in the spring of 1900, upon the death of Henry G.
Nichols, the senior partner of that firm. I then became associated with Hutchins and Wheeler and was trial lawyer with
them and continued this association until December 31, 1908,
when I formed a corporation with Charles C. Bucknam, Esq.,
under the name and style of Berry and Bucknam. We started
in January 1, 1909, at 84 State Street, Boston, and have been
engaged in corporation practice, which has steadily increased
since that time. In a few years we moved our office to 85 Devonshire Street, Boston, where we have been in practice ever
since. On January 1, 1923, we took into partnership with us

Charles F. Lovejoy, Esq., and the firm name commencing January 1, 1923, has been Berry, Bucknam and Lovejoy.

During the last five years my legal residence has been at Lynn and I have lived at Lynn, Massachusetts, during the winters. I have lived during the summers in Topsfield. Massachusetts.

During the last five years besides being actively engaged in corporation law practice I have been pretty actively connected with a number of concerns in Lynn, Massachusetts. In particular I have been active as a Director in the Central National Bank of Lynn and also as a Trustee, Vice-President and member of the Investing Committee of the Lynn Five Cents Savings Bank. I have also been connected with the Lynn Chapter of the American Red Cross. having been Chairman for two years out of the five. I have also become incidentally connected with certain business concerns, acting as a Director and Vice-President of the Richmond Lace Works, a concern for the manufacture of machine made lace in Rhode Island with a sales office in New York City. I have also been a Director of the Lynn Gas and Electric Company, as well as a Manager of the Lynn Hospital. I have acted as counsel for Lynn Hospital, for Central National Bank of Lynn and for Lynn Five Cents Savings Bank.

I have kept in good trim by keeping pretty steadily at exercises in my spare time. I still play tennis to a certain extent and have taken considerable interest in golf during the last two or three years, my home golf club being the Tedesco Country Club at Swampscott, Massachusetts.

Edgar Francis Billings

See Report VI. Page 28.

RUDOLPH MICHAEL BINDER

Born at Hetzeldorf, Hungary. 11 March 1865, of Johann Binder (farmer) and Sarah Orben.
Fitted himself.
Class Status: Freshman. 1891-92. Senior, 1892-93.
Degrees: A.B. 1893: S.T.B. (Univ. Chicago) 1897; Grad. Gen. Theol. Sem., N. Y., 1898: Ph.D. (Columbia) 1903.

Married Garnette Faye Brammer at Cincinnati, 10 June 1913.   Children:
    James Rudolph, born 7 April 1914.
    Brammer, 7 September 1915.
Now professor in sociology at New York University.

After graduation I held a pastorate at West Park on Hudson,
New York, for two years. While there I became intimately acquainted with John Burroughs, the naturalist—a friendship
which lasted until the latters death in 1921. Spent two years
at the University of Chicago; one year at General Theological
Seminary, New York; two years as assistant to Dr. William
Reed Huntington, Grace Church, New York; one year at Oxford
University, England; two years at General Theological Seminary as teaching fellow; four years at St. Bartholomew's Church
with the late Bishop David H. Greer and Dr. Leighton Parks.
Then I started my real life's work—the teaching of sociology at
New York University in 1906 after having prepared myself for
that task by acquiring the Ph.D. at Columbia University in
1903. I have been lecturer, assistant, and associate professor,
and am now full professor of sociology. During the World War
I was a pronounced anti-German as the Report for 1918 shows.
I was married in 1913 and we have two boys. Taking care of a
family is no joke but it has compensations far outweighing the
troubles. Teaching and writing have been my principal voca-
tions, with gardening as an avocation.

In 1920 I published two books—"Major Social Problems,"
and "Health and Social Progress"; another—"Business and the
Professions"—followed in 1922. At present I am under contract for two other books. Have done considerable lecturing as
far west as Parkersburg, West Virginia, and written many
magazine and newspaper articles.

Ralph Bisbee
See Report VI, Page 31.

DEXTER BLAGDEN
Born at New York City, 8 October 1870, of George Blagden [Harvard
    1856] (banker) and Frances Meredith Dexter.
Fitted at A. H. Cutler's.
Class Status: Regular.
Degree: A.B. 1893.
Married Mrs. Mabel (Whitney) Sabin at New York City, 1 April 1918.
Now broker at New York City.

Since graduation I have been continuously in the banking and. brokerage business at New York City, at first with Hoskier, Woods and Company, then with Clark, Dodge and Company, then with Rhoades and Richmond. In 1906 became a partner in Charles Head and Company, where I remained till 1914, when I joined the firm of McGraw, Blagden and Draper. Now have my own offices at 111 Broadway. I am still a member of the New York Stock Exchange, endeavoring to earn an honest. living. Am old-fashioned and still remain married.

[CHARLES] ARTHUR BLAKE

Born at Boston, 26 January 1872, of John George Blake [Harv. Med. 1862] (physician) and Mary Elizabeth McGrath.
Fitted at Boston Latin.
Class Status: Regular.
Degree: A.B. 1893.
Married Leslie Appleton Knowles at Boston, 7 September 1910. Children::
    Harriette Appleton, born 23 November 1912.
    Leslie, 12 December 1913.
    Arthur, Jr., 6 June 1916.
    John Knowles, 2 February 1918.
    Mary Alice, 7 August 1921.
Now in insurance at Boston.

After reading Plutarch's Lives and the lives of the candidates for Harvard Overseers, I feel rather bashful about speaking about myself. I have been in the insurance business ever since I left college and am still in it, although so far it hasn't given me Cullinan's beautiful facility of expression.

After I graduated I became interested in the militia and was, connected with it for about fifteen years, most of it in the field artillery. During the war I spent about twenty-two months in. the Navy, where I served without distinction. I wish I were a hero like Charlie Cummings. But I have always loved the sea and have sometimes been known to use nautical words. I have five children at home from ten years old down. The two oldest are girls and when they won the rope climbing contest in their school recently (climbing thirty feet) it pleased me much more than if they had excelled in some landlubber's accomplishment.

Having no honors or high public positions and not desiring any, I think the pleasantest time of my life is the time between:

daylight and dark, which I always spend with my wife (have a very beautiful and accomplished wife), and children.

Sports: Rowing, sailing and swimming. Travel: To Athens in 1896 with first Olympic team and several trips to Europe.

FRANCIS STANTON BLAKE

Born at Milton, Massachusetts, 26 May 1872, of George Baty Blake [H. C. 1859] (banker) and Harriet Johnson.
Fitted at G. W. C. Noble's.
Class Status: Regular.
Degree: A.B. 1893.
Married Eugenie Marie Stringfellow White at New York City, 16 October 1902.
Now living at Cap Martin, France.

From October, 1917, to June, 1919, I was in France with headquarters in Paris as Chief of Bureau of Canteen of the A. R. C. This work increased rapidly with the arrival of the A. E. F. It grew from a personnel of 70 A. R. C: workers in four Canteens in October, 1917, with 135,000 men served per month, to a personnel of 496 Canteen workers in 67 Canteens with a service of 1,818,650 per month in October, 1918. After the Armistice it was necessary to continue this work, as in many cases it was then more urgently needed than during the war. I therefore carried on until the end of May, 1919. During this time, October, 1917, to June, 1919, the Bureau spent 29,855,704 francs, which constituted a per capita cost of less than one franc per head. So much for these dry and out-of-date statistics. One especial event must be mentioned which was the twenty-fifth gathering of '93 at the Cercle Unies Interallies in Paris on June 20th. This had been arranged by the able executive and organizer C. C. Goodrich. Although the Boche was then knocking at the door, that did not trouble him, so Fearing, Fiske, Dunn, Denny, Thomas, Goodrich, and myself occupied a large table, highly decorated with flowers and fizz in the center of the dining room, flanked by envious Generals of the Allied Forces, who evidently and correctly considered the gathering to be of supreme importance. Have been home each summer, 1919-20-21-22, returning to the South of France for the winter. My great regret is that all our reunions take place in the winter, and suggest Monte Carlo a good bet for the next one. I will attend to the posting if Sam will do the rest.

GEORGE BATY BLAKE

Born at Boston, 28 September 1870, of George Baty Blake [Harvard
1859] (banker) and Harriet Johnson.
.Fitted at Groton.
Class Status: Regular.
Degree: A.B. 1893.
Married Margaret Hunnewell at Wellesley, Massachusetts, 30 June 1902.
Children:
George Baty, Jr., 20 September 1916.
Now living at Lenox, Massachusetts.

Margaret Hunnewell, born 1 August 1904.
Julia Overing, 8 March 1907.
George Baty, Jr., 20 September 1916.
Now living at Lenox, Massachusetts.

Since my last report have been living in Brookline (29 Colchester Street) in the winters, and Lenox in the summers. Joined the Motor Corps at the time of the Boston Police Strike and served as a traffic policeman for over two months. Did some work in the interests of General Wood's candidacy in the Presidential primaries, and attended the Republican convention at Chicago as an onlooker. For the last two years have not been well. Have spent the present winter in Santa Barbara, California.

HENRY FORDYCE BLAKE

Born at Belmont, Massachusetts, 27 February 1872, of Thomas Dawes
Blake (manufacturer) and Susan Price Symonds.
Fitted at Boston Latin.
Class Status: Regular.
Degrees: A.B. 1893; LL.B. 1896.
Married Alice Christine Riley at Manchester, New Hampshire, 9 September 1897. Children:
Sallie Ropes, born 28 May 1898 (married Frank Cullen Brophy
(Yale 1917) 3 May 1919).
Thomas Dawes, 2d, 28 June 1899 (died 28 August 1900).
Alice Ainsmere, 17 July 1901.
Phyllis Marie, 13 January 1903.
Mary Fordyce, 2 August 1909.
Now living in Seattle.

Have nothing to report since my last one except that my oldest daughter, Sallie Ropes Blake, married Frank Cullen Brophy (A.B. Yale, 1917) May 3, 1919, and they have two children: Alice Blake Brophy, born May 10, 1920; Ellen Patricia Brophy, born January 19, 1922. I have retired from the active practice of law, but continue to reside at Seattle.

David Blaustein

See Report VI, Page 36.

WILLIAM MILLER BOOTH

Born at Clayville, New York, 4 September 1870, of William Moss Booth
   (farmer) and Irena Miller.
Fitted at Utica Free Academy and Hamilton College.
Class Status: Special, 1890-91; Scientific, 1892-93.
Degree: S.B. 1893.
Married Marian Booth Foster at Cleveland, 29 December 1896.
Now chemical engineer at Syracuse, New York.

In common with many other professional men, I found the
years 1918-21 unusually difficult with all new business pro-
jects postponed. During this national re-construction period,
I decided to study and wait. The mills are now busy again and.
likewise, I have my time fully employed with problems of production and new business. It has been my plan to do some writing in connection with my professional work.

Mrs. Booth accompanied me upon about eighty automobile
trips covering New York State and much of New England.
Three vacations were spent upon Cape Cod. This territory is
our greatest vacation discovery during the past twenty-five
years. We intend to make an annual trip. Last summer at
the earnest solicitation of Mrs. Booth, I purchased a few acres.
of fruit east of this city. Here we expect to spend our summers.
commuting between this place and Syracuse.

AUGUSTUS JESSE BOWIE, JR.

Born at San Francisco, 10 December 1872, of Augustus Jesse Bowie
   [Freiberg] (mining engineer) and Elizabeth Friedlander.
Fitted at Adams Academy.
Class Status: Regular.
Degrees: A.B. 1893; S.B. (Mass. Inst. Tech.) 1896.
Now an engineer at San Francisco.

Not heard from. And after all—

Robert Pendleton Bowler

Born at Cincinnati, Ohio, 25 January 1871, of George Pendleton Bowler
   [Kenyon 1866] (railroads) and May Williamson.
Fitted at St. Paul's.
Class Status: Regular.
Degrees: A.B. 1893; LL.B. 1896.
Died at New York City, 28 May 1919.

Robert Pendleton Bowler died at New York City of kidney and liver complications May 28, 1919. His great-great-grand-father, Metcalf Bowler, was an East Indian merchant of New-port, R. I., and lost a fortune by privateering in the Revolution. Two generations later the family moved to Cincinnati, where Robert was born, Jan. 25, 1871, of George Pendleton and May (Williamson) Bowler. His mother was descended from the founder of Newport, Ky., and his grandmother was Miss Pendle-ton of Virginia. At twelve he went to St. Paul's School, whence he entered Harvard as a regular member of '93· Proceeding to the Law School he took his LL.B. in 1896 with high rank. He was admitted to the New York Bar in 1897, and spent two years in the office of Bowers and Sands. In the spring of 1899, following a severe attack of typhoid, he went to Europe, and was shortly appointed special assistant to the Attorney-General to represent the Department of Justice at Madrid, where he helped to draft the new consular, maritime, extradition, and commercial treaties with Spain made necessary by the War of 1898. He then came back to America and spent some time in out-door life and travel, mostly in California. Returning to New York City about 1906 he became actively interested in the development of coal lands in Virginia and Kentucky and in the manufacture of coke. This led to the opening up of large and valuable mining properties on the northeastern coast of Cuba, producing iron, copper, manganese, and chrome nickel. Of the company formed, the Moa Bay Iron Co., he became presi-dent, with headquarters still at New York. Much of his early youth he spent abroad (he spoke French before English) and

David Blaustein

See Report VI, Page 36.

WILLIAM MILLER BOOTH

Born at Clayville, New York, 4 September 1870, of William Moss Booth
(farmer) and Irena Miller.
Fitted at Utica Free Academy and Hamilton College.
Class Status: Special, 1890-91; Scientific, 1892-93.
Degree: S.B. 1893.
Married Marian Booth Foster at Cleveland, 29 December 1896.
Now chemical engineer at Syracuse, New York.

In common with many other professional men, I found the
years 1918-21 unusually difficult with all new business pro-
jects postponed. During this national re-construction period,
I decided to study and wait. The mills are now busy again and
likewise, I have my time fully employed with problems of production and new business. It has been my plan to do some writing in connection with my professional work.

Mrs. Booth accompanied me upon about eighty automobile
trips covering New York State and much of New England.
Three vacations were spent upon Cape Cod. This territory is
our greatest vacation discovery during the past twenty-five
years. We intend to make an annual trip. Last summer at
the earnest solicitation of Mrs. Booth, I purchased a few acres
of fruit east of this city. Here we expect to spend our summers
commuting between this place and Syracuse.

To a questionnaire sent in January, Bowie replies in June:
"I have been engaged in the manufacture of high tension
electrical apparatus for transmission lines, including switches,
lightning arresters and fuses The power development in California is increasing very rapidly, calling for new equipment to
meet the changed conditions, demanding strict attention to the
work in which I am engaged. Altho the recent decision of
Governor Smith will cause a general exodus to the state of New
York and much as I should like to join therein it is impossible
at the present time."

Robert Pendleton Bowler died at New York City of kidney and liver complications May 28, 1919. His great-great-grand-father, Metcalf Bowler, was an East Indian merchant of Newport, R. I., and lost a fortune by privateering in the Revolution. Two generations later the family moved to Cincinnati, where Robert was born, Jan. 25, 1871, of George Pendleton and May (Williamson) Bowler. His mother was descended from the founder of Newport, Ky., and his grandmother was Miss Pendleton of Virginia. At twelve he went to St. Paul's School, whence he entered Harvard as a regular member of '93· Proceeding to the Law School he took his LL.B. in 1896 with high rank. He was admitted to the New York Bar in 1897, and spent two years in the office of Bowers and Sands. In the spring of 1899, following a severe attack of typhoid, he went to Europe, and was shortly appointed special assistant to the Attorney-General to represent the Department of Justice at Madrid, where he helped to draft the new consular, maritime, extradition, and commercial treaties with Spain made necessary by the War of 1898. He then came back to America and spent some time in out-door life and travel, mostly in California. Returning to New York City about 1906 he became actively interested in the development of coal lands in Virginia and Kentucky and in the manufacture of coke. This led to the opening up of large and valuable mining properties on the northeastern coast of Cuba, producing iron, copper, manganese, and chrome nickel. Of the company formed, the Moa Bay Iron Co., he became president, with headquarters still at New York. Much of his early youth he spent abroad (he spoke French before English) and in later life his frequent visits to Cuba, added to various travels in England, France, Canada, the Panama Zone, etc., with his residence in Spain, made him thoroughly cosmopolitan. Of a notably genial and sociable temperament, he was a natural club man, and a welcome member of many of the best organizations in New York, Boston, Cincinnati, and Washington. He was passionately fond of open-air sports, especially shooting, fishing, sailing, riding and golf. His legal domicile was Bar Harbor, Maine, where he owned much real estate and spent almost every summer. He was deeply interested in class affairs, and his sunny and roguish presence added to many a gathering a zest which can never be replaced. He was unmarried. [His second name of Bonner he dropped in youth.]

Ralph Hartt Bowles

Born at Cherryfield, Maine, 7 February 1870, of Henry Haviland Bowles
  (merchant) and Abbie Adams Wakefield.
Fitted at Phillips Exeter.
Class Status: Regular.
Degrees: A.B. 1893; A.M. 1896.
Married Namee Clopton Henderson at Washington, District of Columbia,
  20 December 1901. Children:
  　Ralph Hartt, Jr., born 1 May 1903.
  　Donald Henderson, 19 June 1905.
  　John Eliot, 11 January 1911.
Died by drowning near Caldwell, New Jersey, 31 August 1919.

Ralph Hartt Bowles was drowned on Aug. 31, 1919, while
rowing on the Passaic River, near Caldwell, N. J.　He was
born at Cherryfield, Maine (the family having long been associated with Machias), on February 7, 1870, of Henry Haviland
and Abbie Adams (Wakefield) Bowles.　He fitted at Phillips
Exeter, and was a regular member of the Class.　Two years
immediately following graduation he spent in Constantinople,
as private tutor in the household of a naturalized Armenian,
a man of wealth and influence.　He thus obtained an intimate
knowledge of a phase of life little understood in America.　He
made memorable horseback trips through the Troad and other
parts of Asia Minor.

Returning to Harvard he took a year in the graduate school
and received the A.M. in 1896.　For another year he was instructor in English in the Lake Forest Academy, Illinois, then
going back to Exeter and taking the same post there.　Here
he remained for several years, editing various texts for school
use and serving as official reader in English for the College
Entrance Examination Board, besides his regular work.　But
as his family increased he found it impossible to maintain them
on his salary, and in 1907 he resigned, to become educational
editor for Charles Scribner's Sons in New York City; he made
his home at Montclair, N. J.　In addition to his editorial work
he did a large amount of original writing for children's periodicals and school books.

He was active in civic and community movements near his
home, and was president of several local associations of that
nature.　In outdoor pursuits he was fond of tennis and tramping, and kept up his interest in music; in College he had sung
tenor on the Glee Club, and he used to refer to the ''western

trips'' as the pleasantest of his reminiscences. His death removes with startling suddenness a bright, warm-hearted, and interesting personality; he had closed his last report by saying, ''I am enjoying life as never before, feel full of vigor and hope, and plan for new work in the years to come.'' On December 20, 1901, at Washington, D. C., he married Namee Clopton Henderson, who with three sons survives him. The eldest, Ralph, is a junior at Harvard, and the second, Donald, is preparing at Exeter.

Southwick writes: ''Bowles was one of my few intimate friends in our class. I met him a week or so after entering the class. Ralph, to me, was a sort of liberal education. Frequently we took long walks—and I was always amazed at the varied knowledge which he had acquired at school. He was essentially a scholar, without being pedantic or assertive, and was always willing to listen—a great virtue. His was a most lovable nature —always cheerful, calm and serene, and his sense of humor was by no means small. Those who knew him well still mourn his untimely death.''

GEORGE HALE BRABROOK

Born at Taunton, Massachusetts, 21 August 1871, of George Brabrook (Treasurer) and Eliza Hale Knowles.
Fitted at St. Paul's.
Class Status: Regular.
Degree: A.B. 1893.
Married Grace Bradford White at Taunton, Massachusetts, 15 February 1895. Children:
   Barbara, born 4 December 1895.
   Harwood, 28 December 1900.
Now silver mining in Nevada and Montana.

My business is still the development and sale of mining properties and my travels in the past fifteen years have been confined to the mountains of our western states.

To illustrate the curious chances of the mining game I mention that the last property I developed had lain for forty years under the eagle eyes of the engineers of the Anaconda Copper Mining Company who could have bought the entire ground for $50,000. Today, after two years active development of this ground by the able organization to whom I transferred the title, a gross value of $15,000,000 worth of ore has been indicated by a total expenditure of $125,000, including purchase price on the bonds.   A five hundred ton mill has just started operations and results show that mining and milling costs will be as low as any of the best run properties.

I am looking forward this summer to investigating some of the new British Guiana discoveries which promise some very profitable mines.

CALVERT BREWER

Born at Bergen Point, New Jersey, 2 October 1871, of William Augustus Brewer [Harvard S.B. 1854] (insurance) and Bella Calvert Fisher.
Fitted at Dearborn Morgan School.
Class Status: Regular.
Degree: A.B. 1893.
Married Mary Mandeville Minott at South Orange, New Jersey, 10 February 1902. Child:
       Mary Calvert, born 15 October 1917.
Now banker at New York City.

Entered employ of the United States Mortgage and Trust Company, October, 1893, and have been with that company in various capacities from office boy up to present position as vice-president in charge of trusts.   Member of Council and Treasurer of University Settlement, 1916-1921.   Member of Executive Committee and Treasurer, American Society for Control of Cancer.   Member of Executive Committee and Treasurer of New York Stock Transfer Association.   Member of Executive Committee of Corporate Fiduciaries Association.   Director Standard Insurance Company.   Since marriage in 1902 have had seven trips to Europe and one to Honolulu and Japan. European trips have covered England, France, Spain, Italy, Switzerland, Algeria, Tunis, Egypt, Greece, Turkey, Austria, Hungary, and Dalmatia (Jugo-Slavia).   Clubs: Racquet and Tennis, New York; Piping Rock (golf); The Recess (lunch club); Harvard Club of New York.

Stewart Meily Brice

See Report VI, Page 40.

HENRY MORGAN BROOKFIELD

Born at Brooklyn, New York, 17 October 1871, of William Brookfield (glass manufacturer) and Kate Morgan.
Entered from Columbia.

Class Status: Entered Sophomore, 1891-92. Joined Class Senior year.
Degree: A.B. 1893.
Married Louise Lord at Orange, New Jersey, 15 February 1906. Children:
William Lord, born 8 February 1908.
Henry Morgan, Jr., 11 April 1911.
Samuel Lord, 6 September 1915.
Now President of Brookfield Glass Company (retired) at New York City.

Not having had a job with royalty like Fanny Burney or Pepys, I have never kept a diary. As near as I can remember, my brother and I have been running the business that was started by my grandfather and father. Soon after graduation I became its vice-president, and in due course of the revolving years its president. In 1917 my brother beat me to it and went into the Army. Oh! During 1919-1920 I was quite ill and decided to retire from business. I have not taken up any new business, being busy enough at present, in looking after my three sons. What bothers me just at present is the recent action of the Overseers on the racial question. There are a number of colleges which are ninety per cent. Anglo-Saxon. The boys will go to those places instead of to Harvard.

ARTHUR NICHOLSON BROUGHTON

Born at Jamaica Plain, Massachusetts, 20 December 1870, of Nicholson
Broughton (customs officer) and Aravesta Susan White.
Fitted at Boston Latin, 3 years; Roxbury Latin, 3 years.
Class Status: Regular.
Degrees: A.B. 1893; M.D. 1897.
Married Lillian DeWolf Pingree at Jamaica Plain, Massachusetts, 21 December 1898. Adopted Frances Broughton in 1909.
Now practising medicine at Jamaica Plain, Massachusetts.

Four years (1893-1897) in the Harvard Medical School, two years (1897-1898) surgical house officer in the Massachusetts General Hospital. In general practice ever since in Boston (Jamaica Plain). Assistant Surgeon of Faulkner Hospital (seventy-five beds) which is rated Grade A by the American College of Surgeons. My practice has been that of a modern general practitioner, with enough of all kinds of special work, surgery, obstetrics, etc., etc. Intensely interesting, very hard, very well worth while. I have had for some years a full-time assistant, of great value.

We have been abroad twice, and over the Canadian Pacific and to Alaska. Other summers I have spent at Gloucester, Massa-

chusetts, where we have a very pleasant home near the golf
links. I have also been fishing for several years at the St. Bernard Fish and Game Club in Canada, which I joined and which
gives me the most complete vacation.

During the war I had charge of the Radio and Naval Hospital sick who filled our own hospital. For a year, also I went
back as Assistant Surgeon to the Out-Patient Department of
the Massachusetts General Hospital, to take the place of younger men sent across. I was one of the Red Cross unit sent to
Halifax at the time of the explosion.

The past five years have been merely an increasing amount
of daily routine work, with no opportunity for travel. Good
vacations at Gloucester, fishing in Canada, shooting in North
Carolina this winter, have served to keep me fit. My daughter,
at thirteen, is going through Miss Winsor's, my wife has been
well, and in general we are well content. My most severe responsibility at present is in caring for the Winsors, Dodges,
Nutters, Pearsons, and others of my classmates and their families. A very heavy burden.

PHILIP TURNER BROWN

Born at Boston, 21 December 1870, of Frederick Turner Brown (broker)
     and Caroline Vose Emmons.
Fitted at Berkeley School, New York.
Class Status: With class four years.
Degree: A.B. 1895 as of 1893.
Now doing nothing at New York City.

Too busy to reply—as usual.

ROYAL BENTON BROWN

Born at Troy, New York, 17 May, 1871, of Charles Ambrose Brown (mer-
     chant) and Mary Frances Ball.
Fitted at Albany Academy.
Class Status: Special, 1889-91.
Married Margaret Stanley at Troy, New York, 12 March, 1920.
Now travelling in the West.

When the legislators of this great and free country decided to
leave only the "dumb" and cut out the "free" from freedom,
to keep from being blackmailed by the "Women's League," or
whatever it is called, one naturally got good and sore and

thought why not go back again, to where one's forefathers came from in order to have a bit to say about their own manner of living, since it can't be done here. The thought prevails. In regard to returning to the cradle of the tribe, that may come later, but one would like first to see conditions rather more settled in Europe before making very definite plans toward settling so far from the source of supplies. Later on, perhaps, Old Horace might be found in Switzerland, renewing his intellect, at the old school of his youth. Eh, What?

In 1921 I sold my farm near Albany, and later the place in town. In 1922 I sold the mill plant and machinery and other business, in which I was interested, and started to wander. Have worked West, stopping so long as convenient at several places, and when this reaches you, will be in California, D. V., motoring about, more or less, to see the country. I may settle down somewhere and do a little painting, if I havn't forgotten how, and I may not care enough for the climate and life to remain, but this may depend largely upon how my health is affected, for I have been in rather poor health for most of the past year. Have attempted to paint and also write, since I left the East but have been unable to stick to either because the moment I become interested, anything that is gained in health takes wings and leaves me; however, it may be different in the relaxing climate of the West Coast.

ARTHUR TABER BROWNE

Born at Des Moines, Iowa, 7 October 1867, of Hamilton Browne (coal operator) and Mary Louise Napier.
Fitted at Phillips Exeter.
Class Status: Regular.
Degrees: A.B. 1893; LL.B. (Univ. Wis.) 1894.
Married Clara Louise Holmdale at Minneapolis, 9 October 1901. Children:
        Hamilton, 2d, born 26 June 1905.
        Betty, 23 February 1909.
Now in Insurance at Chicago.

Practised law in Chicago, 1894-1897. Went to Boone, Iowa. Practised law there until 1904. Was Referee in Bankruptcy for Story, Boone and Greene Counties. Attorney for railroad and coal companies. The last two years of my stay in Boone were chiefly taken up in franchise and right of way work. In 1904

returned to Illinois. In same line of work until 1913, when I
went with Sherman and Ellis, Inc. We write compensation,
public liability, automobile and fire insurance on the inter-in-
surance plan.

I await with interest the forthcoming Report and shall have
much pleasure in reading of the "principal doings" of my
classmates. I can conscientiously and regretfully report that I
have had none.

JAMES ABERCROMBIE BURDEN

Born at New York City, 16 January 1871, of James Abercrombie Burden
[Yale Sheff.] (iron manufacturer) and Mary Proudfit Irvin.
Fitted at Cutler's.
Class Status: Special, 1889-91. With '95, 1891-92. Joined Class Senior
year.
Degree: A.B. 1893.
Married Florence Adele Sloane at Lenox, Massachusetts, 6 June 1895.
Children:
Emilie Vanderbilt, born 12 May 1896 (died 12 August 1906).
James Abercrombie, 3d, 12 July 1897.
William Douglas, 24 September 1898.
Florence Irvin, 20 August 1902.
Now President of the Burden Iron Company at Troy, New York.

Have little of interest to report. Served on the Advisory
Committee on Steel of the Council of National Defence during
the war. Am a director of the American Iron and Steel Institute. Besides being president of the Burden Iron Company
(with which I have been continuously connected ever since graduation), to which office I succeeded on my father's death in 1906,
I am chairman of the Eastern Steel Company. I am connected
with various other companies of the same general character.

CHARLES ROLAND BURGER

Born at Iowa City, Iowa, 7 December 1867, of Henry Burger [Heidel-
berg Univ.] (miner) and Caroline Mohr.
Entered from University of Colorado.
Class Status: I. Graduate School, 1892-93.
Degrees: Ph.B. (Univ. Colorado) 1892; A.B. 1893.
Married Orville Marie Maxwell at Boulder, Colorado, 5 October 1895.
Children:
Ray Maxwell, born 27 October 1897.
Charles Roland, Jr., 19 September 1899.
Now Registrar, University of Colorado.

Instructor, mathematics, High School, Denver, Colorado, 1893-1902; graduate student, Clark University, Worcester, Massachusetts, 1902-1903; Professor of mathematics, Colorado School of Mines,1903-1917; Assistant Principal, Colorado State Preparatory School, 1918-1919; Registrar, University of Colorado, 1920—; on leave of absence, August 1, 1922, to August 1, 1923.

Got into a notorious mix-up at the Colorado School of Mines in 1917 and eight members of the faculty, including myself, were invited to leave. The story is long and uninteresting excepting to those immediately concerned, the State of Colorado and the teaching profession in general. Suffice it to say that the American Association of University Professors after thorough investigation exonerated the faculty and severely criticized the President, V. C. Alderson, and the Board of Trustees (see report). Am now registrar as above.

George Ebenezer Burgess
See Report VI, Page 46.

Ernest Gisborne Burke
See Report VI, Page 48.

PERCY FLETCHER BURROWS

Born at Lowell, Massachusetts, 14 September 1872, of Henry Burrows and Elizabeth Spenser.
Fitted at Lowell High.
Class Status: Entered Sophomore.
Degree: A.B. 1893.
Now in business at New York City.

I was employed by a wholesale carpet commission merchant for a few months until he retired from business. After that I travelled abroad for three months. In 1895 I was employed by the New York Mutual Gas Light Company, and remained with them for sixteen years as a clerk and accountant. I afterwards worked as an accountant, and then in conjunction with a lawyer, I assisted in the promotion of several small enterprises. At present I am connected with a real estate company, which has erected stores in New Rochelle. Though not active now, will probably do more construction work in the future. I am unmarried and reside at the same address.

EDWARD ANGUS BURT

Born at Athens, Pennsylvania, 9 April 1859, of Howard Fuller Burt
   (miller) and Miranda Forsyth.
Fitted at Albany State Normal School.
Class Status: Entered Junior.
Degrees: A.B. 1893; A.M. 1894; Ph.D. 1895.
Married Clara Mary Briggs at Laurens, New York, 21 August 1884.
   Children:
         Angus Edward, born 20 June 1885. (Married 14 July 1910;
            died 11 July 1911).
         Albert Forsyth, 30 July 1890.
         Farlow, 24 November 1896.
         Howard, 5 December 1900.
Now in botanical research at St. Louis.

I remained in Harvard two years after our commencement
and then became Professor of Natural History at Middlebury
College, Vermont, a region most favorable for field study, collection, and preservation of the higher fungi, to which I devoted as much time as my college duties with large classes would
permit. After eighteen years of such work in Middlebury, I
needed more freedom from class work, a complete botanical
library for reference, and time to work over, round out and
prepare for publication, this accumulated mycological matter.
In 1913 there was an opportunity at an increase in salary
(which, however, has not equalled the increased expenses), to
become a member of the research staff of the Missouri Botanical
Garden and official head of its library of over 90,000 volumes
and pamphlets—the best botanical library in the United States.
   The last five years have not differed materially from the pre-
ceding five. These ten years constitute a period of continuous
production. Principal publications of this period are: The
Thelephoraceae of North America, parts I-XII, 457 pages, 174
text figures, 16 plates; North American Tremellaceae, Dacry-
omingcetaceae and Auriculariaceae,—36 pages, 1 plate; Merulius
in North America, 61 pages, 38 text figures, 3 plates; North
American Species of Clavaria, 78 pages, 12 plates. The high
regard in which this work is held was expressed by Carleton
Rea, author of *British Basidiomycetae*, in his presidential address since published in British Mycological Society Transactions, vol. 8, p. 15, 1922.
   Series of the higher fungi have been sent to me for determina-

tion from all parts of North and South America and the West Indies, from mycologists in various countries of Europe, and South Africa, Ceylon, Java, Japan, New Zealand, and the Hawaiian Islands.

Fellow of American Association Advancement of Science; member Botanical Society of America; secretary Botanists of the Central States; honorary member Boston Mycological Club, Societé Mycologique de l'Est.

Shall be eligible to retirement in 1924.

My son Farlow married, 22 June, 1918, and has a son Farlow Bergland, born 21 October, 1920. Is not this the first grandchild in the class?

CHARLES SHOREY BUTLER

Born at Boston, 6 July 1870, of Charles Shorey Butler (merchant) and Elizabeth Nancy Cummings.
Fitted at G. W. C. Noble's.
Class Status: Regular.
Degrees:A.B. 1893; M.D. 1898.
Married Margaret Parker Hubbard at Boxford, Massachusetts, 31 January 1901. Children:
    Elizabeth, born 17 January 1904.
    Charles Shorey, Jr., 25 September 1908.
Now physician (retired) at Boston.

1893 entered Harvard Medical School; graduated 1897, and continued medical studies, doing laboratory work, in bacteriology at Harvard Medical School until November, 1897, when I entered the Massachusetts General Hospital, Boston, surgical service. After graduating from hospital, 1899, started practice, Boston. So continued, although practice was slow, as is usual in big city. Had married in 1901, and continued to live in Boston. Two children born, one in 1904, one in 1908. In following years, travelled considerably, both through United States, north, west and south; and to Europe. Life, as a doctor, in Boston, continued a routine, pleasant and without difficulty; in brief, for me, a very happy, married life. Then, 1914 bringing the "World War" in August, changed my even routine of comfort and freedom from serious cares. Went to France, March, 1915, and worked among French wounded, under French Red Cross till summer of 1915, when (my service having expired) I returned to Boston.

[The present condition in Germany, where there is no devasta-

tion of homes; with the insolence of the junkers and the whin-
ing of the boche leaders (laughable as much as it is irritating),
should be compared with the contrasting condition in Belgium
and in *France especially,* during those four cruel years of boche
occupation and deliberate destruction. Let Germany acknowl-
edge her war guiltiness; let her even try to keep her promises, if
she be sincere; and, MAKE HER PAY! She deserves all that's
coming to her and more!]

Returned to France during the war, 1915, October; and as before worked for the French wounded, in different hospitals,
(with intermissions to return to Boston) until March, 1917.
Called into active service of United States Army, June, 1917,
as captain, medical, and continued till April, 1919, when I was
honorably discharged at Garden City, New York, as Major,
Medical Corps, U. S. A. Since then, in Boston, have continued
to live, quietly, at home, with my family and gradually retired
from practice.

HOWARD FULTON BUTLER

Born at West Hancock, Maine, 22 January 1864, of James Monroe But-
ler (carriage builder) and Mary Robinson Gray.
Entered from Brown University.
Class Status: "Four years in three."
Degree:A.B. 1892.
Married Maude Lillian Drake at Boston, 11 October 1892. Children:
Howard Fulton, Jr., 30 March 1905.
Mary, 7 June 1908.
Now practising law at Boston.

I have been a lawyer in Boston with varying success since
October 2, 1896. I have had a general business with perhaps a
little more corporation work than any other line.

I have travelled a little. In 1907 I made a trip to Florida,
stopping first at St. Augustine. I stopped a few days at Ormond, Palm Beach, and Miami. Went to Havana for a week,
then to Mexico City, stopping at Vera Cruz and Orizaba. After
a week in Mexico City I came home by train, stopping at New
Orleans, Washington, D. C., and New York City. In 1907 I
made a trip to the chief ports in the West Indies and two places
in South America. In 1910 I took a six weeks' trip to the Mediterranean, stopping at Maderia, Gibralta, Algiers, Monte Carlo,
Nice, Genoa, Venice, Florence, Rome, Naples, and other Italian

cities. Since graduation I have made twenty-three trips to the North Woods after big game, and have made a few fishing trips.

Other than the above trips my chief recreations have been chopping wood and playing auction bridge. Both of the latter games have been very profitable. In all of the above statements I have told the truth but not the "whole truth."

Guy Stevens Callender
See Report VI, Page 51.

PATRICK THOMAS CAMPBELL

Born at Jersey City, New Jersey, 14 April 1871, of Thomas Campbell and Mary Houghton.
Fitted at Boston Latin.
Class Status: Regular.
Degree: A.B. 1893.
Married Edith Hayes at Boston, 28 August 1899. Children:
Thomas, born 7 April 1902.
Edith, 9 February 1910.
Now Head Master Boston Latin School.

Instructor, Latin and Greek, Medford High School, Medford, Massachusetts, 1893—September, 1897. Junior Master, Boston Latin School, 1897-1908. Head of Department of History 1909-1920; Headmaster, Boston Latin School, 1920-September, to date.

When Henry Pennypacker, '85, was chosen Chairman of Committee on Admission I had the great good luck to be chosen to succeed him as Headmaster of the Boston Latin School. From this position I have not been removed. Have a son Tom in class of '24. Hope he makes the baseball team this spring!

Everett Pascoe Carey

Born at Port Elgin, New Brunswick, 19 December 1868, of Henry Carey (farmer) and Arabella Goodwin.
Entered from Mt. Allison University.
Class Status: Entered Senior.
Degrees: A.B. (Mt. Allison) 1892; A.B. 1893; S.B. 1894.
Married Elizabeth Beharrell at Lexington, Massachusetts, 1 November 1896. Children:
Dorothy Beharrell, born 18 October 1898.
Donald Agassiz, 20 December 1900.
Henry Dana, 3 February 1903.
Died of sarcoma, 20 January 1923, at Delhi, California.

Everett Pascoe Carey died of sarcoma January 20, 1923, at Delhi, California. He was born December 19, 1869, at Port Elgin, New Brunswick, son of Henry and Arabella (Goodwin) Carey. He fitted at Upper Sackville School, and attended Mount Allison University (New Brunswick), receiving his degree of A.B. in 1892, at the head of his class. He came to Harvard to qualify for teaching science, took the A.B. in 1893 and the S.B. in 1894. His home at that time was at Bay Verte, New Brunswick. He then studied zoölogy and geology in the Graduate School for a year. After this for four years he taught in various high schools in Michigan, then removed to California to take the chair of chemistry and physics at the University of the Pacific at San José. After two years there he returned to high school work at Redwood, Petaluna, etc., and in 1904 became teacher of physical geography at the San José High School. In 1908 he entered upon a ten-year term in the Polytechnic High School at San Francisco. In 1918 he was a teaching secretary in the Y. M. C. A. Becoming interested in agriculture, he studied the subject, set up a dairy ranch in Delhi, Merced County, California, in 1920, and followed dairying, with the assistance of his sons, up to the time of his death. He contributed to scientific journals various papers on geography, the San Francisco Earthquake of 1906, etc. On November 1, 1896, at Lexington, Mass., he married Elizabeth Beharrell of Amherst, Nova Scotia, who with three children survives him.

Edward Heman Carpenter

See Report VI, Page 53, and Supplement, Page 126.

FREDERICK JAY CARR

Born at New Lisbon, Wisconsin, 13 March 1869, of Willard Philip Carr
  (banker) and Caroline Sophia Ramsey.
Fitted at Phillips Exeter.
Class Status: Special, 1889-90. With class Sophomore year.
Married (1) Ada Couch Elwell at Brooklyn, New York, 21 April 1892
  (died 27 September 1913).
Married (2) Mary Adalaide Boardman, at Montpelier, Vermont, 24 January 1917. Children:
      Daughter, born 9 April 1919.
      Frederick Jay, Jr., 6 January 1923.
Now bank president at Hudson, Wisconsin.

After leaving college I went to a small place, Hammond, Wisconsin, and with others started the bank of Hammond, of which I became cashier. Remaining in this position four years I resigned to accept the position of cashier of the National Bank of Hudson, Wisconsin. Later was promoted to vice-president and then to president which position I now occupy.

In 1906 I was elected president of the Wisconsin Bankers Association, and a year later Wisconsin member of the executive council of the American Bankers Association. In 1914 with others organized the Wisconsin Mortgage and Securities Company of Milwaukee for the handling of Wisconsin farm loans, and a few years later with others organized the Bankers Joint Stock Land Bank of Milwaukee and have served as vice-president of these institutions since organized. These organizations have been a factor in the development of Wisconsin as they have handled upward of one hundred million dollars of loans to farmers over the state since organized. The mortgages are made at six per cent. and deposited with a Trust Company and bonds issued at five per cent. and all sold within the state. The borrower, the investor, and the stockholder have all been served and satisfied. My experience has been that nothing stands up unless service is rendered, and work constructive.

I think I must be close to the record in our class for having the youngest child, which was born January 6th, 1923. Can anyone beat it? We are happy and planning to send our daughter to Vassar where my wife graduated, and of course Frederick J. Carr, Jr., will go to Exeter and Harvard.

Joseph William Carr

See Report VI, Page 55.

Raymond Wilbur Carr

See Class of 1894, Report VI, Page 272.

LEWIS CLINTON CARSON

Born at Detroit, Michigan, 16 July 1870, of William Carson (merchant) and Hannah Wynkoop.
Entered from University of Michigan.
Class Status: I. Graduate School, 1892-93.

Degrees: A.B. (Univ. of Michigan) 1892; A.B. 1894 as of 1893; A.M.
   Univ. of Michigan) 1899; A.M. 1900; Ph.D. 1901.
Married Adele Ball Rowe at Detroit, Michigan, 8 July 1909.
Now pastor of First Unitarian Church, Santa Barbara, California. ,

I was ordained to the ministry in the Unitarian Church in
January, 1915. My ordination took place in Detroit, and I immediately became associate minister of the Second Church in
Boston. In September, 1915, I was called to the pastorate of
the Church of the Messiah, Montpelier, Vermont, where I remained until 1919. From 1919 to 1921 I was pastor of the First
Unitarian Church of Albany, New York. In 1921 I was called
to the pastorate of the First Unitarian Church of Santa Barbara, California, where I am now located and where I hope to
remain for many years to come. Thus my life since leaving college divides itself into two parts, that of teaching (see the Sixth
Class Report) and that of the ministry of religion.

WALTER CARY

Born at Milwaukee, Wisconsin, 26 April 1871, of Alfred Levi Cary (law-
   yer) and Harriet Maria Van Slyck.
Fitted at Milwaukee High.
Class Status: Regular.
Degree: A.B. 1893.
Now in electrical business at New York City.

With a lumber company in Northern Wisconsin during the
winter of 1893-94. Secretary of the Gibbs Electric Company,
Milwaukee, Wisconsin, manufacturers of dynamos and motors,
from 1894 to 1898. Vice-president and afterwards president of
the Milwaukee Electric Company, manufacturers of dynamos
and motors, from 1899 to 1904. General manager and afterwards vice-president of the Westinghouse Lamp Company, New
York City, from 1904 to date. Vice-president of the Westinghouse Electric and Manufacturing Company, from 1917 to date.
During the last fifteen years my business has made it necessary for me to make frequent trips to Europe, except during
the period of the war. One of my most interesting trips was to
Russia in 1907, where I spent nearly four months in St. Petersburg and Moscow, in connection with the electrification of the
tramways in St. Petersburg. The responsibility was great and
the work difficult, for it was no easy matter for a foreigner to
make much headway with the group of government and munici-

pal officials that was in charge of affairs at that time in Russia. a country full of intrigue and graft.

During the last four years my business has taken me almost every year to Vienna, Austria. My trips there have been extremely interesting but sad. as the condition of the city and people now presents such a terrible contrast to the beautiful city and happy people that were there before the war.

For recreation I am still trying to play golf but am becoming an "easier mark" every year. Nevertheless I enjoy the game. I am not married and am becoming so particular and so undesirable that I don't suppose I ever will be. Whatever hopes I ever had in this direction are slowly vanishing.

I am a member of the following clubs: Harvard Clubs. New York and Boston: University. Union. and Racquet and Tennis Clubs of New York.

WILLIAM ERNEST CASTLE

Born at Alexandria, Ohio. 25 October 1867, of William Augustus Castle
  (farmer) and Sarah Fassett.
Entered from Denison University.
Class Status: Entered Senior.
'Degrees: A.B. (Denison) 1889; A.B. 1893; A.M. 1894: Ph.D. 1895:
  ScD. (hon.) Wisconsin. 1921; LL.D. (Denison) 1921.
Married Clara Sears Bosworth at Wellsville, Kansas, 18 August 1896.
  Children:
    William Bosworth, born 21 October 1897.
    Henry Fassett, 23 July 1900. (Died Nov. 1919.)
    Edward Sears. 25 December 1903.
Now Professor of Zoölogy at Harvard.

I came to Harvard already committed by three years experience to teaching as a life work. I came here to get the best possible preparation for it. I took in three successive years the Harvard degrees of A.B.. A.M. and Ph.D. I found here inspiring teachers. wonderful opportunities for original investigation. and entire absence of restraint in thought and speech because of religious or social terrorism. I enjoyed thoroughly this new freedom. and I resolved never to give it up. wherever I went. even if I went out of teaching. I took a job (a very small one) as instructor at the University of Wisconsin. where I remained one year, then went as professor of biology to Knox College. Galesburg, Illinois. taking along a wife

to help me fill this large contract. Here, too, I remained a single year, surrendering the job then to worthier hands, those of
my classmate, H. V. Neal. I came back to the department of
zoölogy at Harvard, beginning as an instructor, hard-worked
but happy, and rising through the various grades (as a result
of longevity and the kindness of friends) to the rank of professor. This rank brings wonderful opportunities for investigation
and for inspiring contacts with bright young men who come here
for graduate study. Because of what I have been able to do in
this favoring environment, Wisconsin has been willing to over-
look my deficiencies as a young instructor and has given me an
honorary ScD., and Denison, closing her eyes momentarily to
my interest in the godless doctrine of Darwin, has made me
an LL.D. But of all the diplomas I have ever received, I prize
most those which bear the firm, methodical signature of Charles
William Eliot. These mean to me freedom, reality, truth. I
hope to end my days where such ideals prevail.

Charles Samuel Chase

Born at Roxbury, Massachusetts, 16 October 1869, of Leverett Milton
    Chase [Dartmouth] (teacher) and Anna Melina Marion.
Fitted at Boston Latin.
Class Status: Freshman year only.
Married Ida Etherington Swansbury at Shelburne, Nova Scotia, 27 June
    1914. Child:
        Sarah Elizabeth, born 13 February 1916.
Died of epilepsy 3 January 1919 at Westboro, Massachusetts.

Charles Samuel Chase died at Westboro (Mass.) Hospital of
a sudden attack of epilepsy Jan. 3, 1919. He was born at Roxbury, Oct. 16, 1869, of Leverett Milton and Anna Melina (Marion) Chase; the family had long been associated with Haverhill.
He prepared at the Boston Latin School and entered Harvard
with the Class in 1889, intending to fit himself for his father's
profession of teaching. He left at the end of freshman year,
however, and went into the employ of the Standard Electric
Supply Company in Boston; thence going to the Narragansett
Electric Lighting Company of Providence, where he remained
for two years. In 1896 he made a prospecting trip to Montana,
but returned after an extended tour on the Pacific coast. He
then took a farm at Salisbury, N. H., where he raised apples

for export to Europe, also speculating profitably in lumber. At this period he traveled extensively both in the United States and in South America. About 1905 he removed to Franklin, N. H., and entered the florist business, again traveling extensively. In 1913 he went to Shelburne, N. S. Here he began to suffer from hardening of the arteries and a deranged heart. After spending the winter of 1916-17 in hospital he went to Loon Lake, Me., for a long convalescence; as the results were not encouraging, he returned to Westboro the next year. Besides his horticultural work, which he found very congenial, he was much interested in music, and belonged to a number of musical societies. On June 27, 1914, he married Ida Etherington Swansbury of Shelburne, who with one daughter survives him.

CLIFFORD HOFFMAN CHASE

Born at Haverhill, Massachusetts, 21 November 1871, of Robert Stuart Chase (accountant) and Ada Harvey.
Fitted at Haverhill High.
Class Status: Regular.
Degree: A.B. 1893.
Now health-seeking at Newton Highlands, Massachusetts.

Since the close of the war, I have been in Newton Highlands, Massachusetts, with Dr. S. L. Eaton, M.D., where I have been occupied chiefly with essay-writing. I hope to have a volume entitled "Compensations" finished soon. It will contain twelve essays dealing with subjects of contemporary interest. Some of the titles are: "The Significance of Life"; "The Value of Experience"; "The Evolution of Progress"; The Waste of War"; "The Utility of Peace"; "The Reality of Religion".

I also have a novel and a book of short stories nearly completed. I am planning a collected edition of all my works, both published and unpublished, to appear perhaps in 1930. I contributed a poem called "Once Upon a Time" for the Twenty-fifth anniversary class dinner at the New York Harvard Club in 1918; and am sending another one entitled "The Days of Long Ago" for the thirtieth anniversary class dinner at the same club.

Samuel Chew

Born at Philadelphia, 28 April 1871, of Samuel Chew (treasurer) and
Mary Johnson Brown.
Fitted at St. Paul's.
Class Status: Regular.
Degrees: A.B. 1893; LL.B. (Univ. Penn.) 1896.
Died of heart disease 5 July 1919 at Philadelphia

Samuel Chew died at Philadelphia, July 5, 1919, after a
short illness. Coming from an ancient and distinguished family, he was fourth in line of descent from Chief Justice Benjamin
Chew of Pennsylvania, who in 1772 built the historic Chew
mansion, Cliveden. In the Battle of Germantown, 1777, the
house was bombarded by the Americans, the British having
taken refuge inside, and it still shows plainly the shot and
shell marks suffered in the battle. Sam inherited the place,
where he lived a part of each year, and in which he took great
pride and interest.

Our classmate's education previous to entering college was
at Penn Charter School, Philadelphia, and at St. Paul's School,
Concord, N. H. At seventeen he passed his entrance exams for
Harvard, but spent a year abroad tutoring, as his family
thought him too young to go to college. Entering Harvard in
1889, he soon became, through his personal magnetism and
manly qualities, one of the most prominent members of the
class. He was very fond of athletics; he played on the University Cricket Team, three years on the class football eleven, and
senior year rowed on the class crew. Most of us remember his
exhibition of fearlessness in the class races, when after breaking his oar he dove into the cold May waters of the Charles—
hoping that thereby his crew might win.

But Chew's talents were of a social rather than of an athletic
nature. His "hail fellow well met" geniality won him a large
circle of friends, and this, combined with his ready wit, made
him the life of social gatherings of every kind. He had an
enormous sense of the ridiculous, and thoroughly enjoyed a
humorous situation, which he loved to impart to others. He was
on the first ten of the Dickey, and among other societies belonged to the A.D., the Alpha Delta Phi, the Pudding, etc.

On graduation he returned to his home, attended the U. of
P. Law School, and was admitted to the Philadelphia Bar.
Soon afterwards he became an assistant city solicitor, a posi-

Newell   Upton   *Moore*   *Trafford*   Lewis   Mason   Shea
                    (mgr.)   (capt.)

tion which he resigned after several years to take up private practice and to aid in the management of his family affairs. At home, as in college, he was very prominent in club life and in all social affairs. He maintained his love for out-of-door exercises, being particularly fond of riding to hounds. He was an inveterate traveller, and had been pretty much everywhere in Europe and in this country. When the Spanish War broke out he was in the Klondyke, and to join his regiment, the Philadelphia City Troop, he made alone a remarkable, almost fool-hardy, return over the Valdez Glacier; getting caught in a blizzard he reached human habitation empty-handed, after forty-eight hours continuous climbing, He then served as corporal with the Troop in Porto Rico.

Chew was intensely patriotic and a keen soldier. He attended the Plattsburg and Oglethorpe Camps with the greatest enthusiasm, and it was the disappointment of his life that his age debarred him from getting a commission with the army in the World War. He wrote me in July of 1917, ''What is needed are men on the fighting line, and I am one that could fill that bill.'' When all else failed he went to France in January 1917, and drove an ambulance for six months until he broke his wrist in cranking his car under heavy fire, and was forced to return home. He was then promised a commission in Col. Roosevelt's Division, which unfortunately never materialized. But he did not cease in his efforts, and after we entered the war received an appointment with the Red Cross. He returned to France in October, 1918, and did legal work in Paris and Tours until the Armistice was signed. He was decorated by special medal presented by the French minister of war in recognition of voluntary services.

It may be a gratification to those who were unable to attend, to know that at his funeral our class wreath lay at the head of his grave. I like what a friend of his wrote: ''The aching hearts left behind are a far higher tribute to his memory than any expressed words could possibly be.'' And yet, as I write this humble tribute, my mind reverts to thirty years of more than intimate friendship, in which there never was a break. The memory of our many good times, our travels, as well as the more serious sides of life, will ever be dear while memory lives in me. I think of his innate refinement and courtesy, of

the beautifully delicate things he could do, of his devotion to
his adoring mother;—in fact he loved as few could love, and
was loved as is given to few to be loved. Generous to a fault,
in no way spoiled by his great popularity, most tender with
old and young, the best and staunchest of friends, he stands
before me the embodiment of courage, loyalty, and devotion.

C. G. W.

Donald Churchill

See **Report** VI, Page 61, and Supplement, Page 126.

PAUL CLAGSTONE

Born at Chicago, 28 September 1871, of James Clagstone and Abby Colby.
.Fitted at Phillips Andover.
Class Status: Joined Class Sophomore year, from '92.
Degree: A.B. 1893.
Married Cora Kirk at Burlingame, California, 7 May 1904. Children:
          Pauline, born 28 February 1905.
          Kirk, 6 March 1906.
Now Western Secretary, United States Chamber of Commerce, San
          Francisco.

Since my last report, have closed out my ranch interests in
Northern Idaho. The life was delightful, but my property was
located in a region with too much snowfall to make it pay. In
1917 I was offered a position with the United States Chamber
of Commerce, and found the work very interesting. There are
several Harvard men on the staff at Washington. In 1917 I was
given the position of Western District Secretary in charge of
the work in the seven states west of the Rockies, with an office
in San Francisco. I am very glad to be living again in San
Mateo, California, where I was married and where our two children were born. My son, Kirk, though just seventeen, is one of
those big, six-foot Californians, plays a rattling good game at
right end for his school, and performs well with discus, shot
and high jump. He will enter Harvard in two years. One
daughter, Pauline, is at Mills College, but will finish at Smith.
We are all very well, and happy to be here in this wonderful
state—but you have probably heard this sort of thing before.

WILLIAM ANTHONY CLARK

Born at Mineral Point, Wisconsin, 13 July, 1868, of William Henry Clark (insurance) and Jane Nancolas.
Fitted at Northwestern University, Evanston, Illinois.
Class Status: Entered Junior with 1892. Joined Class Senior year.
Degree: A.B. 1893.
Married Frances Marie Freese of Hartford, Connecticut, at Boston, 10 February 1894 (died 20 November 1895). Child:
William Anthony, Jr., born 16 November 1894. (Harvard 1916, Mass. Inst. Technology 1921).
Now in real estate work in New York City.

The first fifteen years out of college were devoted to educational, social, and philanthropic work as head of Lincoln House, Boston, and Gordon House, New York. The next ten years were given to business. Usually, in association with others, sometimes independently, I became interested in organizing various business enterprises. Certain substantial mining interests in Mexico were lost owing to the revolution there, and the Great War put two other promising enterprises out of business. In a business way War has been hell for me. But War and I are quits, because my great opportunity for adventure came through the War. I served in France as Hut Secretary from January, 1918, to July, 1918, and was then transferred to the American Red Cross. After the Armistice I was appointed Manager of Relief for the North East of France, including Alsace-Loraine, with headquarters in Verdun. Within eight weeks, twenty-six sub-warehouses were established with French committees in charge. About $2,000,000 worth of relief material was given away through these centres.

The lure of the soil brought back many refugees to villages wholly destroyed. Not infrequently the members of the little family brought in their wordly possessions on their backs. Frequently you saw a group standing on the site once called home, now nothing but a pile of stones. A dug-out, stove, a few cooking utensils left by the Boche, a loose board here and there for flooring and furniture, and the new "home" was started. The courage, faith and patience of these home-loving little people made you want to work your head off for them. You saw evidences of military heroism around the hills of Verdun, but this was different and hit me even deeper.

My God, how you wanted to help personally! But the job was a big wholesale one, and you had to steel yourself against

it, organize against time and weather and sentimentality and
constantly inflamed by the needs of the little shivering people
do the impossible and not even think about it.

After returning I spent two years with the Federal Board
for Vocational Education. Part of the time I was head of the
Division for the Rehabilitation of Disabled Ex-service Men in
New York, Connecticut, New Jersey, and part of the time as-
sistant in administration for the whole country. I succeded Sid
Farwell in the New York office of the board.

And now this bright little chapter is closed and a very prosy
business one is being written. I am frank to say the 'Rainy
Day Fund'' is beginning to look important, but not too important.

ALBERT SIDNEY GREGG CLARKE

Born at Iowa City, Iowa, 5 February 1872, of Rush Clarke [Washington
  and Jefferson] (lawyer) and Sidney Ormsby Robinson.
,Fitted at the Gunnery School, Washington, Connecticut.
Class Status: Regular.
Degrees: A.B. 1893; LL.B. (N. Y. Law School) 1901.
Married (1) Florence Nightingale Kline at Washington, Connecticut,
  28 October 1896 (died 20 July 1904). Children:
    Rush, born 19 August 1897.
    Gregg, Jr., 29 May 1899 (died 2 November 1900).
    Florence Gregg, 30 October 1901.
    Frederick Lawrence Mansfield, 20 July 1904 (died 20 July 1904).
Married (2) Mrs. Suzanne Carlyle (Anderson) Barstow, at Ashville,
  North Carolina, 25 January 1906. Child:
    Margaret Ormsby, 21 December 1916.
Now in summer camp business at Washington, Connecticut.

After graduation, I taught in my old preparatory school for
several years, meanwhile studying law. In 1900, I began the
practice of law and have since continued it. I have been Town
Counsel of my home town, Washington, Connecticut, and Judge
of the Probate Court for my district.

The year I graduated, I took an extended canoe trip in Maine,
with Tarrant King, '91, and Chouteau Dyer, '94. From this
trip grew up the Keewaydin Camps and Canoe Trips, in which
I have been vitally interested ever since. Although there were
one or two other camps started before Keewaydin, ours is the
oldest camp in America with a continuous life under the same
management. These have grown and extended continually, and
they now consist of a camp in Canada for older boys, one in

Vermont for younger boys, one in Vermont for girls, and one in Canada for adults. Many '93 men and their sons and daughters have been at our camps; among them being Wilder, Hume, Gans, Walcott, Nash, Trafford, and Chew. These camps have really become my life work, and I have had the satisfaction of being a pioneer in a new profession and of having established the camps that have been characterized by *Country Life in America* as the "Standard Camps of this Country."

HENRY LIVINGSTON COAR

Born at London, England, 16 June 1862, of Firman Wood Coar (dentist)
and Lucinda Elizabeth Blake.
Fitted at Cologne Gymnasium for Johns Hopkins.
Class Status: Graduate School and Instructor, 1892-95.
Degrees: A.B. 1893; A.M. 1894; Ph.D. (Univ. Ill.) 1903,
Married Mary Elizabeth Coar at Ednor, Maryland, 29 December 1887.
Children:
Marjorie Belle, born 4 January 1890.
Helen Ruth, 6 December 1891.
Henry Osgood, 20 January 1896.
Now Professor of Mathematics and Astronomy at Marietta College, Ohio.

I was born in London (England) of American parents. Until my eighth year I resided in Germany, where my father practised his profession. Returning to this country in 1870, we settled in Yonkers, New York, where I attended the Yonkers Military Institute until 1875, when we returned to Germany and settled in Cologne. In the spring of 1876 I entered the Kaiser Wilhelm Gymnasium in that city and continued at that institute (with the exception of one term) until I graduated in the spring of 1884. Thereupon I entered the University of Bonn for one term to study mathematics and the natural sciences. In the fall of 1884 I returned to this country and entered the graduate department of Johns Hopkins University, where I continued the work commenced at Bonn. I found it, however, expedient to devote considerable of my time to the natural sciences, as my training at the Gymnasium had been entirely of a classical nature. At the end of two years I was obliged to give up my work in Baltimore owing to a lack of funds, and settled in Springfield, Massachusetts, where I conducted a college preparatory school for five years. I was married in 1887. In 1891 I was called to take charge of the mathematics department of Smith Academy (the preparatory department of Washington University) St. Louis, Missouri. At the end of the year I decided to take up my mathematics studies again at Harvard, and entered the Graduate School in 1892, graduating with the Class of 1893. Served as instructor in mathematics and in German for two years, while continuing my studies. Left college in 1895 to serve as Instructor in mathematics at the University of Michigan 1895-1897. Served in the same capacity at the University of Illinois 1898-1906. In 1906 I came as Professor of Mathematics and Astronomy to Marietta College, where I still am.

As for the rest, like all of you, I have grown older in years, but trust I am growing younger in spirit. The children have all flown from the home nest, so we have to expend more of our sympathy on others. Fortunately the students offer an outlet. with their vagaries and problems. Thirty years that seem like a dream, that have passed like a flash; thirty years more, and we shall all know more.

ALEXANDER LYNDE COCHRANE

Born at Malden, Massachusetts, 25 April 1870, of Alexander Cochrane (merchant) and Mary Lynde Sullivan.
Fitted at Groton.
Class Status: Regular.
Degree: A.B. 1893.
Married Vivian Wessell at New York City, 10 August 1917. Children: Nancy Lynde, born 16 August 1918.
Lucy Douglas, 19 February 1920.
Alexander Lynde Jr., 22 May 1921.
Now corporation treasurer at Boston.

My life has been a very simple, uninteresting one. '93-96, West. '96-1907, business. In 1907 retired on account of health. Married in 1917 and have three children, two girls and one boy. Business again, 1921, associated with my brother as treasurer of New England Oil Company, Limited, a subsidiary of the New England Oil Refining Company.

JOHN IRA COCHRANE

Born at East Dorset, Vermont, 31 March 1870, of John Luther Cochrane (farmer) and Sarah Elizabeth Roberts.
Fitted at Burr and Burton Seminary.
Class Status: Regular.
Degrees: A.B. 1893; M.D. (Univ. Va.) 1897.

Married Mary Randolph Jones. at Charlottesville, Virginia, 16 August
1898. Children:
    Sarah Roberts, born 29 January 1901.
    David Duke, 20 September 1902.
Now practising medicine and writing stories at East Dorset, Vermont.

Taught in Westminster School, '93-95. Studied medicine at
University of Virginia and put in a couple of years in New York
hospitals. Since then I have practised medicine in rural Vermont, and at present I occupy the ancestral acres and halls that
have seen five generations of Cochranes. I am the first, however,
to make fiction pay, and of late it has paid better—and that's
about all I know about me.

As to fame—well—I expect the stunt I pride myself upon
most is winning *Everybodys' Magazine's* prize for the best finish of O. Henry's posthumous story "The Unprofitable Ser-
vant." And nobody else ever heard about that!

Edward Russell Coffin
See Report VI, Page 65.

GILMAN COLLAMORE
Born at New York City, 25 December 1871, of Gilman Collamore (mer-
chant) and Mary Alethea Jenkins.
Fitted at Wilson and Kellogg's.
Class Status: Regular.
Degrees: A.B. 1893; A.M. 1894.
Now with New York Life Insurance Company at New York City.

The Arbiter of '93 speaks: "A casual skimming of Colly's
last two Class Reports gives him an E— on lucre ability et al.
He has engaged in certain business, but not so much, with his
Aromatic Uncle A. L. Causse in the Fragrant District of Franklin and Hudson Streets, New York City; he has dabbled with
such foolish avocations as billballs, writing letters on athletic
topics to newspapers, the stage, music, and '93 dinners—all in
a purely dilletante and irrelevant manner; he tore himself away
from the Teutonic atmosphere of Brown's Chop House during
the war and hung out his shingle at the Harvard Club. where
the ignorant placed him in positions of some authority. Mark,
as stated above, holds."

Colly loq: "The Arb speaks truth, since I have read the reports and write for him. But speaking for him and in re-
sponse to the plea of our long suffering and beloved Sam of

the Clan of Batch, I must needs add the catalogue of ships, brief and unimportant though it be: That Colly has given up the business of working at play for that of playing at work; that under pressure (?) and persuasion (?) of a good friend in the Class of '99, he is now, to paraphrase the words of Willie Keeler, better than whom, trying to find 'em where they aint; that, when the New York Life Insurance Company seeks the address of a policy holder or, worse than that, the location of one who has seen fit to wander from the fireside, Colly tries to find him. The play business in which I am now engaged brings to mind the Committee on Admissions, in that the unexpected is always bobbing up serenely—and otherwise. Tomorrow, Thursday, the 26th of April, Colly attends the Committee Dinner as an Ex-Cathedra with four years experience of the Portuguese, the Argentines, and the Greeks (kind permission of Harley Parker). The powers have thrust a prodemotion on Colly, whatever that may mean, by putting him on the Board of Managers of the Harvard Club of New York City (June, 1922), where his main endeavor to date has been to bring a smile to the lips of the austere, an impossibility in the circumstances, as '93 well knows the inelastic grimness of Colly's attempts at humor.

I regret to report that New York went from 1918 to 1923 without a dinner. Four years, and then the rift, the breaking of the clouds before the clear skies of our meeting in June. Colly spoke for one classmate who was too full of gratitude for utterance; he can speak for no other, but hopes that none regrets the journey to a wicked city.

CHRISTOPHER WALTER COLLIER

Born at Westbury, Wiltshire, England, 23 February 1866, of David Allen Collier (farmer) and Louisa Slade Collier.
Fitted at Betts Academy, Stamford, Connecticut.
Class Status: Entered Senior.
Degrees: A.B. (Williams) 1892; A.B. 1893; S.T.B. (Yale) 1896.
Married Jennie Orcelia Wheeler at Williamstown, Massachusetts, 6 September 1893.
Now Minister of Hancock Church, Lexington, Massachusetts.

After leaving Harvard went to Yale Divinity School for professional training in Theology, graduating in 1896. Acting Pastor of the Congregational Church, East Hampton, Conn., 1893-

1897. One semester University of Berlin, 1897-1898. Pastor, Central Congregational Church, Orange, Massachusetts,. 1898-1905. Pastor, Hammond Street Congregational Church, Bangor, Maine, 1905-1916. Pastor, Hancock Congregational' Church, Lexington, Massachusetts, 1916 till present time.

On leave of absence from Church, went overseas, July, 1917, in American Field Service. Was on staff in Paris, but made several ambulance expeditions along the front. Returned in· January, 1918. Getting second leave of absence from my Church (for one year) went over seas in Red Cross, October, 1918. Was Acting Chaplain at Base Hospital No. 30, Royat (Clermont-Ferrand) France. Armistice having been signed. returned in January, 1919.

JOHN LAWRENCE SARSFIELD CONNOLLY

Born at Somerville, Massachusetts, 1 January 1870, of John Sarsfield' Connolly (grocer) and Margaret Patten.
,Fitted at Somerville High.
Class Status: Regular.
Degrees: A.B. 1893; LL.B. (Boston Univ.) 1899.
Married Gertrude Lomasney at Somerville, Massachusetts, 15 May 1902..
Children:
Marguerite, born 18 March 1905.
John Lewis, 28 June 1907.
Gertrude Florence, 1 February 1914.
Ruth, 6 August 1916.
.Now practising law at Somerville, Massachusetts.

For a few years after graduation was engaged in civil engineering but entered Boston University Law School and re-- ceived the LL.B. in 1899. Was at once admitted to the Massa-- chusetts Bar, and have practised uninterruptedly in Somerville, Massachusetts. I have nothing special to report this time. I have four children—Marguerite at Radcliffe, John Lewis at Somerville High, preparing for Harvard, Gertrude Florence and Ruth in the elementary schools. I enjoy excellent health and continue to practice law.

ARTHUR CLIFTON CONRO

Born at South Hero, Vermont, 13 February 1870, of Bertrand Adelbert·. Conro and Martha Wing Clifton.
Fitted at Tabor Academy.
Class Status: Regular.
Degree A.B. 1893.

Married Margaret Jane Wray at Worcester, Massachusetts, 12 July 1905.
Child:
    Wray Clifton, born 26 July 1906.
Now practising medicine at Attleboro, Mass.

After graduating, taught for three years, then took medical course at University of Virginia and Chattanooga Medical College, graduating with highest honors in 1901. (And it is a cussed curious thing the Harvard Quinquennial don't recognize my degree there). Settled in East Longmeadow, Massachusetts, and practised there for eight years; also trustee of the public library. But the East Longmeadonians were too cussed healthy; so I ups killick and steers for Attleboro, Massachusetts. Aha, some town! Much sickness. Many additions to the population of stalwart burgers. Office doorstep worn to splinters. Night-bell pulled out by the roots. During Big War was on Medical Advisory Board of District 47. Always advised 'em to wade in and give 'em hell. Have probably killed more Germans by proxy than any other man in town. Now am getting so tired of filling out all the blanks necessary for a "good" prescription (worse than a cussed Class Report) that am thinking of retiring. Only one thing restrains me—*auri sacra fames.* How's that, Mr. Umpire?

Voice of Umpire (off stage): Balls!

FREDERICK SHEPHERD CONVERSE

Born at Newton, Massachusetts, 5 January 1871, of Edmund Winchester Converse (merchant) and Charlotte Augusta Albree.
Fitted at E. H. Cutler's.
Class Status: Regular.
Degree: A.B. 1893.
Married Emma Cecile Tudor at Brookline, Massachusetts, 6 June 1894.
Children:
    Emma Louise, born 1 April 1895.
    Charlotte Augusta, 7 September 1896.
    Marie Tudor, 2 November 1897.
    Virginia, 16 February 1899.
    Frederick Shepherd, Jr., 12 January 1903 (died 10 September 1910).
    Elizabeth, 26 November 1904.
    Edmund Winchester 2d, 4 October 1915.
Now composing music at Westwood, Massachusetts.

Graduate Royal Academy of Music in Munich, 1902. Teacher of composition New England Conservatory for two years. Instructor of Music, later assistant professor at Harvard, 1903-

1907. 1906 gave up teaching and devoted myself entirely to composition. Helped to organize Boston Opera Company and served as vice-president for five years. Wrote first American opera to be performed at Metropolitan Opera House in New York. Served during the war in Massachusetts State Guard— first in Motor Corps, then in 13th Regiment; also member of National Committee on Army and Camp Music in charge of music in all camps. Took up teaching at New England Conservatory in 1920 as Head of Theoretical Department and am still engaged in this work.

New works: Symphony in C minor, first produced 1920. Symphony in E major, first produced 1922. Tone Poem, "Song of the Sea," not yet produced. Song for male chorus: "Harvard, Sovereign Mother," in collaboration with M. A. DeWolfe Howe. Two Songs for Soprano Voice, "Wild Rose," and "Love's Homing." Sonata for Violoncello and Piano. Fantasie for Piano and Orchestra, first performed in 1922; still in manuscript.

CHARLES EMERSON COOK

Born at Parsonsfield, Maine, 22 July 1869, of James William Cook (express) and Sarah Josephine Emerson.
Fitted at Boston English High.
Class Status: Regular.
Degree: A.B. 1893.
Married (1) Margaret Quincy Greene at Norwich, Connecticut, 17 October 1893. Child:
    Dorothy Quincy, born 17 May 1897.
Married (2) Grace E. Greenwood of West Medford, Massachusetts, at New York City, 3 April 1900.
Married (3) Gladys Hanson Snook at Atlanta, Georgia, 12 April 1916.
Now in publicity business at New York City.

After graduation went to New York City and engaged in newspaper work and play-writing, one of his first productions being the book and lyrics for the comic opera, "The Walking Delegate." This was followed (1898) by "The Chorus Girl." Later (1903) came the very popular "Red Feather"—music by De Koven—which played throughout the country for four years; followed by "The Rose of the Alhambra," which played two years. In 1900 also took up theatrical management and advance work, associating himself with David Belasco. Was for some time the advance man for Mrs. Leslie Carter; later for Blanche Bates,

David Warfield, etc. In 1906 organized the first successful club
of theatrical business men, known as "The Friars," with
a club-house in New York City; and was its president or Abbot.
Was for several years business manager of the Belasco Theatre,
afterwards (1908) adding the Stuyvesant Theatre. In 1916 was
director of publicity of the "Yale Pageant" at New Haven and
in 1918 independent manager for Lou Tellegen. About this
time incorporated himself as "Charles Emerson Cook, Inc.,
Publicity," at 110 East 42d Street New York City, which is his
latest (1923) business address. Resides at Jackson Heights,
Queen's Borough, New York.

GEORGE CRAM COOK

Born at Davenport, Iowa 7 October 1873, of Edward Everett Cook
   [Hobart] (lawyer) and Ellen Katharine Dodge.
Entered from Iowa University.
Class Status: Entered Senior.
Degrees: A.B. (Univ. Iowa) 1892; A.B. 1893.
Married (1) Sara Herndon Swain at Chicago, 19 May 1902.
Married (2) Mollie A. Price at Chicago, 21 January 1908.
Married (3) Susan Glaspell of Davenport, Iowa, 14 April 1913.
Now director of the Provincetown Players in New York City.

After graduation studied and travelled in Germany (Heidelberg), Switzerland (University of Geneva), etc., for two years.
In September of 1895 became instructor in English at the University of Iowa, where he remained four years. Served in the
Spanish War with the 50th Iowa Infantry. In 1902-1903 was
instructor at Leland Stanford. Then returned to Davenport
and devoted himself to writing novels and plays, in the intervals
of farming until 1910. In 1911 became associate literary editor
of the *Chicago Evening Post,* living at New York City. In 1915
became director of the "Provincetown Players," of MacDougal
Street, New York City, a theatrical venture organized not as a
public theatre but as a private club, which has had much success
in producing plays unsuited for commercial use in regular thea-
tres. For this experiment he has written a number of plays,
some in collaboration with Susan Glaspell. His summer home is
at Provincetown, Massachusetts, but he is at present travelling
in Greece, and the secretary has not been able to get into com-
munication with him.

HOWARD HAMBLETT COOK

Born at Salem, Massachusetts, 1 November 1870, of William Stevenson
   Cook (expert accountant) and Sarah Elizabeth Mansfield.
Fitted at Salem High.
Class Status: Regular.
Degrees: A.B. 1893; A.M. 1894; Ph.D. 1896.
Now assistant secretary, American Iron and Steel Institute at New York.

Remained in the Graduate School for three years after graduation, receiving the degree of A.M. in 1894 and Ph.D. in Division of Political Science in 1896. Soon after was made assistant to the Massachusetts State Commission on Taxation, of
which Professor F. W. Taussig was a member. This Commission investigated the system of taxation then existing and recommended changes in a report made in the following year. In
1897 became Chief Clerk of the Department of Municipal Statistics, City of Boston, a department then just organized, with
the purpose of giving full publicity to all municipal activities.
In 1907 was appointed Special Agent of the Bureau of Corporations, Department of Commerce, Washington, D. C., and was
assigned to the investigation of production costs and general
economic conditions affecting the Steel Industry in this and
foreign countries. In 1910 was appointed Assistant Secretary
of the American Iron and Steel Institute, the trade association
of the steel companies of the United States, Canada, and Mexico. During the war was Assistant Secretary of the Committee
on Steel and Steel Products organized to direct the production
of war material and regulate prices under the supervision of
the Council of National Defense. Also appointed as Expert
by War Industries Board and assigned to duty as Assistant to
the Chief of the Tin Section, War Industries Board, with control over the importation, distribution and sale of pig tin
whether for war purposes or otherwise. In 1915 served as a
member of the International Jury of Awards, Panama-Pacific
Exposition, in San Francisco.

Irving Jabez Cook
See Report VI, Page 72.

LOUIS CRAIG CORNISH

Born at New Bedford, Massachusetts, 18 April 1870, of Aaron Cornish
   (physician) and Frances Virginia Hawkins.
Fitted with G. D. Hale.

Class Status: Special 1889-91 and 1892-93.
Degrees: ''Certificate without academic degree'' 1893: A.B. (Stanford)
    1894; A.M. (Harv.) 1899; D.D. (St. Lawrence Univ.) 1922; D.D.
    (Meadville Theol.) 1922; Dean of Dicsoszentmarton, Transylvania
    (Roumania) 1922.
Married Frances Eliot Foote at Boston, 14 June 1906.
Now Secretary of the American Unitarian Association at Boston.

1893-94, a student and instructor at Stanford University.
1894-98, Secretary to the Bishop of the Protestant Episcopal
Church in the Diocese of Massachusetts. 1898-99, Harvard
Divinity School. Ordained in King's Chapel, Boston, to the
Unitarian ministry, 1899. 1900 to 1916, minister of the First
Parish in Hingham. Massachusetts. 1915-17, Secretary-at-large
of the American Unitarian Association. 1917 to the present,
Secretary of the American Unitarian Association. 1915, President of the Tuckerman School for the Training of Parish Workers. 1919, by invitation of the British Unitarian Association,
official representative of the American and Canadian Unitarian
churches to many of the Unitarian churches in England. Ireland, Scotland. and Wales, and ''McQuaker Lecturer.'' 1922,
Chairman of the Unitarian Commission appointed to investigate
the condition of religious minorities in Transylvania (Roumania). (For account of the work of the Commission see my
book ''Transylvania in 1922,'' Beacon Press. Boston, 1923).

These headings will sufficiently indicate all I have to report
that is in any way outside of the interesting and varied work
of my ministry. Looking back over the thirty years, I doubt
if any man in the class has enjoyed greater variety or more
absorbing interests than have come to me. I mean this statement not as a tribute to my work, but as a testimony to the
value to the man himself of the Christian ministry as a profession. The Secretary's request for information intimates that we
must speak now or forever after hold our peace. which I hope
will excuse a certain valedictory tone in these brief comments.

JAMES COPPINGER COTTER

Born at Castine, Ohio, 1 September 1869, Terence Coppinger Cotter
    (civil engineer and railroad official) and Hannah Driscoll.
Fitted at High School, Paducah, Kentucky, and at Camberwell, England.
Class Status: Special. 1888-91. Joined class Junior year.
Degrees: A.B. 1893; LL.B. 1895.

Married Victoria Charleville Whyte at St. Louis, 27 November 1901.
  Child:
    John Maurice Esmonde Coppinger, born 13 December 1902 (H. C.
    1922).
Now practising law at Indianapolis.

On the 18th day of September, 1894, while yet in the Harvard Law School, I was admitted to practice at the bar of the Supreme Court of Indiana. On the 21st. I was admitted to practice in the United States District Court for the District of Indiana. On December 20, 1895, the Supreme Court of Massachusetts, "holden at Boston, within and for said County of Suffolk," admitted me to the practice of law in the Courts of the Commonwealth. The Circuit Court of the United States on September 16, 1896, admitted me to practice in the United States Courts for Massachusetts. In December, 1901. I was admitted as an attorney and counsellor of the Supreme Court of the United States.

After having been admitted to the Suffolk Bar. 1895, I practiced in Boston for a year and during the same time I continued studies at Harvard in the Graduate School. In the fall of 1896. I returned to my home in Indianapolis. For two years, 1897-1899, I was instructor in the Indiana Law School. Indianapolis. Courses: Trusts and Real Property.

In 1897 and for a few years thereafter. I took an active part in local politics and was an aspirant for the Democratic nomination for mayor. I soon discovered that politics were a growing interference with systematic law work and I thenceforth confined myself to my regular vocation. Since I was admitted to the Massachusetts Bar in 1895. my work has been the practice of law and attending to business affairs connected therewith. I have been an official of a number of companies in Indianapolis and New York; but as such my duties have been strictly those of legal counsel.

Of late years I have given very little time to clubs or sports as such. My social life has been largely inter-family, with relatives and friends in Indianapolis and in other cities. In spite of the pressure of work. I have never lost my student spirit and have kept up my systematic study in subjects allied to law, in some branches of science. historical researches, and in literature. This has been one of my chief relaxations.

In June. 1922, I made my first visit to Boston in twenty

years (my son was to be graduated in the Class of 1922). Once again I lived Harvard. Once again I had the happiness of meeting my classmates as fellows and friends, at the delightful Class Supper at the Boston Yacht Club, in the Yard, at their homes, offices, casually;—in the joys of the resumed companionship, the years out in the world fell away. I will not forget. There was regret too; some did not come, some can never come.

William Norman Cottrell

See Report VI, Page 74.

Alfred Frazer Coulter

See Report VI. Page 75.

JOHN FERGUS CROSBY

Born at Neponsett, Illinois, 30 January 1862, of Thomas Crosby (farmer) and Eliza Parker.
Entered from Andover Theological.
Class Status: Sophomore year only. Joined 1894.
Married Eva Elizabeth Hale at Barrington, New Hampshire, 22 June 1892. Children:
> Eliza Hale, born 18 April 1893 (married Lt. Harry B. Sherman, 22 June 1917).
> Robert Shakford, 16 March 1895 (married Beatrice J. Costello, 6 June 1920).
> Ethel May, 1 September 1896 (died 19 August 1897).
> Gerald Parker, 1 January 1898.
> Thomas Prince, 17 October 1899.
> Evelyn Hayes, 22 March 1901 (married Clyde W. Chapman, 20 Nov. 1919).
> Howard Fergus, 22 July 1902.
> Lucy Bell, 14 May 1904.
> Lester, 30 May 1905 (died 30 May 1905).
> Gilbert Stanforth, 2 April 1909.
Now farming at Arcade, N. Y.

The first six years after leaving College I spent in the work of the ministry, having the pastorates in Barrington, New Hampshire, and Second Congregational Church, West Medway, Massachusetts. In 1898 bought farm in Madbury, New Hampshire. When in 1905 our place was destroyed by fire, bought the Elm Hurst Farm in Dover, New Hampshire, where we lived until 1920. Bought land in Northwest Canada, also Maple Lawn Dairy Farm Arcade, New York. Lost what little money he had in the wreckage of the New England Railways, Boston and Maine, New York and New Haven etc. The last five years I have spent largely in Canada and on our farms in Arcade and Dover, New Hampshire. Now our oldest boy has taken over the farm at Dover and I shall confine my efforts to Arcade (dairying) and Canada (wheat farming).

Last year (1922) I was afraid I was growing old and to test out my power of endurance engaged with a threshing crew and worked (at full pay of $4.00 a day) 68 days. And looked after my own harvesting meanwhile. No! We are not old. "We are 20 tonight."

EDWARD CONWAY CULLINAN

Born at Groveland, New York, 14 November 1869, of Jeremiah Cullinan (merchant) and Margaret Conway.
Fitted at Phillips Exeter.
Class Status: Left after Sophomore year.
Married Helen Whiteside at New York City, 8 December 1903.
Now in insurance at New York City.

That I was born of poor but honest parents; that my valedictory at the Geneseo Normal School was "unconquered Ireland"—now, as a Czecho-Slovak I marvel at my adolescent daring in fussing with fiery and untamed peoples;—that I ventured from "Main Street," out there in the wide open spaces, to Exeter for finishing; that I spent the pimpled months under "Bull" and "Brad" in the damndest finest school in our well-known country: that I took all educational hurdles in my stride, was a cracking good pool-player as well as an able inhaler of cigarettes, and that I finally entered Harvard with only two conditions, may be a matter of interest. (It is hell to bare one's soul to the public, to one's pals. I pen manfully under roweling but I'm worried to death about split infinitives and the niceties that obtain in cultural writing).

My earlier reports speak gladness. Sadness, by design, is sunk. Since the last report not much is to be added. As Director I did carry the Harvard Club of New York through war years. I know I did a good job! I then returned to insurance. I may only add that I eat regularly, drink modestly and attempt to grow old gracefully. Degrees I have not experienced,

except of heat and cold! Distinctions? I am probably the only
white man of our time who didn't know all the "Floradora"
Pretty Maidens.

Of travels since the last report I only enthuse about one, my
months spent abroad, two years ago with Tom Slocum, '90,
also a loyal honorary member of '93· No two he humans could
have had a better time. We saw Western Europe, afield, afloat
and awing! In Wales I think I came upon the basic notion of
Yale cheers, when we motored into Bettws-Y-Coed! Try it on
your Victrola! Then when you digest that, bust hell out of the
machine with Ffestiniog and Llannachllyn!!!

CHARLES KIMBALL CUMMINGS

Born at Boston, 25 September 1870, of Charles Amos Cummings [Van
    Rensselaer Polytechnic] (architect) and Margaret Kimball.
Fitted at Roxbury Latin.
Class Status: Regular.
Degree: A.B. 1893.
Married Lydia Lyman Paine at Boston, 18 May 1898. Children:
    Francis Hathaway, born 22 April 1899.
    Charles Kimball, Jr., 27 November, 1901.
    Ethel, 16 December 1903.
    Evelyn, 14 March 1907.
    Margaret, 9 July 1910.
Now practising architecture in Boston.

At Brest, during the war, the navy censor when in a pleasant
mood occasionally allowed officers to cable home, "Am well.
Love." It seemed to us pretty meagre; but the censor was in-
exorable and used to reply to protests, "It's all you need to
say, anyway." (If only Samuel Francis Batchelder were more
like that censor, we unliterary people would not have to sit
biting our pencils and wondering how to write autobiographies
and "make them snappy").

During the past five years I have been still practising architecture in Boston, relieved by one journey to Europe and several shooting and fishing trips. I find myself growing each
year fonder of gardening. My family is growing up: one son
who graduated from Harvard two years ago is now studying
law; another is expecting to graduate this year. My eldest
daughter is at Radcliffe and the two younger ones in school.

FRANK JOSSLYN CURRIER

Born at Lynn, Massachusetts, 8 June 1872, of Benjamin Willis Currier
   (merchant) and Louise Carlton Martin.
Fitted at Lynn High.
Class Status: Regular.
Degree: A.B. 1893.
Married (1) Marie Ingalls Newhall at Lynn, Massachusetts, 30 April
   1908.
Married (2) Grace Elizabeth Silsbee, at Lynn, 15 January 1921.
Now travelling in Europe.

For three years after leaving college I worked at and studied
store management. Then went into the shoe manufacturing
business in which I continued until 1915. Went to Chicago
and entered the brokerage business. After trying for months
to get into the regular service, in the fall of 1918, I joined the
American Red Cross as a chauffeur, and very shortly was sent
abroad. Was on the water when the Armistice was signed. I
was sent almost immediately to Coblentz where as assistant manager of the A. R. C. warehouse I had three interesting months
and very hard work. Was then sent to Paris in March, 1919,
and went into the paymaster's department. Later on was chief
paymaster of the Transportation Department and continued
as such until this work was taken over by the general paymaster
in March, 1920. The next two months of my service was occupied in convoying a trainload of automobiles from Paris to
Vienna—the most interesting and enjoyable experience I had
"over there." Sailed for home in May, arriving in New York
early in June, 1920. Went into the brokerage business in Boston.

On January 15, 1921, I married Miss Grace Elizabeth Silsbee
of Lynn, Mass. This has proved to be the crowning achievement in a heretofore rather fruitless struggle, and I am still
amazed at why I should be given such happiness. We came
abroad in November, 1921, for an indefinite stay. Landing in
France, went to Paris, Italian Rivera, French Rivera (had a
nice little visit with Frank Blake at Cap Martin), Island of
Jersey, England, back to Paris, Switzerland, Florence, where we
are lingering on. I expect that we will spend some time in Rome
and sail from Naples some time in May.

GEORGE DE CLYVER CURTIS

Born at Chester, Pennsylvania, 27 November 1870, of Edward Curtis
(physician) and Augusta Lorler Stacy.
Fitted at F. G. Ireland's.
Class Status: Regular.
Degree: A.B. 1893.
Married Josephine Denver Jones at San Diego, California, 8 September
1917.
Now bee-keeping and farming at Lakeside, California.

After graduating I spent three years in rather uncoördinated
study and travel, and then took a position as assistant librarian
on the staff of the New York Public Library. For the next ten
years I worked at arranging and calendaring the manuscript
collections of the library, cataloging rare and curious volumes,
etc. During this time I lived with my father and mother, my
brother and sisters, in the old house which my grandfather had
bought in the 1830's, in a once quiet street far down town, until business finally compelled us to move. Our summers at Rock-
away were very pleasant with boats and bathing and tennis.
I accompanied my sister Natalie on her visit to the western and
southwestern Indian tribes in 1904-05, during which she collected much of the material embodied in her monumental work,
The Indian's Book. In 1907, when she was ordered to Southern
California for her health, I went with her, and remained in this
part of the country, passing one year on a cattle ranch in Arizona. (I wrote a little book containing my impressions of the
life and country, published under the pen-name of Gregory Mar-
word) and in 1910 I "homesteaded" a bit of California mountain land, where I have lived ever since. I have cleared part of
the land, planted vines and olives, and keep poultry and bees.
A few months after graduation I enlisted in Company K of
the Seventh Regiment, and served in it until I left New York—
nearly fourteen years. In 1916 and 1917 I tried in various ways
to get back into service, but as I had never accepted promotion
in my old regiment, the age-limit debarred me from the line,
either as officer or private, and I had no business training that
would have qualified me for the staff. However, after my re-
jection by the Army, I found acceptance in another quarter,
and in the autumn of 1917 married Josephine Denver Jones.
Since then we have built a house in the Spanish style, with a
patio. We live quietly, very close to nature, with Persian cats

and Airedales for company, and occasional trips to San Diego.
I had a serious illness two years ago, with operations on nose
and throat, but my health is almost completely reëstablished,
and I cherish a hope that some day I may be able to travel eastward for a Class Reunion.

Walter Howard Cushing

Born at Medford, Massachusetts, 8 February 1871, of Henry Harrison
  Davis Cushing (packer) and Anna Bramhall Herriot.
Fitted at Medford High.
Class Status: Regular.
Degrees: A.B. 1893; A.M. 1899.
Married Frances Louise Dudley at Medford, Massachusetts, 15 November
  1894. Children:
    Howard Randolph, born 21 February 1896 (died 21 November
    1897).
    Sydney Hall, 30 September 1897.
    Walter Kenneth, 15 November 1902.
Died of paralysis at Framingham, 6 December 1921.

Walter Howard Cushing died at Framingham December 6,
1921. He was born at Medford February 8, 1871, son of Henry
Harrison Davis Cushing and Anna Bramhall Herriot. Fitting
at the local high school he entered Harvard in 1889 and was a
regular member of the Class graduating *magna cum laude*. Immediately afterwards he began teaching history at the Medford
High School. From 1897 to 1899 he was a graduate student in
history, and in the latter year received his A.M. In 1901 and
1902 he was an assistant in the same subject. The next year he
was elected head master of the Framingham High School, where
he remained until the close of his active career, filling the post
with great success, and in his own words "devoted to raising the
quality rather than the quantity of the population." About six
years before his death he suffered a nervous breakdown from
which he never recovered. He was deeply interested in his
chosen field of American History, was a member of numerous
historical societies, one of the editors of the *History Teachers'
Magazine,* and for many years secretary of the New England
History Teachers' Association. His zeal and ability brought
him a high reputation in his profession, and his fine character
and sympathetic nature the affection and respect of all who
knew him. November 15, 1894, at Medford, he married Frances
Louise Dudley, who with two sons survives him.

FREDERICK WILLIAM DALLINGER

Born at Cambridge, Massachusetts, 2 October 1871, of William Wilber-
    force Dallinger (city treasurer) and Elizabeth Folsom Kingman.
Fitted at Cambridge Latin.
Class Status: Regular.
Degrees: A.B. 1893; A.M. 1894; LL.B. 1897.
Married Blanche Lucy Russell at Lovell, Maine, 29 August 1900.
    Children:
        John Russell, born 8 October 1901.
        Anna Elizabeth, 20 July 1903.
        Lucy Kingman, 17 January 1905.
        William Stearns, 3 September 1908.
Now member of Congress, 8th Massachusetts district.

In November, 1893, I was elected to the Massachusetts House
of Representatives from one of the Cambridge Districts and
served in that body during the years 1894 and 1895. In 1895
I was chosen State Senator from the Cambridge District and
was reëlected in 1896, 1897, and 1898, serving on many important committees and being for three terms Chairman of the Joint
Committee on Metropolitan Affairs, at that time the most important committee of the Legislature. During my third term in
the Senate I barely escaped being elected its President.

In 1897 I finished my book entitled "Nominations for Elec-
tive Office in the United States" which was published by the
University as Volume 4 of the Harvard Historical Studies.
The same year I was admitted to the Bar and began the practice of my profession with our classmate Arthur P. Stone, under
the firm name of Stone and Dallinger.

After my retirement from the State Senate our law firm was
enlarged by the admission of Hugh Bancroft, Harry N. Stearns,
and Frederick W. Fosdick, the first two being Harvard men and
the latter being a graduate of the Harvard Law School. The
name of the new firm was Stone, Dallinger and Bancroft, which
carried on a large and successful general practice for a number
of years. This firm was later dissolved, Bancroft and Fosdick
being associated together, Stone forming an association with his
nephew, Mason Stone, and Stearns and I continuing the business at the old stand, under the firm name of Dallinger and
Stearns.

In 1912 I was the Republican candidate for Congress from the
8th Massachusetts District and was defeated by Frederick W.
Deitrick, a Harvard Law School man, by 1200 plurality. I ran

again in 1914 and was elected to the 64th Congress and reëlected to the 65th, 66th, 67th, and 68th Congresses by large majorities. The people of my District have been exceedingly good to me and the recent Democratic tidal wave apparently did not affect me at all, for which I am profoundly grateful.

During the last two Congresses I have been Chairman of the Committee on Elections and am also a member of the Committees on Education, and on Indian Affairs. In the 64th Congress I achieved "nation-wide notoriety" as the man who twice kept Victor Berger, the friend of Lenine, out of Congress for giving aid and comfort to the enemy during the World War.

Edward Crosby Darling

Born at Hudson, Ohio, 23 September 1869, of George Darling [Union 1846; Princeton Theol. 1849] (clergyman) and Katherine Elizabeth Crosby.
Entered from Ripon College, Wisconsin.
Class Status: Entered Sophomore.
Degree: A.B. 1893.
Married Elizabeth Patton Kent at Wytheville, Virginia, 1 December 1898.
Children:
Kent Crosby, born 12 November 1890.
George Edward, 15 July 1902.
Died of cerebral tumor 5 August 1922 at Philadelphia.

Edward Crosby Darling died of cerebral tumor at Philadelphia, August 5, 1922. He was born at Hudson, Ohio, September 23, 1869, the son of George Darling, a Congregational clergyman and graduate of Union College, and Katharine Elizabeth Crosby. He went to Ripon College, Wisconsin, first in the preparatory department, and then entered as a freshman in the fall of 1887. He was anxious, however, to earn enough money to attend an Eastern college. In 1889 one of his aunts moved to Cambridge, and this enabled him to live with her and enter Harvard in 1890 as a Sophomore. Her house was too far away for him to take much part in undergraduate life, but he received his degree with '93 in regular course. The week after graduation he began work with the Pittsburgh Reduction Company, at New Kensington, Pa., the sole concern manufacturing aluminum in this country. This proved to be his life-work. In three years he was promoted to be superintendent. The company changed its name to the Aluminum Company of America, and its business increased to such an extent that in 1908

Darling was sent to London as its European manager. Here
he was also director of the Northern Aluminum Company, Ltd.
In 1916, owing to war conditions, he returned to this country,
but was at once sent to Russia to explore the aluminum fields
of the Caucasus region to the east of the Black Sea. The next
year he located in Pittsburgh as the company's manager there.
He was also interested in the American Bauxite Company at
Philadelphia. Although unable to attend Class gatherings he
was always a loyal Harvard man; and his business career,
steadily rising from humble beginnings to a position of international importance, is one in which '93 may take an honest
pride. December 1, 1898, he married Elizabeth Patton Kent,
of Wytheville, Va., who with two sons survives him. The elder
son, Kent Crosby Darling, has just graduated from Harvard.

BRADLEY MOORE DAVIS

Born at Chicago, 19 November 1871, of Charles Wilder Davis (publisher)
and Emma Moore.
Entered from Stanford University.
Class Status: Graduate School, 1892-95.
Degrees: A.B. (Stanford) 1892; A.B. 1893; A.M. 1894; Ph.D. 1895.
Married Annie Elizabeth Paret at Germantown, Pennsylvania, 22 Sep-
tember 1908. Child:
Margery French, born 17 October 1912.
Now Professor of Botany at the University of Michigan.

After taking my doctorate at Harvard in 1895 I taught for ten
years at the University of Chicago. Then came a period of
five years employed in part in the preparation of two texts—
"The Principles of Botany" and "A Laboratory and Field
Manual of Botany." At this time I became interested in plant
genetics and began in 1908 my studies with evening primroses
on principles of inheritance, variation, etc., which are still in
progress. These five years were divided between Cambridge
and Woods Hole and greatly widened my professional interests.
I became connected in 1911 with the University of Pennsylvania, spending seven delightful years in the fine old city of
Philadelphia. For the year 1918 I had the good fortune to be
in Washington with the Statistical Division of Food Administration.

In 1919 an attractive call drew me to the University of Michigan, where I am pleasantly situated with a little house and

some land to improve and my daughter growing up under happy surroundings. This is a brief outline of a professor's quiet life which has resulted in a considerable list of technical papers. It has been punctuated with bits of travel in Europe, Egypt, and more recently in western America. Such travel with its opportunities for sketching and rough life has been my chief pastime.

Of various professional organizations the American Society of Naturalists has been for me a source of great interest and pleasure, since for thirteen consecutive years I have been an officer, most of this time as secretary. Of the prominent honor societies I am a member of the American Academy of Arts and Sciences and the American Philosophical Society. I recall with great pleasure active interest of earlier years in the Chicago Literary Club and Loyal Legion. I am also a member of the Botanical Society of America, New England Botanical Club, Ends of the Earth, etc.

PHILIP WHITNEY DAVIS

Born at Jamaica Plain, Massachusetts, 27 June 1871, of William Whitney Davis (merchant) and Julia Wilder Robinson.
Fitted at Browne and Nichols.
Class Status: Regular.
Degrees: A.B. 1893; S.B. 1895.
Now metallurgical engineer at Boston.

After graduating with the A.B. degree in 1893, I spent the next two years in the Scientific School, graduating in 1895 with the degree of S.B. in electrical engineering.

I was in the service of the West End Street Railway—subsequently the Boston Elevated Railway—from 1896 to 1900. Then I was with the Electric Storage Battery Company of Philadelphia as engineer of their Boston office until 1905. In 1905 I became connected with the consulting engineering office of Charles K. Stearns. In 1907 I was one of the incorporators of the Eastern Metal and Refining Company, the others being the owners of Richards and Company, metal dealers in Boston. This concern engaged in metallurgical processes as a subsidiary of Richards and Company, who sold the products. I continued to manage this plant until 1916-1917, when I gave up most of my time to studying the methods and apparatus used in smelting South American tin concentrates to produce pig tin. In

1918-1919 I built for Richards and Company a smelter for handling tin concentrates imported from Bolivia, and successfully smelted some 4,000 tons producing a product which commanded a premium in the market over similar products of nominally the same grade imported from England.

In 1921 as a result of financial reverses due to the sudden deflation of prices and inventories, the Eastern Metal and Refining Company was merged with Richards and Company. The mines in South America closed down and no more ore being obtainable, the smelter also closed down and has not since reopened.

SAMUEL CRAFT DAVIS

Born at St. Louis, Missouri, 13 June 1871, of John Tilden Davis (merchant) and Maria Jeannette Filley.
Fitted at Smith Academy.
Class Status: Regular.
Degree: A.B. 1893.
Married Emma Whitaker at St. Louis, Missouri, 16 July 1904. Children:
  Alita, born 11 November 1905.
  Samuel Craft, Jr., 20 January 1910.
Now trustee at St. Louis, Missouri.

As you suggest, "Same old story, nothing new." My time is taken up with hard working (my friends always smile when they hear me say that) during the winter months with occasional hunting or fishing trips and then some polo and yachting during the summer to keep my health in good enough shape to get back for our 30th. As to "business, profession, or official position," I am technically President of the Davis Estate. I am afraid you would consider me in the semi-retired class, as most of my time is taken up in looking up investments and financial matters for different members of my family. Last summer was devoted to reading our Secretary's article on Harvard Celebrities, or characters of "Ye Ancient Tyme."

WILLIAM HORACE DAVIS

Born at Holyoke, Massachusetts, 21 July 1871, of George Washington Davis [Univ. of Vt. Med.] (physician) and Julia Rawson Hastings.
Entered from Amherst.
Class Status: Entered Sophomore.
Degrees: A.B. 1893; M.D. 1897.

Married Mabel Amanda Crown Johnson at Milton, Vermont 3 December 1898. Children:
Crown Hastings, born 9 June 1900.
George William, 9 June 1901.
Dorothy, 6 August 1904.
Roger Maxfield, 22 November 1905 (died 15 September 1906).
Richard Mackworth, 12 June 1908 (died 26 October 1908).
Kenneth } 29 August 1910.
Barbara }
Gordon, 18 March 1914.
Now Chief Statistician for Vital Statistics, Census Bureau, Washington, District of Columbia.

1897: M.D., Harvard. 1898, December 1: Completed service as House Officer, Massachusetts General Hospital, West Surgical Service, under Doctors H. H. A. Beach, Maurice H. Richardson, and Samuel J. Mixter. 1898, December-1899, October: Abroad for pleasure and study. 1900, January-June: Practised medicine in Dès Moines, Iowa. 1900, August-1916, September: Practised medicine in Boston, Massachusetts, serving at times as District Physician and in the Out-Patient Departments of the Massachusetts General Hospital. 1908: Medical Inspector, Boston Health Department. 1908-1916: Vital Statistician, Boston Health Department. 1916, September to date: Following Civil Service examination, Chief Statistician for Vital Statistics, Bureau of the Census, Washington, D. C. 1918: Chairman, Joint Influenza Committee (composed of representatives of the Army, Navy, United States Public Health Service, and the Bureau of the Census). 1919: Chairman, Advisory Committee on Medical Nomenclature. 1920: Chairman, Vital Statistics Section, American Public Health Association. 1920: Vice-President, International Commission charged with the decennial revision of the international list of causes of sickness and death, Paris, October 11-15, 1920.

George Lawrence Day

Born at Haverhill, Massachusetts, 11 October 1870, of George Whitefield Day (shoe manufacturer) and Marie Zoe Blaisdell.
Fitted at Phillips Exeter.
Class Status: Special, 1889. Left college 27 February 1890.
Married Della Isabel Joyce of Peekskill, New York, at Newport, Rhode Island, 14 August 1918.
Died of acute dilatation of the heart, 6 January 1921, at Fort Wadsworth, New York.

George Lawrence Day died at Fort Wadsworth, New York, January 6, 1921, from acute dilatation of the heart. He was born at Haverhill, October 11, 1870, of George Whitefield Day, a shoe manufacturer, and Maria Zoe Blaisdell. He fitted at Phillips Exeter and entered Harvard in 1889 as a special student, but did not do well in his studies, and left College at the mid-years,—not, however, "under discipline." After a period of roving about the world, including a trip to England on a cattle steamer, he enlisted in the navy. Not making a success of this, he assumed the name of John Mapes Adams, and joined the Marine Corps in 1897. Here he found his niche, was promoted to corporal the next year, and to sergeant in 1900. During the Spanish War he served aboard the "Mayflower," was gunnery sergeant in the Philippines during the insurrection there, was in the China Relief Expedition during the Boxer Rebellion, and also took part in the West Indian Campaign. In 1902 he was discharged with "exceptional" record and "excellent" character. He at once reënlisted, was discharged in 1906, enlisted again and was discharged in 1909. He then changed his branch of service and enlisted as a private in the Coast Artillery Corps, again rising to the grade of first sergeant.

When this country entered the World War, he took a commission as second lieutenant in the Coast Artillery in June, 1917. In August of 1918 he sailed for France with the 54th Artillery, and after the Armistice served with the Army of Occupation at Coblenz until October, 1919. He then returned suffering from chronic myocarditis, went into hospital, and was honorably discharged from his active commission in December, but was immediately commissioned second lieutenant in the Reserve Corps. He continued as first sergeant of Coast Artillery, and was assigned to Fort Wadsworth.

In the service he was known as an unusually intelligent man, very capable along technical lines, and an enthusiastic athlete, especially in baseball, which had been his hobby since school days. He was efficient and popular, had a great knack in handling men, and was an excellent organizer and manager. The commanding officer at Fort Wadsworth writes: "His service as a soldier in the United States Army and Marine Corps was of exceptional merit, and a great credit to himself and the United

States of America.'' His most famous exploit was during the
siege of Tientsin, when on July 13, 1900, as a sergeant of
Marines, under heavy fire, he rescued his wounded captain. In
recognition of this intrepid feat he was awarded the Congres-
sioual Medal of Honor ''for distinguished conduct in the presence of the enemy in battle.''

Thus ''Chicker'' Day, or ''Foggy'' Adams, as he was known
for most of his life, stands a unique figure in the records of the
Class—perhaps of the whole University—a typical ''gentleman
ranker'' and one of the very few Harvard men who ever received the highest military decoration within the gift of our
Government. August 14, 1918, two days before sailing for
France, he married at Newport, Rhode Island, Della Isabel
Joyce, a trained nurse, of Peekskill, New York, who survives
him.

JASPER NEWTON DEAHL

Born at Kasson, West Virginia, 19 April 1859, of Henry Deahl (far-
mer) and Catherine Kline.
Entered from University of Nashville.
Class Status: Special, 1891-92. Joined Class Senior year.
Degrees: A.B. (Univ. Nashville) 1889; A.B. 1893; A.M. (Hon.) (Univ.
Nashville) 1894; A.M. (Columbia) 1899; Ph.D. (Columbia) 1906.
Married Mary Anderson at Wingo, Kentucky, 1 August 1901. Children:
Martha Kline, born 21 June 1904.
Henry George, 1 April 1907.
Now Professor of Education at West Virginia University.

After leaving Harvard I was principal of the Normal School,
West Liberty, West Virginia, 1893-1898. At the end of 1898 I
resigned my position and entered Columbia University where
I continued my studies for two years, holding a scholarship the
first year, and a fellowship the second. In 1900-1901 I taught
school a part of the year in West Virginia and a part of the
year in New York City. In 1901 I was appointed Division
Superintendent of Schools in the Philippine Islands, but accepted an appointment in West Virginia University as Professor of
Education. I have held that position since 1901. I have taught
in the university summer schools of Texas, Pittsburgh, and New
Jersey. My addresses are for the most part educational, before
high schools and organizations, teachers, and civic bodies.

My travelling has been within the United States from ocean

to ocean and from Lakes to Gulf, including most of this country—only one sojourn of any length, a winter in Florida. My
recreations are tennis and golf. For eleven years I was a member of the State Board of Education of West Virginia and for
five years I was a member of the State Book Commission. I
have been State Director in the National Education Association
and in the National Pilgrims Association and President of the
State Educational Association of West Virginia. I am a member of the Phi Beta Kappa and of the Masons.

Ambrose Collyer Dearborn

Born at Melrose, Massachusetts, 31 January 1873, of George Henry Dear-
born (insurance) and Bessie Berry Godfrey.
Fitted at Melrose High.
Class Status: Regular.
Degree: A.B. 1893.
Married Louise Frances Beane at Melrose, Massachusetts, 29 July 1906.
Died of diabetes, 19 September 1920, at New York City.

"Amby" Dearborn died at his home in New York City after
a very brief illness. He had been back at his desk but a few
days after a summer holiday, returning well-bronzed by the sun
and boasting that he had never felt better in his life. He was
at his office until three days before his death.

His business career, after a few years of newspaper work and
teaching, was entirely with the firm of Henry Holt and Company, publishers. At the time of his death he was the Secretary
and a Director of the Company, which placed upon its minutes
that he had made himself "an integral and important part of
the business, to the growth and success of which he devoted the
energies of the best part of his life." He was in charge of the
educational department and personally edited many scores of
text-books.

"Amby" entered College very young, did much newspaper
work, particularly for the Boston Globe, while in college, and
had a large acquaintance. He retained in later life most of his
undergraduate enthusiasms, and was always "regular" in anything pertaining to Harvard or to '93. When the offices of
his firm were moved to the building next door to the Harvard
Club it was easy for him to drop in and gratify his fondness for
association with other Harvard men. Both parents survived

him at their home in Melrose, Mass., and his visits there permitted him to keep in touch with many of his friends of college days.

The star that will go beside his name in the next Quinquennial marks the passing of a modest, manly, four-square citizen who was a loyal friend and delightful companion. He never made an enemy. His death was sudden, but his record needed no apology. His memory recalls no asperities—only cheerfulness, good-will and durable satisfaction of life.

F. R. M.

HARTLEY DENNETT

Born at Saco, Maine, 15 September 1870, of Roscoe Gilpatric Dennett and
   Annie Olivia Berry.
Entered from Technology.
Class Status: I. Graduate School 1892-93.
Degrees: S.B. (Mass.. Inst. Tech.) 1892; A.B, 1893,
Married Mary Coffin Ware at Boston, 20 January 1900 (divorced 1913)..
   Children:
      Carleton, born 23 December 1903 (died 31 December 1903).
      Devon, 12 May 1905.
Now farming at East Alstead, New Hampshire.

[Extract from latest *Gazetteer of New Hampshire*.]

East Alstead, pleasantly situated in the depths of the New Hampshire marshes, thirteen miles from Bellows Falls. Easily reached by raft during freshets on Dennett Creek. H. Dennett, postmaster. This town is said to have been founded about 1893 by the family of one Dennett, a refugee from Harvard during the reign of terror of *Les Examinations d'Une Heure.* The church (Rev. Dennett, pastor) and the public library (Hartley Dennett, Esq., trustee) are fine specimens of the work of the well-known architect Dennett. The latter is believed to contain the only complete set of the multitudinous works of Dennett the Socialist, copiously annotated by his disciple John the Orangeman. Here also is a curious college term-bill rendered H. Dennett, '93, and endorsed, "Received on account, three dozen eggs. Charles F. Mason, Bursar," supposed to be the last example of the ancient custom of paying tuition fees "in kind." One of the sights of the town is the snapping-turtle breeding and stock breeding his pets for their snapping powers, as the stumps of farm in the depths of "Mill Hollow," owned by Mr. Hartley Dennett. Mr. Dennett, who is an enthusiastic turtologist, is.

several of his fingers testify. When fully developed, this power, he hopes, will form a successful commercial proposition, and his stock will be placed on the market as the Dennett Live Wire-cutters.

Clarence Bigelow Denny

Born at Boston, 7 August 1871, of Daniel Denny [H. C. 1854] (merchant) and Mary De Forest Bigelow.
Fitted at J. P. Hopkinson's.
Class Status: With '93, 1889-90. With '94, 1890-91.
Married Elizabeth Winsor Tilden at Boston, 1 June 1897. Child:
    Daniel, born 29 May 1898 (died July, 1914).
Died 22 November 1920, at Dedham, Massachusetts.

Denny was born August 7, 1871 at Savin Hill, Dorchester, Mass., and died November 22, 1920, at Dedham, Mass. The cause of his death was convulsions due to a severe blow on the head, received in Paris while doing Red Cross work in the previous year. His father was Daniel Denny, a Boston merchant, and his mother Mary DeForest (Denny). The early years of his life were spent in Dorchester and Milton. He fitted for college at Hopkinson's private school, entered college with our Class, but left at the end of Sophomore year.

After leaving College he worked for two years with the Boston & Albany R. R., but after the death of his brother, Daniel, in 1896, he left the B. & A. to help his father in the Boston firm of Denny, Poor & Co. His father died the following year, the firm was dissolved, and Denny took up insurance work. This did not hold his interest, and in 1898 he began work with the Submarine Signal Co. This work interested him intensely. He soon became Secretary of the Submarine Signal Co. and from 1899 to 1917 he did some valuable and important work, spoken of in the most flattering terms by his colleagues in this company. While in this capacity he did considerable travelling, going to Bermuda, Canada, Panama, London, etc.

In January, 1917, he entered war service, volunteering for the American Ambulance Field Service under A. Piatt Andrew. He drove an ambulance at Verdun for several months, while Mrs. Denny served in a hospital in Paris. He received an injury to his foot which nearly resulted in an amputation at the hospital in Paris to which he was transferred. Having then completed the six months term of his enlistment with the

Parker
  Hand

Cummings Robb

Trafford

Ware Farwell

Upton

Fearing

CLASS DAY OFFICERS, 1893

Ambulance Service, he joined J. M. Perkins, '92, head of the Military Department of the Red Cross at Paris, and helped to organize the Bureau of Military Affairs of the Red Cross. He came to America for a short time in January, 1918, but returned in a month and remained in Paris at Red Cross Headquarters for the rest of the War.

Denny was a good sportsman, being chiefly fond of horses and canoeing. As a horseman he was remarkable, being an excellent rider, and an expert driver of four-in-hand or tandem. On the water, he made several long canoe trips both in this country and in England. He always did things with his hands. He was always using carpenter's tools. He became very much interested in cement work and invented a system which he established as a business under the name "Sideways Studios" on Boylston Place, Boston, where he made fountains, garden benches, jars and other artistic cement articles. He was made a "Master Craftsman" of the Arts & Crafts Society. His interest in the Boy Scouts was very keen. He felt that it was the hope of this country, and the greatest thing in the world for destroying "muckerism" and giving boys the proper kind of training. He was kind, gentle and noticeably self-effacing and modest, a merry and genial companion and a sincere and honest friend. He married in June 1897, Elizabeth Winsor Tilden of Boston; and a beautiful and remarkable boy, Daniel Denny, was born May 29, 1898. The death of this boy, by drowning, while at a summer camp in July, 1914, was a terrible blow, from which Denny never entirely recovered, although his bravery in enduring his loss was remarkable.

F. A.

CHARLES LUNT DE NORMANDIE

Born at Portsmouth, New Hampshire, 26 September 1870, of James De Normandie (Antioch 1857) (clergyman) and Emily Farnum Jones.
Fitted at Roxbury Latin.
Class Status: Regular.
Degrees: A.B. 1893; LL.B. 1897.
Now practising law at Boston.

For the last five years my life is much as it was at the twenty-fifth anniversary, though since then I have made my all-the-year home in the country at Lincoln. I am sorry I have nothing of interest to say.

LOUIS LEE DENT

Born at Short Bend, Missouri, 21 September 1870, of James Munro
   Dent (merchant) and Mary Jane Springer.
Entered from University of Missouri.
Class Status: Entered Junior.
Degrees: Litt.B. (Univ. Mo.) 1892; A.B. 1894 as of 1893.
Married Mary Elizabeth Barrett at Minneapolis, Minnesota, 26 May
   1899.
Now practising law at Chicago.

Studied mathematics in the Graduate School, 1893-94, and
was in the Law School 1895-97; then began practice in Chicago
with the firm of Hoyne, Follansbee ('92) and O'Connor. In
1900, after a year in Colorado, Idaho, and Wyoming, opened an
office by myself; a few years later joined the firm of Sheriff,
Dobyns and Freeman, at present Dent, Dobyns and Freeman.
I have been and am very busily engaged in the practice of my
profession.

In 1898 published "Federal Control over Interstate Commerce," and in 1902 was made Assistant Professor of Law in
the Northwestern University Law School; later Professor of
Law, Equity Pleading and Practice, which chair I still retain.
Member of Chicago Club, Chicago Historical Society, and other
clubs and societies not quite so well known as these.

LOUIS EUGENE DESBECKER

Born at Buffalo, New York, 2 April 1871, of Samuel Desbecker (mer-
   chant) and Marie Weil.
Fitted at Central High School and with tutor, Buffalo.
Class Status: "Four years in three."
Degrees: A.B. 1892; LL.B. (N. Y. Law School) 1894.
Now practising law at Buffalo, New York.

I am still unmarried. 1917 I was appointed a member of
the Board of Education of the City of Buffalo and have been
re-appointed twice since. It is a board (unpaid) consisting of
five members. I am now president of the board. Before 1917
things educational were run as a part of the City Government.
Under the State Law passed in that year the "board" was created with large powers, but still subject more or less to the City
Council as to finances. It seemed impossible to make the City
Government understand that it no longer controlled the School
Department, the result was continual friction. Within the past

few months the highest court of New York State by a decision in favor of the board has settled many of our difficulties. I am still giving considerable of my time to this "labor of love."

I served as a director of the Chamber of Commerce and I am a director of the Buffalo Eye and Ear Infirmary, Children's Aid Society, Society of Natural Sciences, Buffalo Club and other similar organizations. In 1920 I was chosen as one of the four delegates at large from the State of New York to the Democratic National Convention held at San Francisco. I attended and had an interesting and enjoyable time. So between practising law and giving my time to these and other outside interests I manage to keep reasonably busy. My law firm is now Desbecker, Fisk, Newcomb and Block. All the members of the firm are Harvard men, either Academic or Law School or both.

Clubs and societies: Buffalo Club, University Club, Park Club, Buffalo Athletic Club, Buffalo Country Club, Buffalo, New York; Wanakah Country Club, Wanakah, New York; Niagara Falls Country Club, Lewiston, New York; Harvard Club, New York City.

BRADFORD COLT DE WOLF

Born at San Francisco, 21 February 1871, of Francisco Eugene De Wolf and Isabella De Wolf Colt.
Fitted at Phillips Exeter.
Class Status: Special 1889-91.
Married Elizabeth Lindsey Burness at London, 14 December 1893.
Child:
Francis Colt, born 28 October 1894.
Now living at Bristol, Rhode Island.

I lived in Brussels, Belgium, for fifteen years and corresponded for the "New York Times," "New York Herald," and "Evening Post." I translated Sprelberch de Lovenjoul's work on Balzac. "Un Roman d'Amour," the love story of Balzac and Madame Hanska, published serially in the "Bookman" (New York) in 1902. Since my return to this country I have corresponded for the "New York Times," "Evening Post," and "Boston Transcript," political and literary questions of the day. I have travelled considerably in France, Switzerland, Germany, Hungary, and Italy, and written on current questions of the day in these countries to the above-mentioned newspapers.

A descendant of the first governor of Rhode Island, William Bradford, and Mary Bradford, *née* Le Baron I have been at work for some time on a history of the Bradfords and Le Barons in Rhode Island. Have devoted much time, incidentally, to Dr. Francis Le Baron, born in Provence, France, the "Nameless Nobleman" of Jane Austin's novel, who never revealed his real name—thought to be "de Montamand."

Arthur Wyman Dexter

See Report VI, Page 89.

ALBERT JAMES DIBBLEE

Born at San Francisco, 25 February 1870, of Albert Dibblee (powder
mills) and Annie Meacham.
Fitted at J. P. Hopkinson's.
Class Status: Regular.
Degrees: A.B. 1893; LL.B. 1896.
Married Ethel Rodgers at Columbus, Ohio, 19 April 1899. Children:
    Anne Rodgers, born 1 December 1900.
    Margaret Jane
    Marian Eliza   twins, 23 June 1909.
Now practising law at San Francisco.

Since graduating from the Law School I have been continuously engaged in the practice of law in San Francisco. My residence has been in Ross, Marin County, but we have spent many of the winters in San Francisco. My daughter, Anne Rodgers, married Frederick Hope Beaver of San Francisco, October 1, 1921, and on September 21, 1922, presented me with a fine husky grandson, who, I hope, will be at Harvard about eighteen years hence. Since becoming a grandfather I feel very aged, but I am not yet tottering and am still able to enjoy out of door exercise and sports such as fishing, shooting, and motoring. My health is fine. Owing to advanced age my war work was confined to examination of candidates for the military training camps, and Liberty Loan, Red Cross and Y. M. C. A. drives, and work in connection with an organization for the investigation of persons suspected of disloyalty and of rendering assistance to the enemy. The only public office which I have ever held is that of City Attorney of Ross, which position I have filled since 1909. Am a member of the San Francisco Bar Association, California State Bar Association and the American Bar Association, and of the following social organizations: Pacific Union Club, University Club, Marin Golf and Country Club, Lagunitas Country Club, Harvard Club of San Francisco and the Harvard Club of New York.

JOSEPH PHILLIPS DIMMICK

Born at Montgomery, Alabama, 28 September 1872, of Joseph Wesley
  Dimmick (clerk of court) and Annie Savage.
Entered from University of Alabama.
Class Status: Entered Sophomore.
Degrees: A.B. (Univ. of Alabama) 1889; A.B. 1893.
Married Nora Spann at Montgomery, 18 February 1909.
Now Treasurer and General Manager of Alabama Central Railway.

For a number of years after graduation I was assistant to my father, Clerk of the United States District Circuit Court for the Middle District of Alabama, at Montgomery. In 1906 I was appointed by President Roosevelt to be Postmaster of Montgomery, an event that caused considerable interest, as I was only thirty-three years old (the youngest man who ever held the position) and belonged to the "lily white" party, which was supposed to be *non grata* with the administration. In 1914 my commission expired and I took up farming in a small way. Was also an officer in three local corporations. When I filled out one of those blanks and reported that my occupation was the manager of a very short line railroad, I did so with considerable hesitancy; because the little road I am interested in is such a miserable apology for an honest-to-goodness railroad. However, I so stated, because it represents my occupation. I still have the farm—about four miles from the centre of this city—but I do not live on it. I farm after a fashion; it has not been a howling success but it is a source of some pleasure. City-dwelling farmers usually have great expectations, and this measures their success as farmers; my farming experience has not been an exception to this rule. This sort of farming, though, has one redeeming feature, it inculcates optimism; you always expect a fuller measure of success next year.

I am also President of a coal mining company, mining bituminous coal. Our company mined in excess of 162,000 tons of coal during 1922. I, however, cannot claim to be a coal operator, because I do not reside in the mineral district of this State and òur company has a very efficient manager in charge of operations. I am also Secretary and Treasurer of the Black Warrior 'Coal Company, a corporation owning and leasing coal lands. Now that I have about chronicled my business activities, I cannot say that I am a very active business man: I have considerable leisure time. I am married but have no children. I enjoy good health, live in my own home, enjoy the good things of life in moderation and have few worries. My chief tribulation is that I weigh more than 230 pounds. Looking backwards, I feel that while in my life I have not achieved the heights of success, I have kept out of the morass of failure.

Silas Dinsmoor

Born at Bellevue, Kentucky, 30 September 1852, of Thomas Hill Williams
   Dinsmoor (farmer) and Nancy Eugenia Wadsworth.
Entered from University of Missouri.
Class Status: Senior year only.
Degrees: B.S.D. [Bachelor of Scientific Didactics] (State Normal School,
   Kirksville, Mo.) 1885; A.B. 1893; D.O. (American School of Osteo-
   pathy, Kirksville, Mo.) 1900; M.D. (University of Ky.) 1906.
Married Laura Brashear Bulkley at Higginsville, Missouri, 29 April
   1895. Child:
      Daughter (died at birth), 4 October 1896.
Died of accidental injuries, 17 September 1921, at Pittsburgh.

Silas Dinsmoor died Sept. 17, 1921, at Pittsburgh, Pennsylvania, from injuries originally received in a fall from a wagon five years before. He was born Sept. 30, 1852, at Bellevue, Boone County, Kentucky, the son of Thomas Hill Williams Dinsmoor (whose father was a native of Windham, N. H. and a graduate of Dartmouth) and Nancy Eugenia Wadsworth. As a young man he attended the State Normal School of Missouri, and from 1879 to 1889 taught various schools in that state, usually as principal. In the latter year he became a student in the University of Missouri and the next year an instructor in chemistry there. He entered Harvard in our senior year to make further studies in chemistry, working mostly in the Graduate School, but taking his A. B. with '93·

After this he returned to the University of Missouri until 1897, when he became interested in the recent development of Osteopathy, entered the American School of Osteopathy at Kirksville, Missouri, received his degree of D. O. in 1900, and began practice in 1901 at Louisville, Kentucky. Meantime he continued his medical studies, and in 1906 took his M. D. from the University of Kentucky, and was for a year a lecturer on medical chemistry there. In 1908 he removed his practice to Pittsburgh, Pa., and a few years later to Sewickley in that state. On the outbreak of the Great War in 1914 he went to San Benito, Texas, settled on a ranch he had bought some years before, and devoted himself to raising food-stuffs and cotton,— "a position," as he put it, "in the Ancient and Honorable Order of Agriculturalists, the present hope of the world." It was while thus engaged that he met with the accident which ultimately caused his death. At about the end of the War he returned to Pittsburgh, where his wife had been carrying on his practice.

In coming to Harvard, Dinsmoor was influenced by several of his fellow teachers at the University of Missouri, who had spent leaves of absence there, and was especially attracted by "Harvard's liberal policy with respect to the A. B. degree." Though he was in Cambridge only one year, he found that year "made a lasting impression on me." He once wrote of that time, "I met comparatively few of my class, but I recall with pleasure my Thanksgiving dinner at Prof. Lyon's, in company with two or three other students from Missouri; a reception given by the late Prof. Cook for his pupils; Prof. Norton's Christmas reception to all Harvard students who could not go home for the holidays; the Class and Commencement dinners; and the reception at Pres. Eliot's. I mention these merely because my experience has doubtless been that of many other students who were at Harvard only a year or two."

Dinsmoor kept up his interest in Harvard and '93 till the end. He was a conscientious correspondent, writing with a delightful modesty and an equally delightful quiet humor. Asked on one questionnaire, "Do you smoke?" he replied, "No but I get smoked rather too often for comfort." In his death, '93 loses its oldest member, but one whose loyal spirit was still young. On April 29, 1895, he married Laura Brashear Bulkley at Higginsville, Missouri, who survives him.

ROBERT GRAY DODGE

Born at Newburyport, Massachusetts, 29 July 1872, of Elisha Perkins
   Dodge (manufacturer) and Katharine Searls Gray.
Fitted at Newburyport High.
Class Status: Regular.
Degrees:A.B. 1893; A.M. 1895; LL.B. 1897.
Married Alice Woolley Childs at Amesbury, Massachusetts, 11 Sep-
   tember 1900. Children:
        Katharine Gray, born 1 July 1901.
        Eleanor Childs, 13 November 1902.
        Sarah, 24 April 1907.
        Alice Langdon, 30 April 1910.
Now practising law at Boston.

1893-94: Travelling in Europe.   1894-97: Harvard Law
School. 1897 to date: Practising law in Boston. No degrees,
distinctions or publications, and but slight experience of public
office. Was a city councilman of Newburyport many years ago,
served four years as an assistant attorney general of Massachusetts, and was for one term a member of the State Ballot
Law Commission.

   For the past thirteen years I have been a member of the firm
of Storey, Thorndike, Palmer and Dodge, occupied mainly
with trial work and kindred matters. Have had a constant
succession of varied and interesting experiences in the practice
of law. I have taken occasional trips to Europe—two of them,
in the earlier days, with Ned Coffin. For an outdoor sport I am
still playing tennis, as poorly as ever. No change in family
record.

HUGH DODSON

Born at Fort Smith, Arkansas, 10 December 1866, of John Dodson
   (real estate) and Elizabeth O'Keefe.
Entered from Johns Hopkins.
Class Status: Special, 1889-91.
Married Katharine Weston Boltwood at Van Buren, Arkansas, 14
   February 1900. Children:
        Boltwood, born 1 December 1900.
        Joseph, 22 September 1902.
Now teaching at St. Louis.

   Left college in 1891—no profession nor occupation in mind—
for two years a man of leisure—dancer, cotillion leader, trip to
Europe, etc. In 1893 bought half interest in Fort Smith

Daily Times—three and a half years Arkansaw editor *a la* Opie Read—my editorials do not set the Arkansaw prairies or woods afire. In 1897 give up paper—have higher aspirations—enter Kenrick Seminary—study philosophy two years—leave the Seminary and the higher aspirations in 1899. Loafer for a year and a half—fall in love—get married—find out I have to go to work. Solicitor for a year and a half—find it interesting but not profitable.

In 1902 fall into the arms of Uncle Sam. After twenty years in the postal service am just now leaving Uncle Sam for a better boss. Am joining the staff of my wife's "Dodson School of Private Tutoring," so bid fair to end my days as a "jolly old pedagogue."

Physically, the cessation from active manual labor is adding to my rotundity. Financially, my home being one block from St. Louis's night centre, Grand and Olive, I am hoping to sell at $1,000.00 a foot; however, I am no centipede.

My younger boy is in his freshman year at St. Louis University; my elder boy expects to be graduated this June from the United States Naval Academy at Annapolis as a future Admiral.

My religious activities center around the Jesuit Church on the next corner.

Henry Waldo Doe

See Report IV, Page 69.

John Joseph Dolan

Born at Boston, 18 February 1872, of Lawrence Edward Dolan (mechanic) and Catherine Dunn.
Fitted at Boston Latin.
Class Status: Regular.
Degrees: A.B. 1893; LL.B. (Boston Univ.) 1895.
Married Annie Grace Spencer at Boston, 31 December 1896. Child:
Grace, born 15 August 1898.
Died of pulmonary tuberculosis at Wolfboro, New Hampshire, 20 July, 1919.

John Joseph Dolan died of consumption at Wolfboro, New Hampshire, on July 20, 1919. Until his last months, which he spent in the New Hampshire country in his vain search for health, he had lived always in Boston. Even during his college years he lived for the most part at his mother's home in town, and, apart from playing on the freshman nine, took little part in college activities. After receiving his degree with the class he studied at the Boston University Law School from which he graduated in 1895. He practised law in Boston for some years as a partner of his brother Matthew, under the firm name of Dolan and Dolan. After his brother's death, he was for a while law editor of the Boston Daily Law Journal, and then resumed practice by himself, continuing until poor health caused his retirement some half dozen years ago. He was found to be suffering from tuberculosis, and his last years were spent in a brave struggle—pathetic indeed to those who knew the circumstances—against the inroads of the disease. In 1918 he wrote: "I hope to put in a few useful years on this earth yet. That's all I'm doing now—just hoping." He kept up his courage, and his letters from Wolfboro continued to express hopefulness until the last.

He married Annie Grace Spencer in 1896 and had one child— a daughter Grace—born August 15, 1898, who survive him.

R. G. D.

CHARLES THURSTON DOLE

Born at Charlestown, Massachusetts, 6 March 1869, of Charles Augustus Dole (manufacturer) and Edith Veronica Dalton.
Fitted at Berkeley School, Boston.
Class Status: Special, 1889-92.
Married Susan Adelaide Gage at Pepperell, Massachusetts, 20 September 1893. Children:
    Dorothy Cutter, born 14 July 1894.
    Charles Minot, 18 April 1899.
Now manufacturing paper at Lawrence, Massachusetts.

Since leaving college my business interests have been confined to the manufacture of surface coated paper for half-tone printing. The Champion Card and Paper Company was the name of the company when I joined the organization, the mill being located at East Pepperell, Mass. My father-in-law, Mr. C. M. Gage, a pioneer in the manufacture of this grade of paper, being president of the company at that time. Until June, 1898, I lived in Pepperell, removing that year to Tyngsboro, Massachusetts.

In 1902 the Champion Card and Paper Company was consolidated with the pulp and paper mills at Lawrence, Massachusetts, owned by the International Paper Company, under the name of Champion-International Company. In order to be nearer my business I moved to Andover, where I now reside. As manager of sales of this company I am a frequent visitor to New York, Philadelphia, Washington, and Chicago, but outside of business trips I have no travelling to report that would be interesting. I have been a vestryman of Christ Church, Andover, for twenty years. I am a member of the Harvard Clubs of Andover and New York, also the Aldine Club and National Republican Club of New York.

WALTER CAZENOVE DOUGLAS, JR.

Born at Liberty, Virginia, 17 July 1870, of Walter Cazenove Douglas (Gen. Sec. Y. M. C. A.) and Ellen Johnson.
Fitted at Berkeley School, Boston.
Class Status: Regular.
Degrees: A.B. 1893; LL.B. (Univ. of Pennsylvania) 1897.
Married Ellen Hewson at Philadelphia, 1 June 1908. Children:
    Ellen Hewson, born 21 April 1909.
    Lucy Clabaugh, 16 June 1914.
    Katharine Clabaugh, 28 December 1915.
Now practising law at Philadelphia.

University of Pennsylvania Law School, 1894-1897; practised law in Philadelphia, 1897-1900; and in Lancaster County, Pennsylvania, 1900-1906; Assistant United States Attorney, Philadelphia, 1906-1914; Professor of the Law of Torts, Insurance, and Common Law Pleading, Temple University Law School, 1912-1916; Referee in Bankruptcy, 1915 to date; Pennsylvania State Board of Law Examiners, 1916 to date; Secretary and Treasurer State Board of Law Examiners, 1923. My family is the same as at the date of the last report, i.e., my wife and three daughters, aged respectively fourteen, nine and seven. My profession, with incidental connections, and my family, absorb my time very fully.

HENRY ABIJAH THOMPSON DOW

Born at Woburn, Massachusetts, 7 July 1871, of Stephen Henry Dow (leather manufacturer) and Emma Tryphena Thompson.
Fitted at Woburn High.
Class Status: Regular.
Degree: A.B. 1893.

Married (1) Mary Celende Whitcher at Woburn, Massachusetts, 5 April
  1898 (died 20 April 1902). Child:
      Henry Kenneth, born 18 February 1901.
Married (2) Etta May Willard at Cambridge, Massachusetts, 6 June
  1904. Child:
      Lois Willard, born 24 September 1905.
Now corresponding secretary for trustees under the will of Mary Baker
  · G. Eddy, at Boston.

The business career which I expected to enter upon about the
middle of the year 1893 did not start until March 1, 1894. From
that time until February, 1914, I was connected with one of
the large banking institutions of Boston. I resigned my position in order to become the business agent and later the corresponding secretary for the trustees under the will of Mary
Baker Eddy. In these capacities I have had and still am having much joy and satisfaction.

All of my ancestors for generations have lived and labored
in or near the "hub of the universe," and because I have always
admired the conservative New England characteristics and
habits I do not know the desire for chance and change. Consequently my homes (three in number) have all been located within fifteen miles of Boston. Since 1909, however, we have spent
about ten weeks each summer at Salisbury Cove, five miles from
Bar Harbor, Maine. These vacations have afforded opportunities for close contact with nature in her great variety of moods
and have been for me both sport and pastime on land and
water.

I have never been a joiner, although I am a member of the
Ancient Order of Free and Accepted Masons. Since the last
Report my son has entered Bowdoin College. He is now in his
junior year and a member of a fraternity composed of young
men with high ideals of manhood. He has been singing in the
Glee Club and also taken part in other college activities. While
my sense of disappointment that my son did not choose Harvard was keen, it has been dispelled because the arguments advanced in favor of the Maine college have so far fully justified
his choice. Our daughter is headed for Wheaton College, expecting to enter in 1924.

Charles William Downing

See Report VI, Page 96.

TRACY DOWS

Born at New York City, 2 November 1871, of David Dows (merchant) and Margaret Esther Worcester.
Fitted with J. A. Browning.
Class Status: 1889-92, special; 1892-93, with '95; 1893-94, with '96; 1894-95, 1 Law.
Degree: A.B. 1894.
Married Alice Townsend Olin at Rhinebeck, New York, 11 November 1903. Children:
Stephen Olin, born 14 August 1904.
Margaret, 15 April 1906
Deborah, 27 October 1914.
Now a trustee at Rhinebeck, New York.

There is little to add to what I have written for previous reports. The conditions of my life remain practically unchanged. During the World War I served as a member of Local Board No. 2 for Dutchess County and as Fuel Administrator for Northern Dutchess County. I have become keenly interested in local affairs and am affiliated with the Rhinebeck Savings Bank as trustee and with the Rhinebeck Cemetery Association as trustee and secretary. With my family I passed the winter of 1921-1922 in France.

WILLIAM DUANE

Born at Philadelphia, 17 February 1872, of Charles Williams Duane [Univ. of Penn.] (clergyman) and Emma Cushman Lincoln.
Entered from University of Pennsylvania.
Class Status: Entered Senior.
Degrees: A.B. (Univ. of Penn.) 1892; A.B. 1893; A.M. 1895; Ph.D. (Berlin) 1897; Sc.D. (honorary) (Univ. of Penn.), 1922.
Married Caroline Elise Ravenel at Philadelphia, 27 December 1899. Children:
William, Jr., born 17 October 1900.
Arthur Ravenel, 16 November 1901.
Charles Prioleau, 28 July 1909.
Margaretta, 3 May 1911.
Now Professor of Bio-Physics at Harvard.

During the last five years I have still been trying to lessen some of the ills of mankind by projecting rays through those suffering from malignant disease and also trying to find out something more about radiation. The National Research Council in Washington elected me as chairman of its Physics Division and I have also been elected to membership in the National Academy of Sciences and the American Philosophical Society.

The University of Pennsylvania presented me with an honorary
Doctors degree. I have also been awarded the John Scott Prize
of $800 and the Comstock Prize of $1,500. Why they gave
them to me I do not know, but this did not deter me from ac-
cepting them. I have also been elected a member of the Council
of the French Physical Society and an Honorary Fellow of the
American Radiological Society.

I have made two trips to California and back, to organize
radiation institutes and to deliver lectures, visiting the chief
natural wonders in the United States and Canada on the way.
I have also attended scientific meetings in various cities to read
papers, etc.

With regard to pastimes there is nothing to report except
some automobile tours through some of our Eastern States.

DIVIE BETHUNE DUFFIELD

Born at Detroit, Michigan, 3 March 1870, of Henry Martyn Duffield
    [Williams 1861] (lawyer) and Frances Pitts.
Fitted with H. G. Sherrard and G. L. Gorton and at Phillips Exeter
    Academy.
Class Status: Regular.
Degree: A.B. 1893.
Now practising law at Detroit, Michigan.

Lawyer associated with my father, General Henry M. Duffield, from 1895 to his death in 1912; since then alone. Was
active in rowing from graduation to and including 1912. Have
won important championships in singles, doubles, pairs, fours,
and eights. Since 1912 have coached the crews of the Detroit
Boat Club as an amateur coach, without remuneration. Have
had one or more winning crews each year. Favorite winter
sport—curling. In my old age have taken up golf.

Member of Detroit Library Commission for twenty years,
three times president, now serving my fourth term of six years.
President of Charter Commission, which framed present City
Charter. Corporation Counsel for the city, 1918. Twice reform candidate for mayor. beaten both times but the reforms are
here.

Served as enlisted man in United States Navy in 1898, at
Havana, Guantanamo Bay, Santiago and Porto Rico. Commissioned Officer Michigan Naval Brigade and six years command-

ing officer. Put on retired list December, 1913, after nineteen years service.

Detroit Club, Detroit Athletic Club, Detroit Boat Club, Detroit Curling Club, Meadowbrook Country Club, Prismatic Club. No publications or speeches. Have shown consideration for the public! Unmarried.

MORRILL DUNN

Born at Fort Leavenworth, Kansas, 26 June 1871, of William McKee Dunn (United States Army) and May Ella Morrill.
Fitted at G. W. C. Noble's.
Class Status: Freshman year only. Joined '94.
Married Anna Chapman at Chicago, 27 May 1899. Children:
Anita, born 16 August 1900 (married Keith Carpenter of Chicago, 15 October 1921).
May Morrill, 15 February 1904.
Morrill, Jr., 21 December 1906 (died 23 February 1908).
William McKee, 16 October 1908.
Now operating gravel-mine at Natchez, Mississippi.

1893-1894: Portland, Maine, Electric Light Plant. 1894-1896: Apprentice Westinghouse Electric and Manufacturing Company, Pittsburgh. 1897 to date: Manufacturing railroad and automobile supplies, Chicago and Detroit.. Two interims in last period are October, 1917, to November, 1918, Air Service (not flying) in France, and March, 1921, to the present time, trying to pull out an alleged gold mine in the form of a gravel business for good road purposes in Louisiana, which my associates and myself in an enthusiastic moment got into and are now trying to get out of with a whole skin. I am glad to say it now looks as though we would. I was picked on for the job; hence the residence of myself and Mrs. Dunn for the past two years, at Natchez, Mississippi.

Additions to my family are: a son-in-law, Keith Carpenter, of Chicago, and a grand-daughter, born to Anita Dunn Carpenter, September, 1922. May Morrill Dunn is a sophomore at Bryn Mawr, and William McKee Dunn is headed for Harvard, I hope via Milton.

DANIEL OSBORNE EARLE

Born at Worcester, Massachusetts, 3 September 1869, of Timothy Keese Earle and Caroline Cartland Osborne.
Fitted with G. E. Gardner and W. F. Abbot.
Class Status: Regular.
Degree: A.B. 1893.

Married Grace Howard King at Providence, Rhode Island, 21 December
1899. Child:
     Osborne, born 10 November 1904 (H. C. 1925).
Now salesman for Packard Motor Car Company at Boston.

*Extract from the diary of Mr. Sam Pepys, inventor and sole
distributor of the original Pepysin Gum.*

June ye 1. Mrs. P. to the Home Beautiful Convention, so I
a-joy-riding with Baby Doll, her second cousin (or so she claim-
eth.) But lo! in Cambridge tire trouble came upon us, and we
were fain to alight hard by a great house. Then comes me forth
out of the house one Earle, and well named, for he is truly one
of nature's noblemen. Also he knoweth more about cars than I
did conceive possible; for he told me he was a salesman thereof
at 1089 Commonwealth Avenue, Allston, though in former days
treasurer of the Shirtmakers Guild at Westerly, Rhode Island.
And he is verily a genial soul and obliging, ready to aid friend
and stranger alike, and as merry a heart as you shall find in a
summer's day. So while his hinds dealt faithfully with the car,
he entreated us within his manor and did entertain us right
royally. He hath here an ice-house of a bigness such as I never
did see, and all the contents ranged in order upon shelves,
mighty pleasant and convenient. And he is a monstrous good
performer with the cork-screw. But when I had sampled his
dandelion wine, as ancient Horace saith, *O Puer!* So no more
this day.

June ye 2. Set forth from Cambridge about two of the clock,
which was as soon as I could drive. And at parting, mine host
did coyly put a paper into mine hand, though what it was I
wist not then. Natheless, all the way home I had a presenti-
ment I had been choused. And when I got me down and had
come fully to myself, I found that it was so indeed; for the
paper was a reckoning for eighty-seven ducats. Moreover, I had
left Baby Doll behind.

HORACE AINSWORTH EATON

Born at Quincy, Massachusetts, 13 October 1871, of Horace Eaton (mer-
     chant) and Rebecca Phipps Baxter.
Fitted at Adams Academy.
Class Status: Regular.
Degrees: A.B. 1893; A.M. 1897; Ph.D. 1900.

Married Emily Russell Lovett at Brookline, Massachusetts, 3 September
1902. Children:
    Rebecca, born 11 June 1903.
    Sidney Lovett, 1 May 1906.
    Robert Endicott, 11 June 1910.
    Elizabeth Russell, 25 May 1912.
Now head of the Department of English at Syracuse University.

After graduation, I entered the Harvard Divinity School intending to enter the Unitarian ministry. After two years I
turned to teaching instead. I taught one year at a small
school in Pomfret, Connecticut, and then spent four years
in the Harvard Graduate School, taking my A.M. in 1897 and
my Ph.D. in 1900; and teaching part of the time during
1899-1900 in Boston University. The following year, I spent in
Italy, doing some work in the libraries there, but chiefly having
a good time. I returned to go to the University of Vermont as
instructor in English and German, and stayed there two years.
In 1902 I married Emily Russell Lovett of Brookline. In 1903
I came to Syracuse University as instructor in English—and I
have been here ever since, rising through all grades until I
reached my present position of Head of the Department of English in 1916.

Summer vacations I have spent with my wife and four children at Sargentville, Maine, where we have an old farm on
Penobscot Bay, less devoted to farming than to sailing. Latter-
ly the high cost of living has obliged me to teach in summer
schools, usually at Syracuse. But two years ago I crossed the
continent to teach in the University of Oregon at Eugene, my
first taste of the west. This coming summer I am going back
to teach in the summer session of the University in Portland,
Oregon, the reason why I shall be unable to attend the thirtieth
reunion of '93·

I have done little literary work—publishing merely occasional articles in learned and educational magazines. I have,
however, done a good deal of work for the community in which
I live, serving upon all sorts of committees and holding offices
in all sorts of organizations. At present I am Honorary President of the Syracuse Drama League (it bought and established
a Little Theatre while I was President); President of the Faculty Club of the University; Chairman of the Board of Directors
of the Seventeenth Ward Civic Association. For many years

I was Secretary of the Syracuse Harvard Club and then President. The Club is at present sleeping—but I am not even a nominal officer.

I am a liberal, firmly convinced that we must decidedly change the world in which we live if our civilization is to persist. I am even eager to see Christian principles really tried in solving the world's problems!

JOHN EDGAR EATON

Born at Truro, Nova Scotia, 26 February 1871, of David Hamilton Eaton
  (merchant) and Carrie Matilda Eaton.
Entered from Acadia College.
Class Status: Entered Senior.
Degrees: A.B. (Acadia) 1890; A.B. 1893; LL.B. 1896.
Married Anna Marie Hathaway at Westerly, Rhode Island, 20 March,
  1897. Children:
      Ruth Hathaway, born 6 June 1898.
      John Edgar, Jr., 8 March 1901.
Now practising law at Boston.

Since graduation from Harvard Law School in 1896 I have practised law continuously in Boston, as a member of the firm of Eaton and McKnight. My present offices are at 148 State Street, where I have been since 1917. My family remains the same as in my last report, except that my daughter Ruth has married Ralph Richardson, Harvard 1915. My son John is now in his senior year at Harvard. During the last quarter of a century I have averaged about twelve hours a day of hard work, and am still going strong. However, occasional business and vacation trips have carried me over the dry spots. I belong to a number of fraternal societies, and local clubs. I am now past master of Constellation Lodge, A. F. and A. M., Dedham. Massachusetts. I still like to play tennis when time permits, but shall soon have to turn to golf for recreation. The law is a hard mistress, and any young graduate who wants to make money and enjoy life should avoid it. Strange to say my son John is now planning to enter Harvard Law School in spite of my advice.

JOHN WALDO EICHINGER

Born at Decatur, Illinois, 14 February 1870, of Michael Eichinger (stock-
  raiser) and Lucy Helen Huff.
Entered from Eureka College, Illinois.
Class Status: Entered Junior.

Degree: A.B. (Eureka) 1890.
Married Stella Johnson at Marshalltown, Iowa, 10 September 1902.
 Child:
  John Waldo, Jr., born 10 September 1904.
Now Editor for Iowa State Highway Commission, at Ames, Iowa.

Entire time spent in newspaper, news, and editorial work, and for several years past in publicity work. Was doing newspaper work in Iowa for many years after leaving college—at Clinton, Ottumwa, Council Bluffs, and Des Moines. In 1908 was telegraph editor of the *Des Moines Capital*, remaining there till 1912. Then on account of impaired health became manager of a 7,000-acre wheat and stock ranch near Gleichen, Alberta. A few years later, having got into condition again, returned to editorial work as editor for the bulletins of the Iowa State Highway Commission, where I still remain.

SAMUEL WALKER ELLSWORTH

Born at Weymouth, Massachusetts, 29 March 1870, of Alfred Augustus
 Ellsworth (Amherst 1858) (clergyman) and Angelina Clementine Cook.
Fitted at Phillips Andover.
Class Status: Regular.
Degrees: A.B. 1893; M.D. 1896.
Married Mrs. Kate (Anderson) Wadsworth at New Haven, Connecticut,
 30 September 1914.
Now in practice of medicine at Boston.

After graduation from the Harvard Medical School in 1896 I served as Medical House Officer at the Boston City Hospital, and at the Boston Lying-In Hospital, and was Assistant Physician at Adams Nervine Hospital, Jamaica Plain, for one year. I was practitioner of medicine at Quincy, Massachusetts, 1899 to 1910. Since that time I have followed X-Ray work exclusively. My hospital service has been as follows: Visiting Physician to Quincy Hospital, 1902-1910; Director of Roentgen Laboratory, Boston City Hospital; Consulting Roentgenologist, Quincy Hospital; Assistant in Roentgenology at the Harvard Medical School. The supreme achievement of my life, as well as the happiest, was my marriage to Kate Anderson Wadsworth, September 30, 1914. I received a commission as Captain in the Medical Reserve Corps of the United States Army in July, 1917, and was attached to the Boston School of Military Roentgenology, giving instruction in this branch of medicine to both Army and Navy surgeons for six months.

March 25, 1918, sailed from New York with B. H. 116—36
officers, 100 nurses, 250 enlisted men. April 7, arrived Bazoilles-
sur-Meuse, hospital center for 20,000 beds. Three weeks assisting in construction, etc. May 1, temporary duty with Second
Division at Souilly. May 28, American Red Cross Hospital No.
1, Paris, attending wounded from Chateau-Thierry, etc. June
28, headquarters of medical consultants, assistant to senior consultant in Roentgenology, Neuf-Chateau. Visiting the various
American hospitals in France as inspector of X-Ray equipment
and laboratories. Nov. 1, Major, Medical Corps. Jan. 17, 1919,
sailed from Brest. Feb. 12, honorably discharged, Washington,
D. C.

Resumed practice of Roentgenology in Boston, May 1, 1922,
resigned position at Boston City Hospital where I had been
connected with the X-Ray Department for twenty-years and accepted appointment of instructor in Roentgenology at the Boston University School of Medicine, and engaged in private practice at 520 Beacon St., Boston, in partnership with Dr. Frank
E. Wheatley.

Travel: Mediterranean trip to Egypt and Italy in 1913. California, the Yellowstone and Canadian Rockies in 1922. Present condition: Good health. Weigh 183 pounds and wear
glasses. Member of the American Medical and Massachusetts
Medical Societies; Boston Medical Library; American Roentgen
Ray and N. E. Roentgen Ray societies; Megantic Fish and
Game Corporation; Quincy Neighborhood Club; and the Harvard Club of Boston.

SAMUEL DEAN ELMORE

Born at Hartford, Connecticut, 29 December 1868, of Samuel Edward
    Elmore [Williams 1857] (banker) and Mary Amelia Burnham.
Fitted with H. H. C. Bingham.
Class Status: Special, 1889-92. Joined Class Senior year.
Degrees: A.B. 1893; LL.B. 1896.
Married Susan Clifford Cross at Cambridge, Massachusetts, 27 November
    1899.
Now practising law at Boston.

Class reports bring to mind the passing years. But for this
it would hardly have occurred to me that I have been engaged
in the general practice of law in Boston for as many years as
twenty-seven, every one of which, as I reflect upon them, has

brought ever increasing happiness and contentment. The fundamentals instilled in a youthful mind by a Harvard training are still in daily use and of great advantage. They have contributed largely to the personal interest and enjoyment I still have in the practice of law. Since changing my residence from Cambridge my interest in politics and public affairs has become more general and I have held no public office. Outdoor life still has great attractions for me and I play very poor golf. Indulge in travel somewhat as occasion offers. The past five years have been most interesting and absorbing ones to me but are doubtless uneventful from the point of view of others.

Clubs, societies, and public offices: Brae-Burn Country Club, Boston City Club, Colonial Club of Cambridge, Massachusetts Bar Association, Boston Bar Association, Acacia Society, Past Master, Amicable Lodge, A. F. and A. M., Cambridge. City Council of Cambridge, 1905-1906. Massachusetts House of Representatives, 1907-1909.

GUY THORP EMERSON

Born at Waltham, Massachusetts, 11 June 1871, of Warren Frank Emerson (dry goods merchant) and Lilian Thorp.
Fitted at Browne and Nichols.
Class Status: Freshman year only. Joined '94.
Married Mabel Stoddard Eddy at Auburndale, Massachusetts, 29 May 1901.
Now living at Waltham, Massachusetts.

After a variety of experiences ranging from lumberman to art critic, settled into practice of law in 1897 with Hurlbut and Jones of Boston. After two or three years, however, took up farming at Bolton, Massachusetts. In 1910 was sales manager of the H. H. Mathews Company of Boston. Shortly after this, went to New York City, practised law and promoted sundry business ventures. In 1917 returned to Waltham, and in July, 1918, became legal assistant to the Bureau of War Trade Intelligence at Washington, continuing till July, 1919. Since that date have been a broker, living at Waltham.

ROBERT EMMET, D. S. O.

Born at New York City, 23 October 1871, of Thomas Addis Emmet (physician) and Katherine Duncan.
Fitted at F. G. Ireland's.
Class Status: Special, 1889-91. Joined Class Junior year.

Degrees: A.B. 1897 as of 1893; M.D. (Columbia) 1896.
Married Louise Garland at New York City, 25 November 1896. Children:
      Robert, 2d, born 25 September 1897 (died, October, 1915. 2d
         Lieutenant, First Life Guards).
      James Albert Garland, 19 October 1898. (Lieut. 1st Life Guards).
      Thomas Addis, 3d, 19 June 1900. (Royal Navy—retired).
      Aileen, 26 December 1903.
Now farming at Warwick, England.

Ideal but not idle country life. Most of my time has been occupied managing a small patent in which I am interested, fox hunting when possible, and recovering from the great damage to the place and gardens due to unavoidable neglect during the war.

MAURICE HENRY EWER

Born at Dedham, Massachusetts, 24 July 1872, of Alfred Ewer (bank
      examiner) and Elsie Hannah Curtis.
Fitted at Roxbury Latin.
Class Status: "Four years in three."
Degree: A.B. 1892.
Married Gertrude Sophie Durkee at Dorchester, Massachusetts, 6 June
      1894. Child:
      Elinor Gertrude, born 15 December 1897.
Now Vice-President of National Park Bank, New York City.

From 1892 to 1900 I was assistant national bank examiner in Massachusetts (my father's occupation) and lived in Roxbury. I then went to the National Park Bank of New York City and have remained there ever since, rising from auditor to assistant cashier, then to cashier, and in January, 1917, to vice-president. I live in Montclair, New Jersey. My work is hard and exacting and leaves me no time for hobbies or avocations. (Sorry I can give you no "narrative" which would prove of interest).

CLARENCE RUDOLPH FALK

Born at Milwaukee, Wisconsin, 27 November 1869, of Franz Falk and
      Louise Wahl.
Fitted at Milwaukee Academy.
Class Status: Special, 1889-91. Joined Class Junior year.
Degree: A.B. 1893.
Married Margaret Sawyer at Milwaukee, Wisconsin, 14 May 1901.
      Children:
      Louise Sawyer, born 5 March 1902.
      Margaret Sawyer, 10 January 1904.
      Nancy Sawyer, 25 October 1907.
Now manufacturing machinery, etc., at Milwaukee.

After graduating from the class of 1893 I spent a year at the Harvard Law School, after which I returned to Milwaukee to take charge of the Savings Department of the First Wisconsin National Bank. Several years later I resigned that position and, in company with a friend of mine, spent eighteen months in a leisurely journey around the world. Our itinerary after leaving San Francisco, included Hawaii, Japan, China, Manchuria, Singapore, and the Malay Peninsula, Java, India, Ceylon, Egypt, the Holy Land, Constantinople, and Russia. At Moscow we joined Mrs. John A. Logan and party and witnessed the coronation of the czar.

After returning to Milwaukee I accepted a position as dramatic critic on one of our daily papers. Subsequently, I was identified with the Cloos Electrical Engineering Company, and later the brokerage firm of Tracy and Company. It was in 1901 that I first became associated with the Falk Corporation, working my way upward through the various departments of this plant, eventually becoming Works Manager. In 1914 I was made one of the Vice-Presidents and Directors of this Company, which is a corporation engaged in the manufacture of high grade machinery, railroad supplies and steel castings.

In 1916, feeling that this country might be drawn into the war, I attended the training camp at Plattsburg, New York, remaining there until late in October that year. On the first of February, 1917, I was made a Captain of the quartermaster department of the Reserve Corps in the United States Army, assigned in June for duty at the Quartermaster Depot at Jeffersonville, Indiana, in charge of purchases. Early in 1918 I was transferred to the ordnance department at Washington and assigned to the trench warfare section, in charge of design and production of three and four inch Stokes Mortars. This assignment held until I was honorably discharged on December 13th, 1918, with a commission of Major in the Reserve Corps of the Ordnance Department, United States Army.

I am a member of the following clubs: Milwaukee Club, Milwaukee Country Club, Milwaukee Athletic Club, Milwaukee University Club, Milwaukee Press Club, the Town Club, the Fox Point Club, the local Harvard Club, the New York Harvard Club, Milwaukee Order of Elks, life member of the Congressional Country Club of Washington, D. C. I am a member of the

Wisconsin State Historical Society, Milwaukee Order of Foreign
Wars of the United States, and the American Legion. I have
been twice president of the Milwaukee Harvard Club, president
of the Milwaukee Metal Trades Association, and am now president of the Chicago Orchestral Association of Milwaukee. I
assisted Mr. Roosevelt in organizing the American Legion of
Wisconsin, personally aiding and securing the money necessary
to finance the work, chairman of the American Airway Transport Company, and vice-chairman of the Milwaukee Air Board.

In the spring of 1921, accompanied by my wife and three
daughters, I made an extended tour through Europe. While
in the war area, together with my classmate, Walter Cary,
visited all the principal battle fields of France and Belgium.

I might add that outside of the ordinary wear and tear of
bringing up three girls these days of automobiles and the eigh-
teenth amendment, I am physically 100 per cent. perfect and
feeling quite well, notwithstanding the fact that I have not yet
found a good hair restorer; what is left is gradually growing
white. I have purchased a twenty-acre farm some ten miles out
of Milwaukee on the Milwaukee River where I spend my summers, and when I am not busy playing golf and tennis, I am
pruning apple and pear trees, and living the simple life (when
I am allowed to do so).

FRANK EDGAR FARLEY

Born at Manchester, New Hampshire, 25 April 1868, of George Wash-
  ington Farley (machinery) and Lucina Cofran Baker.
Fitted at Lawrence High.
Class Status: Special, 1889-90. Joined Class Sophomore year.
Degrees: A.B. 1893; A.M. 1894; Ph.D. 1897.
Married Mrs. Amy (Elwell) Crane at St. Louis, Michigan, 5 August 1903.
Now Professor of English Literature at Wesleyan University.

From 1893 to 1897, graduate student at Harvard and assistant in English at Harvard and Radcliffe; in 1897-98 instructor
in English at Haverford College; from 1898 to 1903 instructor,
associate professor, and professor of English in Syracuse University; from 1903 to 1918, associate professor and professor of
English at Simmons College; since 1918, professor of English
Literature in Wesleyan University.

Publications: Editor of Paradise Lost, Books I and II, 1898;

author of Scandinavian Influences in the English Romantic Movement, 1903; joint author, with G. L. Kittredge, of an advanced English grammar, 1913, and A Concise English Grammar, 1918.

Since graduation my main interest has been in studying English literature and trying to teach college boys and girls what I have learned. The only interruption to this program came in 1909-10, when I enjoyed fifteen months of foreign travel on sabbatical leave. My life has not been an exciting or a distinguished one. It might have been more fruitful if my health had been better, but I found pleasure in my work, and greater rewards than I deserve. I do not refer to material rewards. The closing years of my professional life seem likely to be spent in an environment which is in many respects ideally suited to a person of my temperament and aims.

The clubs to which I belong and the few offices which I hold are of interest only to the small community in which I live. I have, however, been elected Fellow of the American Academy of Arts and Sciences. and I have kept an active interest in the Delta Upsilon fraternity.

WILLIAM OLIVER FARNSWORTH

Born at Damariscotta, Maine, 27 October 1871, of Lewis Farnsworth (merchant) and Lydia Augusta Mathews.
Fitted at Boston Latin.
Class Status: Regular.
Degrees: A.B. 1893; A.M. 1894; Ph.D. (Columbia) 1913.
Now Professor of Romance Languages, Northwestern University.

After receiving my A.M. in 1894, I began the teaching of French, not realizing then that occupation was to fill my life. I am still at work in the same subject, but with a much bigger appreciation of what it all means. Many of my summers have been spent in travel in Europe, Canada, or in horseback wanderings in the mountains of North Carolina. Among my pleasantest recollections are the six years on the Yale Faculty, the four years at Columbia, where I received a Ph.D. in 1913, and the four years at the University of Pittsburgh just before the war.

In November, 1917, I was commissioned First Lieutenant in what is now the Air Service, and after a period of training in

photographic work at Cornell, was sent abroad, remaining on
duty in France and Germany until August, 1919. My particular task was the organization and maintenance of the Photographic Sections of the Air Service at the front, a rather responsible position which appears to have been satisfactorily filled.
At the same time the war did something important for me, in
showing me that I was not in an academic rut as I had feared.
In May, 1919, I was promoted to a Captaincy, and on my recall
was attached to the War Department in Washington for several
months. In the meantime, I resigned from my position as head·
of the department of Romance Languages at the University of
Pittsburgh, which had given me leave of absence; but changing
my mind about remaining in the Army, I received my discharge
in December, 1919, and went to Cuba for a six months' vacation.

The following fall I came into the department of Romance
Languages at Northwestern University. The last two summers
have been spent in Mexico, which I find fascinating indeed. I
have succeeded in overcoming a constitutional dislike to expressing myself in writing so far as to put forth several books
of more or less interest to a few persons. Yet with this variety
·of experiences the great adventure of all has not come to me—
as yet—and I am still single.

ROBERT DAVID FARQUHAR

Born at Brooklyn, 23 February 1872, of David Webber Farquhar [Har-
    vard temp.] (builder) and Sarah Malvina Joslyn.
Fitted at Phillips Exeter.
Class Status: Regular.
Degrees: A.B. 1893; S.B. (Mass. Inst. Tech.) 1895; Grad. Ecole des
    Beaux Arts, Paris, 1901.
Married Marion Jones at New York City, 29 September 1903. Children:
    David, born 7 July 1904.
    John Percival, 20 March 1912.
    Colin, 28 December 1913.
Now practising architecture at Los Angeles.

Entered Massachusetts Institute of Technology after 1893
and completed course in architecture in 1895. Admitted to the
Ecole des Beaux Arts, Paris, in March, 1896, and graduated
there in 1901, six very enjoyable years before returning to the
United States. In New York architects' offices for three years.
Came to California in 1905 and have practised architecture here

since then. Went to Italy in American Red Cross Service in 1918, and was stationed in relief work in several towns of Northern Italy, principally at Trento, Belluno and Bolzano.

Enjoy life in California and take every opportunity to journey Eastward. My recreations are golf and walking in the country, in the mountains which are close at hand. Serve on the Advisory Board of the Los Angeles Philharmonic Orchestra.

SIDNEY EMERSON FARWELL

Born at St. Paul, Minnesota, 14 April 1870, of George Lyman Farwell
  (merchant) and Sara Gardner Wyer.
Fitted at Phillips Andover.
Class Status: Regular.
Degree: A.B. 1893.
Married (1) Fannie Sophia Rhodes at Lakewood, Ohio, 14 December
  1898 (died 10 January 1900). Child:
      Daughter, born 9 January 1900 (died 10 January 1900).
Married (2) Mrs. Elizabeth Colwell (Beatty) Barrows at West Chester,
  Pennsylvania, 27 December 1906, with children: Wilfred W. Barrows
  and Howard F. Barrows.
Now employment manager at Lord and Taylor's, New York City.

Until the great war, that is to say, more or less twenty-five years after leaving college, I had become accustomed to a free and easy life with little care, and requiring my devoting only twelve to eighteen hours a day to warding off the wolf from my humble doorway.

Though even these comparatively short hours have been getting less popular with men and their wives, I still believe that both men and women should do some work every day. I have no quarrel with play and a good time, but war work got me into bad habits at the time of life when I had pictured myself boating on the Nile, or motoring through or over the Alps.

I am in a fair way to break now all the short hour laws,— my Saturday afternoon is gone,—I am writing this at the hour when I count on being in church,—but think of the pleasure and the opportunity enjoyed in dealing with the employment of 2,000 men and women in a modern Fifth Avenue department store where I am known as the Employment Manager. That is life, I'll say, *somebody's* life problem every minute. Work, pleasure, sorrow, happiness, and what does one need besides—except time to eat and sleep? No monotony, no drudgery, no turmoil

that can't be turned to better coöperation—why think of time
or laws about hours? It is life—full of pep, variety, and opportunity to make or break that very important and somewhat
neglected part of our industrial machine—the human being.
As a reducer of ennui, not even riches can compare. I am
putting in the hours, however, in the hope of getting some of
the riches.

ALFRED CHASE FAY

Born at Natick, Massachusetts, 2 April 1867, of Gilbert Park Fay
     (hatter) and Laura Sophia Brigham.
Fitted at Chelsea High.
Class Status: I. Scientific, 1889-90. Joined '94.
Degree: A.B. 1893.
Married Henrietta Elizabeth Martin at Chelsea, Massachusetts, 24 Novem-
     ber 1894. Children:
          Eliot Gilbert, born 20 January 1902.
          Robert Walcott, 23 June 1907.
Now in automobile business at New York City.

For the past five years I have been associated with the War-
ren-Nash Motor Corporation, and am general manager of the
"Uptodate Specialty Company," dealers in automobile fittings.
Have a son, Eliot, who graduates this year from Harvard, and
another son, Robert, at Boston Latin School fitting for Harvard.

HARRISON GILBERT FAY

Born at Natick, Massachusetts, 10 May 1869, of Gilbert Park Fay (mer-
     chant) and Laura Sophia Brigham.
Fitted at Chelsea High.
Class Status: Regular.
Degrees: A.B. 1893; A.M. 1909.
Married Ella Chloe Colt at Winsted, Connecticut, 31 March 1900 (died
     18 October 1918). Children:
          Henry Colt, born 26 January 1901.
          Priscilla Brigham, 22 February 1902.
          Gilbert Jefferson, 8 April 1912.
Now teaching in the DeWitt Clinton High School, New York City.

The teaching profession still offers a field for my abilities.
Daily contact with young minds inspires optimism and pre-
serves youth.

When the great war broke out the New York Training School
for Teachers where I was an instructor, suffered a rapid decline
numerically in membership. An ever diminishing student body

compelled the transfer of many of us to the high schools of the
city. Good fortune fell to me in being assigned to the De Witt
Clinton High School, said to be the largest in the land. I say
fortune smiled because the war was on in dead earnest, and the
boys generally of foreign extraction did not understand the real
issue. To observe their minds moulded by discussion, swayed
by events, unconsciously stirred by singing the new war songs,
and finally enlisted by appeals till they collectively sold one
million in liberty bonds, was an experience never to be forgotten. I felt like one in a laboratory where the success of an experiment is doubtful and fraught with danger. Ever since the
armistice, history has been a much easier subject to teach to any
body of youth.

My sport, for twenty years, summer and winter, has been
swimming, with a preference for a distance of a few miles. I
am more than convinced that the ivy orator of many years ago
was correct when he declared in the presence of a former president of Harvard, "swimming is the only clean sport."

I am a member of the Broadway Tabernacle Church—a dea-
con, if that is expected—and also of the High School Teachers'
Association, the Pro-League Club, the Commonwealth Club, the
Family Circle, etc.

GEORGE RICHMOND FEARING, JR.

Born at New York City, 20 February 1871, of George Richmond Fearing
[Columbia 1860] and Harriet Travers.
Fitted at A. H. Cutler's.
Class Status: Regular.
Degrees: A.B. 1893; LL.B. 1896.
Married Hester Sullivan Cochrane at Boston, 12 May 1897. Child:
George Richmond, 3d, born 28 March 1898.
Now a trustee at Boston.

After leaving Law School worked for one year in law office
of R. M. Saltonstall. Married in 1897. Toured abroad, spent
one year in Paris; owing to illness, one more winter in Aiken,
South Carolina; went into business with Jackson and Curtis in
1899. Became partner in 1900 and continued with them for
about ten years. In 1915 became special partner in Van Em-
burgh and Whitney, New York; withdrew in 1921 and am at
present engaged in paring down loans and dodging federal

taxes—legally of course. I am and have been President of the
Free Hospital for Women, Brookline, which occupies a great
deal of my time and thought.

JAMES HENRY FENNESSY

Born at New Baltimore, New York, 14 July 1865, of James Fennessy (mer
chant) and Elizabeth Gorman.
Fitted with W. T. Baden.
Class Status: Special, 1889-91.   Law School, 1891-94.
Degree: LL.B. 1895 as of 1894.
Married May Caroline Seep at Titusville, Pennsylvania, 30 January 1900
(died 9 September 1919).   Children:
    Alma Elizabeth, born 5 June 1903.
    Eleanor Seep, 17 October 1905.
    Marcia Seep, 23 October 1907.
    Joseph Seep, 1 March 1910.
Now President Mine and Smelter Supply Company at New York City.

Fennessy is absent on a trip around the world with his children. He still continues as president of the Mine and Smelter
Supply Company, manufacturers and jobbers of mining machinery, assayers' and chemists' supplies, and electrical equipment, with main offices in New York City. Until 1915 he made
frequent trips to the offices and warehouses of the company at
Denver, Salt Lake City, El Paso, San Francisco, and Mexico
City. His residence is still at Greenwich, Connecticut.

OTIS DANIELL FISK

Born at Cambridge, Massachusetts, 29 April 1870, of James Chaplin Fisk
(mill treasurer) and Mary Grant Daniell.
Fitted with M. S. Keith.
Class Status: I. Scientific, 1889-90.   Joined '94.
Married Ethel Fiske at Cambridge, Massachusetts, 10 April 1913.
Now farming at Petersham, Massachusetts.

Although I have really nothing of interest to say still I feel
that the appeal of our Secretary should be heeded in justice, at
least, to the thirty years of faithful endeavor which he has made
for the class. Five years ago I called my occupation farming,
but that was simply a temporary war interest, and my "gainful
occupations" are now, as then, so diversified that they can only
be classified as business management. My business interests are
not centered in the country town where I have spent two-thirds
of the time in the last ten years; but I have taken a great in-

terest in the affairs of that town, and have been connected, in one way or another, with most of the larger questions. · My impression of the management of country affairs is, at present, expressed by the well-known story about a grocer who was a deacon, and who was heard to call down stairs before breakfast to his clerk: " 'John, have you watered the rum?' 'Yes, sir.' 'And have you sanded the sugar?' 'Yes, sir.' 'And dusted the pepper?' 'Yes, sir.' 'And chicoried the coffee?' Yes, sir.' 'Then come up stairs ·to prayers.' "

Clubs: Somerset, Boston Athletic Association, Colonial, Petersham Country.

CHARLES HENRY FISKE, JR.

Born at Boston, 18 February 1872, of Charles Henry Fiske [H. C. 1860] (lawyer) and Cornelia Frothingham Robbins.
Fitted at J. P. Hopkinson's.
Class Status: Regular.
Degrees: A.B. 1893; LL.B. 1896.
Married Mary Duncan Thorndike at Cambridge, Massachusetts, 20 June 1895. (Died 23 February 1923.) Children:
    Charles Henry, 3d, born 3 December 1896. (Died 24 August 1918.)
    Cornelia Robbins, 20 November 1898.
    Rosanna Duncan, 4 July 1900. (Married L. B. Sanderson, Jr., [H. C. 1921] April 1922.)
Now practising law in Boston.

After being graduated at the Harvard Law School in 1896 (I am secretary of my Law School class) I settled in Boston. After a few months in the office of Ropes, Gray and Loring (still a famous firm under changing names) I went into my father's office and have practised by myself ever since.

The war interrupted and I served in France and Washington in 1918 in the army, and while still in service was with the United States Liquidation Commission in 1919 in Paris. I was honorably discharged in September of that year, but remained with the Commission till February, 1920. My army rank was first lieutenant. I refused a proffered captaincy and was recommended for a majority, but the Armistice prevented. I received from the French Government in 1920 the order of Officer of Academy with palm. My son was mortally wounded in action near Fismes (Aisne) August 12, 1918, and died in hospital twelve days later. His body is buried at Suresnes in the

American Military Cemetery. He was a second lieutenant of
Infantry. He received his A.B. degree with 1919, awarded
posthumously.

My father died in January, 1921, and I bought 26 Central
Street, Boston, and moved my offices there April 1. I have been
very fortunate in attracting to the offices a number of active and
successful lawyers. I am an advisory and family lawyer and
hold some property for others. I go to Europe almost every
year and had just returned from a lovely journey in Provence
with Mrs. Fiske when she died of pneumonia after influenza, in
New York City.

I am on the Committee of Management of the Boston Y. M.
C. A., Huntington Avenue branch, and a member of the General
Activities Committee. I am a member of the corporation of the
Church of the Advent, Boston. Hitherto I have been greatly
interested in public speaking, before, during, and since the war.
As for games, golf I like best, and have close contests with Post,
Barlow, and Goodrich—all '93's. I am glad to say that two or
three of my best friends are classmates, and I have kept up my
intimacy so far as I could with every '93 man I could meet. I
try to be alive to the best things in life. Health excellent.

AUSTIN BRADSTREET FLETCHER

Born at Cambridge, Massachusetts, 19 January 1872, of Ruel Haseltine
Fletcher (teacher) and Rebecca Caroline Wyman.
Fitted at Cambridge High.
Class Status: Special 1889-91. Scientific, 1891-93.
Degrees: S.B. 1893.
Married Ethel Hovey at Cambridge, Massachussetts, 1 March 1894.
Children:
    Dorothy, born 12 May 1895.
    Norman, 27 September 1899 (died 7 July 1906).
Now consulting highway engineer at Sacramento, California.

Secretary and Executive Officer, Massachusetts Highway
Commission, 1893-1910; Secretary-Engineer, San Diego (California) County Highway Commission, 1910-1911; State Highway Engineer of California, 1911-1923; President, State Re-
clamation Board of California, 1917-1923; Director of Public
Works, State of California, 1921-1923; first Chief Engineer,
United States Bureau of Public Roads in 1916 for a few months
while on leave of absence from California; delegate from Massa-

Corbett   Hill (mgr.)   Trafford   Sullivan   Abbott   Dickinson

Hallowell   Upton   J. Highlands   A. Highlands   Hapgood
Mason   Cook   Frothingham (capt.)   Wiggin

chusetts to First International Road Congress, Paris, France, 1908; delegate from California to Third International Road Congress, London, England, 1913; president Fourth National Road Congress, Atlanta, Georgia, 1914. Author: "Macadam Roads" (bulletin United States Department of Agriculture), 1906; associate editor Blanchard's "Handbook on Highway Construction," chapter on Drainage (Wiley and Son), and many papers on highway matters. Member Executive Committee of State (California) Council of Defence during the World War. Member American Society Civil Engineers, A. S. T. M., Concrete Institute, Boston Society Civil Engineers, Massachusetts Highway Association (honorary), American Road Builders Association, American Association of State Highway Officials (member of the Executive Committee), A. A. A. S., Association Internationale Permanente des Congres de la Route, fellow American Geographical Society.

Resigned from all public office in California in January, 1923, upon a change in the State administration. Now in private practice and consultation work. In the early months of 1923 engaged in a study of the highway problems of New England with particular regard to the correlation between motor transport and the railroads.

HERBERT LINCOLN FLINT

Born at Cambridge, Massachusetts, 30 October 1870, of Francis Flint (manufacturer) and Celestia Frederika Barnes.
Fitted at Cambridge Latin.
Class Status: Regular.
Degrees: A.B. 1893; M.L.A. 1915.
Married Caroline May Cobb at Cambridge, Massachusetts, 4 October 1911. Child:
      Eleanor, born 16 September 1915.
Now landscape architect at Cleveland.

With the old National Bank of Redemption in Boston 1893-1899. Too confining. Next six years in the open doing various things connected with mining, investigating copper prospects in the Canadian Rockies and hydraulicing gold in Central British Columbia, with trips to Montana, Colorado, etc. Failed to acquire wealth but stored up a host of recollections of fine scenery, rock and earth forms and the beauty of the great out-doors.

Since 1905 have been drawn through successive stages of surveying, superintending, construction, into full fledged landscape architecture and town planning. Was with Warren H. Manning in Boston, 1909-1914, with a comprehensive landscape tour of Italy, Switzerland, France and England in 1913.

1914-1915 found me back at Harvard to acquire the Master's degree in Landscape Architecture and Town Planning. Since 1915 have been located in Cleveland with A. D. Taylor, quietly practising the profession. Most of the work has been in Ohio with some as far away as Wisconsin and more recently in Florida where a new town was evolved between Ormond and Daytona. Other recent work includes the cutting up of Rockwood, the Longworth estate in Cincinnati. The work has been varied but largely interesting, no two problems alike and it may fairly be counted one of the "Durable Satisfactions of Life" that certain portions of the earths surface are a bit more beautiful and not a few workers' families are living in more healthful and attractive surroundings through personal effort. Have hunted and fished and camped as opportunity offered, but have seldom busted into print, and the best club is home.

Louis Bertram Flower

See Report VI, Page 115.

ELMER HOLLINGER FRANTZ

Born at Millersville, Pennsylvania, 12 August 1867, of Abraham Miller
    Frantz (farmer) and Mary Ann Hollinger.
Fitted at Millersville State Normal School.
Class Status: Junior year only.
Married Carrie Smith Bowser at Martinsburg, Pennsylvania, 22 June
    1899.   Children:
        Dorothy Bowser, born 12 May 1900.
        Haller Bowser, 6 August 1902.
        Marion Bowser, 14 August 1907.
        Lillian Bowser, 6 October 1909 (died 30 October 1918).
Now stock broker at New York City.

January 4, 1923.—My present occupation in trading in New York Stock Exchange stocks is representative of my practical employment during the last five years, which involved the general field of investments, together with some teaching of finance for a period. Should I be favored with leisure, I would complete a book which I have begun at the suggestion of a publisher, dealing with "Speculation and its relation to American Industrial Life."

Because of limitations of health I have had to live apart from many of the functions that bring men together in clubs and societies; a fact of deep regret. My travel is just such as has been incidental to business, and has extended through the East only—the eastern states of our country. My sport is plain, old fashioned walking, which tells my story of spartan simplicity. My recreative pastime is seeing a good play. It is truer to say that my real pleasure is found in books. Literature means more to me than business, although I am heartily at home in finance and the financial side of business.

In summarizing the years since I left college I must say life has been just one big struggle between a great ambition and steaming energy on the one hand, and a suffering body on the other. It has been a tragic thing, a huge surprise; but a discipline of the first order. I hope that Harvard will treasure health as well as intellect in the boys she develops and find a way to cut out the infinite waste that goes with ill health. It has been my nemesis.

LOVAT FRASER

Born at Brooklyn, 4 September, 1870 of Charles John Fraser and Mary
   Anna Whitfield.
Fitted at Rutgers College Grammar School.
Class Status: Special, 1889-92.
Now Mine and oil producer at Los Angeles, California.

A detailed account of the business life of an active man since college days would be too long to read let alone print. My own experiences have taken me into many different walks of life. Many times my "book learning" has surprised practical men and has stood me in good stead.

After college I engaged in real estate, and from that to farming, lumbering and quarrying, all in a small way. Naturally my interest in farming led me to study soils, clays, etc., as well as fertilizers. I had an opportunity about 1896 to start in a mineralogical business and learn practically as well as theoretically, concerning ores and gems. The study of the source of minerals drew me into mining and the study of mining engineering, beginning about 1900. By original methods, I made abandoned mines pay a little and gradually worked up some production, operating irregularly from 1900 to the present date. During those years about half of my time was spent in New York City in the office part of corporations. My duties as Secretary-Treasurer or President threw me into frequent contact with corporation lawyers, in fact almost constant work with them. Having been a law student before college days, my interest in the subject was natural and this led to the false report, which is still current, that I was an attorney,—which I was not.

From soils and minerals it was only a glide to oil, especially as I lived much of my boyhood in sight of the oil derricks in Northwestern Pennsylvania. Eventually I became interested in oil as well as in mines. From soils, minerals and oil, chemicals was a natural result.

Chronologically as I remember it off hand, English and Company, New York, mineralogists, 1898 a director; Reynolds Mineral and Chemical Company, 1901, secretary and treasurer; Green Mountain Park and Home Association, 1902, president; Eastern Fluor Spar Company, 1903, secretary and treasurer; from 1903 to about 1913 actively engaged in mining Fluor Spar, copper and various minerals and gems, including emeralds. 1914 to 1917 associated also with Harris Chemical Laboratories, New York City. Quebec Asbestos and Chrome Company, 1917, part owner. Electro Alloys Company, Los Angeles, 1918, president; California Chemical Co., Los Angeles, 1919, secretary-treasurer; Southwest Gem and Jewelry Company, Los Angeles, 1920, president; Golden State Silk Mills, Inc., Los Angeles, 1923, president. That brings my record up to date and I am still actively interested in mines, mineral specimens and oil.

FREDERICK AARON FREEARK

Born at Fosterburg, Illinois, 2 February 1870, of Christian Freeark (farmer) and Frederika Hoffmeister.
Entered from Blackburn University.
Class Status: Entered Junior.
Degrees: A. B. 1893; LL.B. (Northwestern Univ.) 1905.
Now practising law at Chicago.

˜˜˜ ˜˜˜˜ ˜˜˜˜˜˜ in Alton, Illinois, public school. 1894-
Washington University, St. Louis.
)ringfield, Illinois, public high school.
Chicago high school and finished law
University. 1906 to date: Have been
o.
belonging to last five years that are
ζes or travels, no sports or pastimes, no
s, no degrees or distinctions, no publi-
societies or clubs. I have no family—
main a bachelor. In spite of my efforts
I haven't yet succeeded.

Tillingbast French
κeport VI, Page 118.

FRIDENBERG
ζugust 1870, of Louis Edward Fridenberg and

of Cleveland, Ohio, at Buffalo, New York, 9·

ιiladelphia.

ιis thirtieth anniversary report is the ex-
.l interest on the part of our classmates,
ny story is easy. We are interested in
at extent, therefore, anything I can say,
ιowever ˜˜˜˜˜˜, ιy prove interesting. I can refresh your
memory in regard to the facts; but will leave it to you to draw
the inferences. I am still a member of the Philadelphia Bar;
in 1919 formed a professional partnership with Barnie F. Winkelman, of the class of 1915, and our offices are located at 1218
Real Estate Trust Building. I was married in 1914, my wife
is living, we enjoy good health, are housekeeping, but we are
without children. I swing regularly between my home and
my office, and back again. I continue to be busy. The work
changes like the weather, but fortunately is free from big
storms. I do not report any "high lights" as regards personal
profession, travels, sports, public offices, distinctions, publications and clubs.

gineering, beginning about 1900. By original methods, I made abandoned mines pay a little and gradually worked up some production, operating irregularly from 1900 to the present date. During those years about half of my time was spent in New York City in the office part of corporations. My duties as Secretary-Treasurer or President threw me into frequent contact with corporation lawyers, in fact almost constant work with them. Having been a law student before college days, my interest in the subject was natural and this led to the false report, which is still current, that I was an attorney,—which I was not.   •

From soils and minerals it was only a glide to oil, especially as I lived much of my boyhood in sight of the oil derricks in Northwestern Pennsylvania. Eventually I became interested in oil as well as in mines. From soils,   '   '   '   ''   '   '
cals was a natural result.

Chronologically as I remember it off
pany, New York, mineralogists, 189£
Mineral and Chemical Company, 1901,
Green Mountain Park and Home Asso
Eastern Fluor Spar Company, 1903, s
from 1903 to about 1913 actively enɡ
Spar, copper and various minerals anɗ
alds. 1914 to 1917 associated also witƺ
oratories, New York City. Quebec Asƅ
pany, 1917, part owner. Electro Allₑ
geles, 1918, president; California Cheɿ
1919, secretary-treasurer; Southwest ɑ
pany, Los Angeles, 1920, president; G
Inc., Los Angeles, 1923, president. That
date and I am still actively interested ·
mens and oil.

FREDERICK AARON FREEARK

Born at Fosterburg, Illinois, 2 February 1
    (farmer) and Frederika Hoffmeister.
Entered from Blackburn University.
Class Status: Entered Junior.
Degrees: A. B. 1893; LL.B. (Northwestern ι
Now practising law at Chicago.

1893-1894: Taught in Alton, Illinois, public school. 1894-1895-1896: Studied law, Washington University, St. Louis. 1896-1903: Taught in Springfield, Illinois, public high school. 1904-1906: Taught in a Chicago high school and finished law course at Northwestern University. 1906 to date: Have been practising law in Chicago.

There are no details belonging to last five years that are worthy of note. No voyages or travels, no sports or pastimes, no public positions or offices, no degrees or distinctions, no publications or speeches, no societies or clubs. I have no family—having been obliged to remain a bachelor. In spite of my efforts to amount to something I haven't yet succeeded.

Robert Tillinghast French
See Report VI, Page 118.

SOLOMON LOUIS FRIDENBERG

Born at Philadelphia, 23 August 1870, of Louis Edward Fridenberg and
    Brendella Pront Isaacs.
Fitted with T. H. Walls.
Class Status: Regular.
Degree: A.B. 1893.
Married Jeanette Ullman of Cleveland, Ohio, at Buffalo, New York, 9
    June 1914.
Now practising law in Philadelphia.

If it be true that this thirtieth anniversary report is the expression of the mutual interest on the part of our classmates, my task in sending my story is easy. We are interested in each other, and to that extent, therefore, anything I can say, however ordinary, may prove interesting. I can refresh your memory in regard to the facts; but will leave it to you to draw the inferences. I am still a member of the Philadelphia Bar; in 1919 formed a professional partnership with Barnie F. Winkelman, of the class of 1915, and our offices are located at 1218 Real Estate Trust Building. I was married in 1914, my wife is living, we enjoy good health, are housekeeping, but we are without children. I swing regularly between my home and my office, and back again. I continue to be busy. The work changes like the weather, but fortunately is free from big storms. I do not report any "high lights" as regards personal profession, travels, sports, public offices, distinctions, publications and clubs.

If it is a good principle for our classmates to be interested in
each other individually, why isn't it an equally good principle
for all Harvard men to be interested in each other individually?
Loyalty by thought and deed, to our Alma Mater, cannot entirely atone for any indifference of Harvard men towards each
other. To take a concrete example; during the thirty years
since 1893, there has not been any material improvement in the
organization of Harvard men, as such, in Philadelphia, although the city has developed greatly. True there is a local
Harvard Club of which I am a member, which has a membership of several hundred; collects annual dues and sustains
scholarship funds; but it does not have any home and its meetings
consist of an annual dinner, at which the average attendance is
perhaps fifteen per cent. of the membership, and ten per cent.
of the Harvard graduates who are residents. A splendid sum
was realized by way of contribution to the recent Harvard Endowment Fund. Surely that was evidence of our loyalty to Harvard University. But on the other hand we do not have, as we
ought to have, and as other large cities have, a true organization
of Harvard men in Philadelphia. Therefore, that is an evidence
of the indifference among our local graduates toward each other.
May I not hope that in this vicinity we shall experience the
application of not only our institutional loyalty, but also the
classmate feeling for purposes of developing a similar feeling
between the individual Harvard men.

LEE MAX FRIEDMAN

Born at Memphis, Tennessee, 29 December 1871, of Maxfield Friedman
 (merchant) and Mathilda Marks.
Fitted at Roxbury Latin and with M. Winkler.
Class Status: Regular.
Degrees: A.B. 1893; LL.B. 1895.
Now practising law at Boston.

Refuses all secretarial blandishments, so we shall just have to
drag along the best way we can.

LEONARD ALDEN FRINK

Born at Boston, 22 September 1870, of Alden Frink (architect) and
 Roxanna Folsom.
Fitted with A. Hale.
Class Status: Special 1889-92. Law School, 1892-95.
Now practising law at Boston.

It is a brave man who will write his own biography and I would rather call it his obituary. Either he displays undue modesty or develops into a prevaricator of the first magnitude. Both of which fail to do justice to the small amount of good that is in even the worst of us. When one reaches the high noon of life, he may with some justification throw out his chest at his possible successes and achievements. To me such success is that of maintaining our long friendship and to be worthy of the steadily growing love of our old and new friends. As Ingersoll said: "The past, it rises before me as a dream." and like the Dartmouth College student's reply to the Dean who asked what were his relations with women, the student replied: "Very satisfactory, sir, very satisfactory." So I say that my successes during the past twenty-five years of life have been on the whole very satisfactory.

Principal doings as follows, to wit: I have practised law in Boston since 1897. Was editor of the National Sportsman's Magazine, 1900 to 1903. Have written and published various articles from time to time and have been guilty of pouring forth a limited amount of poetry. For seven years I served with the Massachusetts Militia, First Corps Cadets, and during the last war was connected with the Department of Justice. I am interested in lumber and forestry at Hazelmere, my place at Belgrade Lakes, Maine, where the out-door life in all its ramifications can be enjoyed to the limit. I have Masonic affiliations, am a Republican in politics, and a liberal in religion. As this is said to be the last report called for during life, I leave all future facts to the judgment and justice of another biographer.

ARTHUR BOWES FRIZELL

Born at Boston, 14 July 1865, of Joseph Palmer Frizell (civil engineer) and Julia Bowes.
Entered from Technology.
Class Status: Entered Junior.
Degrees: A.B. 1893; A.M. 1900; Ph.D. (Kansas) 1910.
Now teacher of mathematics.

Was instructor in mathematics at Massachusetts Institute of Technology, 1888-1891. Taught mathematics in the Massachusetts Nautical Training School, 1894-1895; in the New York Uni-

versity, 1895-1896; at Harvard (instructor), 1897-1906, taking
my A.M. in 1900.

After serving the University nine years the accumulated income from instruction outside my classes warranted negotiation
with the North German Lloyd for passage to a despotic land.
My sojourn there was begun by attendance at a meeting of the
Deutsche Mathematiker-Vereinigung, 1906, and at its close
I crossed the Alps for IV International Congress of Mathematicians at Rome. King Victor Emmanuel was present at the
opening session.

Returning to Freedom's Altar I accepted a professorship at
a Lutheran College in the Sunflower State (University of Kansas). Later the degree from K. U. led to a position paying
more than Alma had ever given (McPherson College, Kansas,
1911-1917). As professor I crossed the ocean again and read a
paper to the V. International Congress of Mathematicians at
Cambridge, England. This has been followed by others deliv-
ered at New York, Chicago and St. Louis, published in Bulletin
of American Mathematical Society.

I stayed with the good German Baptists up to the bursting of
the war cloud. After the war I taught under my old friend Ira
N. Hollis, at the Worcester Polytechnic Institute, which was
able to pay more than McPherson College. Subsequently (1920-
1922) I imparted instruction for 2 years to Cadets on board
U. S. S. *Nantucket,* the Massachusetts Nautical Training Ship.
Discharged similar duties in the Navy Yard about the same
length of time.

I do not feel affinity for the League as elucidated recently by
epexegesis of Lowell, but rather accept the hermeneutics of
Harding.

LOUIS ADAMS FROTHINGHAM

Born at Jamaica Plain, Massachusetts, 13 July 1871, of Thomas Bum-
    stead Frothingham (trustee) and Anne Pearson Lunt.
Fitted at Adams Academy.
Class Status: Regular.
Degrees: A.B. 1893; LL.B. 1896.
Married Mary Shreve Ames at North Easton, Massachusetts, 8 May
    1916.
Now member U. S. House of Representatives.

1917: Colonel, 13th Regiment, Massachusetts State Guard.
1918: Went to France as one of a commission and established
a bureau for Massachusetts soldiers and sailors. Later, on return to United States, commissioned a Major in the United.
States Army and served until some months after the Armistice.
1920: Elected a member of the Harvard Board of Overseers for
the third time. Also elected a member of the United States.
House of Representatives from the 14th Massachusetts District.
Reëlected in 1922.

WILLIAM HARRY FURBER

Born at Boston, 20 October 1870, of George Edward Furber (merchant)·
and Maria Louisa Ames.
Fitted at Boston Latin.
Class Status: Regular.
Degrees A.B. 1893.
Married ,Mabel Harriet Holden at Brookline, Massachusetts, 27 March·
1901. Child:
  Holden, born 13 March 1903.
Now in lumber business at Boston.

For a short time in the fall of 1893 was in the insurance·
business; balance of that year in advertising department of
Boston Globe, continuing there till the fall of 1894. In January,.
1895, went into the office of my father's firm, Furber, Stockford and Company, as stenographer and bookkeeper, and later·
travelled on the road for them as lumber salesman. At my-
father's death in June, 1901, I became partner with Mr. Stockford and continued in the wholesale lumber business with him
under the firm name, Furber, Stockford and Company, till
1908, when I withdrew. Owing to a nervous breakdown I was:
out of business till September 1st, 1908, when I started independently in the wholesale lumber business again, incorporat-
ing as W. H. Furber and Company, January 1, 1920, and am
still at it.

F[REDRIK] HERMAN GADE

Born at Christiania, Norway, 12 August 1871, of Gerhard Gade [Univ.,
Christiania] (United States Consul) and Helen Rebecca Allyn.
Fitted at Anderssen's Skole, Christiania, and Cambridge Latin.
Class Status: ''Four years in three.''

Degrees: A.B. 1892; LL.B. 1895; Honorary Degree (Kristiania University) 1911.
Married Alice Garfield King at Chicago, 25 May 1897. Children:
    Gerhard, born 30 September 1898.
    Alice King, 9 December 1899.
Now Envoy Extraordinary and Minister Plenipotentiary of Norway at
    Rio Janeiro, Brazil.

After coming, at the request of my government, here to Brazil in March, 1918, to serve, as then appeared likely, only for a limited time as Chargé d'Affaires, I was the following year (July, 1919) on the post being raised to a full legation, appointed as Envoy Extraordinary and Minister Plenipotentiary. During my term of service in this capacity I have had two leaves-of-absence of half a year each time, which in both instances were spent partly in the United States and the remainder in Norway. I feel that the saddest part of being "booked" here for the current year is that I shall miss our thirtieth anniversary as I did the twenty-fifth in leaving for Brazil a few months too early.

ffrank Bernard Gallivan

Born at South Boston, 1 January 1872, of James Stephen Gallivan (carpenter) and Mary Flyng.
Fitted at Boston Latin.
Class Status: With '93 throughout. Assistant and Grad. School, 1893-95.
    Assistant, 1896-97.
Degrees: A.B. 1894 as of 1893; A.M. 1894; Ph.D. 1897.
Married Marie Louise Bayard at Brooklyn, 15 January 1906. Child:
    Helen Adelaide, born 29 November 1906.
Died of heart disease, 11 November 1919, at South Boston.

Frank Bernard Gallivan died at South Boston of heart disease, November 11, 1919. He was born there January 1, 1872, the son of James Stephen and Mary (Flyng) Gallivan, his father being a native of Ireland. He fitted at the Boston Latin School and entered Harvard in 1889, taking his A.B. in 1894, as of 1893. At the same time he took his A.M. During this and the following year he was an assistant in "Chem. 1." In 1895 he was an assistant in chemistry at the St. Louis Medical College, then returned to his former position and took his Ph.D. in chemistry in 1897. He then went to the Brooklyn Polytechnic as assistant professor of analytical chemistry, and was promoted to full professorship in 1899. In 1905 he accepted the post of chemist to the Boston Bureau of Milk Inspection. Feeling convinced that the passage of the "Pure Food Act" would create a demand for chemists with some legal training, he took up the study of law, and was admitted to the Massachusetts Bar in December of 1907; he was, however, disappointed with the results. The next year, owing to a difference of opinion with the Board of Health, he resigned his place, and opened a private laboratory in Boston for testing the purity of foods, etc. Soon afterwards he became associated with the United Drug Company, and at the time of his death was chief of their department of chemistry. Several years ago, in consequence of certain dissatisfactions with the teaching of chemistry at Harvard, he ceased all connection and interest with the College, and formally removed his name from the class list. On January 15, 1906, at Brooklyn, New York, he married Marie Louise Bayard, who with one daughter survives him.

HOWARD SCHIFFER GANS

Born at New York City, 23 October 1872, of Levi Lierberman Gans (manufacturer) and Addie Schiffer.
Fitted with Dr. J. Sachs.
Class Status: "Four years in three."
Degrees: A.B. 1892; LL.B. (N. Y. Law Sch.) 1894.
Married Mrs. Birdie (Stein) Sternberger at New York City, 2 July 1908 with adoptive children: Marion Stein Gans, born 12 June 1889 and Robert Stein Gans, 14 August 1890.
Now practising law in New York City.

Entered the law office of Stern and Rushmore in New York City in autumn of 1892. Matriculated at New York Law School at about the same time. Graduated from Law School and was admitted to the bar in New York State in 1894. Continued to "cub" in law office until 1898. Hung out my shingle in New York without partner and in splendid isolation in 1898. Was appointed a Deputy Assistant District Attorney in New York County in December, 1900. Promoted to office of Assistant District Attorney in 1902; resigned to enter private practice with John H. Iselin, '96' in December, 1905. Continued in private practice until October, 1917 (with John H. Iselin for about two years: thereafter alone). Gave up private practice at that time to go to Washington for war work. Served successively as one of the counsel for the Shipping Board, as legal adviser to one of the Assistant Secretaries of the Treasury, and

as Advisory Counsel to the War Labor Policies Board.   Tried
for overseas service in the Judge Advocate General's Department; and was offered a commission with an assignment which
would keep me on this side of the water—which I declined.
Continued with War Labor Policies Board until February,.
1919.   Was abroad, chiefly in Paris, from end of February,
1919, to August of that year.   For a brief period I was in Poland.   Induced by what I saw there, I associated myself, shortly after my return to the United States, with the work of the
Joint Distribution Committee.   This was an organization for
the relief and rehabilitation of war sufferers in Eastern Europe.
Its funds were collected primarily from the Jews in the United
States and (though many millions were spent on non-sectarian.
activities) devoted primarily to the relief of the Jews in Eastern Europe, who stood in greater need of relief than the Christian population because they had not only shared with their
compatriots of other faiths all the horrors incident to invasion
by hostile troops and were not infrequently singled out for especially harsh treatment by the invaders, but had found themselves, after the war was over, the objects of the wave of Anti-
Semitism which seems once more to be sweeping the world, and
in consequence continued to suffer at the hands of their compatriots.   Administrative work of this organization occupied
most of my time—including a considerable part of that spent
abroad in 1921—until the Spring of last year (1922).   Since
then I have been devoting myself to my own affairs, and to a.
minor extent, to the practice of the law.

James Albert Garland, Jr.
See Report VI, Page 125.

CHARLES MERRICK GAY

Born at Newton, Massachusetts, 23 January 1871, of Charles Merrick Gay
(Univ. of Vt. 1853) and Sarah Maria Shaw.
Fitted at E. H. Cutler's.
Class Status: Regular.
Degrees: A.B. 1893; S.B. (Mass. Inst. Tech.) 1895.
Married Louise Gallatin at Tuxedo Park, New York, 18 September 1909.
Children:
Catherine Gallatin, born 31 August 1910.
Louise Bigelow, 20 January 1912.
Now practising architecture at New York City.

After graduating I went to the Institute of Technology for two years, graduating in Architecture in 1895 with degree of B.S. I then went to Paris and was received as student in the Ecole des Beaux Arts in 1896. I studied at the school until 1900 when I returned to America and entered the office of Carrère and Hastings. I worked there until 1902 when I became a member of the firm of Gay and Nash. This firm was dissolved in 1906 and I became a farmer in the Ramapo Valley, doing some architecture on the side. In 1909 I married Louise Gallatin of New York and now have two daughters.

In 1915 we moved to Santa Barbara, California, where we stayed until 1917. We then came East and I received a commission as Captain in the Engineer Corps, United States Army and was attached to the General Engineer Depot, Washington, D. C. I did not get to France and in the spring of 1919 was discharged. In the autumn of 1919 I entered the office of Clinton and Russell, architects, New York City, where I still am. I still go out to the farm in the summer and still long for the time when old age, physical infirmities or a nervous breakdown will give me an excuse once more to become a farmer. In the meantime I am once more an architect, and feeling younger and physically and nervously stronger than ever.

THOMAS ASHLEY GIFFORD

Born at Springfield, Massachusetts, 25 December 1866, of John Henry
    Gifford [Harvard, temp.] (manufacturer) and Rebecca Anne Gifford.
Fitted with H L. Coar ('93).
Class Status: Regular.
Degree: A.B. 1893.
Now with Motorcraft Engineering Corporation, New York City.

After graduation, I was in business occupation in Springfield, Massachusetts, until 1900, when I came to New York. Here I have been with several corporations, the longest period being from 1905 to 1916 with a fire insurance company as its cashier. In 1916, I left them and helped organize a company to manufacture medicinal chemicals, acting as its treasurer. We had a brilliant chemist and plenty of capital, and, after many delays, we possessed a finely equipped plant, where we turned out some very superior products at a good margin of profit. After the United States entered the war, however, we were unable to get the necessary raw material; poor team-work developed among the officials; the chemist (an Austrian) went back on us; and the concern went up the flue, together with most of my investment. The end came in 1918.

During 1919, 1920 and 1921, I was with an export concern, and began again the studying of geography and foreign exchange. This concern also blew up through force of circumstances. Since then, I have been with the Motorcraft Engineering Corporation, which manufactures and deals in attachments for automobiles.

I am a member of the Harvard Club of New York, and spend the most of my leisure hours there, indulging mainly in bridge and billiards. No voyages, no sports (except the above), no public offices, no degrees, no publications or speeches.

Louis Whitmore Gilbert

Born at Chicago, 3 June 1871, of Selden Gilbert [Tufts] (clergyman) and Sarah Louise Whitmore.
Fitted at Boston Latin.
Class Status: Regular.
Degrees: A.B. 1893; M.D. 1897.
Died at Brookline, 30 March 1919.

Louis Whitmore Gilbert died at Brookline, March 30, 1919, from the progressive results of an early attack of infantile paralysis. He was born at Chicago, June 3, 1871, the son of Rev. Selden and Sarah Louise (Whitmore) Gilbert. The family was of old Maine stock, but after several removes settled in Boston, where Louis fitted for Harvard at the Latin School. He was a regular member of '93, and after graduation at once entered the Medical School, having always had that profession in view. Receiving his M.D. in 1897 he served on the Medical side of the Massachusetts General Hospital, and afterwards at the Boston Lying-In Hospital. He entered active practice in Brookline and attained a high reputation as a general practitioner. His heart was thoroughly in his work. "While the family physician's life affords little excitement," he once wrote, "there is a large measure of satisfaction in trying to make the lives of others easier, and in the firm friendships formed in the course of the daily round." His ability was recognized by many appointments. In 1899-1900 he was assistant in Histology at the Medical School, and at the same time became physician to the Boston Dispensary, where he served for seven years. In 1908 he was made medical examiner to the Brookline municipal gymnasium, and medical school inspector. He was also a councilor of the Massachusetts Medical Society, was physician to the children's outpatient department of the Massachusetts General Hospital, was in charge of the Children's Heart Hospital in Brookline, was visiting physician to the Boston Floating Hospital, etc. Among other avocations he was devoted to sailing, and made many long summer cruises, going as far as the Gulf of St. Lawrence. He was warmly interested in Class affairs and an ever-welcome guest at dinners and reunions. As his malady advanced, he was obliged to relinquish his work, and spent the last year at Pictou, Canada. In his last report he said, "Looking back, I think I should do the same things over again." He never married.

JAMES WATERMAN GLOVER

Born at Clio, Michigan, 24 July 1868, of James Polk Glover (merchant) and Emerette Maria Neff.
Entered from University of Michigan.
Class Status: Graduate School 1892-95.
Degrees: Litt.B. (Univ. of Mich.) 1892; A.B. 1895 as of 1893; A.M. 1894; Ph.D. 1895.
Married Alice Durfee Webber at Ann Arbor, Michigan, 29 August 1900.
Children:
James Webber, born 16 September 1901.
Sanford Webber, 8 October 1903 (deceased).
Now Professor of Mathematics and Insurance, University of Michigan.

Since graduation (after two years in the Graduate School at Harvard) I have been a member of the faculty of the University of Michigan in the department of mathematics. While I have offered courses in pure and applied mathematics my chief interest since 1905 has been in mathematics applied to finance, insurance and statistics. During the last ten years this work has developed rapidly—at the present time there are over six hundred elections annually in these courses. The students come chiefly from the field of business administration although there is a growing demand for elementary training in mathematical statistics by students in education, biology and psychology. The University of Michigan has been particularly prominent in the technical training of actuaries for insurance com-

panies and graduates of this department are scattered all over
the country in positions of responsibility.

The development of actuarial courses has naturally drawn
me into public and professional work, and I have served or am
serving in many public positions.

Had a wonderful time at Harvard last December just after
Xmas when the various scientific societies were gathered there.
All the graduate students in mathematics at Harvard from way
back were there and Professor Osgood made successful arrangements for a grand reunion. Some of the men I had not seen for
twenty-five years. We had a banquet at the Union with President Lowell as guest and every body was in a happy mood—
particularly Mr. Lowell.

PHILIP BECKER GOETZ

Born at Buffalo, New York, 20 July 1870, of George Goetz (merchant)
    and Katharine Hansauer.
Fitted at Buffalo High.
Class Status: Regular.
Degree: A.B. 1893.
Married Linda Alvord Graves at Buffalo, 7 July 1897. Children:
    Theodore Becker, born 23 April 1904.
    Esther Becker, 7 August 1907.
Now Professor in English and Classics at the University of Buffalo.

Taught in local high schools immediately after leaving college, later at the Nichols School (Buffalo), later still (beginning in 1913), helped organize the Arts and Sciences Department of the University of Buffalo. Am directing and teaching
the work in classics and English at this university.

Two years ago began contributing a weekly column of "Com-
ment" to the *Buffalo Evening News*. Have published four volumes of verse "Kallirrhoe" (1896); "Poems" (1898); "In-
terludes" (1904); "The Summons of the King" (1911). Also
pamphlets and various addresses. See "Who's Who" for 1922-
23.

Interested in country life, music, tennis. Son, Theodore B.
Goetz, now at Harvard. Member of the Council of the University of Buffalo; trustee of the Nichols School, Buffalo; trustee
of the Buffalo Seminary; director of the Albright Art Gallery;
trustee of the Grosvenor Library.

CHARLES CROSS GOODRICH

Born at Akron, Ohio, 3 August 1871, of Benjamin Franklin Goodrich
[Univ. of Penn. Medical] (manufacturer) and Mary Marvin.
.Fitted at St. Paul's.
Class Status: Regular.
Degrees A.B. 1893.
Married Mary Anna Gellatly at Orange, New Jersey, 22 April 1895.
.Now a trustee at New York City.

1893-1894: Special course at Massachusetts Institute of Technology in mechanical engineering. 1894-January, 1895: Special course in same subject in Lawrence Scientific School. February, 1895: Began work for the B. F. Goodrich Company at Akron, Ohio, where I continued until August, 1907, when I resigned active connection with this company. Since then I have been one of its directors. August, 1907: Moved to West Orange, New Jersey, which has since been my residence. In 1913 again engaged in business with the Goodrich, Lockhart Company, with which firm I am still associated.

Spent 1918 and early part of 1919 in France as Assistant Chief Purchasing Officer, A. E. F., of the Ordnance Department. In April, 1919, received my discharge from the Army as Lieutenant Colonel and went to London as Agent for the Liquidation Commission of the War Department, where I remained until November, 1919, at which time I returned home.

Spent six months in 1920, six months in 1921, and eight months in 1922 in Europe, partially on business and partially for pleasure, during which visits I travelled pretty generally over Europe, particularly in 1920, when I visited all the Balkan States of Central Europe as well as Constantinople. My interest in sports continues strong, with particular application to golf. Have just received Distinguished Service Medal.

ARTHUR HALE GORDON

Born at Boston, 2 March 1872, of Adoniram Judson Gordon (Brown 1860)
(clergyman) and Maria Hale.
Fitted at Boston Latin.
Class Status: Regular.
Degree: A.B. 1893.
Married Harriet Louise Manning at East Orange, New Jersey, 15 September 1910. Children:
Frances Hale, born 31 July 1911.

John Manning, 19 January 1913.
Elizabeth Eugenia, 5 October 1914 (died 29 July 1915).
David Livingstone, 12 November 1916.
Now in Baptist ministry at Buffalo, New York.

After leaving college spent a year studying in Chicago, then entered Newton Theological Institution, Newton Centre, Massachusetts. After two years left to supply a church in Fitchburg, Massachusetts, for a year. Then spent a year in the Free Church Theological College, Glasgow, Scotland, and several months in Berlin, Germany. Accepted my first pastorate at Ipswich, Massachusetts, where I spent two years (1899-1901). Called to the Immanuel Baptist Church, Cambridge, Massachusetts, where I remained from 1901 to 1909. Removed to the Ponce de Leon Avenue Baptist Church, Atlanta, Georgia, early in 1910, and remained there as pastor till July, 1917. Supplied from August, 1917, till March, 1918, at the First Baptist Church, Los Angeles. California, while the regular minister was absent in war work. Then entered Y. M. C. A. for a year as war secretary. Stationed first at San Diego, California, and then at the Coast Guard Station, New London, Connecticut. In April, 1919, accepted call to the Delaware Avenue Baptist Church at Buffalo, New York, where I still remain as pastor after four years of service.

CLIFFORD ALLEN GOULD

Born at South Orange, New Jersey, 27 March 1871, of William Banks
  Gould (manufacturer) and Eleanor Margaret Allen.
Fitted at Dearborn and Morgan School.
Class Status: Regular.
Degrees A.B. 1893.
Married Helen Fyfe at Nutley, New Jersey, 8 June 1903. Child:
  Margaret, born 6 April 1908.
Now manufacturing hardware at Newark, New Jersey.

Still engaged in the manufacture of hardware. Plodding along merrily at the ripe old age of 52. Took a short trip to England and France last summer to see how their Volstead Acts were working; enjoyed the sunshine tremendously.

FREDERICK LOUIS GRANT

Born at Winsted, Connecticut, 25 December 1871, of James Eugene
  Grant (manufacturer) and Jeannette Maria Watrous.
Fitted at Winsted High.

Class Status: Left Junior year.
Degree: B.D. (Yale) 1895.
Married Ettaline Harriet Ladd at Windsorville, Connecticut, 1 January
1896. Child:
Eleanor Ladd, born 13 November 1896.
Now in Congregational Ministry at Warren, Massachusetts.

After leaving college at the end of junior year, I studied two
years in Andover Theological Seminary and graduated at Yale
Divinity School in May, 1895. In October of that year I was
ordained to the Christian Ministry and became pastor of the
Congregational Church in Northfield, Connecticut. Remained
there till 1906, when I removed to Plainville, Connecticut, as
pastor; then after ten years to the church in East Hampton,
Connecticut, where I was living at the time of the twenty-fifth
reunion of blessed memory. After spending pretty nearly all
my life in Connecticut I decided to try my fortunes in Massachusetts, and became pastor of the First Congregational Church
in Warren in August, 1921. Beyond this I can truthfully say
little news; that is, there have been no marked incidents of more
than personal interest. My work is that of a preacher and student, the second necessitated by the first. Outside of professional lines I have done considerable lecturing on nature study,
and also have done an increasing amount of literary work of a
general character. In addition I have attained a considerable
degree of expertness in photography. My only voyages the last
few years have been to a delightful summer place I own in my
native state. I have not held any offices in the past five years,
and the particular distinction that pertains to me is that of being a Harvard man who is also a graduate of Yale, and so able
to maintain a marked degree of impartiality on either side of
the bowl.

HARRY EDWARD GRIGOR

Born at Taunton, Massachusetts, 30 January 1869, of Edward Grigor
(merchant) and Lucy Peabody Price.
Fitted at Taunton High.
Class Status: Special, 1889-91.
Married Olive Caroline Ambler at Natick, Massachusetts, 4 June 1913.
Now manufacturing paper specialties at Natick, Massachusetts.

When I left college I planned to take up newspaper work.
I found that field at its crowded period, and after working at
several jobs had to give it up for something paying better, and

in 1894 entered the Boston Customs House. This leads me to suggest that the way of the educated young fellow, looking for a toe-hold at the bottom of the Hill of Difficulty, has grown much easier during the last thirty years. The supply of good human material seems less in proportion to the country's stage of economic development. My first ventures in journalism were on country papers; afterwards I was for a time an editorial writer on the Boston Herald.

While my years at the Customs House were uneventful, two European trips and constant wide reading saved them from lack of interest. In 1917 I changed from a dilletante to a hard-boiled business man, taking charge of the Ambler Myriagraph Company, a concern in Natick, Massachusetts, having an exclusive contract to treat Japanese paper for use by the Rapid Addressing Machine Company, of New York. Heading a business with fifty or sixty employees means personal relations. The "boss" is expected to make out income tax returns, assist the foreign to naturalize, urge night-school on the laggards, to advise those in love and those whose family affairs are not smooth. I am struck by the scarcity of boys and girls seeking employment; the desire for education seems almost universal.

But the foregoing are work-a-day reflections. The real perspectives of life appear when business is over, the shades are drawn and the reading-light adjusted. Then the curtain rises on the moving-pictures of the imagination. Because one has never written a book, run for office or "made" a learned society, does not mean that life lacks color and inspiration, for a bookish man with college background may have many and varied adventures of the mind and walk the streets of many El Dorados whose gates open with the key Harvard has given him.

George Griswold, 2d

See Report VI, Page 133.

Michael Henry Guerin

Born at Chicago, 27 December 1871, of John Guerin [Rush Med., Chicago] (physician) and Mary Jackson.
Fitted at Harvard School, Chicago.
Class Status: Regular.
Degrees: A.B. 1893; LL.B. (Chicago College of Law) 1895.

Married Mary Esther Glenn at Oakland, California, 8 April 1896. Children:
> John Glenn, born 2 February 1897.
> Mary Carmelita, 9 October 1898.
> Thomas Edmund, 16 August 1901.
> William Jackson, 26 June 1903.

Died by drowning, 11 September 1919, in Lake Michigan.

Judge Michael Henry Guerin met his death through accidental drowning in Lake Michigan September 11, 1919. He was on his way in his motor boat with his son Tom from his summer home at White Lake to Muskegon, Mich., and, while engaged in repairing a steering gear which had become defective, he was thrown overboard by a sudden lurch of the boat in a rather heavy sea. He was apparently injured or stunned by the boat as it tossed about, so that he was not able to swim or even respond to the efforts of the son who vainly tried to rescue him. His body was recovered a few hours after the accident on a sand bar where it had been washed. And thus passed, without a moment's warning, a man in the fullness of life, whose loss to his family, his friends and the community cannot be told in mere words.

Henry Guerin (by that name he was generally known) was born in Chicago December 27, 1871, one of nine children. His father, Dr. John Guerin, a native of Ireland, came to Chicago early in life, first engaging in teaching as Professor of Mathematics and Natural Sciences in the University of St. Mary's of the Lake and later in the practice of medicine, after a course in the Rush Medical School. The father held at various times several public offices in the city, including that of City Physician and a membership in the School Board, maintaining the latter connection at the time of his death several years ago. Mary Jackson, the mother, was of Revolutionary stock, her forbears first settling in this country in Fairfield County, Conn., in 1679; and her great grandfather, Jonathan Jackson, fought through the Revolutionary War and fell in action at the Battle of Yorktown.

Henry, who was preceded to Cambridge by his older brother, Edmund, a member of the class of 1891, fitted for Harvard in a Jesuit college in Montreal, and at the Harvard School in Chicago. In the former all the courses, were conducted in French, and he had the unique experience, for an American, of studying his first Latin through the French. He took a general course in college, showing a preference for languages,—Latin, Greek, German, French and Italian being among his electives. With his natural ability he easily maintained a good standing in his studies, and, while not a member of any of the college societies, he took an interest in various activities in Cambridge, and at one time was a runner on the Track Team. At the close of the Junior year, having completed the full course required for a degree with the exception of two courses, he went abroad and spent his senior year in Europe in travel and study, remaining most of the time in institutions in Berlin and Vienna.

He returned to Cambridge in time to graduate with the class, and, after completing a course in the Chicago College of Law, he entered upon the practice of his chosen profession in Chicago in 1895.. He steadily acquired a lucrative law practice and soon won for himself a prominent place at the Bar. He was co-author of the Little Giant Index Digest of Illinois decisions; Professor of Law in the Chicago College of Law from 1898 to the time of his death; Master in Chancery of the Circuit Court for a period of five years; and in 1917 he was elected Judge of the Superior Court of Cook County, Illinois, for a term of six years. Thus he made steady progress to positions of trust and honor in the community. While he was fortunate in early life, as the son of well-to-do parents, in being reared in comfortable surroundings, his sturdy character and indomitable spirit soon showed themselves, so that his real worth was early evident. He became an exceptionally successful trial lawyer and advisor, winning many important cases. His interest in his work and his loyalty to his clients were such it was once said of him, that while engaged in a trial, before entering the court room he left all his friends on the outside.

He was both high minded and fair minded, thorough and sincere, hating sham and hypocrisy, but most considerate in his dealings with others. His persistence and his devotion to duty were marked characteristics, and these, together with his integrity and ability easily won him the place he deserved; and finally the election to the Judgeship, a position that he had much desired and which he was filling at the time of his untimely death. During the War he gave much time from his

busy life to the various drives and other patriotic enterprises
and he served as one of the 4-minute speakers in raising money
for the Red Cross, Y. M. C. A., K. C., etc. He naturally took
an active part in local politics and was identified throughout
his career with the Democratic Party.

For many years he maintained a summer home across the
Lake in Michigan, and his friends from Chicago and elsewhere
always found a warm welcome there. He was athletically inclined through his life, in yachting, swimming and walking; but
his principal sport was golf, and his membership in several golf
clubs permitted him to enjoy the game in so far as his busy life
would permit. In addition to the country clubs he was a member of several city clubs, both social and political, and his life
was thus rounded out to the fullest. While his material and
temporal success was marked, the other side,—the home and
social side—was equally appealing. In either case was in
evidence his efficiency, his rugged character, his high moral tone,
and at the same time his kindliness. His devotion to his family, his happiness with them, his planning for his children and
his interest in their future, all now pass in review; and these
indeed leave no doubt as to the loss that these dear ones sus-
tained in the tragedy of his untimely death. And he seemed
naturally to assume the responsibilities of many of his friends
also. To these he was ever a source of comfort, whether they
came to him professionally or otherwise. For his intimates
a light went out in his passing. To them his comradship, rare
wit, excellent judgment and sympathy meant more than can be
described.

H. J. C. '84

Frederick Putnam Gulliver

Born at Norwich, Connecticut, 30 August 1865, of Daniel Francis Gulliver
[Yale 1848] (physician) and Mary E. Strong.
Fitted at Norwich Free Academy.
Class Status: Graduate School, 1892-96.
Degrees: A.B. 1893; A.M. 1894; Ph.D. 1896.
Died of pneumonia 8 February 1919, at Philadelphia.

Frederick Putnam Gulliver died of pneumonia at Philadel-
phia, February 8, 1919. He was born at Norwich, Connecticut,
August 30, 1865, the son of Dr. Daniel Francis and Mary
(Strong) Gulliver. He fitted at the Norwich Free Academy and

entered the Massachusetts Institute of Technology in September, 1883, as a student in the Mining Department. He established a high record, but left in February, 1886, before taking a degree, to become assistant topographer in the United States Geological Survey and was promoted to topographer in 1889. His work led him into nearly every State east of the Mississippi. In 1892 he entered the Graduate School to continue his professional studies, took his A.B. in 1893, and continued a resident student until 1896, when he took his Ph.D. Receiving an appointment to a travelling fellowship,.he spent a year in Europe, and was a member of the International Geological Congress in Russia. In September, 1897, he became Science Master at St. Mark's School, where he taught with much success for eight years, leaving on account of a severe case of appendicitis. This permanently impaired his health; but after a long convalescence he became geographer to the Pennsylvania Commission on the "Chestnut Tree Blight" in September, 1912. Here he remained until forced to give up all regular occupation. He held many high professional positions, among them secretary of the geological section of the American Association for the Advancement of Science, memberships in foreign societies, etc. He was much interested in local history, and was chairman of the Historical Committee for the 250th celebration of the founding of Norwich. He was unmarried

ANDREW HAHN

Born at Newton, Massachusetts, 1 December 1869, of John Hahn (carver)
    and Elizabeth Itchner.
Fitted at Newton •High.
Class, Status: Regular.
Degrees: A.B. 1893; S.T.B. 1896.
Now living at Newton, Massachusetts.

My Gracious Petercats (I never swear!) what is there to tell in the life of a country parson—and retired at that? Flat, flatter, flattest. After getting my degree at the Divinity School, I was ordained to the Unitarian ministry at Wolfboro, New Hampshire, May 19, 1897. Continued pastorate there till August 31, 1902. Flat. I then resigned and went home to Newton for three years, being technically known as "unsettled." (This does not refer to my intellect—get me?) Flatter. In 1905 I took the Old First Parish Church at Duxbury, Massachusetts (also instructor in Powder Point School) and might be there yet, except that during the war I was careless enough to say that the Germans were right. Argal (as saith poet Shakspere) —resignation on April 1, 1918. Back to Newton again and still "unsettled." Flattest. Expect to be buried under a lilac bush in my own back garden—super-flat!

ALBERT HALE

Born at Jamaica Plain, Massachusetts, 19 April 1872, of Albert Hale [H. C. 1861] (teacher) and Katharine Davenport Wood.
Fitted at Hale's School.
Class Status: Regular.
Degree: A.B. 1893.
Married Mabel Stedman at Brookline, Massachusetts, 19 June 1922.
Now in bond business at Boston.

On graduating from college I entered the bond business in Boston and after a few years became manager of the bond department of Parkinson and Burr. remaining in this position for some fifteen years. Subsequently, I engaged in the same business on my own account under the name of Albert Hale and Company—my present occupation. During this time little out of the ordinary has occurred. In 1915 I attended the first Plattsburg Training Camp but the following year a serious injury prevented my continuing the training. In 1918 I volunteered for service but was not accepted. In June, 1922. I married Miss Mabel Stedman of Brookline.

JOSEPH HENRY HALL

Born at Norwich, Connecticut, 31 August 1870, of Joseph Hall (manufacturer) and Sarah Rogers.
Fitted at Berkeley School, New York.
Class Status: Special, 1889-92.
Married Grace Manning Smith at Brooklyn, New York, 13 June 1897.
   Children:
      Joseph Henry, Jr., born 17 June 1898.
      Lloyd Grosvenor, 9 July 1899.
      Philip Sidney, 5 January 1902.
Now manufacturing woolens at Norwich, Connecticut.

Have resided in Norwich, Connecticut, ever since leaving college, with the exception of a few trips and a year abroad. Have remained in same business, that is, manufacturing woolen

cloth. Am now connected with Joseph Hall and Son, Inc., and
no longer have interest in Hallville Mills. Two oldest sons are
now through college, one having degree from Yale and other
from Sheffield Scientific School. Youngest is about to enter.
My chief interest now seems to be golf. Residence address is
now 160 Broadway, Norwich, Connecticut.

SAMUEL PRESCOTT HALL

Born at South Boston, Massachusetts, 13 September 1872, of David
    Prescott Hall (lawyer) and Florence Marion Howe.
Fitted with J. Leal, Plainfield, New Jersey.
Class Status: Regular.
Degree: A.B. 1893.
Married Sarah Kidder Thomson at Ossining, New York, 21 December 1901.
    Children:
        David Prescott, born 5 April 1904 (died 5 April 1904).
        Maud, 27 October 1905 (died 1 November 1905).
        Eleanor Florence, 17 January 1907.
        Samuel Gridley Howe, 11 January 1909.
Now   U. S. Appraisal Engineer at Columbus, Ohio.

Practised at Columbus, Ohio, as senior partner of Hall and
Bush, architects and engineers until last June, when I was appointed Appraisals Engineer, Income Tax Section, Internal Rev-
enue Bureau. Am "on the road" or "in the field" most of
the time, appraising the large bulk of the war-industries which
still survive, and some which do not. Work is very interesting,
and experience almost invaluable. Am in Washington part of
the time, but mostly not.

Have two children, Eleanor Florence and Samuel Gridley
Howe, and they keep me busy. Have taken but little part in
public life, and done little writing, except technical. · Bulk of
my work since last report has been in consulting work, investigation of properties for bond issues—and against them—income
tax work, invested capital, industrial accounting, and so forth.
Have never grown very rich in this world's goods, but have led
a busy, happy, and, at least to some extent, a useful life, and
hope so to continue.

Thomas Hall, Jr.

See Report VI, Page 138.

FRANK WALTON HALLOWELL

Born at West Medford, Massachusetts, 12 August 1870, of Richard Price
  Hallowell (merchant) and Anna Coffin Davis.
Fitted with W. Nichols.
Class Status: Regular.
Degree: A.B. 1893.
Married Jessie Coburn Donald at Chestnut Hill, Massachusetts, 27
  June 1896. Children:
    Richard Price, 2d, born 15 December 1897.
    Cornelia, 23 March 1901.
Now in wool business at Boston.

On leaving college, immediately went into the wool business.
Became member of the firm of Hallowell and Donald in 1898
and have been in the wool business ever since, and am still very
actively engaged in it. During the war felt that I could be of
more service using my knowledge of wool than in any other
way; was member of syndicate created by War Department for
importing wool from South America for the Government, and
when all wool in the United States was taken over by the War
Department, was a Government Valuer.

Have always been a Republican in politics but the party is
becoming so hide-bound and behind the times, wish an Independent Liberal Party (Liberal in italics) would be started
which I could vote for instead of being forced into the Democratic ranks. I continue my interest in athletics, play considerable golf and play a better game of tennis than when I graduated. Enjoy each year more and more as time goes on meeting
the old faces at Class dinners, reunions, etc. Member of the
Union Club and Harvard Club of Boston, Brookline Country
Club, and various fishing clubs, etc. Trustee Franklin Savings
Bank of Boston.

George Daniel Hammond

See Report VI, Page 140, and Supplement, Page 126.

[BILLINGS] LEARNED HAND

Born at Albany, New York, 27 January 1872, of Samuel Hand [Union]
  (lawyer) and Lydia Coit Learned.
Fitted at Albany Academy.
Class Status: Regular.
Degrees: A.B. 1893; A.M. 1894; LL.B. 1896.

Married Frances Amelia Fincke at Utica, New York, 6 December 1902.
C**h**ildren:
    Mary Deshon, born 28 March 1905.
    Frances Lydia, 9 April 1907.
    Constance, 21 July 1909.
Now United States District Judge for the Southern District of New
    York. ·

Law School, 1893-1896; law clerk with Matthew Hale, Albany, New York, from October, 1896 to March, 1897; law clerk with Hun and Johnson, Albany, New York, from March, 1897, till January 1, 1899; partner of Hun, Johnson and Hand from January 1, 1899, till November 17, 1902; law clerk with Zabriskie, Burrill and Murray, New York, from November 17, 1902, till January 1, 1904; partner with Gould and Wilkie, New York, from January 1, 1904, till April 28, 1909; appointed United States District Judge for the Southern District of New York, April 28, 1909, in which position I still am serving..

Travelled in Europe with D. R. Vail, December, 1896; with my family in England, 1911; again in England and the Continent, 1922. Went west to Montana in 1913, to New Mexico in 1917, to Wyoming in 1919. Have very often spent some part of summer in Murray Bay Canada. Otherwise spend my summers at Cornish, New Hampshire. Sports—chiefly walking, a little tennis and less golf. Public positions—none but as judge. No degrees or distinctions. Have published some articles before 1909 in *Harvard Law Review*. Clubs: Harvard Club of New York, University Club of New York, Century Club of New York.

JOHN GODDARD HART

Born at Newport, Rhode Island, 12 February 1870, of James Nicholas:
    Hart (boat-builder) and Annie Frances Goddard.
Fitted at Rogers High, Newport.
Class Status: Regular.
Degrees: A.B. 1893; A.M. 1894.
Married Ethel Hastings at Andover, Massachusetts, 13 June 1899.
Now Instructor in English, Harvard.

Ever since graduation has been connected with the English Department at Harvard. For many years was also secretary to the Faculty of Arts and Sciences, and secretary of the Committee on Admissions. These posts he has now resigned and is, devoting himself to teaching, attending to all the mechanism which had to be established on account of the new rules for general examinations for those who concentrate in a particular field. His official position is Instructor in English.

JOHN HENRY HARWOOD

Born at Newton, Massachusetts, 4 June 1869, of George Shaw Harwood, (manufacturer) and Ellen Anne Barnard.
Fitted at Newton High and E. H. Cutler's.
Class Status: Regular.
Degrees: A.B. 1893; LL.B. 1896.
Married Annie Bowlend Reed at Chicago, 14 April 1904. Children:
     John, born 24 September 1905.
     Reed, 1 September 1907.
     Sydney, 7 April 1909.
     Mary Reed, 10 November 1914.
Now manufacturing woolen machinery at Boston.

After graduating from the Law School in 1896 I was for a few months in the office of Hayes and Williams, Boston, then for a year with Matthews and Thompson, then for a time alone, and then joined forces with R. G. Dodge, '93, under the name of Harwood and Dodge, with offices in the Tremont Building, Boston. July 1, 1901, gave up the practice of law and accepted an interest in the firm of George S. Harwood and Son, 53 State Street, Boston, manufacturers of woolen machinery. Was also treasurer of "Lewando's," Boston, and president of the Harwood and Quincy Machine Company, Worcester. I am still making and selling woolen machinery, and have suffered and enjoyed pretty much the ordinary run of vicissitudes, difficulties, and successes that most business men have been through this last five years.

My family is just exactly the same, except that my children are growing up altogether too fast. My eldest son enters Harvard next fall. In the last five years I have had two really good vacations. One summer I spent with my eldest son in the Rocky Mountains riding horseback through Glacier Park and Rocky Mountain Park, and the other (last summer) with my wife and two oldest sons fishing, motoring, climbing mountains and playing golf in Scotland and England.

Drayton Franklin Hastie
See Report VI, Page 142.

HORATIO HATHAWAY, JR.

Born at New Bedford, Massachusetts, 12 September 1870, of Horatio
  Hathaway [Harvard 1850] (merchant) and Ellen Rodman.
Fitted with L. B. Stedman and at Groton School.
Class Status: Special, 1889-91.
Married Mabel Lovering at Taunton, Massachusetts, 15 January 1898.
  Child:
        Lovering, born 8 November 1899.
Now trustee and investor at Boston.

I do not know how to improve upon the last report with its
bright additions and wise deletions supplied by the Secretary.
My activities are the same as noted there; except that, with the
end of the war, my military and nautical responsibilities
ceased. My principle sport is riding to hounds and I also enjoy
small boat racing at Dark Harbor, Maine, where I now spend
my summers with my family. My "principal occupation" is
the care and re-investment of funds in various trusts created
by my father's will.

Charles Sumner Hawes

Born at Chelsea, Massachusetts, 7 June 1869, of William Hawes (lumber
  merchant) and Marianna Jane Locke.
Fitted at Chelsea High and Winchester High.
Class Status: Regular.
Degree: A.B. 1893.
Married Frances Wilson at Winchester, Massachusetts, 15 December 1897.
Died of apoplexy at Chicago, 22 April 1921.

Intending to be a physician, Hawes spent a year in hotel
work (which he greatly enjoyed) and another as a travelling
tutor—visiting the Mediterranean lands as far east as Syria—
and then entered the Medical School. After two years there,
he left in 1897, hoping to return, and took the post of auditor
at Memorial Hall. Two years later again, he declined a good
position in a large hotel to accept a clerkship in the Adjutant
General's office at Washington, whence he could attend the
evening sessions of the Columbian Medical School. Government service appealed to him strongly, however, and in 1900
he took an executive position in the Census Office, and three
years later became a special agent for the Department of Com-

merce and Labor. Among his assignments here was the collection of statistics for manufactures in Pennsylvania, for marriage and divorce in Greater New York, for women and child labor in the south, for cotton mill operatives in New England, etc. In 1909 he went into business with the Spirella. Waist Company of Meadville, Pennsylvania, and spent several years in organizing their trade in Minnesota and Wisconsin. In 1913 he joined the Chicago branch of the Library Bureau, planning and equipping library interiors. In 1918 he went into war work, and became office manager and research assistant in the Bureau of Research, War Trade Board (afterwards transferred to the State Department) at Washington. He specialized in the questions relating to the dye industry; and it was on a journey undertaken for this purpose that he was suddenly stricken down. His genial social nature and warm interest in Class affairs will be remembered no less than his unusual ability as an executive and investigator. On December 15, 1897, he married Frances, daughter of John T. Wilson, of Winchester, Massachusetts.

OSCAR BROWN HAWES

Born at Montclair, New Jersey, 24 February 1872, of George Lenox
 Hawes [Coll. City of N. Y. 1859] (dentist) and Adelaide Dunning.
.Fitted at Mrs. Shaw's School, Boston.
Class Status: Regular.
Degree: A.B. 1893.
Married Anne de Pourtales Day at Germantown, Pennsylvania, 17 February 1903. Children:
 Adelaide Dunning, born 21 November 1903.
 Elizabeth Day, 3 April 1908.
 Eleanor Cope, 3 April 1911.
'Now Unitarian minister at Summit, New Jersey.

Harvard Divinity School, 1893-1894. Taught at Mitchell's. Boys' School, Billerica, Massachusetts, 1894-1895. Travelled abroad during summer of 1895, returning in October. January 1, 1896, became minister of Unitarian Church in Greeley,. Colorado. In fall of 1896 went to Toronto, Canada, and in May, 1897, was ordained as Minister of the First Unitarian Church there. Summer of 1900 travelled abroad, including a visit to Greece. January 1, 1901, became minister of Unitarian Church in Germantown, Philadelphia. February 17, 1903, married Anne de Pourtales Day, of Germantown. Three daughters,.

born respectively, November, 1903, April, 1908, and April, 1911. Organized Nicetown Club for Boys and Girls in Philadelphia, and took part in reform movement in politics, work of Civil Service Reform Association, etc. there. Went abroad with family in 1910, attending International Congress of religion in Berlin and in London. Became minister of Unitarian Church in Newton Centre, Massachusetts, September, 1916. Went to France and served as Director of Foyers du Soldat with French army at and near the front November, 1917, to July, 1918. Hut Director, Y. M. C. A., Hut No. 1, Camp Montoir, St. Nazaire, August-November. Sent to various camps to "interpret" France and to speak of French army to our soldiers. Returned home immediately after the Armistice. Became minister of All Souls' Church, Unitarian Universalist, Summit, New Jersey, February, 1921. Chairman of All Souls' Forum. Honorary member Canoe Brook Country Club. Spent summers in delightful companionship with my family at my summer home on Lake George, and after 1912 in the colder and more bracing climate of Hancock Point, Maine. Summer of 1916 attended summer school at Harvard, taking Chapel services for one week. Attended Theological summer school of 1920. Have won no new degrees or distinctions, but have enjoyed my work and the companionship with my family which the ministry allows. One daughter now in Vassar and the other two preparing. Still enjoy golf and tennis, fishing and boating during the summer, and preaching at any time!

JOHN HEISS

Born at Crestline, Ohio, 5 October 1863, of John Heiss (contractor and builder) and Elizabeth Pottiger.
Entered from Wittenberg College.
Class Status: Entered Senior.
Degrees: A.B. (Wittenberg) 1892; A.B. 1893; A.M. 1900.
Married Maud Souders at Dayton, Ohio, 3 September 1900. Children:
John Paul, born 7 January 1906.
Elizabeth Madeleine, 1 May 1907.
Ruth Miriam, 17 February 1910.
Frederick Hubert, 24 January 1913.
Now Professor of Modern Languages at Purdue University, Lafayette, Indiana.

Professor of Modern Languages twenty-three years on the same spot—nothing but hard work in winter—reading, rusticat-

Queen: Heaven! What do my eyes behold?

Hamlet: Madam, you are gazing at probably the toughest lulu in the history of Denmark.

"HAMLET"—H. P. C. PLAY, 1893

ing and ruminating in summer—make three hundred words out
of that if you can!

In the last five years I have not taken a single trip worth
talking about, except to blow up and down the country in the
Buick with the kids once or twice in a while. If I told you
that my greatest achievement was to bring up four of the health-
iest, finest kids that I (naturally) ever saw, you fellows would
give me the merry ha-ha! Well, all right! As long as all concerned are happy, "good" is the word. I still feel as young as
in '93, and the daily harness fits me without rubbing. I have
no idea when I shall retire.

FREDERICK GRANTHAM HENDERSON

Born at Brookline, Massachusetts, 21 May 1873, of Clarks Alan Hender-
son (British Consul) and Helen Elizabeth Power.
Fitted with C. L. Rideoute.
Class Status: 1889-90, Sp. Sci. 1890-92, with '94. Joined Class Senior
year..
Degree: A.B. 1893.
Married Johanna Swanton at Dorchester, Massachusetts, 15 February
1914. (Died 19 February 1923).
Now farming at West Medway, Massachusetts.

No member of the Class can possibly have led a more uneventful life than mine. I began as treasurer of the Henderson
Dairy Company at Brookline. In 1903 I took up the piano
business, first with Chickering and Son, and in 1910 with the
Bowen-Henderson Company, both at Boston. Shortly after this
latter change went into farming, first at Ellis, Massachusetts,
on my own account, and then for another man at West Medway,
Massachusetts. I am still living in the country and farming for
some one else. The over-shadowing event of the last five years
of my life is the death of my wife which occurred on February 19th of this year. My sole interest in life is centered
in my seven-year-old boy, Lawrence, and I hope to live to see
him enter Harvard. I also hope that when he graduates he
may not be quite such a nuisance to his Class Secretary as
I have been to mine. (The Class Secretary will appreciate
the meaning of this.)

WILLIAM JULIAN HENDERSON

Born at Lima, Peru, 10 February 1871, of Clarks Alan Henderson
(British Consul) and Helen Elizabeth Power.
Fitted at Walnut School, Brookline.
Class Status: 1891-92, II. Sci. Joined Class Senior year.
Degree: A.B. 1893.
Married (1) Ethel Josephine Garey at Newton Centre, Massachusetts,
22 August 1899 (died 22 January 1907).
Married (2) Mrs. Mabel Louise Reynolds at Hyde Park, Massachu-
setts, 21 November 1911. Child:
Richard Buffum, born 13 October 1916.
Now manufacturing electrical apparatus at Hyde Park, Massachusetts.

Since leaving college my principal occupation for the first
fifteen years was teaching in high schools, and I believe that this
was one of the worst occupations for me that I could have chos-
en, mainly because of my physical unfitness. During the second
fifteen-year period my principal occupation has been carrying
on a small electrical manufacturing business involving a very
large amount of experimental work on transformers, rectifiers,
etc.

During the World War, was not consulted by the President
regarding his general policy and was not specifically responsible for the defeat of Germany. Furthermore, I do not claim
to know all about the best methods of defeating the recent dry
amendment to the Constitution. (No, I cannot definitely recommend any particular bootlegger in this district, and feel
rather offended than otherwise at being called on as an expert
on such a subject).

Oliver Bridges henshaw

See Report VI, Page 147.

WILLIAM CARTER HEYWOOD

Born at Boston, 23 February 1872, of George Alpheus Heywood (lumber
merchant) and Martha Carter.
Fitted with J. C. Patton and at Phillips Exeter.
Class Status: Regular.
Degree: A.B. 1893.
Now practising law at New York City.

After graduation studied law and was admitted to the bar
of Hampden County, Massachusetts, in 1896. Practised for
some time at Holyoke, Massachusetts, under the firm name of

Green and Heywood. For the past twenty years have led a quiet
and uneventful existence, practising law in New York City, my
office having been all that time in Wall Street. The only
breaks have been a month each year spent in the mountains of
North Carolina. Still unmarried.

JAMES HENRY HICKEY

Born at Boston, 13 October 1871, of William James Hickey and Cath-
erine Amelia Graham.
Fitted at Boston Latin.
Class Status: Regular.
Degrees: A.B. 1893; LL.B. 1896.
Married (1) Gertrude Elizabeth Morse at Newtonville, Massachusetts, 3
June 1903 (died 19 December 1916).
Married (2) Gertrude Magdalen Fox, at Palm Beach, Fla., Feb. 26, 1919
(died Dec. 4, 1920).
Now practising law at New York City.

1893-1896: Harvard Law School. 1896: Entered office of
Duer, Strong and Jarvis, 50 Wall Street, New York City.
1897: Admitted to New York Bar. Entered office of Hayes and
Williams, 28 State Street, Boston. 1898: Admitted to Massachusetts bar. 1899: Opened law office, 53 State Street, Boston.
1899-1903: Practised in Boston. 1903: Law partnership, Morse,
Hickey and Kenny, 28 State Street, Boston. 1904: Opened law
office, 43 Exchange Place, New York City. 1904 to date: Practised in New York City.

Have been practising law continuously at No. 43 Exchange
Place, New York City, independently, since 1904, work em-
bracing general practice, both court and office work. 1907-
1908: Revised, with former Surrogate Robert Ludlow Fowler,
the well-known work "Gerard on Title to Real Property." Was
formerly, 1904-1910, active in Republican politics, during last
two years acting by special appointment as Special Deputy Attorney General for the State of New York. Otherwise never
sought or held public office, though as a progressive in 1912,
did my part and was nominated for Congress, and later for
Supreme Court, without, however, any chance for election.

Have travelled abroad and in United States considerably, but
mainly have kept hard at the practice of law, especially during
the last five years. Member: Harvard and University Clubs of
New York.

John Ashley Highlands

Born at Fall River, Massachusetts, 25 December 1869, of John Jay High-
lands (contractor) and Elizabeth Sanders.
Fitted at Fall River High.
Class Status: Special, 1891-92. IV. Scientific, 1892-93.
Degree: S.B. 1893.
Died of angina pectoris, 15 April 1920, at New York City.

"Big Jack,"—no wonder everyone knew and liked him.
With his enormous stature, his ever-smiling face, his pictur-
esque conversation and his simple affectionate disposition, few
men of Harvard have enjoyed a wider circle of friends. It is
significant that his closest friends were his oldest ones.—those
who grew up with him long before he became conspicuous as
an athlete. He had one outstanding characteristic which endeared him to his intimates,—a high degree of loyalty. When
a difficult situation arose on the baseball field or in private life,
he immediately absolved his associates of all blame, assumed
more than his share of responsibility and threw himself heart
and soul into the crisis. In a tight game, with his team making
errors, he would look around with a grin, saying "somebody's
got to play a little baseball," and then strike out the opposing
batters in one, two, three order. The same spirit actuated him
in his every day life. No sacrifice was too great for him to
make, once he had given his friendship.

A student of much more than average ability, an expert in
many sports, perhaps the greatest Harvard pitcher of all time,
he will long be remembered as an unselfish, lovable and great-
hearted friend.

B. W. T.

HENRY ARTHUR HILDRETH

Born at Lowell, Massachusetts, 7 September 1871, of Henry Albert Hil-
dreth (manufacturer) and Marion Estelle Welch.
Fitted at Boston Latin.
Class Status: Regular.
Degree: A.B. 1893.
Now living at Boston.

Topic "business life" covers entire history. August 18, 1893,
entered employ of The National Manufacturing Company, Worcester, Massachusetts, manufacturers of wire goods. January
17, 1894, elected secretary and to board of directors. Septem-

ber 6, 1894, elected President. January 18, 1905, was retired. September 1, 1905, entered employ of Library Bureau as general manager steel department. July 1, 1907, resigned. February 1, 1912, entered employ of Empire Paper Company, Boston and Ithaca, New York, as treasurer. May 1, 1914, resigned. April 23, 1915, recalled to Worcester to again become president of The National Manufacturing Company. September 1, 1922, resigned.

There has been literally nothing in my life since leaving college outside of business activities. In 1915 I was recalled to Worcester to again take up the management of the company with which I became associated upon leaving college but which had in the meantime been virtually wrecked by parties who forced me out in 1905. This company, The National Manufacturing Company, was merged in 1916 into The Morgan Spring Company. This consolidated company was merged in 1919 into The Clinton Wright Wire Company, and in 1920 all the consolidated companies were merged into The Wickwire Spencer Steel Corporation of which I became the export manager,—also continuing as head of the wire goods department represented by the products of the former National Manufacturing Company. On September 1, 1922, the management moved the general offices from Worcester to New York City, and as after forty years of residence in Boston I could not see my way clear to change it to New York, I resigned my position.

Having been for more than seven years with literally not a single day's vacation,—(except the 25th anniversary celebration) I am now enjoying a very thorough rest, with a little attention to some personal interests very much neglected during the last eight rather strenuous years. My present occupation (not "gainful") is looking for a new job.

John Lewis Hildreth, Jr.

Born at West Townsend, Massachusetts, 17 August 1870, of John Lewis Hildreth (Dartmouth 1864) (physician) and Achsah Beulah Colburn.
Entered from Dartmouth.
Class Status: I. Graduate, 1892-93.
Degrees: Litt.B. (Dartmouth) 1892; A.B. 1893; L.M. (Dartmouth) 1894.
Married Harriet Munson Bigelow at New York City, 1 June 1897. Children:

Harriet Smith, born 3 February 1900.
John Lewis, 3d, 4 June 1906.
Robert Faulkner, 11 August 1909.
Elizabeth Bigelow, 22 July 1911.
:Died of influenza, 3 December 1920, at Bayonne, New Jersey.

Although John Lewis Hildreth, Jr., received his Litt.B. degree from Dartmouth in 1892, and was only with us in our Senior year, receiving his degree from Harvard in 1893, he was well known to those members of the Class who were residents in Cambridge. He lived in Cambridge until after graduation and prepared for college at the Cambridge Latin School. His father was a prominent Cambridge physician living in the immediate vicinity of the College.   Hildreth was one of those men in school or college who possessed sterling and substantial qualities, had the respect of everyone, the liking of many, and the warm affection of those who knew him best.   In Dartmouth he was an athlete of some distinction, playing on his varsity football team.   During the year he spent at Harvard, without losing his loyalty to Dartmouth in any degree, and while he applied himself more particularly to his studies than to social activities, he was a loyal supporter of the College and a thorough believer in it.   He valued his Harvard degree all his life and from the conversations which the writer had with him it is evident that he appreciated his affiliation with the Class of 1893. Naturally modest, even at times to the degree of shyness, it was not to be expected that in one year he would acquire many new friends.   He did, however, renew his acquaintance with his older friends who had been at school with·him and they found him the same likeable fellow that he was in school.

After leaving Harvard he attended the Massachusetts Institute of Technology for some time, where he completed his professional training, although he did not pursue his studies to the extent of obtaining a degree.   He was a hydraulic engineer by profession.   For a short time he was in the employ of the Water Department of the City of Cambridge and then for several years was connected with the Metropolitan Water Board in Massachusetts.   His next work was with the Metropolitan Water Board of New York, being engaged on the ground water supply at Jamaica and Babylon, Long Island, and on tunnel construction at Cornwall-on-Hudson.   He was then engaged in the construction of the lower part of the Passaic Valley sewer in New Jersey. During the war he was employed in construction work for the government terminal at Port Newark. At the time of his death he was at the Bayonne plant of the Standard Oil Company of New Jersey. In all of these positions he was engaged in active executive work in the field, his particular ability being shown in the active construction work rather than upon the theoretical side of his profession. He was a member of the American Society of Civil Engineers and of the Harvard Engineering Society.

Although his death was premature, his life was a cause of congratulation for all who knew him. In school, in college, and in life he played a man's part in the world. He lived a clean, wholesome, active life and lived it well. If his career is to be measured in years it was comparatively short; if measured in service to his fellow men it was full and complete.

A.P.S.

ERNEST OSGOOD HILER

Born at Jamaica Plain, Massachusetts, 4 December 1871, of Thomas
  Greenleaf Hiler (cashier) and Mary Jane Clark.
Fitted at Roxbury Latin.
Class Status: Regular.
Degrees: A.B. 1893; LL.B. 1896.
Now practising law at Boston.

Have continued practice of law at 35 Congress Street, Boston, specializing in corporations, estates, and conveyancing. 1919: Visited Big Horn Forest Reservation and Yellowstone Park. 1920: Big Horn Forest, Yellowstone and Lion National Park. 1921: Porto Rico. 1922: Saddle and camping trip to Belly River Region, Glacier Park.

Sports, trail riding in the West and snow-shoe trips with Appalachian Mountain Club. Chairman, Music Committee, Harvard Club of Boston. Chairman, Entertainment Committee, Harvard Musical Association. Member, Board of Governors St. Botolph Club. In charge of music at all three clubs. Librarian, Harvard Musical Association. Member, Photo Guild of Society of Arts and Crafts, and of Camera Club of Boston Young Men's Christian Union.

David Hoadley

See Report VI, Page 151.

JAMES EDWIN HOLLAND

Born at Cincinnati, 1 May 1871, of John Holland (manufacturer)
and Catherine Elizabeth Ohlen.
Fitted at St. Xavier's Jesuit College.
Class Status: Special, 1889-93.
Now in business at New York City.

On January 1st, 1917, retired from the vice-presidency of
my father's business (fountain pens) in Cincinnati, after
twenty-three years' most active duty, having been general manager ever since leaving college in 1893. I retired upon medical
advice to travel for two years. That year I went to Florida,
and Cuba. In July, 1918, I took a 2,500-mile auto tour
through New England with our classmate C. P. Huntington.
As he was in a very nervous condition, I went to Florida with
him for the winter; but his health continued to fail after
his return to New York, and he passed away in October, 1919.

I remained in New York experimenting with various business propositions, one of which included a trip to Sweden for
six months, but ended most disastrously for me, owing to the
world collapse of prices in July, 1920. In the fall of 1922 I
learned of an opening where my business experience would fill
a need, a newly incorporated electric illuminating fixture concern, The Thompson Manufacturing Company, whose headquarters are in Washington, with commercial office in New
York City. I have high hopes of success with this venture, of
which I am sales director.

Throughout my residence in Cincinnati my spare time was
devoted to horseback riding for the most part and I was most
active in directing the Cincinnati Riding Club, of which I was
a vice-president. I played at golf some, but never performed
in a manner to be enthusiastic about. I belonged to the University, Queen City, Riding, Cuvier-Press Clubs in Cincinnati;
and in New York to the Harvard Club, which is my best address. I am in excellent health and spirits, and hope to enjoy
much in life here and in travel, which has always been my
greatest love.

JOSEPH CLARK HOPPIN

Born at Providence, Rhode Island, 23 May 1870, of Courtland Hoppin.
  [Brown 1855] and Mary Frances Clark.
Fitted at Groton.
Class Status: Regular.
Degrees: A.B. 1893; Ph.D. (Munich) 1896.
Married (1) Dorothy Woodville Rockhill at Washington, District of
  Columbia, 26 November 1901.   Child:
      Courtland, born 12 March 1906.
Married (2) Eleanor Dennistoun Wood at Islip, New York, 20 July
  1915.
Now living at Pomfret Center, Connecticut.

Between graduation from Harvard and our Twenty-fifth
Anniversary my life consisted in the main of study in Europe,
and teaching archaeology in the United States at Wellesley and
Bryn Mawr College. The winter of 1910-11 I acted as assistant to Richard Norton, '92, in the excavations at Cyrene, North-
Africa, which were carried on under him by the Archaeological
Institute of America. During the war I was called back to my
old position at Bryn Mawr to take the place of a man who had
been drafted. I resigned the position in the spring of 1919 and
since then have held no active position. I spent the winter of
1919-1920 in South America. The next winter (1920-1921) I
was sent to the Pacific Coast as one of the lecturers for the
Archaeological Institute and lectured on various topics before
the different societies of the Institute, from Vancouver to San
Diego. The summers of 1920 and 1921 I spent in Europe.

Two years ago an ulcerated tooth caused an illness which subsequently developed into cancer and for over a year my time
has been spent in and out of the hospital, undergoing no less
than five large and small operations, besides suffering perpetual
and intense pain. Thanks to the skill of my doctors, excellent
nursing and the constitution of an ox, the fight has been a
successful one, as far as can be told at present, and I think I
am safely out of the woods, though a few more months must
elapse before my cure is absolutely certain. The last operation has involved the removal of the entire jaw-bone, together
with most of the surrounding tissue.

As soon as my health permits, it is my intention to go to
Greece and conduct an excavation on the site of the Heraeum at

Argos. As I am no longer tied down in this country I hope to
do a good deal of independent work in both Greece and Egypt
in the years to come.

TRACY HOPPIN

Born at Providence, Rhode Island, 9 January 1871, of Frederick Street
    Hoppin [Yale 1856] (lawyer) and Clara Tracy.
Fitted at Berkeley School, Providence, Rhode Island.
Class Status: Regular.
Degree: A.B. 1893.
Married Constance Burlingame at New York City, 23 April 1907. Chil-
    dren:
        Philip Burlingame, born 13 September 1912.
        Barbara, 7 May 1916.
Now painting at New Hope, Pennsylvania.

After graduation and one year in the Harvard Law School,
I went abroad with the idea of returning to the Law School in
the autumn. Unfortunately I had a complete physical breakdown in Europe and spent the next eight years there in the pursuit of health. I returned in 1902 with a certain amount of
knowledge of the arts and a decided taste acquired for painting, and settled in New York City, where I began to study
seriously to become an artist. In 1907 I married Constance
Burlingame and continued to live in New York for ten years,
during which time I became the proud father of a future Harvard undergraduate. My health, however, was not quite equal
to the strenuous life in New York with its many distractions,
so I moved my family to New Hope, Pennsylvania, which is a
community of artists and afforded me great stimulus and companionship in my work. The real country conditions also give
me other jobs beside my painting for I find myself becoming
an expert on refractory furnaces and water pipes. In 1916
my daughter was born. Such is a brief account of my life up
to the last Class Report. The last five years have been peaceful,
happy and interesting to me, though there is nothing especial
to record. I have had the opportunity and pleasure of watching and helping on the development of my children and I have
made a decided advance in my work and received a certain
amount of recognition. There is nothing truer than the old
saying—"Ars longa, vita brevis est."

ELWIN LINCOLN HOUSE

Born at Lebanon, New Hampshire, 4 April 1861, of Jerome Bonaparte House (manufacturer) and Nancy Jane Fowler.
Entered from Boston University.
Class Status: Senior year only.
Degrees A.B. 1893; S.T.D. (Boston Univ.) 1894; D.D. (Furman, S. C.) 1899.
Married Sherlie De Forest Grow at Lebanon, New Hampshire, 10 May, 1883. Children:
Elmer Elwin, born 8 December 1884, A.B. Harvard, 1907.
Ray, 1 March 1887 (died 28 March 1887).
Arthur Everett, 16 November 1896.
Now lecturer and writer on Christian Psychology at Hood River, Oregon.

Entered the Congregational ministry after college and have been paster at Portland, Maine; Attleboro, Massachusetts; Providence, Rhode Island; Portland, Oregon; Spokane, Washington. Became Chaplain of the Fifth Massachusetts, U. S. A., Spanish American War.

Entered the lecture field, 1913, on Religious Psychology, and have written sixteen books and booklets .on this subject that have had a sale of two hundred and fifty thousand. I am still in this same field, touching the larger cities of the country. This will continue to be my life work. I have invitations now to go to England and Australia with my work, but have been unable to fill all the invitations in this country. My latest books are "The Psychology of Orthodoxy," "The Drama of the Face," "The Mind of God," "The Glory of Going On," "Simplified Psychology."

Philip Barthold Howard

See Report VI, Page 155.

WLLIAM DE LANCEY HOWE

Born at Fort Washington, Maryland, 19 November 1869, of Albion Paris Howe [West Point 1841] (United States Army) and Elizabeth Law Mehaffey.
Fitted at Browne and Nichols.
Class Status: Special, 1889-92. Joined Class Senior year.
Degrees: A.B. 1893; LL.B. 1896.

Married Clara Horton May at Cambridge, Massachusetts, 1 June 1901..
   Children,:
      Elizabeth May, born 5 March 1903.
      Katharine, 5 September 1905.
      Margaret De Lancey, 16 April 1907.
      Dorothy Sewall, 16 December 1912.
Now practising law at Boston.

This is the most taxing return of all, covering a period of thirty years, containing no items or schedules that can be answered intelligently by the word "None," allowing no deductions, and not even permitting the usual one and one-half per cent. personal exemption. It simply says: "Write about three hundred words" and "Sign here." It's wicked. (About 100).

After leaving the Law School in 1896 I spent three years. with a firm in Boston. In June, 1901, I was married to Miss. Clara H. May of Cambridge. In the fall of that year three other Harvard men and I opened the office we still occupy at 53 State Street. In 1903 Mrs. Howe and I moved from Boston to old Concord Town, expecting to stay there about a year, but. remaining twenty. Our children are all duly entered as Item 1, 2, 3, and 4 under Schedule C in the return filed in 1918.

During the last five years I have discovered no Pharaoh's: tomb, no theory of relativity, no twinkling little star many light-years away, no new concepts of the order and dimensions of the universe. And yet, in spite of these careless omissions, the years have been the fullest and happiest of all; closer companionship at home, larger and more responsible interests: abroad, and friendships ever stronger and more enjoyable.

IRA WOODS HOWERTH

Born in Brown County, Indiana, 18 June 1860, of John Howerth (farmer) and Elizabeth Amelia Bright.
Fitted at North Indiana Normal School.
Class Status: Entered Junior.
Degrees: A.B. 1893; A.M. (Univ. Chicago) 1894; Ph.D. (Univ. Chicago). 1898.
Married Cora Olive Cissna in Wayne County, Illinois, 16 August, 1881..
Now Professor Sociology and Economics in Colorado State Teachers College, Greeley, Colorado.

After leaving Harvard in 1893 I entered the University of Chicago, where after taking the A.M. and Ph.D. degrees I remained until 1912, with the exception of two years' leave, during which I served as secretary of the Illinois Educational Commission. I spent one vacation in Europe.

In 1912 I was called to the University of California as Professor of Education and Director of the University Extension Division. In this year I published two books. In 1918 I went to Europe and served in the Educational Corps of the A. E. F. I am now Professor of Sociology and Economy in the Colorado State Teachers College. During the past five years I have travelled extensively by automobile through the scenic portions of this country. Other details in former reports.

CHAUNCEY GILES HUBBELL

Born at New York City, 16 November 1870, of John Edward Hubbell (merchant) and Elmira Ostrander.
Fitted with D. Morgan.
Class Status: Regular.
Degree: A.B. 1893
Married Alice Denslow Slade at Cambridge, Massachusetts, 1 July, 1896.
    Children: .
        Richard Van Arsdale. born 27 March 1897.
        Roger Kingsley, 23 May 1898.
        Ruth Elsa, 14 October 1899.
        Rosalind Elizabeth, 26 May 1902.
        Ronald Edward, 16 October 1903 (died June 1912).
        Ednah Eloise, 24 June 1905.
Now in Massachusetts Registry of Motor Vehicles, at Boston.

Since leaving Cambridge, 1893, two years in Public Charity Bureau in Brooklyn, New York. Twelve years in active ministry in one parish of New Church or Swedenborgian denomination. Fifteen years with our Massachusetts Automobile Department. now called the Registry of Motor Vehicles, first as examiner and inspector, now as statistician and publicity man for the well-known chief of this department, Frank A. Goodwin.

JOHN HOMER HUDDILSTON

Born at Cleveland, Ohio, 9 February 1869, of George Kennedy (farmer) and Armina Robinson. Adopted by Adam Huddilston.
Entered from Baldwin University.
Class Status: Senior year only.
Degrees: A.B. (Baldwin, Ohio) 1890; A.M. (Baldwin, Ohio) 1892; A.B. 1893; Ph.D. (Munich) 1897,

Married Roselle Baker Woodbridge of Berea, Ohio, at London, England,
8 May 1896. Children:
  Rachel, born 7 February 1905.
  Homer, 10 March 1909.
Now Professor of Greek Language and Literature, and Art History, at
University of Maine.

The years in the life of a college instructor are quite likely to
glide by uneventfully, one much the same as the others. In my
own case the family relations indicated above continue to shed
their blessings and we all live cosily on our farm, troubled
neither about provisions for old age pensions nor the price of
coal. Mother earth in right measure and with the proper adjustments represents the best antidote for old age ills as they
usually crowd about the pathway of the underpaid teacher. Of
course we have to buy transportation to Boston before we are
fully conscious of being out in the cold world and where if we
had to stay and pay the butcher and the baker and the rest of
those fellows whose names do not begin with B the financial
distress would soon rob the four of us of most of that optimism
with which we view life.

I spent my first two years after leaving Harvard as Instructor in Greek at Northwestern University where I wrote ''Essentials of New Testament Greek,'' and which has had, I suppose, the most remarkable sales in the thirty years of its existence that any book of its kind has had. A text-book usually
lives a decade or so and gives way to others or such revisions as
means another book. This little book will sell further in its
third decade than in the first and second together. It went into
Chinese in 1917.

I went to Berlin and Munich, 1895-1898, where I made my
degree, returned to Bryn Mawr for a year (the usual length
of time in those years for one who failed to be ''interesting'')
and then came to Orono as the first Professor of Greek on the
change of the Maine State College to the University of Maine.
My wife and I returned to Italy, and I made another trip including Egypt and the Holy Land in 1912. These last few
years have been marked by the stay-at-home habit, promoted by
good health and wonderful Maine weather.

JOHN THOMAS HUGHES

Born at Watertown, Massachusetts, 24 August 1871, of Michael Hughes
and Sarah Dolan.
Entered from Boston College.
Class Status: Regular.
Degree: A.B. 1893.
Married Margaret Anna Purcell at Cambridge, Massachusetts, 19 October
1898 (died 11 April 1923). Children:
John Thomas, born 21 September 1899 (died 29 September 1901).
Edward Francis, 24 March 1901.
Thomas John, 16 April 1904.
Now practising law at Boston.

From 1893 to 1895 was in the Law School. Since that time
has steadily practised law at Boston. Wife, Margaret A., died
April 11. 1923.

GEORGE EDGAR HUME

Born at Indianapolis, Indiana, 19 March 1869, of James Madison Hume
and Mary Elizabeth Culley.
Fitted at Boston Latin.
Class Status: Regular.
Degrees: A.B. 1893; LL.B. (Univ. Indianapolis) 1895.
Married Lucy Fitzhugh Holliday at Indianapolis, Indiana, 16 November
1898. Children:
William Mansur, born 6 June 1900.
Jaquelin Holliday, 17 July 1905.
Now in insurance at Indianapolis, Indiana.

Returned to Indianapolis after graduation. Entered Indiana
Law School and took LL.B. degree. Practised law for several
years—firm name, Gates and Hume. Organized Indiana Title
Guaranty and Loan Company. Acted as its secretary-treasurer
for three years. Became treasurer of American Central Life
Insurance Company, which office I still hold. Organized Hume,
Mansur Company, of which I have been president for seven
years. Took my family to Europe in 1913, to the Orient in
1919, and to Hawaii in 1922. Have two sons. William, who is
living with Mrs. Hume and me in Pasadena, California. and
Jack, who is now in Phillips Exeter.

JOHN STROTHER HUMPHREYS

Born at Bardstown, Kentucky, 28 April 1872, of Samuel Carpenter
Humphreys [Georgetown] (Clergyman) and Mattie Scott Thurman.
Fitted at Georgetown, Kentucky.
Class Status: Entered Senior.
Degrees: A.M. (Georgetown) 1892; A.B. 1893; A.M. 1894.

Married 'Sue Hite Maxey at Louisville, Kentucky, 22 December 1896.
Children:
> Samuel Maxey, born 13 August 1898.
> Attie Eugenia, 18 August 1902.
Now Professor of Classical Languages at West Texas State Normal
College, Canyan, Texas.

I left Harvard in 1895 to accept a position in Boys' High
School, Louisville, Kentucky. After three years entered Chicago as candidate for degree of Doctor of Philosophy. Moved
to Texas in 1901 to accept position as co-Principal Howard
Payne College, Brownwood. Elected President Howard
Payne College, 1908; elected President Burleson College,
Greenville, Texas, 1913; elected President College of Marshall,
1918. Elected Registrar and Professor of Classical Languages
in West Texas State Normal College, 1921. This position I now
hold. During my more than twenty years in Texas, I have had
the usual experiences attendant upon the promotion of the denominational small college in the earlier stage of its development; in just three of them. No one of them passed out under
my administration. At last reports, they were all still living.
In my present position, I am not resting but I am enjoying freedom from financial cares. In the West Texas State Normal College there are each year over 2,000 students. There are still
just four in my family.

EDWARD LIVINGSTON HUNT

Born at New Orleans, 2 February 1871, of Carleton Hunt [H. C. 1856]
(lawyer) and Georgine Cammack.
Fitted at Phillips Exeter.
Class Status: Regular.
Degrees: A.B. 1893; M.D. (Columbia) 1896.
Married Margaret Emily Tobin at Austin, Texas, 8 October 1902. Child:
> Edward Livingston, Jr., 26 October 1904.
Now specialist in nervous and mental diseases at New York City.

Upon leaving college I entered the medical department of
Columbia University and in 1896 received the degree of M.D.
After two years of hospital service I began to practice medicine in New York City. During the past fifteen years I have
limited my practice to nervous and mental diseases. I am now
teaching neurology in Columbia University and am neurologist
to the Lincoln, City, French, and St. Luke's Hospitals. My address is 41 East 63rd Street, New York.

Robert William Hunter

See Report VI, Page 161.

Charles Pratt Huntington

Born at Logansport, Indiana, 22 November 1871, of Edward Staunton
Huntington (editor) and Julia Ann Pratt.
Fitted at Adams Academy.
Class Status: Regular.
Degrees: A.B. 1893; Certificat d'Etudes, Ecole des Beaux Arts, Paris,
1900.
Married (1) Maude Mary Bayly at Florence, Italy, 5 May 1894 (divorced
1913). Child:
    Vivienne Maude, born 25 April 1902.
Married (2) Eleanor ("Moretti") Rogers at New York City, 11 September 1913.
Died of pulmonary tuberculosis, 15 October 1919, at New York City.

Charles P. Huntington died at Bronxville, N. Y., on Wednesday, Oct. 15, 1919, after a brief illness, although he had not been in robust health for twelve or fourteen months. He spent the winter of 1918-19 at Passe-a-Trille, Florida, with James E. Holland '93, returning to New York in the spring somewhat benefitted by his sojourn in the south; but those who knew him best noted at the time that he was far from a well man. However, his death was entirely unexpected.

After graduation from Harvard, Huntington went abroad, and on May 5, 1894, married Maude Mary Bayly, daughter of General Abingdon Bayly of Camberly, England, at Florence, Italy, one child, Vivienne Maude, was born to them on April 25 1902. From 1895 until 1902 he made his home in Paris, where he studied at the Ecole des Beaux Arts. In 1904 he began the practise of his profession in New York, in which he was engaged until a short time before his death. In 1913 he married Eleanor Rogers, whose stage name was Eleanor Moretti of New York.

Charley, "Bunty," as he was known to his pals, had already won well-merited success as an architect when death stayed his heart and hand. The group of buildings at Broadway and 155 St., composed of the Hispanic Museum, the Church of Our Lady of Hope, the Numismatic Museum, etc., etc., will ever stand as a monument to his architectural ability. He was a firm friend of Archer M. Huntington, whose munificent generosity made possible the erection of the noteworthy structures that dominate the heights of Riverside Drive.

As a man he was loyal and devoted to his friends, a charming companion, with a sense of humor which served on many occasions to relieve the often necessary drabness of every day life. He never failed to be present at the class reunions in New York, and it was evident that he genuinely enjoyed these meetings. His death is a distinct loss to the Class—and to Harvard.

H. C. S.

Harold Hutchinson

See Report VI, Page 163, and Supplement, Page 127.

LINCOLN HUTCHINSON

Born at San Francisco, 10 April 1866, of James Sloan Hutchinson (banker) and Coralie Demorest Pearsall.
Entered from University of California.
Class Status: Graduate School, 1892-94; 1898-99.
Degrees: Ph.B. (Univ. California) 1889; A.B. 1894 as of 1893; A.M. 1899.
Now Professor of Commerce, University of California, and Special Investigator.

1894-1898: Ill-health; foreign travel and ranch life. 1898-1899: More graduate study, and degree of A.M. 1900-1923: member of faculty of University of California, at first as instructor in history and economics and since 1913 as professor of commerce. At various periods, absent on leave in the following occupations: 1905-1906: Special Agent, United States Department of Commerce, in Latin America. 1912-1913: Extensive travel investigating economic conditions. 1915-1916: Commercial Attaché, United States Embassy, Brazil. 1917-1918: United States War Trade Board and United States War Industries Board, Washington. 1918: Member of War Industries Board, Mission to England and France. 1919: Chief, American Relief Administration Mission, Czecho-Slovakia. 1920 January-August: Commercial Attaché, United States Embassy, London, August, 1920—September, 1921: Technical Advisor Government of Czecho-Slovak Republic. September, 1921, to date: Special Investigator American Relief Administration, Russian Unit, involving travel of some 20,000 miles in Russia.

At various intervals, travel in many parts of the world, studying economic conditions.

Clubs, etc.: Faculty Club, Berkeley; Bohemian Club, Harvard Club, and University Club, San Francisco; Cosmos Club, Washington; Savile Club, London; Fellow Royal Statistical Society, London; member, American Economics Association. Publications: "Panama Canal and International Trade Competition" 1913, and sundry articles in scientific and other periodicals. Still unmarried.

CHARLES EDWARD HUTCHISON

Born at Boston, 29 September 1872, of Charles Edward Hutchison and Mary Ann Elizabeth Sargent.
Fitted at E. H. Cutler's.
Class Status: Regular.
Degrees: A.B. 1893; S.T.B. (Epis. Theo. School, Cambridge) 1897.
Married Louise Humphreys Kendall at Cambridge, Massachusetts, 26 June 1902.
Now in Episcopal ministry at Christ Church, East Orange, N. J.

I was for one year a master at Pomfret School, and three years. a student at the Episcopal Theological School, Cambridge. Graduated there in 1897 and was ordained into the Episcopal ministry. For two years an assistant on the staff of Calvary Church, New York City. Work most interesting and varied. An excellent training for a beginner. 1899-1902, Rector of Grace Church, Avondale, Cincinnati, in a suburban residential district among very delightful people. 1902-1906, Vicar of the Church of the Ascension, Boston, on Washington Street, in the South end. Interesting and strenuous. 1906 to the present, Rector of Christ Church, East Orange, New Jersey; a parish of considerable size, which keeps me very busy.

Alpheus Hyatt, Jr.

See Report VI, Page 165.

GEORGE HOADLEY INGALLS

Born at Boston, 28 July 1872, of Melville Ezra Ingalls [Harv. Law 1863] (railroad president) and Abbie Stimson.
Fitted at Franklin School, Cincinnati.
Class Status: Regular.
Degree: A.B. 1893.

Married Katherine Davis Hinkle at Cincinnati, Ohio, 12 November 1898.
  Children:
      Katherine Elizabeth, born 6 September 1899.
      George Howard, 13 August 1904.
      Melville Ezra, 2d, 25 December 1906.
      Louise, 25 April 1908 (died 15 July 1909).
Now Vice-President New York Central Lines at New York City.

Went to work on the Chesapeake and Ohio, October 1, 1893,
at Richmond, Virginia, remaining there until April 1, 1895,
when I went with the same company at Huntington, West Virginia; after a year spent there, went to Cincinnati and worked
in my father's office, and in the fall of 1896 was appointed
assistant to the President in charge of the coal and coke traffic,
resigning in the fall of 1899. On January 7, 1900, was appointed Assistant General Freight Agent of the C. C. C. and St.
Louis Railway, and in the fall of 1902 was made General
Freight Agent. November 1, 1906, was made Freight Traffic
Manager of the New York Central Lines, west of Buffalo,
which position I held until in August, 1917,, when I was made
Traffic Manager. When the Government took over the operation of the railroads during the war I was appointed Resident
Traffic Assistant, then in February, 1919, Traffic Assistant and
in June, 1919, Senior Traffic Assistant to the Regional Director
of the Eastern Region. During that period I had a most interesting time; the work was hard but of such a nature as to be
interesting and all together a most valuable experience. November 1, 1919, I was appointed Vice-President of the Corporation of the New York Central Lines. Upon return of the carriers to the owners was appointed Vice-President of the various
lines composing the New York Central System in charge of
traffic, with headquarters in New York. During the process of
reorganizing the carriers upon their return have held a number
of positions in addition to that of Vice-President of our lines,
namely: Chairman of the Executive Traffic Committee of the
Eastern Territory; Chairman of the Traffic Division of American Railway Association, which represents all the railroads in
the United States. In addition to my railroad duties am Vice-
President of Virginia Hot Springs Company. Have not had
much opportunity for travelling for pleasure since leaving college, having made only one trip to Europe. My chief diversions
are riding and golf, and am now having difficulty in preventing

my boys from beating me in golf. My two boys are at St. Mark's School, the oldest one entering Harvard in the fall and the other in two years. We spend our summers at Murray Bay, Canada, where certain things that go to make life enjoyable are obtainable and of a good quality.

William Henry Isely

See Report VI, Page 167.

FREDERICK GIBBS JACKSON

Born at Lowell, Massachusetts, 22 October 1870, of Edward Payson Jackson [Amherst 1863] (teacher) and Helen Maria Smith.
Fitted at Boston Latin.
Class Status: Regular.
Degree: A.B. 1893
Married Ida Singer Robinson at Dorchester, Massachusetts, 25 July 1894.
    Child:
        Karl Frederick, born 18 December 1895.
Now teaching at Dorchester, Massachusetts.

The first two years out of college I spent in teaching sciences in the Lincoln, Nebraska, High School. Then followed two years in the Springfield, Mass., High School, a year and a quarter in Montclair, New Jersey, and since December, 1898, in the Dorchester High School, Boston, Massachusetts, where I have been head of the Science Department since 1906. Having spent the summer of 1905 in bicycling about in Europe, I felt that I was qualified to serve as an exchange teacher in Germany; so I spent from the Easter to the summer vacation, 1909, teaching in the Gymnasium Andreanum at Hildesheim, hard by the Harz Mountains. With my family I passed the balance of the summer travelling over the ground I had previously bicycled over. Again in 1913 I personally conducted a small party in Europe under the auspices of the Bureau of University Travel.

Having established this quadrennial custom of visiting Germany, I could not fail to maintain it by sending my son in 1917 as an officer in the 101st Engineers; and he was well on his way toward the Rhine when the Armistice stopped him at the Meuse. My own military share was performed as private and sergeant in the Massachusetts State Guard.

My summers, with only occasional exceptions, I spend at my
little cottage at Newfound Lake, New Hampshire, motor boating on the lake, and autoing and tramping about the foothills
and notches of the White Mountains. It is here also that I have
done some summer camp work both as a counsellor and a lecturer on scientific subjects at the boys' and girls' camps about
the lake.

PATRICK TRACY JACKSON

Born at Cambridge, Massachusetts, 7 November 1871, of Patrick Tracy
    Jackson, Jr., [Harvard 1865] (cotton merchant) and Eleanor Baker
    Gray.
Fitted at Browne & Nichols.
Class Status: Regular.
Degree: A.B. 1893.
Married Anne Smoot at Chicago, 11 April 1898. Children:
    Anna Loring, born 5 October 1904.
    Patrick Tracy, Jr., 19 November 1906.
    Jonathan, 3 September 1913.
Now cotton merchant and manufacturer at Boston.

I spent the first five years after graduating in a machine shop
and various cotton mills learning cotton manufacturing, and
the next four with Harding, Whitman and Company. In
1902 bought control of the Lowell Weaving Company, a tire
fabric mill and settled in Lowell. In 1908, organized the Warner Cotton Mills and Leroy Cotton Mills, spinning mills, and
combined the three into the Bay State Cotton Corporation.
Also organized Boston Yarn Company as commission house.
In 1909 helped reorganize the Passaic Cotton Mills. In 1910
helped organize the International Cotton Mills, composed
of the Consolidated Cotton Duck Company, Bay State Cotton Mills, Boston Yarn Company, and two Canadian mills,
I being manager of the last three. This year we moved to Cambridge. In 1911 helped organize American Textile Company,
later the American Tire Fabric Company. For the next few
years was busy developing and increasing production in the
cotton mills, and also spent considerable time inventing and developing machinery for a properly reinforced waterproof paper.

In 1917 withdrew from the International group and became
manager of the American Tire Fabric Company, my war work
consisting in organizing this mill to make gas mask duck and
running day and night. On my father's death in 1918, my

brother and I incorporated the P. T. Jackson Company, cotton merchants, which my grandfather had started fifty years before, and I became president. In 1920, started a company for manufacturing reinforced paper and after some hard struggles have gotten it on a successful basis.

The next year I became president of a land company in the Florida Everglades to grow sugar cane. Development is slow but prospects for the future are excellent. Last fall I bought a ranch in New Mexico and shall stock it with cattle this year, a play ground for my children as they get older. Am now organizing a company to develop fruit lands and lumbering in Honduras.

My wife and I have taken two European trips and have spent several vacations camping in Florida and cruising along the West Coast and Keys. We have taken two cruises among the off islands of the Bahama group and have been on several camping trips in Northern New Mexico. Play tennis, also yacht racing with the children in the summer.

Clubs: Harvard Club of Boston, Harvard Club of New York, Union Club, Boston; Lunch Club, Boston; Eastern Yacht Club, Manchester Yacht Club, Oakley Country Club, Military Order, Loyal Legion of United States.

THOMAS AUGUSTUS JAGGAR, JR.

Born at Philadelphia, 24 January 1871, of Thomas Augustus Jaggar [Gen. Theol. Sem.] (clergyman) and Anna Louisa Lawrence.
Fitted at Delancey School, Philadelphia.
Class Status: Regular.
Degrees: A.B. 1893; A.M. 1894; Ph.D. 1897.
Married (1) Helen Kline at San Francisco, 15 April 1902. Children:
    Kline, born 29 September 1905.
    Eliza Bowne, 2 November 1911.
Married (2) Isabel Peyran Maydwell at Hilo, Hawaii, 17 September 1917.
Now Director of Hawaiian Volcano Observatory and Volcanologist of the U. S. Weather Bureau.

I left College to study geology in Germany. Returned to Harvard (1895) as instructor in field and experimental geology, took a doctor's degree, worked summer times on the Geological Survey in western mountains and deserts, taught field summer schools, taught outside in Wellesley and Tech, became Regent and Assistant Professor at Harvard (1903) and then went over to Technology as Professor and Head of their geological department (1904). During this experience the two events that I now prize most were my acquaintance with President Eliot in the college office and faculty, and a trip to Martinique in 1902 that decided me on adopting the field study of geophysics as lifework. I became interested in education through some association with the university extension movement, entitled "Massachusetts College," an institution chartered by the legislature, but inoperative through lack of adequate endowment.

Numerous expeditions under Harvard and Technology to volcanic lands finally landed me in Hawaii (1911) and brought about the founding of the volcano observatory here, the establishment of a corporation known as the Hawaiian Volcano Research Association, and the joint control by this Association and Technology of a permanent station for volcano study. In 1919 by voluntary act of Congress this station was taken over by the U. S. Weather Bureau and volcano recording became a new activity of our Government. I remained in charge and the Research Association now supplements the Government work, still aided generously by Technology, in experiments and explorations. We assisted in founding the Hawaii National Park, and have made investigations of the lava tide, the depth and temperature of the lava lakes, the collection and analysis of volcanic gases, underground temperature by boring, and all the earthquake and eruption changes recordable during twelve years. In 1920 visited New Zealand in interests of the Pan-Pacific volcano observatory campaign.

My son is a freshman at Washington State University and my daughter is in school at San Francisco. The boy very properly wants to go to Harvard for professional studies and his interests are commerce and shipping; he has already been assistant engineer on a power plant and freight clerk on a steamship to South America.

I have come to believe that the most vital needs of the world are engineering and agriculture. Hawaii has both and is something of a paradise. These things are the fundamental, outdoor, human aims for all education.

Albert Cheney Johnson

See Report VI, Page 171.

George Fulton Johnson

See Report VI, Page 172.

PHILIP VAN KUREN JOHNSON

Born at Boston, 29 March 1869, of Charles Everett Johnson [Harvard 1853] (shoe manufacturer) and Marianne Webster.
Fitted at J. P. Hopkinson's.
Class Status: Scientific 1889-91.   Special, 1891-92.
Degrees: A.B. 1903 as of 1893; M.D. (Columbia) 1900.
Married Martha Therese Fisk at Port Chester, New York, 12 April 1904 (divorced 1919).   Child:
  Charles Everett, 2d, born 7 January 1905.
Now practising medicine at Los Angeles.

THE SECRETARY TO A CLAM

O Philip, always, up to now,
  Uncertain, coy, and hard to spot,
When pain and anguish wring my brow
  A ministering angel—not,
Again you shirk my frenzied call;
I think you do not care at all!

Yet Harvard gave you her degree,
  And bore your father on her roll;
And many a friend in '93
  Acounted you a genial soul.
"Noblesse oblige" would fit your case—
At least you might have saved your face.

I fancy had I asked your bill
  For curing me of ache or pain,
You would have answered promptly, Phil—
  But this is something else again.
When you must give, not take, the loot,
The shoe is on the other foot.

Well, go thy ways! The class will live
  In history, even though you pout.
And if you do not wish to give
  Your history, I can leave it out.
I don't suppose it matters much—
But Phil, your manners beat the Dutch!

Edward Renshaw Jones, Jr.

See Report VI, Page 174.

JAMES FRANCIS JONES

Born in Carmarthenshire, South Wales, 1 June 1864, of Benjamin Jones
    (minister) and Margaret Evans.
Entered from Marietta College.
Class Status: Scientific, 1892-93.
Degrees: V.S. (Ontario Veterinary Coll.) 1886; S.B. (Marietta) 1892;
    B.S. 1893; M.D. (Univ. of Cincinnati) 1896.
Now writing and lecturing at New York City.

At age of twenty entered the Ontario Veterinary College at
Toronto, completed the two-year course, and received its degree
of V.S. in 1886.   Practised veterinary medicine at Zanesville,
Ohio, 1886-89.   Entered Marietta College at Marietta, Ohio, and
received its degree of S.B. in 1892.   Was a fourth-year student
of anatomy and physiology in the Scientific School 1892-93
(registering from Greenville, Ohio), and received the degree
of B.S. in 1893, *cum laude*.   Entered the medical department
of the University of Cincinnati and received its degree of M.D.
in 1896, with license to practise in Ohio.   At the same time
(1893-96) was lecturer in the Ohio Veterinary College at Cincinnati and instructor in biology at Marietta.   From 1896 to
1899 was assistant professor at Marietta.   During this period
was also interested in study of social questions, and was one of
the "Committee of Fifty for Investigation of the Liquor Problem."   (See its publications by Houghton, Mifflin & Co.).   His
leading preoccupation, however, was the Welsh movement in this
country.   At Marietta he worked hard to establish a Cambrian
or Welsh professorship, for instruction and research in Welsh
history, literature, and art.   In 1901 he became secretary of the
"Pan-Racial Institute," organized at Philadelphia under the
auspices of David Starr Jordan, Hugo Munsterberg, Jacob A.
Riis, Theodore S. Woolsey, and others, and consisting mainly
of a Welsh or Cymric department.   In 1908 the Institute shifted
its headquarters to Chicago.

He now reports: "From 1912 to 1916 was ranching in New
Mexico, associated with the late C. J. (Buffalo) Jones, than
whom no one is generally credited with having achieved more
for the rescuing of the American bison from extinction.   Volun-

teered, on America's entrance into the War, for any service deemed qualified to render in either Army or Navy, but with negative result. Entered the overseas service of the Y. M. C. A. and sent to France. Assigned to the Cinema Department at Brest; transferred to the Social Hygiene Department and as-signed to lecture at 'Post Schools', located at Bar-sur-Aube, St. Joire, and other points in France; transferred to Coblenz and assigned to the Second Division with headquarters at Neuwied, finally transferred to the Third Division with headquarters at Andernach. Returned to America in August, 1919, and took up residence at New York City. Since concerned largely with the elaboration of the art concept of life, and with ways and means for its practical expression in the daily affairs of exist-ence, individual and collective. This under the assumption that 'It is only as human behavior expresses itself in terms of high art that life at its best can come into being.' This approach to life and its problems and possibilities has received the earnest endorsement of many of the most eminent thinkers and men and women of practical affairs in the country, and has resulted in the formation of 'The Greater Art League.' ''

Edgar Alonzo Rabarl

See Supplement to Report VI, page 127.

GEORGE HOWARD KELTON

Born at Hubbardston, Massachusetts, 20 September 1861, of Elihu
    Kelton, Jr. (farmer) and Susan Jane Hathorn.
Entered from Middlebury College.
Class Status: Left Senior year.
Married Ruth Sarah Coolidge at Petersham, Massachusetts, 24 March
    1893. Children:
        Margaret Susana, born 24 October 1894 (married Norman C.
            Linden of Baltimore, 14 February 1920).
        Elihu Howard, 4 January 1897.
        Lawrence Eliot, 22 December 1899 (died 15 December 1901).
        Richard Coolidge, 13 June 1902.
Now farming at Hubbardston, Massachusetts.

There is ''nothing to add to the last report,'' except in addi-tion to my farming I have been connected with the State Fer-tilizer Inspection, for several years as Deputy-Inspector. Also, in a very small way for some time I have been doing some little work for the Bureau of Crop Estimate of the United States Department of Agriculture. In my farming, I am starting a herd of pure bred Herefords.

My son, Elihu Howard, enlisted in the aviation service of the Army and soon went to France in active service through the war and is now about to finish his course in the Harvard Engineering School.

JOHN MARTIN KENDRICKEN

Born at Boston, 25 November 1870, of Paul Henry Kendricken (mechanical engineer) and Cecilia Garvey.
Fitted at Boston Latin.
Class Status: Regular.
Degrees: A.B. 1893; LL.B. 1896.
Married Mrs. Priscilla (Alden) Kimball at New York City, 15 October 1919.
Now practising law at Boston.

In the summer of 1894 I took a bicycle trip through France, Belgium, etc., In 1895 travelled through the British Provinces, camping on St. John River, etc. In March of 1897, after finishing my course at the Law School and taking the degree of LL.B. the previous year, I entered on the practice of law in the Tremont Building, Boston. On January 1, 1901, I formed with W. S. Bangs ('92) the law firm of Bangs and Kendricken, with offices in Barristers Hall, Boston. This partnership lasted until 1905 and on June 1, 1906, I removed my offices to the Exchange Building, Boston. In 1918 I removed to 68 Devonshire Street, Boston, where I remain at this writing. These dates mark the milestones in a busy professional life. I have continued to practice law diligently for the past five years. During that period I have travelled very little, but I have got married and set up an establishment at 199 St. Paul Street, Brookline.

I have kept up my interest in trap shooting, hunting, and yachting. I hold no public position or offices nor do I seek any. During the past year I was elected to the council of the Massachusetts Commandery of the Military Order of the Loyal Legion of the U. S. A., and also to the Council of the Massachusetts Commandery of the Naval Order of the U. S. A.

RICHARD HUNTER KENNEDY

Born at Little Rock, Arkansas, 25 May 1868, of James William Kennedy [Univ. of Virginia] (publisher) and Mary Venable.
Entered from Vanderbilt University.
Class Status: Entered Sophomore.
Degree: A.B. 1896 as of 1893.
Married Clara Ellen Gill at Brockton, Massachusetts, 28 June 1892.
Children:
  Olivia Poindexter, born 14 May 1893.
  Louise Venable, 25 July 1895.
  Richard Merrill, 15 November 1896 (died 8 February 1919, at Evacuation Hospital No. 9, A. E. F.)
  Theodore Adams, 20 April 1898 (Private, 1st class, 27th Co., 166th D. B., A. E. F.)
  Alfred Gill, 20 June 1899.
  Laura Payne, 1 June 1902.

Kennedy entered the preparatory department of Vanderbilt University (Nashville, Tennessee) in the autumn of 1886, but in 1889 came to the theological department of Boston University, where he studied for a year, preaching meantime at West Abington, Mass. The next year he entered Harvard as a sophomore. In January, 1892, he began work with the Congregational church of Linden, a part of Malden, Mass., and in September was ordained there, having married in June. An attack of illness just before Commencement, 1893, prevented him from taking his degree in course. During the next two years he studied in the Divinity School, and in 1895 took the pastorate of Pepperell, Mass., where he remained for two years. He then accepted a call to San Mateo, California, thence going to Albany, Oregon. In 1902 he moved to Forest Grove, Oregon, preaching in Hillsboro near by. Two years later he removed to Cornwallis, Oregon, and gradually gave up the ministry in favor of lecture work, managing Lyceum courses, etc. Losing all his belongings by fire he removed to Salem. Oregon, about 1908, where he engaged in poultry farming. In 1912 he took a farm at Newberg, Oregon, and in 1913 went to the Indian School at Chemawa, Oregon, where he remained four years in charge of the religious instruction. He then went to Portland, Oregon, and returned to Chatauqua and Lyceum lecturing with the Redpath Bureau. He was last heard from at Chicago in 1918, while engaged in this work. Since then all efforts to locate him have been unsuccessful, and he occupies the unique position of being the only ''lost man'' now on the secretary's list.

WILLIAM HOWLAND KENNEY

Born at Leominster, Massachusetts, 22 July 1871, of Clarence Kenney
(manufacturer) and Elizabeth Carver Howland.
Fitted at Leominster High.
Class Status: Special, 1889-90.
Married Grace Lawrence Burrage at Leominster, Massachusetts, 15 Sep-
tember 1903. Children:
  Elizabeth Burrage, born 25 August 1905 (died 13 September 1906).
  William Howland, 2d, 29 October 1907.
Now teaching at Emerson College of Oratory, Boston.

Began as a public singer and teacher of singing in New York
City. Then became interested in teaching the speaking voice.
After several years of this, left the New York field, came to
Boston, and in 1900 became associated with Emerson College,
since when there has been no change in positions held, or occupation. The Commonwealth of Massachusetts in 1919 granted
us (Emerson College) the privilege of conferring the degree of
B.I.L. (Bachelor of Literary Interpretation). Our degree
work is accepted by accredited colleges and universities
throughout the country; in some instances credits for as much
as three years being allowed on a B.A. or B.S. course. Our
graduates are serving as teachers of oral and written English
in leading institutions in every state. This recognition of our
effort is no small compensation for years of hard constructive
work in building an institution, which today is recognized as
the leading school of its kind in the world. I hope my son will
be a Harvard man of the Class of 1930.

WILLIAM EDWARD KENT

Born at Binghamton, New York, 17 October 1870, of George Albert
Kent (cigar manufacturer) and Nancy Jane Dietrick.
Fitted at Phillips Andover.
Class Status: Special, 1889-93.
Married Mary Louise Roberts at Binghamton, New York, 20 January
1900. Children:
  William Edward, Jr., born 9 December 1900.
  Robert Percy, 26 December 1902.
  Beatrice Jane, 24 June 1904.
  Gertrude Louise, 27 October 1905.
  Richard George, 26 December 1907.
  Donald James, 19 September 1909.
  John Walter, 20 November 1911.
  Harold Paul, 24 October 1913.
Now ''leading a retired life'' at Binghamton, New York.

After leaving college made four trips abroad, studying sing-- ing among other things. Engaged in the piano and music busi- ness with his brother, H. F. Kent, at Binghamton, New York.. Was then in Philadelphia for awhile tutoring. During the Spanish War joined Battery A of Philadelphia, composed of college men, and served in Porto Rico. On his return went to work in his father's factory at Binghamton, New York, but was compelled to give up the position on account of his eyes. Tried out-of-door life and the real estate business in Philadelphia.. About 1903 returned to Binghamton and took up farming,. where he has been located ever since, being still troubled with bad eyes.

Charles Walter Keyes

Born at Newton, Massachusetts, 16 January 1871, of Henry Keyes (rail-- roads) and Emma Frances Pierce.
Fitted with W. Nichols and Hopkinson's.
Class Status: Special, 1889-91. Joined Class Junior year.
Degree: A.B. 1893.
Married Phebe Everett Reynolds at East Orange, New Jersey, 21 August 1912. Child:
    Phebe, born 23 July, 1916.
Died of angina pectoris at East Pepperell, Massachusetts, 14 August 1921.

Charles Walter Keyes, the third son of Henry Keyes and Emma Frances Pierce, was born at Newton, Massachusetts, January 16, 1871. He attended Chauncey Hall School, William Nichols' private school, and finished his preparation at Hop- kinson's School, entering Harvard as a Special Student in the fall of 1889. He joined the Class of 1893 at the beginning of the Junior year and graduated with it. In August, 1894, he entered the employ of the Nashua River Paper Company at East Pepperell, Massachusetts, later becoming Secretary of this com- pany, of which his brother, George T. Keyes, was President, and took a very active part in its management on the produc- tion. In this occupation, with the exception of a few months in 1912 during which time he temporarily retired from business, he spent the rest of his life.

In January, 1912, Keyes was one of a party, of which I was a member, to make a trip to Hawaii, Japan and Korea, and thence by the Trans-Siberian Railway to Russia, returning home through Germany, France and England. The close association on this trip brought out very strongly Charlie's many attractive traits as a companion, always interested in the doings of the moment and ready at all times for adventure of any sort. Miss Reynolds, whom he married in August, 1912, was also a member of the party and they met for the first time as we boarded our train in New York.

Charlie was deeply interested in athletics and sports of all kinds, and in his first year in college took an active part in rowing as a member of the Freshman crew. An accident in which he seriously injured his knee unfortunately put a stop to further rowing after his Freshman year. Although at times greatly handicapped by this disability, Charlie seized every opportunity for shooting, coon hunting and field trials, in which sports his love for dogs and his skill in handling them gave him his greatest pleasure. His "Hillcrest Kennels" at East Pepperell were well known. He was by nature an excellent judge, not only of dogs but cattle, sheep and horses as well, and his ability was greatly increased by careful study and training. For many years he was considered one of the best judges of dogs in the American Kennel Club.

As a friend, those who were fortunate enough to break through his natural reserve, which made him careful and deliberate in admitting others to intimate relationship, found him sympathetic, loyal and ready to make any sacrifice on behalf of others. In his family he showed particularly that spirit which was apparent in other intimate relationships. Devoted to his mother and sisters, and maintaining a wonderfully intimate and affectionate relationship with his two brothers, he thoroughly enjoyed home and home life, and when he married and his daughter was born his happiness in his domestic relations was complete. The courage with which he faced his final illness and the anxiety he showed to spare his family were just those qualities all who knew him realized were fundamental to his character.

C. C. G.

Frederick Palmer Kidder

See Report VI, Page 178, and Supplement, Page 128.

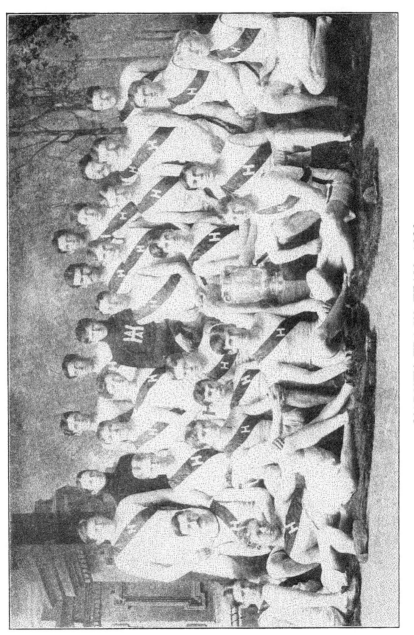

VARSITY TRACK TEAM, 1893

DAVID KIMBALL

.Born at Boston, 7 July 1870, of David Pulsifer Kimball [Harvard 1856] (lawyer) and Clara Millet Bertram.
.Fitted at Hopkinson's.
Class Status: Regular.
Degrees: A.B. 1893; A.M. 1897.
Married Amalia Ingeborg Gardiner at Bath, New Hampshire, 21 September 1903.
Now writing plays in Europe.

Took a trip round the world in 1893-94. From 1894 to 1897 was a student of literature and history in the Graduate School, taking his A.M. in the last named year. The next year was in the Law School. In 1899-1900 passed two terms at Oxford and one at Cambridge, England; 1900-'01 in Italy and Austria; 1901-'02 at Stanhope-Wheatcroft Dramatic School, New York City, and received its diploma. Since that time has been interested in playwriting. Owing to Mrs. Kimball's health, spent much of time since marriage in France, largely at Berck-Plage. Also took in various interesting foreign events, such as the Passion Play in 1910, the coronation of King George V. in 1911, etc. In 1914-15 studied playwriting at Cambridge with Professor Baker. Went to California and spent till 1919 at Santa Barbara. Since then has been mostly abroad again, sometimes in London and sometimes in Paris or the south of France; still interested in dramatic work.

WILLIAM GHOLSON KITTREDGE

.Born at Cincinnati, Ohio, 22 October 1869, of Edmund Webster Kittredge [Dartmouth 1852] (lawyer) and Virginia Gholson.
.Fitted at Adams Academy.
Class Status: Left during Sophomore year.
Degree: LL.B. (Cincinnati) 1895.
Married Katharine Leaman at Cincinnati, Ohio, 16 June 1898 (died 9 January 1920). Children:
    Virginia, born 7 April 1899.
    Robert Leaman, 29 January 1901.
    Margot Gray, 26 May 1902.
    William Gholson, 27 January 1904 (died 10 March 1908).
    Edmund Webster, 3 July 1905 (died 24 June 1906).
    William Gholson, 13 January 1909.
    Edmund Webster, 5 December 1910.
    Kitty Phillips, 15 January 1913.
Now residing at Cincinnati, Ohio.

Was obliged to leave college in March of our Sophomore year
on account of pneumonia. Then went to the University of
Bonn for five semesters. In 1892 I entered the Law School of
Cincinnati College and in 1895 received the degree of Bachelor
of Law, with grant to practice in the State of Ohio. For several years, accordingly, I was in my father's law firm at Cincinnati. In 1901 removed to "Ridgeway Plantation" near
Cole's Ferry, Virginia, and took up farming. Did fairly well,
but our most successful crops were boys and girls. I returned
with my family to Cincinnati in December of 1919, having lived
for nineteen years in Virginia. I am engaged in no "business,
profession, or official position" at present. I have a little to do
in looking after my property. We spend two months or more
in Maine nearly every year.

ROBERT EVERETT KLINE

Born at Miamisburg, Ohio, 17 February 1868, of Jonathan Henry Kline
   and Mattie Stanfield.
Entered from Otterbein University.
Class Status: III Scientific 1892-93.
Degrees: A.B. (Otterbein) 1892; S.B. 1893.
Married Agnes Louise Lyon at Dayton, Ohio, 5 June 1895. Children:
   Robert Everett, Jr., born 29 April 1898.
   Donald Chenoweth, 23 May 1904.
Now with U. S. Shipping Board, Emergency Fleet Corporation, at Wash-
   ington.

Associate engineer, Dayton, Ohio, Sewer System, 1893-1894-
1895. County engineer, Dayton, Ohio, 1895-1901. Chief Engineer, construction of a number of inter-urban railways, at
Dayton, Ohio, 1901-1905. Contracting and engineering structures, bridges, railways, sewers, highways and streets; also consulting engineer, 1905 and 1907-1917, at Dayton, Ohio. City
engineer, Dayton, Ohio, 1906-1907. President Ohio Society of
Civil Engineers, 1906-1907. With United States Shipping
Board Emergency Fleet Corporation, 1917 to date. Plant engineer, Philadelphia, 1917-1918; district plant engineer, Boston, 1918-1919. Manager Eastern District Supply and Sales
Division, 1920. Special assistant to chairman, 1921. Head
claim section, and special assistant, 1921 to date.

THEODORE WESLEY KOCH

Born at Philadelphia, 4 August 1871, of William Jefferson Koch (merchant) and Wilhelmina Bock.
Entered from University of Pennsylvania.
Class Status: Entered Senior.
Degrees: A.B. (Univ. Penn.) 1892; A.B. 1893; A.M. 1894.
Married Gertrude Priscilla Humphrey at Lansing, Michigan, 27 November 1907. Child:
Dorothy Alden, born 17 August 1913.
Now University Librarian, Northwestern University, Evanston, Illinois.

Assistant, Cornell University Library, 1895-1900, in charge of the Fiske Dante Collection (compiled catalogue, published in two volumes). Published "Dante in America," 1897. Spent 1900-1901 at the University of Paris and the Collège de France. Assistant, Catalogue Division, Library of Congress, 1902-1904. Assistant Librarian, University of Michigan, 1904-1905. Librarian, University of Michigan, 1905-1915. Chief, Order Division, Library of Congress, 1916-1919. Librarian, Northwestern University, 1919 to date.

Publications: A Portfolio of Carnegie Libraries, 1907; Library Assistants Manual, 1913; Books in Camp, Trench and Hospital, 1917; A Book of Carnegie Libraries, 1917; British Censorship and Enemy Publications, 1917; War Service of the American Library Association, 1918; War Libraries and Allied Studies, 1918; Books in the War, the Romance of Library War Service, 1919 (of which a French translation was published: Les Livres à la Guerre, 1920); Les Bibliothécaires d'Antan, 1922; The Leipsig Book Fair; Rebuilding the Louvain Library, 1923.

Favorite recreation: European vacation travel. Goes across whenever he can get leave of absence, the money, and the family's permission.

GAILLARD [THOMAS] LAPSLEY

Born at New York City, 14 November 1871, of Howard Lapsley (stockbroker) and Katherine Aldis Willard.
Fitted at Berkeley School.
Class Status: Regular.
Degrees: A.B. 1893; A.M. 1894; Ph.D. 1897; Hon. M.A. (Cambridge Univ. England) 1904; M.A. (Cambridge) 1920.
Now Fellow, Lecturer, and Tutor of Trinity College, Cambridge, England.

October, 1893 to June, 1894: Harvard Graduate School.
1894-1895: Travelling in Europe. 1895-1897: Harvard Graduate School. 1897-1898: Research in London. 1898-1899: Study
and writing in New York. 1899-1900: Instructor at Harvard.
October, 1900 to January, 1901: Instructor at Harvard. January, 1901 to June, 1901: Assistant Professor at Leland Stanford, Junior, University. August, 1901, to June, 1903: Instructor, and afterwards Assistant Professor at University of California. 1903-1904: Assistant Professor, University of Pennsylvania. 1904 to date: Fellow and Lecturer, and afterward Tutor in
Trinity College, Cambridge.

From the early part of 1908 until the autumn of 1910 I was
prevented from working by a serious illness. I passed the winter of 1908-1909 in Colorado and California, and that of 1909-
1910 in Egypt. Before this and up to and including 1917, I
habitually passed my summers in America. Since I took the
responsibilities of the tutorship, it has been impossible for me
to go far away or for a long period. The word "tutor" does
not mean here what it did to us in our undergraduate days,
and this is an illustration of the truth that what really keeps
England and America apart is the fact of having a common language.

The five years that have elapsed since the black days of
March, 1918, have been a reconstruction which has made it
clear to many of us that we are no longer even middle-aged men.
There are moments when one resents that and is tempted to
protest that though old one is not yet senile. But such times
are rare and one finds that there is still a great deal of work
to be done, and that it is still full of an interest and even an
excitement that cannot be explained to people who have not
voluntarily chosen the teaching profession and stuck to it.
When one is in sight of the end of one's active life—I shall be
superannuated in nine years time if I live so long—it's some
thing, indeed it's a very great deal, to feel that I have kept in
pretty close relation with certain Harvard friends, one of the
closest, as is fitting, a classmate. Since the war there have
been many of the younger generation here and some of them,
including all the scholars who have come on Charles Fiske's
generous foundation, have been in my charge.

I am not married and I do not expect to be—but I am

aware that the world contains a good many silly women and some desperate ones. In 1920 the University adopted a statute making it possible to confer the full degree of M.A. upon men who like myself were neither qualified to incorporate nor holding a University office. Thereafter they took me before the Vice-Chancellor, who made an honest man of me.

RALPH CLINTON LARRABEE

Born at Kalamazoo, Michigan, 5 December 1870, of McIvah Larrabee (merchant) and Abbie Josephine Glover.
Fitted at Boston English High.
Class Status: Regular.
Degrees: A.B. 1893; M.D. 1897.
Married Ada Perkins Miller at Newton, Massachusetts, 17 September 1900. Child:
    Martin Glover, born 25 January 1910.
Now practising medicine at Boston.

For the past five years I have kept right on with my professional work—whose racy details I may not divulge. I am still on the staff of the Boston City Hospital, but I resigned my position at the Medical School at the close of the war. About this time the hospital established a laboratory and special clinic for the study of diseases of the blood, and I am at the head of this work.

No "voyages and travels" worthy of note, and no "sports and pastimes" except wood-chopping and such mountain-climbing in New Hampshire as is possible for a fat man of fifty-two. In connection with this hobby I have been interested in the "sport of trail-building" in the White Mountains, and have had charge of the construction of one or two trails for the Appalachian Mountain Club. As chairman of this club's Guide-Book Committee I have been in charge of the publication of the fourth and fifth editions of its "Guide to Paths in the White Mountains." Apart from this guide-book I have published nothing but a few medical articles dealing mostly with diseases of the blood.

GEORGE WARRINGTON LATHAM

Born at Port Byron, New York, 28 September 1870, of George Warrington Latham (banker) and Mary Smith Kelly.
Fitted at Auburn High, New York.
Class Status: Regular.

Degree: A.B. 1893.
Married Alice Brockway of Moravia, New York, at Waukegan, Illinois,
    20 July 1902. Children:
        Allan, born 21 February 1906.
        Sylvine Elizabeth, 16 June 1909.
Now Associate Professor of English at McGill University, Montreal.

Latham, afflicted with sudden shyness, persistently refuses
to send any information for this report. The following facts
are culled from his previous excellent reports:

1893-94, teacher of Greek and Latin at Delaware Institute,
Franklin, New York. 1894-1900, teacher of Greek and English
in High School at Auburn, New York. 1900-01, student of
English at University of Chicago. 1901-07, instructor in English at Brown. 1907 to date, teaching English at McGill University, Montreal—for many years as lecturer, now as associate
professor.

ARTHUR GORDNER LEACOCK

Born at Lehman, Pennsylvania, 27 May 1868, of John Clarke Leacock
    (clergyman) and Lydia Gordner.
Entered from Syracuse University.
Class Status: Graduate School, 1892-94, 1896-97, 1898-99.
Degrees: A.B. (Syracuse) 1892; A.B. 1893; A.M. 1894; Ph.D. 1899.
Married Anne Adams Brown at Little Boar's Head, New Hampshire, 24
    August 1911.
Now teaching at Phillips Exeter Academy.

The first six years after graduation I spent partly in the
Graduate School, partly in getting experience in teaching, and
partly in travel in Greece and Italy. A portion of my sojourn
in Europe was to study at Munich, at a time when there was
still thought to be virtue in the German Universities. After
receiving my final degree in the classics at Harvard in 1899 I
came to Exeter where I have remained until the present time,
engaged in the pleasant work of teaching Greek to high-spirited
American boys. As one of the older men in the school I have
had an increasing amount of committee work to do. Am Curator of the portraits and other art objects of the Academy, a
member of the Scholarship Committee, Chairman of the Library
Committee, and a member of the Problem Committee—the latter an organization somewhat like the Homeric Council of Eld-
ers.

When I married in 1911, I turned architect. I remodeled

a decrepit colonial house to live in and developed an old-fashioned perennial garden. At the sea-shore, a little later, I built a bungalow after my own plans. I have held no offices in the State, although I received one vote as Sheriff of Rockingham County last fall. In the Church, I am treasurer of Christ Church Parish, Exeter. My avocation is music. I play the 'cello in the Faculty Trio. We are all amateurs, but for us no technical difficulties exist, or if they do, we treat them with high disregard.

Any success I may have had in these various activities is due to Harvard College, the study of Greek, and contact with the powerful thinkers of the class of 1893.

Walter Augustus Lecompte

See Report VI, Page 184.

CHARLES HENRY LINCOLN

Born at Millbury, Massachusetts, 22 April 1869, of William Henry Lincoln [Bowdoin Med.] (physician) and Eunice A. Reid.
Fitted at Worcester Academy.
Class Status: Regular.
Degrees: A.B. 1893; A.M. 1894; Ph.D. (Univ. of Penn.) 1896.
Married Mary Frances Angell at Lewiston, Maine, 28 August 1901.
Now in geneological and historical work at Worcester, Massachusetts.

Upon graduating I taught history and economics at Bates College in 1894-1895, following with three years in the University of Pennsylvania, the first as candidate for Ph.D., the last two as Senior Fellow with work of instruction in American history. I then went to the Library of Congress, where from 1898 to 1907 I was engaged in arranging, calendaring, and editing for publication historical manuscripts. After 1907 I was busy at the American Antiquarian Society in Worcester, doing like work upon the manuscripts of that institution and supervising the publication of some of its most valuable documents until the autumn of 1910.

Since 1910 I have been engaged as archivist and historian along the same lines but in broader fields. Among my published books are: "The Revolutionary Movement in Pennsylvania"; "A Calendar of John Paul Jones Manuscripts";

"Naval Records of the American Revolution"; "Manuscript
Records of the French and Indian War"; "The Correspondence of William Shirley, Governor of Massachusetts"; "Early
Narratives of Colonial Indian Wars"; besides various magazine
articles and press contributions. During 1914 and 1915 I gathered for the National Government the originals or secured
photostat copies of original manuscripts in Massachusetts
dealing with her participation in the Revolutionary War.

In 1916 and 1917 I was arranging for the University of Illinois its collection of historical manuscripts. With the outbreak
of the war I returned to Worcester and served on several committees for French relief and correspondence with volunteers.
I was also treasurer of a fund for fatherless children in France.
Since then my father-in-law, a former professor in Bates College, now eighty-five years of age and retired, has been with me
and I have remained in Worcester. I am also a Chautauqua
lecturer. I am ninth by descent from Thomas Lincoln, "the
miller" who came from England to Hingham, Massachusetts in
1635. Mrs. Lincoln is eighth from Miles Standish of Plymouth.
Member: American Historical Association, Naval Historical
Society. Worcester Enonomic Club, Worcester Historical Society, Worcester Harvard Club.

ERIC ISIDORE LINDH

Born at Chicago, 30 July 1870, of Oliver Lindh (clergyman) and Brita
      Mary Byberg.
Fitted at Berlitz School of Languages.
Class Status: Special, 1889-90. Joined Class Sophomore year.
Degrees: A.B. 1893; A.M. 1896.
Married (1) Harriet Evelyn Critchett at Cambridge, Massachusetts, 28
      August 1893 (died 8 January 1910).
Married (2) Carrie Josephine Collins at Alton, Rhode Island, 10 July
      1912. Children:
            Mary Josephine, born 18 June 1913.
            Caroline Elizabeth, 9 January 1923.
Now in Congregational ministry at Quincy, Mass.

My time for the first five years out of college was divided
pretty evenly between my church work and seminary and graduate work. The next seven years were in one pastorate where
the specially significant work was a leadership in a clean-up
campaign against disorder and lawlessness, involving three

townships in Southern Rhode Island. From 1905 to 1913 I was,
in Pawtucket, Rhode Island, where the real thing was the organization of an institutional church and the erection of a large
new edifice equipped thoroughly for social as well as religious
work. From 1913 to 1917 I was at Gary, Indiana, preaching at
the First Congregational Church, lecturing on sociology at the
Y. M. C. A. to a class averaging thirty-five, and serving also for
two years as lecturer in the celebrated Gary Schools. Came
East in 1917 and during the war served as speaker for the Government, delivering in all one hundred and seventeen addresses
concerning matters of public interest involved through the war.
Then after some months of field work in New England for the
Congregational denomination, I settled in Quincy in December,
1919, where I have been plodding along with fair progress ever
since.

A matter of special interest would be my reënrolment in the
Graduate School at Harvard for special work in Philosophy, beginning in September, 1917. This divided my time with the
duties of government speaker, as I spent two days a week in
Cambridge. Hence in all I have been a registered student at
Harvard for thirteen years—College, Divinity School, and
Graduate School. Am continuing the work referred to in last
report—may publish results ten or fifteen years hence. A new
arrival in my family since the twenty-fifth—Caroline Elizabeth,
born in Quincy, January 9, 1923. Hence besides wife have two
daughters to brag about.

EDWARD LIVINGSTON

Born at New York City, 26 September 1871, of Edward Livingston and
Frances Hazeltine.
Fitted at Berkley School, New York.
Class Status: Regular.
Degrees: A.B. 1893; LL.B. (Columbia) 1896.
Married Mabel Drake at Garrison, New York, 1 July 1913 (died 27 Oc-
tober 1915).
Now farming at Manitou, Putnam County, New York.

In the summer of 1918 I was very ill and it took me a long
time to "come back," but by spending the winters in Florida
and the summers quietly at Manitou, I have now completely recovered. I have really nothing else to report.

HARRY CHAMBERLAIN LOW

Born at Salem, Massachusetts, 5 August 1870, of Daniel Low (jeweller)
    and Elise Jane Stevens.
Fitted at Salem High.
Class Status: Regular.
Degrees: A.B. 1893; M.D. 1899.
Married Mabel Converse Chipman at Boston, 18 June 1902.   Children:
    Daniel Story, born 30 April 1903.
    Carolyn, 18 March 1905.
Now practising medicine at Boston.

Brief summary of my life since graduation:—The first four
years at Harvard Medical School, the next four in Boston
hospitals, a year in London, then married. Pathologist at Boston City and Children's Hospitals, and for the last fifteen
years in Orthopedic Service of Massachusetts General Hospital.
Now Visiting Surgeon at Massachusetts General Hospital with
especial charge of Infantile Paralysis Clinic.

Long connected with Children's Island Sanatarium and
have established a similar free hospital of forty beds for sun-
light treatment at North Scituate. Interest in several other
charitable institutions fills in my time and leaves only too little
for family and farm.

My boy is not at Harvard, because of the nearness of the
home town of Brookline and the call of the country. At Amherst he is preparing for his post-graduate course in the Harvard School of Business Administration.

Francis Crump Lucas

Born at Columbus, Indiana, 14 November 1868, of William Jones Lucas
    (banker) and Elizabeth Crump.
Fitted at Phillips Exeter.
Class Status: Regular.
Degrees: A.B. 1893; LL.B. (Indiana Law Sch.) 1895.
Married Mrs. Jessie Lynne (Lincoln) Ballard at Chicago, 2 December
    1901.   Child:
        Jessie-Lynne, born 22 May 1903.
Died of paralysis, 12 June 1920, at New York City.

After graduation, Lucas studied law at the Indiana Law
School, took his LL.B. in 1895, and began active practice at
Indianapolis, specializing in probate law. · In 1898 he removed
to New York City, but shortly afterwards established himself
at Columbus, Indiana, doing literary as well as legal work.

This led him into the publishing business, which he took up in 1903 at Washington, D. C. After two years he returned permanently to New York and became secretary and treasurer of the Alpha Manufacturing Company. Later he entered the banking house of W. N. Coler and Company. In 1911 he went into the bond market, at first independently, but subsequently affiliating with Martin Berwin and Company. He lived at Leonia, New Jersey, and in his leisure time wrote several books of a religious nature, including "The World Destroyer," "Spiritual Interpretations," and "Key to Eternal Life." About a year ago he suffered a stroke of paralysis, but seemed at the time to recover. He was an active member of the New York Harvard Club and much interested in Class affairs. Interment was at Columbus. On December 2, 1901, at Chicago, he married Mrs. Ballard (Jessie Lynne Lincoln) of Los Angeles, California, by whom he had one daughter.

Of his college days, Southwick writes as follows: "Frank Lucas I knew intimately. My room was next to his, in a house in Cambridge Street, and consequently I saw him every day. He was a most agreeable and unusual man—though often whimsical—very much interested in philosophy, and quite a friend of Professor Royce, who, on more than one occasion, came to see him at his room. Frank knew but three or four score of men at Harvard, but those who did know him will remember him as a kind-hearted, sincere and loyal man."

WILLIAM LUCE

Born at Fort Smith, Arkansas, 21 October 1868, of John Bleecker Luce (lawyer) and Cornelia Priscilla Forester.
Fitted at Berkeley School, Boston.
Class Status: Left Senior year.
Married Katharine Williams McKinney at Fort Smith, Arkansas, 28 October 1908. Children:
      John Bleecker, born 7 July 1909.
      Stephen Bleecker, 30 January 1911.
      William Falconer, 12 January 1915.
      Charles McKinney, 18 July 1916.
Now in coffee business at Sherman, Texas.

Old man Gray prophetically hit me off when he coined the phrase "Short and simple annals of the poor." I could not dig up the price of one of his "animated busts," in fact I could not finance a very dull bust, now that bust-producing liquor

is so costly. In spite of the fact that I draw a reasonable salary, as drummer salaries go, I have strictly obeyed the scriptur-
al injunction to ''lay not up for yourselves treasures upon the
earth.'' In fact my treasures are like the jewels of Cornelia—
boys.

The pension attorneys remind me that I served in the Spanish-American War, but, as I have a full complement of eyes,
legs, arms, and general good health, their importunities fail to
interest me. If any Ulysses of '93 undertakes an Odyssey into
the vastness of Texas, he will find hearty, though simple, welcome at 1223 East King Street, Sherman, and will be furnished
a well broke Ford to inspect the Long Horns of the Black
Lands.

HOWARD LYON

Born at York, New York, 21 May 1860, of Ira Goddard Lyon (farmer)
     and Henrietta Powers.
Fitted at Geneseo State Normal School.
Class Status: Entered Junior.
Degrees: S.M. Hon. (Lafayette) 1890; A.B. 1893.
Married Miriam Gould at East Aurora, New York, 20 August 1884.
     Child:
          Madeline, born 18 July 1886.
Now with Welsbach Company at Gloucester, New Jersey.

Took position of the Department of Science in the State Normal School, Oneonta, New York, in September, 1893, and continued until June, 1909. July, 1909, assumed the duties of research expert with the Welsbach Company, and have continued
the employment since that time. My duties have had relation
to the development of devices for the utilization of gas in the
production of light and heat. Have travelled only moderately.
In 1916 spent three months in the island of Jamaica. On this
trip especialy my recreation was the study of botany, in
which I am much interested. My recreations are mainly golf
and walking trips. The greater interest in the latter is directed
toward botany, and incidentally the enjoyment of wholesome
exercise out of doors.

Have lectured from time to time on Illuminating Engineering and other scientific subjects. Some addresses have been published. No other publications except an article on Sap Pres-

sure while at Oneonta. Member: Illuminating Engineering Society. On various committees on Illumination. American Gas Association; Country Club, Woodbury, New Jersey.

RICHARD MACALLISTER

Born at Calcutta, India, 10 January 1870, of Richard Macallister (consul general) and Alma Charity Mears.
Fitted at C. W. Stone's.
Class Status: Special 1889-90. With 1894, 1890-92. Joined Class senior year.
Degree: A.B. 1893.
Married Josephine Anne Dickson at Ottawa, 12 October 1905. Children: Alma Carol, born 2 March 1910.
Richard Dickson, 8 September 1912.
Now Assistant Chemist at Port Colborne, Ontario.

Since last report, put in underground electric service, cables, manholes, etc., for Foundation Company at International Nickel Company's plant at Port Colborne. Then rebuilding ore bridges for Canadian Furnace Company and electrifying same. Thence went with British American Shipbuilding Company at Welland, where we built five steamers. All above war work. Then back again to Department of Railways and Canals at Government Elevator for two years. Just quit and am now assistant chemist at Canadian Furnace Company. For three years have been Assessor or Assistant Assessor and Collector for this burg.

GEORGE GRANT MACCURDY

Born at Warrensburgh, Missouri, 17 April 1863, of William Jasper MacCurdy (farmer) and Margaret Smith.
Fitted at Warrensburgh State Normal School.
Class Status: Special Sci., 1891-92. Joined Class Senior year.
Degrees: A.B. 1893; A.M. 1894; Ph.D. (Yale) 1905.
Married Glenn Bartlett at New York City, 30 June 1919.
Now Curator of Anthropology and Research Associate in Prehistoric Archeology with Professorial rank in Yale Univ.

Student, University of Vienna, 1895-1896; School of Anthropology, Paris, 1896-1897; University of Berlin, 1897-1898. Connected with Yale University since 1898. Member International Jury of Awards, St. Louis Exposition, 1904. Secretary, American Anthropological Association, 1903-1916. Fellow and past Vice-President American Association for the Advancement

of Science. Corresponding member: Society of the Institute of
Coimbra (Portugal), School of Anthropology (Paris), *Société
des Américanistes* (Paris), Numismatic and Antiquarian Society of Philadelphia, Anthropological Society of Washington,
Missouri Historical Society, *Société Historique et Archéologique
de la Charente* (France). Member Supervisory Board, American Year Book Corporation, 1911-1919. Member of a Committee to investigate evidence bearing on the antiquity of man at
Vero, Florida, 1916; First Director, American School in France
for Prehistoric Studies, 1921-1922. Chairman, Governing
Board, American School in France for Prehistoric Studies.
Author of a number of papers and memoirs on anthropological
subjects, including: The Eolithic Problem (1905), Some Phases
of Prehistoric Archaeology, 1907, Antiquity of Man in Europe
(1910), A Study of Chiriquian Antiquities (1911), The Cult
of the Ax (1916), The Octopus Motive in Ancient Chiriquian
Art (1916), The Dawn of Art (1916), Some Mounds of Eastern
Tennessee (1917), The Problem of Man's Antiquity at Vero,
Florida (1917), Human Skeletal Remains from the Highlands
of Peru (1923). Special research interest: Human Origins.

WALTON BROOKS McDANIEL

Born at Cambridge, Massachusetts, 4 March 1871, of Samuel Walton
    McDaniel [Law School] (lawyer) and Georgiana Frances Brooks.
Fitted at Cambridge Latin.
Class Status: Regular.
Degrees: A.B. 1893; A.M. 1894; Ph.D. 1899.
Married Alice Corinne Garlichs at Saint Joseph, Missouri, 2 August,
    1899.
Now Professor of Latin at University of Pennsylvania.

My professional life has naturally assumed a more settled
character as I near a quarter-century of service in one institution, the University of Pennsylvania, although an increase of
students from around 3,000 to nearly 15,000 has made some
duties more exacting. Most of my teaching is still in the Graduate School, but I always carry a load of administrative work
connected with the college and with our departments of it.
Public lecturing has also much engaged me and I have attended
meetings of professional societies rather faithfully. Recently
I served as president of the American Philological Association
and I have long been interested in our other national societies,

the Classical League and the Archaeological Institute of America, being vice-president of the local branch of the latter. Besides committee and council work in these I have had similar activities in the American Philosophical Society. A half dozen other social and professional clubs claim some of my time. In 1920-1921 I served as a professor in the American Academy in Rome. My wife and I found our temporary home upon the Janiculum so wholly happy that I was strongly tempted to make it permanent, when the headship of the Classical School in the Academy was offered me. But professional and social ties in America were too strong to sever. During our fifteen months abroad, I spent all my time in Greece and Italy, and, after so many visits, the land of the ancient Romans seems almost a second home.

Publications in English, American and Italian periodicals have come from my pen when possible in my busy life, some of a popular character, others technical. A book is about to be born—probably a still birth—one can never tell.

Our winter house affords me all the disagreeable exercise that I want, but our summer cottage at the water's edge of Martha's Vineyard gives me the rowing, swimming and canoeing that I have always loved. It is there and during my explorations of the classic lands that I really and truly live.

GEORGE LEARY McELROY

Born at New York City, 11 April 1867, of William Patrick McElroy (merchant) and Annie Dougherty.
Fitted with B. R. Abbott.
Class Status: Regular.
Degree: A.B. 1893.
Now interior decorator at New York City.

No! *Please* don't spring the old joke about "interior decoration"! That's my job, but think what it required to learn it. First—four years at the Beaux Arts in Paris, as a gay young stoodent in the Latin Quarter. Mong Doo! Then a long apprenticeship with our classmate, C. P. Huntington, in his office at New York City. Then the plunge into independent practice of architecture with my own office in this Teutonic burg— Mein Gott! Then, about 1915, the great adventure—the Sign on the Door—the Client—excuse me, I mean the clients—the momentous questions, shall the bath room be pink or blue? Shall the garage be Louis XIV or neo-Babylonian? How shall we "treat" the coal cellar? And oh my dear friends, you don't know what these questions mean until you've discussed 'em with a fat Hebrew dowager—whose son, by the way, wants his room at Harvard "done over" in a style that shall proclaim his loyalty to his Alma Mater. Believe me, *moi qui parle*, it's a solemn responsibility, this supplying taste to the tasteless, this casting of pearls before swine. Sometimes I feel the future of American culture depends on me—even as my own future depends on my ability to collect my little accounts rendered.

STEPHEN ANDREW McINTIRE

Born at Charlton, Massachusetts, 19 April 1871, of Stephen Waters
    McIntire (merchant) and Elizabeth Rich Woodbury.
Fitted at Phillips Exeter.
Class Status: Regular.
Degrees: A.B. 1893; LL.B. 1900.
Now practising law at New York City.

Have continued to pay office rent and telephone bills with fair degree of regularity. Knock wood.

FREDERICK CHASE McLAUGHLIN

Born at Bergen Heights, New Jersey, 9 December 1871, of Robert Wil-
    liam McLaughlin (sea-captain) and Emily Louise Meredith.
Fitted at Somerville High.
Class Status: Regular.
Degrees: A.B. 1893; A.M. 1895; LL.B. 1898.
Married Sarah Sands Clarke at Binghamton, New York, 27 December
    1898. Children:
        Elizabeth, born 23 October 1899.
        Frederick Chase, Jr., 21 March 1901.
        Samuel Clarke, 3 July 1902.
        Robert Meredith }
        Richard Meredith } 14 August 1904.
        Margaret, 8 August 1906.
Now practising law at New York City.

Came to New York City immediately after graduation from Harvard Law School in 1898. Have been here ever since. Started my own law office in 1899 and for nearly twenty years have been a member of firm of McLaughlin, Russell and Sprague, No. 25 West 43rd Street, New York City. Have lived

at White Plains, New York, since August, 1900. I am president
of the Common Council of that city and have been a member of
the council continuously since the city charter was obtained
in 1915. Also president of the Westchester Golf Club, ex-pres-
ident White Plains University Club, and identified with much
that goes on in that small city. Particularly interested in municipal government. Have four boys in college this year. One in
senior class at Harvard. Daughter graduated from Wellesley
in 1921 and another enters next year. An active law practice
in New York City, an absorbing interest in the life and problems of an ideal small city, and the job of educating a large
family of children spells out my existence.

Wayne MacVeagh, Jr.

See Report VI, Page 194, and Supplement, Page 128.

George Butler Magoun

See Report VI, Page 194.

LLEWELLYN JOHN MALONE

Born at London, England, 16 December 1864, of Edward Malone [Cam-
bridge Univ.] (barrister) and Annie Clara Jones.
Fitted at Phillips Andover.
Class Status: Left class Senior year.
Married Fermine du-Buisson Baird at Boston, 9 December 1899·
Now trustee and investor at Boston.

Originally intended to study literature but spent 1893-96
in the Law School. In 1897-98 was fifteen months prospecting
with Chew, '93, on the Copper River, Alaska; without noticeable
results at the time, though it afterwards turned out that we
had staked claims over the very location of the present great
Kennecott Copper Mines, the richest in the world! Of course
at that time Alaska was mostly known as a fur country and
with the experience I gained there I entered the fur business
in Boston which I continued for several years. At my place
at Wells, Maine, I became interested in raising standard bred
poultry, and gradually built up the largest plant of its kind
in the State. But there is no money in this sort of thing unless managed with intelligence; and I found that though during
my frequent absences I could hire labor I could not hire in-

telligence—at least not in Wells. So I ultimately sold out just
before the War—most fortunately, as the price of grain (the
prime factor in poultry raising) had already begun its upward
march.

As an American citizen who was born a British subject,
naturally I was very much interested in the late unpleasantness.
There seemed but little opportunity to help in Maine, so during
the war I passed most of my time in Boston. I wanted to take
up aviation, but was given to understand my aspirations were
too high. So I did a little in minor ways, helping among other
things to put the castors under that human skunk, Dr. Muck,
with a few successes of the same sort that give me keen satisfaction to look back upon.

The mining interests which I began in Alaska have come to
absorb most of my time. I have served without pay on the
directorates of three corporations. Although my office is at
30 Huntington Avenue. Boston, yet (owing to a little difference
in opinion with the tax collectors) my legal residence has been
for years at Wells. where I pass much of my time and which
is my best address. I have accumulated but little of "this
world's goods," but have everything one needs, a few luxuries.
moderately good health. and am very happy.

PERCIVAL MANCHESTER

Born at Chicago, 15 January 1870, of George Otis Manchester [Hamilton]
    and Ella Boynton.
Fitted with W. N. Eayrs.
Class Status: Left Junior year.
Married Nena Adele Tillson at Evanston, Illinois, 6 June 1901.
Now farming near Winter Haven, Florida.

After leaving college, spent a year in California with the
thought of going into fruit growing. Decided. however, to go
to Chicago and in the summer of 1894 went into the employ
of the Sargent Company, iron and steel founders. In 1905
joined with other interests and formed the Quincy, Manchester,
Sargent Company, becoming secretary and treasurer and afterwards vice-president. In 1909 formed the Railway Appliance
Company of which I was president. In January, 1915, having
had a serious eye trouble I gave up my business and spent the
next two years and a half travelling, the winters being spent
in Florida.

In 1916 attended the Officers' Training Camp at Plattsburg.
June 15, 1917, was commissioned Major in the Ordnance Department and assigned to Frankfort Arsenal, Kentucky. October 3 sailed for France and was Base Ordnance Officer at St.
Nazaire; afterwards commanding Intermediate Ordnance depot at Gievres. Honorably discharged May 17, 1919, with distinguished service medal and citation; also received from the
French Government the Order of L'Etoile Noire, grade
d'officier.

For a year and a half, or from May, 1919, until December.
1921, I acted as New York manager for Richards and Company,
a Boston concern engaged in the metal business.

About this time a long cherished plan of a "life out of doors"
came to a head and I set out for Florida. Six months were occupied looking over different localities and the vicinity of Winter Haven finally selected. We now have (as I have a partner.
a former Yale man) a grove that is large enough to occupy all
of our time except for an occasional fishing or shooting expedition.

JOSEPH MANLEY

Born at Mount Vernon, Iowa, 13 June 1871, of Samuel Hamilton Manley
(teacher) and Louise Catherine Albright.
Fitted at Illinois State Normal School.
Class Status: Regular.
Degrees: A.B. 1893; Hon. A.M. (Marietta) 1898.
Married Florence Bosworth Lane at Cincinnati, 26 June 1901. Children:
Edward, born 8 April 1904.
Lucia, 6 February 1907.
Now Professor of Political Science at Marietta College.

The secretary has to admit defeat in this case. Good old Joe
has beaten him, and takes the prize as the Human Oyster. To
every appeal he has remained dumb, and when as a last resort
the secretary sent him a long telegram "collect," beseeching
him to reply for the sake of '93: Foxy Joe countered by refusing
to pay the charges. thereby setting the secretary back several
simoleons. Upon which the secretary took the count, and the
descendant of William the Silent was unanimously declared the
winner.

To be sure. there wasn't much to say. Ever since September
of 1893 Joe has been a professor at Marietta. For years and

years it was Greek, then in 1914 Greek, English, and Mediæval
Political History, then in 1916 Greek and Political History,
next year Political History alone and now Political Science.
(The secretary gleans these facts from the Quinquennial, not
from Joe). But what he really needs is a course in English
Composition and Expression. Good luck to you, anyway, Joe!

ERNEST LINCOLN MANNING

Born at Jamaica Plain, Massachusetts, 25 December 1870, of William Way-
    land Manning (estate agent) and Abby Ripley Hobbs.
Fitted at St. Marks.
Class Status: Freshman year only.
Married Lillian Blanche Quincy at Rutland, Vermont, 21 August 1915.
Now in banking at Boston.

On leaving college I returned to my home at Marquette,
Michigan, there for three years having charge of Assessments
and Taxes on Estate Properties in the Upper Peninsula. I
then went to California to acquire some financial knowledge of
the beet sugar business at the factories, three years later becoming treasurer of one of the companies in New York City.
Relinquishing this in 1905, I entered the investment business
in association with my brother, at Boston, first as representatives, then as junior partners, of a New York House. In 1919
we established our own firm, and on the retirement of my brother, I became and now am, associated with a Chicago banking
house, at their Boston office.

SAMUEL HUBBARD MANSFIELD

Born at Gloucester, Massachusetts, 27 June 1870, of Alfred Mansfield
    (fisheries) and Sarah Jane Hubbard.
Fitted at Gloucester High.
Class Status: Special, 1889-90.
Now Proprietor of Old Colony Mercantile Agency, Boston-Gloucester.

After leaving college, about 1891 I went to New York City
in employ of the Holmes Electric Protective Company (Bur-
glar Alarm Company), and about 1894 entered the grocery business and later dealt in lubricating oils and engineers' supplies,
till about 1901. Was with Roger W. Babson, dealing in investments in his early days. About 1903 became associated with
the Huff Electrostatic Separator Company of Boston (an elec-

trical process for concentrating ores) and later became its treasurer after holding various offices. In 1916 I went into business
for myself, establishing the Old Colony Mercantile Agency for
commercial credits and mercantile collections in which business
I am now.

Henry Orlando Marcy, Jr.

Born at Cambridge, Massachusetts, 2 July 1871, of Henry Orlando Marcy
  [Harv. Med. 1864] (surgeon) and Sarah Elizabeth Wendell.
Fitted at Boston Latin.
Class Status: Regular.
Degrees: A.B. 1893; M.D. 1897.
Married Eleanor Hunnewell Nichols at Newton, Massachusetts, 15 May
  1909. Children:
    Eleanor Beatrice, born 11 August 1914.
    Henry Orlando, 3d, 27 October 1915.
Died of after-effects of influenza, 29 May 1922, at Newton.

Henry Orlando Marcy, Jr., was born in Cambridge, Massachusetts, July 2nd, 1871, the son of Henry Orlando and Sarah
(Wendell) Marcy. His father, still living but now retired from
active practice, has been one of Boston's most distinguished surgeons. He fitted for college at the Boston Latin School. On
graduating from college he entered the Harvard Medical
School. After completing the four years course there he was
appointed House Surgeon at the Roosevelt Hospital in New
York City, serving under the distinguished surgeon, Dr. Charles
McBurney. On his return to Boston he associated himself with
his father in surgical work. He was appointed Assistant in
Anatomy at the Medical School and was considered one of the
best teachers in the Anatomical Department. He was made a
Fellow of the American College of Surgeons.

Marcy was a fine student and always stood well in his classes.
I can well remember in Latin School days how many times
Marcy would be called upon to stand up as the recipient of honors at the annual school exercises. He was awarded his degree of
A.B. *Magna cum Laude* and was elected a member of the Phi
Beta Kappa. In the Medical School he stood fourth in his class.
He possessed a well disciplined mind. He was quick to grasp the
essentials of a subject and his memory was remarkably reten-
tive. His health was never robust and he was frail in body. For
this reason he never engaged much in sports. One of his chief
characteristics was his loyalty to his friends. He was not one who

made many friends, but to those whom he chose to call friends, he gave himself without reserve. While taking a course at the Massachusetts Institute of Technology he was elected a member of the Tech .chapter of the D. K. E. Fraternity. He entered into the spirit of this fraternity life with a great deal of zest and endeared himself to a large number of Tech men through this association.

On May 15, 1909, he married Eleanor Hunnewell Nichols of Newton, a sister of our former classmate, Howard Gardner Nichols. His married life was a most happy one. His family and his home were all in all to him. He was very fond of Lake Placid in the Adirondacks and it was his custom to spend his summers with his family at their beautiful place on this lake. There he had as near neighbors Secretary Hughes and Chief Justice White. In the spring of 1922 he suffered an attack of influenza which eventually affected his heart and caused a severe anemia. He put up a brave fight but his frail body was not able to overcome the severe infection and he passed away on May 29, 1922. His wife and a son and daughter survive him.

One could not be thrown much with Marcy without discerning the strength of principle and the high ideals which actuated his life. He was an active member of the Old South Congregational Church. His pastor, Dr. George A. Gordon, in a personal letter, tells how highly he was regarded in this church. We have lost a most loyal classmate, and one who leaves a memorial of high esteem.

F. M. S.

Charles Guy Martin

See Report VI, Page 198.

FREDERICK ROY MARTIN

Born at North Stratford, New Hampshire, 17 November 1871, of John Douglas Martin (merchant) and Caroline Taylor Thompson.
Fitted at Lowell (Mass.) High.
Class Status: Regular.
Degrees:A.B. 1893; A.M. Hon. (Brown) 1902.
Married Anna Frances Wayne at Cambridge, Massachusetts, 9 September 1909. Child:
Nancy, born 31 January 1911.
Now General Manager of The Associated Press, New York.

My thirty years divide into five years with the extinct Boston Journal, fourteen years in charge of the Providence Journal, and eleven years with the Associated Press. I came to New York in 1912 as Assistant General Manager; in 1920 became Acting General Manager, and in April, 1921, General Manager. I have travelled in every State in the Union and much in Europe—my work there in the first two years of the war period having been particularly diversified and interesting.

I have continued my interest in Harvard alumni affairs; have been a member of the Board of Managers of the Harvard Club of New York and have served on many of its committees; have been a vice-president of the Alumni Association and am now a director of the Alumni Association and on the *Bulletin* board; have also served three years on the Standing Committee on the Nomination of Overseers.

My Lares and Penates are out in Westchester in Bronxville, where I own a home, a garden and a few trees. I am a member of more clubs and organizations than I can afford, but the list would not particularly interest the class. I have tried to do my share on boards of libraries, hospitals, and other non-paying directorates. In the course of my work I have accumulated one honorary degree and a few foreign decorations. My health continues above par. I have not missed a day from my work in thirty years on account of illness, except when shot by burglars in Providence and once when I was held up for two months in Chicago by a siege of typhoid—all of which is gratefully recorded. C'est tout!

SELDEN ERASTUS MARVIN, JR.

Born at Albany, New York, 1 December 1869, of Selden Erastus Marvin
  (steel treasurer) and Katharine Langdon Parker.
Fitted at J. P. Hopkinson's.
Class Status: Regular.
Degree: A.B. 1893.
Now living in New York City.

Master, in charge of English Department and Second Form, Albany Academy, 1893-1894. Military Secretary, State of New York, 1895-1896. Private Secretary to Lieut. Governor, State of New York, 1897. With B. F. Goodrich Company, Akron, Ohio, 1898. Secretary and Treasurer, Franklin Boiler Works Com-

pany, Green Island, New York, 1899-1910. Military Secretary,
State of New York, 1905-1906. Secretary to Governor, State
of New York, 1906. Treasurer Ore Recovering Company, Pottstown, Pennsylvania, 1911-1914. Assistant Treasurer Pan American Munitions Corporation, 1915-1918. First Vice-President, American Mercantile Corporation, 1919. Sent to Scan-
dinavia, Denmark and Finland to arrange for branch offices—
returned to find Corporation ruined through gross neglect and
worse. No regular position 1920-1921. Ill for five months
(February-June) 1922. Offered and accepted the position of
manager in charge of Correspondence Department in newly organized firm of C. P. Holzderbie and Company, also had charge
of advertising—publicity—getting out of reports, firm letters,
etc. Firm dissolved, owing to changes in condition among
members, November, 1922. Have been looking for a position
since.

WALTER EFFINGHAM [HOLLISTER] MAYNARD

Born at New York City, 17 November 1871, of Effingham Maynard (pub-
    lisher) and Helen Maria Hollister.
Fitted at Berkeley School.
Class Status: Regular.
Degree: A.B. 1893.
Married Eunice Ives at New York City, 19 April 1903. Children:
    Walter, born 19 April 1906.
    Audrey, 24 November 1908.
Now in financial business at New York.

After leaving college, I continued the publishing business inherited from my father—Maynard, Merrill and Company. In
1907 I sold out my business and bought an interest in the old
Fifth Avenue Hotel property at Fifth Avenue and 23rd Street.
The demolition of the old hotel and the erection of a large office
building on its site, and its management and financing occupied
me pretty actively till 1917. During the war I was absorbed
in propaganda, publicity and periodical work—especially anti-
radical activities, and throughout I was closely identified with
many forms of relief work in France, in recognition of which I
was given the Legion of Honor. At present I am occupied in
financial work of various kinds and am a director or trustee of
a number of civic organizations including the New York Orthopedic Dispensary and Hospital, the Fifth Avenue Associa-

tion, the National Weekly Corporation (publishers of the "Independent"), Beaux Arts Institute of Design, etc., etc.

I travel a good deal, play more than I used to—enjoy art, especially architecture and music. I will close with most cordial greetings to all members of the class of '93, and best wishes for their health and prosperity.

Charles Merriam

See Report VI, Page 200.

JAMES ANDREW MERRILL

Born in Rockcastle County, Kentucky, 6 April 1861, of Andrew Hanson Merrill (miller) and Ann Eliza Eustin.
Fitted at Missouri State Normal School.
Class Status: IV. Scientific,. 1892-93.
Degree: S.B. 1893.
Married Nellie Agnes Lowen at Trenton, Missouri, 23 December 1895.
Children:
    Robert Lowen, born 1 August 1900 (deceased).
    George Lowen, 9 April 1902.
    Helen Elizabeth, 11 January 1909.
Now president of State Normal School at Superior, Wisconsin.

After graduation I spent four years as teacher of natural sciences in State Normal School, Warrensburg, Missouri. In 1897 I left this position to accept the chair of natural sciences in the Manual Training High School in Kansas City, a new school with a new idea back of it. Its purpose was to make manual training a part of the curriculum just as physics, English or algebra are a part of the curriculum. It succeeded wonderfully and the idea is now a common factor in education. In 1900 I came to Superior State Normal School where I have remained ever since. In 1902 I was appointed vice-president, and on July 7, 1922, was elected president. Since coming here I have been active along many lines. I have done much geological work in all the states west of the Mississippi River except New Mexico and Texas, especially on the iron ranges in Minnesota. In 1921 I made a journey of exploration for oil fields to Pence River, and went as far north as latitude 58 degrees. I found that country a most fascinating one. Aside from its possibilities for oil it is a most wonderful agricultural country and for wild game it is equal to the forests of Labrador.

I have written many articles of scientific and general interest, and have been especially active in teachers' associations and institutes. Have written three books on geography of Wisconsin, the last one, "An Industrial Geography of Wisconsin," has had rather a large sale.

My chief recreation is motoring and roaming the woods, with enough fishing to afford variety and excitement. I still have a summer cottage on the Buck River, America's most famous trout fishing stream, to which my Harvard classmates are most cordially invited.

My admiration for Harvard and my devotion to its ideals have grown with the years, and I have done what I could to send strong western men to its halls. Long live the Class of 1893 and may its service to humanity grow greater with its years!

ALBION LEROY MILLAN

Born at Cambridge, Massachusetts, 18 October 1870, of Alexander Millan
　　(merchant) and Hannah Doane Townsend.
Fitted at Cambridge Latin.
Class Status: Regular.
Degrees: A.B. 1893; LL.B. 1896.
Married Anna Elouisa Dane at New Boston, New Hampshire, 26 June
　　1900. Children:
　　　　Hollis Bailey, born 1 August 1901 (died May 1918).
　　　　John, 10 August 1902.
Now practising law at Boston.

I have been active in practising law ever since I graduated from the Law School. There are two reasons for this. I like the work and I have to make my living. As a diversion, I have had a few hens, cows, horse, and dog on the small farm in Acton, Massachusetts, the next town to Concord, where we live all the year. I have read how hard it used to be for a drunkard to go by a bar-room, and I find a similar trouble at this time of the year in going by a window where little chickens are for sale. If I did what I should like, I would buy them all and take them home. I am fortunate in seeing many of our classmates often, because they live in and around Boston. In college, Professor Wendell always objected to a few ideas imbedded in too many words. So I must close with best wishes to you all.

RALPH GIFFORD MILLER

Born at New York City, 24 September 1872, of Benjamin Rush Miller (varnish maker) and Almira Louise King.
Fitted at St. Paul's, Garden City, New York.
Class Status: Regular.
Degree: A.B. 1893 *cum laude.*
Married Alice Bowers Lee at Southampton, New York, 30 September 1896.
Children:
Alice Lee, born 19 July 1897.
Ralph Gifford, Jr., 23 December 1900.
Now lawyer at Los Angeles, California.

Spent winter of 1894-1895 abroad, then commenced practice of law with Bowers and Sands, New York City. Attorney for Whitney-Ryan Transportation Companies for ten years. Left practice in New York City in 1910. Bought hunting box in Wyoming and raised white faces until 1915 when I sold and practised law in Denver until 1917 when I opened law office in Los Angeles, California. Gave up law practice when the United States went into war, as lawyers did not help much with the war. Bought ranch, 2,500 acres, on McKenzie River, Oregon, at Leaburg, near Eugene, Oregon, and raised beef and pork for the boys at the front. 1921-1922, for the winter did law work for Mortgage Guarantee Company here and took care of my ranch in Oregon from June to November. Now just settling into practice in Los Angeles again, practising on my own account and on retainer from Equitable Bond and Mortgage Company, 706 South Hill Street, as its secretary and on retainer from Universal Producer Syndicate, as its president. The latter is an oil company with drilling about to start and we expect to make at least a 5000-barrel well and then our fortunes. At any rate, the company will be run honestly and I have so arranged matters that the actual investors get back one hundred per cent. on the dollar before any promotion stock will be recognized or paid dividends.

CHARLES EDWARD MOODY

Born at Canterbury, New Hampshire, 29 October 1865, of Howard Moody
(clergyman) and Cornelia Ann Clough.
Fitted at Phillips Andover.
Class Status: Regular.
Degree: A.B. 1893.
Married Irene Greenleaf Hartwell at Lowell, Massachusetts, 4 September
1901. Children:
Howard Hartwell, born 6 August 1905.
Emily, 5 June 1909.
Paul Lyman, 23 April 1911.
Now in telephone work at New York.

Since leaving college, substantially all my work has been in
the telephone business, first with the New England Telephone
Company and for the last twenty years with the American Telephone Company, seven years as travelling auditor with headquarters at 125 Milk Street, Boston. During those years I visited nearly all of the Bell Telephone Companies in the United
States, auditing their books and making general and special reports on the operating and financial condition of the companies.

For the last thirteen years I have been located in New York
in charge of the Division of Bell System Reports. All the
monthly and annual statistical and financial reports of the Bell
Companies are received in my office. Special analysis and studies from these reports are made for our executives; statements
prepared for various financial publications and figures furnished
for the quarterly and annual reports of the American Company,
etc. Supervision of this work claims about all my time for elev-
en months in the year, the other month, generally August, I
spend at my dug-out in New Hampshire. My oldest enters Harvard this fall.

William Vaughn Moody

See Report VI, Page 204, and Supplement, Page 128.

FRED WADSWORTH MOORE

Born at Independence, Iowa, 7 March 1870, of Lorenzo Moore (merchant)
and Ellen Wadsworth.
Fitted at Phillips Andover.
Class Status: Regular.
Degrees: A.B. 1893; LL.B. 1896.
Married Mrs. Louise (Toby) Becker at New York City, 27 July 1921.
Now Graduate Treasurer and Secretary of Committee on Regulation of
Athletic Sports at Harvard.

Harvard Law School, LL.B. 1896. Graduate Manager Athletics at Harvard, 1894-1896. Practised law in Boston, 1897 to 1917. Graduate Treasurer Harvard Athletic Association, 1913 to date. Went in to Military Intelligence Service as civilian, fall of 1917. Commissioned Captain, Quartermasters Corps, January 29, 1918 and assigned as Assistant Intelligence Officer, New England Department, Boston. Appointed Intelligence Officer, New England Department, March 30, 1918. Promoted to Major, August 5, 1918; some job. Honorably discharged, February 25, 1919. Have since continued to act as Graduate Treasurer, giving up law entirely, as I find that the oversight of forty-five intercollegiate teams keeps me fairly busy. Married July 27, 1921, at New York, to Louise Becker (nee Toby).

WILLIAM CHARLES MOORE

Born at Lawrence, Massachusetts, 9 August 1864, of William P. Moore (machinist) and Esther Ashworth.
Fitted at Bridgewater State Normal School.
Class Status: Scientific, 1890-93.
Degrees: S.B. 1893; A.M. 1908.
Married Lora Gertrude Davidson at Salem, Massachusetts, 19 November 1898.
Now Superintendent of Schools at Newburyport, Massachusetts.

All my college work was planned in preparation for teaching. On graduation, therefore, I entered immediately upon that work and have continued in it ever since. I am now making arrangements to retire from active service on the first of next September.

During the thirty years since graduation I have held teaching positions in Worcester Academy, the State Normal and Training School, Oswego, New York, the State Normal School, Salem, Massachusetts, and Mount Holyoke College. I have also been Superintendent of Schools in Southington, Connecticut, and in Newburyport, Massachusetts. My most important posts have been in the Salem Normal School, Mount Holyoke College, and in Newburyport. These three positions together cover a period of nearly twenty-five years.

The Quinquennial Catalogue makes it appear that I have spent a number of years at Harvard in graduate study. Most of this work was done incidentally, however, while teaching in the Salem Normal School. As a matter of fact I was in residence in Cambridge only during the year 1907-08. In June, 1908, I received the Master of Arts degree in Education.

Just now I am greatly in need of a prolonged rest. In 1912 I had a serious nervous breakdown which kept me out of service for three years. To ward off, if possible, a similar condition I am now giving up my position as Superintendent of Schools in Newburyport.

ROLAND J[ESSUP] MULFORD

Born at Friendsville, Pennsylvania, 27 May 1871, of Elisha Mulford (Yale 1855) (author) and Rachael Price Carmalt.
Fitted at Cambridge Latin.
Class Status: Regular.
Degrees: A.B. 1893; LL.B. 1896; Ph.D. (Johns Hopkins) 1903.
Married Margaret Biddle Guest Blackwell at Baltimore, 21 December 1901.
    Children:
        Helen Blackwell, born 6 January 1904.
        John, 1 August 1907.
Now Instructor in Latin, Princeton University.

For the last five years I have been Headmaster of Ridgefield School, in Connecticut, preparing boys for Harvard, Princeton and other colleges. The school, which with the help of Howard C. Smith, I started in 1907, has had a full complement these last years. Last June I resigned as Headmaster and was given a sabbatical year, which I am spending studying Latin at Princeton. I had an opportunity to sell out my interest in the school last winter and did so to one of the alumni of the school.

The graduate work has proved very interesting, and profitable in finding the new methods and learning the new work that has been done. I am a strong advocate of the sabbatical year. At the mid-years there was a vacancy in the Latin department and I was asked to become instructor for the half-year. I have found the work most interesting, and am confirmed in what has always been a strong belief that teaching is the finest profession in the world.

LOUIS CHRISTIAN MULLGARDT

Born at Washington, Missouri, 19 January 1866, of John Christian Mullgardt (harness manufacturer) and Wilhelmine Haeusgen.
Class Status: Special, 1889-90.
Married Laura Rosette Steffens at Chicago, 9 June 1897. Children:

Alexander Steffens, born 3 January 1899.
John Louis Christian, 24 August 1906.
June,—June 1914.
Now practising architecture at San Francisco.

I realize, perhaps more than anyone else, that the Class Report would fall flat if it failed to contain my roundelay. I adore talking about myself (laudatiously, of course). The discouraging features are,—getting away with it,—and being the only reader of one's own stuff.

I will begin diplomatically by stating that your documents reached me in Rome, whilst I was making a deep study of Italian wines, and their effect upon Class Legislation, to be followed by a Class Report, accompanied by Demosthenese lantern slides. This will probably constitute my last research work on the omega leg of a world tour (which began in San Francisco in May, 1922), the time required being concordant with my letter of credit. I might say, with some measure of pride, that my journey has made a deep impression upon the world, like a canal, but unfortunately too much like a canal, its banks are of sand, which caves in and will obliterate the swath, even before this reaches your printer; otherwise, a Crooks' Tour, through it, might have constituted one of our little pleasure trips, during the next Class reunion.

I smoke and drink, and had an unmitigated respect for the Constitution before it became diluted. Architecture is my long suite. It is the finest profession in the category, next to lauding oneself. As a student, I have always been a shining success if failure to acquire a single degree has any merit attached to it. I have practised architecture in St. Louis, London, San Francisco and Honolulu. Some of the things which I have done are already indelibly recorded in the Class Reports, but the extent to which my clients have been done, has, for the general good of the Class, been kept out of its records.

I write frequently on things Architectural, in fact, too frequently, in the opinion of my contemporaries; but a habit once acquired takes more strength of will-power to resist than I care to possess. Writing is fun, if done seriously; and awful, if done funnily. I am a recognized authority on the latter, and therefore always write seriously.

My family has been increased by one, since the last report of three. This one is another male, a Boston bull-terrier, which is the nearest point attained by myself, thus far, to being the proud possessor of a Harvard offspring. My eldest son will probably get his degrees this year. He has tried three universities, and has found them all below the exalted mark set by what he heard his father say about Harvard, when I 'thought he wasn't listening.

Edward Stanton Mullins

See Report VI, Page 209.

DAVID SAVILLE MUZZEY

Born at Lexington, Massachusetts, 9 October 1870, of David Wood Muzzey (real estate) and Annie Woodbury Saville.
Fitted at Boston Latin.
Class Status: Regular.
Degrees: A.B. 1893; B.D. (New York Univ.) 1897; Ph.D. (Columbia) 1907.
Married Ina Jeanette Bullis at New York City, 20 September 1900.
Children:
    David Saville, Jr., born 6 September 1902.
    Elizabeth, 23 February 1904.
Now Professor of History at Columbia University, and Assistant Leader of the Society of Ethical Culture, New York City.

1893-1894; Tutor of mathematics in Robert College, Constantinople. 1894-1897; Student at Union Theological Seminary, New York, special work in church history. 1897-1899; Fellow of Union Seminary. First studied at Berlin under Harnack and Gencke, then at Paris (Sorbonne). 1899-1905; Teacher of English and Latin, Ethical Culture School, New York. 1905-1911; Teacher of history, Ethical Culture School, New York. 1911; Lecturer, 1912-1920; Associate Professor, 1920-1923; Professor of history at Barnard College. 1907; Degree of Ph.D. from Columbia. Published a "Life of Thomas Jefferson" in 1918.

Spent spring of 1919 in Florida and Virginia for my health—case of persistent bronchitis. In 1920 promoted to full professorship in Barnard College. Same year published Revised Edition of "American History." In spring of 1922 published first volume of a college history of the United States. My son, David, Jr., will graduate from Harvard in June, 1923. My daughter, Elizabeth, entered Smith College in September, 1922.

VARSITY GLEE CLUB, 1893

I am to have a sabbatical vacation in 1923-1924, during which I shall finish my history of the United States (Volume II). When I return to Columbia in 1924, shall give up my undergraduate teaching at Barnard and do only graduate work in American history in the Faculty of Political Science at Columbia. For recreation I still play tennis as nimbly as I did thirty years ago. Spend part of every summer at Annisquam, Massachusetts.

HOWARD PERVEAR NASH

Born at Roxbury, Massachusetts, 8 December 1871, of Osborn Preble Nash (clerk) and Abby Annie Pervear.
Fitted at Chelsea High.
Class Status: Regular.
Degrees: A.B. 1893; LL.B. (Boston Univ.) 1896.
Married Emma Augusta Jones at Brooklyn, New York, 26 July 1899.
Children:
    Howard Pervear, born 8 September 1900.
    Osborn Preble, 5 November 1902.
    Alexander Allaire, 12 June 1904.
    Winifred May, 31 July 1907.
Now a lawyer at Brooklyn, N. Y.

1893-1896: Law student. 1896-1900: Editor of Encyclopedia of Forms and Precedents. 1900-1903; Editor of Cyclopedia of Law Procedure. 1903-1905: Assistant to William D. Guthrie, Esquire. 1905-1909: Lawyer, New York City firm Wells (E. H., Yale, '93) and Nash. 1909-1918: City Magistrate, Borough of Brooklyn, New· York City by appointment of George B. McClellan, Mayor. 1919: Judge County Court, King's County, New York, by appointment of Governor Alfred E. Smith. 1920 to date: Lawyer, Brooklyn, New York, firm of Nash and Gottesman (S..M., Cornell, 1908).

HERBERT VINCENT NEAL

Born at Lewiston, Maine, 3 April 1869, of John Neal (bookbinder) and Caroline Augusta Noyes.
Entered from Bates College.
Class Status: Senior year only.
Degrees: A.B. (Bates) 1890; A.B. 1893; A.M. 1894; Ph.D. 1896.
Married Helen Phillips Howell at Southold, New York, 8 June 1899.
Children:
    Margaret } twins, born 26 February 1901.
    Helen
    John Howell, 13 July 1906.
Now Professor of Zoology, Tufts College, Massachusetts.

Graduate student, Cambridge, 1893-1896. Student, University of Munich and Naples Biological Station, 1896-1897. Professor of biology, Knox College, 1897-1913. Professor of zoölogy, Tufts College, 1913-1923. Assistant Director, Harpswell Laboratory, 1907-1917. "Y-guy" in Italy, 1918-1919; discharged, September, 1919, New York.

Completing this year the twenty-fifth year of college professorship. Sabbatical year 1921-1922 spent in England, chiefly at Universities of Oxford and London.

ALBERT WOODARD NEWLIN

Born at Bloomingdale, Indiana, 13 June 1869, of Kersey Newlin (farmer) and Luranah Woodard.
Entered from Earlham College.
Class Status: Senior year only.
Degrees: Ph.B. (Earlham, Ind.) 1892; A.B. 1893.
Married Beatrice Hortense Roos at New Orleans, 5 September 1904.
Children:
    Albert Kersey, born 17 June 1905.
    Lucille Luranah, 20 June 1907.
    Nestor Behrman, 18 February 1913.
    Clifton Roos, 23 June 1915.
    Floyd Woodard, 3 April 1918.
    Robert Ewing, 31 March 1922.
Now on editorial staff Daily States at New Orleans.

From 1893 to 1906, engaged in newspaper work entirely, first in Boston, then in New Orleans; edited the Lake Charles (La.) Press for one year, returning to staff of New Orleans Picayune in 1897; took active part in campaigns against yellow fever in 1897-1898 and 1905; when Justice Newton C. Blanchard left the Supreme Court to run for Governor in 1903, I campaigned the state with him, travelling in every parish (county) of the state. In 1906, Governor Blanchard made me secretary of the Southern University Board, a state institution; also named me a major on the Governor's staff, Louisiana National Guard; 1909 to 1912, engaged in newspaper work in New Orleans; 1912 was elected secretary of the Democratic State Central Committee of Louisiana, which position I still hold, having been reëlected in 1916 and in 1920. In 1912, Governor L. E. Hall appointed me jury commissioner for the parish of Orleans, and Governor Pleasant re-appointed me in 1916, serving until 1919. In March, 1920, I was appointed United States Naval Officer of

Customs for the Port of New Orleans, by President Woodrow Wilson, and served until November 15, 1922. During the years of the World War, I was appointed by the Governor of Louisiana a member of the Council of Defense for Orleans Parish and a member of the War Gardens Committee for New Orleans, engaging in many other war activities.

Howard Gardner Nichols

See Report VI, Page 212.

Joseph Longworth Nichols

Born at Cincinnati, Ohio, 10 November 1870, of George Ward Nichols and Maria Longworth.
Fitted at St. Paul's.
Class Status: Regular.
Degrees: A.B. 1893; M.D. (Johns Hopkins) 1897.
Married Mary Morgan at Saranac Lake, New York, 5 April 1910.
Died of tubercular cerebral meningitis, 17 June 1918, at Saranac Lake, New York.

After leaving Cambridge Nichols studied medicine at the Johns Hopkins Medical School, graduating in June, 1897, at the head of his class and being appointed to a fellowship in pathology. He remained at Johns Hopkins another year, working under Dr. Welch, and then went to Berlin for further study. In the spring of 1900 while in England, where he had gone intending to work in the London hospitals, he developed pulmonary tuberculosis, from which he suffered all the rest of his life.

The next few years were chiefly spent in Switzerland, Colorado and Arizona. While in Arizona he met Dr. Edward L. Trudeau of Saranac Lake, New York, and at his suggestion went there in August, 1903, to engage in research work connected with tuberculosis. In the spring of 1905 he again went abroad, spending the following winter in Egypt, and in August, 1906, he returned to Saranac Lake, bought a house and except for occasional absences (including a short wedding trip to Europe in 1910) lived there until his death, which occurred on June 17, 1918, after a brief acute attack of tubercular cerebral meningitis. He is survived by his wife and by his mother, Mrs. Bellamy Storer, and a sister, married to the Marquis de Chambrun, a descendant of Lafayette and a prominent member of the French Chamber of Deputies.

Nichols never . practised medicine. He always intended to devote himself to research and for a number of years after settling in Saranac Lake he worked regularly in the laboratory, where he showed marked ability. But his interests were not confined to research and he gave much time to public and philanthropic work, being at the time of his death president of the Saranac Lake General Hospital, treasurer of the Society for the Control of Tuberculosis, a director of the Boys' Club, and a vestryman of St. Luke's Church. He gave much to the community in which he lived and in return was universally respected and loved.

Compelled to spend so many years in practical exile, Nichols never, even to his most intimate friends, uttered a word of complaint or regret. He cheerfully accepted the limitations imposed by his health, and led a useful, and (especially from the time of his marriage) a happy life. Of an unusually lovable nature, he inspired the warmest friendships; and his death, coming the day before the twenty-fifth anniversary reunion of '93, was a great shock to his classmates and was felt by many as an irreparable personal loss.

C. L. B.

Walter Clark Nichols

See Report VI, Page 214.

MAXWELL NORMAN

Born at Newport, Rhode Island, 21 April 1871, of George H Norman
(civil engineer) and Abbie Durfee Kinsley.
Fitted at A. Hale's.
Class Status: 1889-91, with '93; 1891-93, with '95; 1893-94, with '94.
Degree: A.B. 1895 as of 1894.
Now trustee and investor at Newport.

His legal residence continues to be Newport, Rhode Island, though he has a summer place at Hamilton, Massachusetts, spends much of the winters at Palm Beach, and makes a trip to Europe every year—sometimes two. Occupation chiefly co-trustee of his father's estate; also trustee of Newport Water Works, director of Old Colony Trust Company, etc. Interested in golf.

ALLEN ALVIN NORTH

Born at Greenville, Ohio, 26 February 1870, of Allen North (farmer) and
  Mary Ann Fry.
Entered from Ohio Wesleyan University.
Class Status: Senior year only. Law School, 1893-96.
Degrees: A.B. (Ohio Wes.) 1892; LL.B. 1896.
Married Hester Ellen Ryan of Piqua, Ohio, at Greenville, Ohio, 24 June
  1896. Children:
    Allen Alvin, born 4 September 1902.
    Annetta Ardis, 4 July 1904.
Now in insurance at Troy, Ohio.

Immediately after graduating from the Law School settled in
his home town, Greenville, Ohio, married, and in June of 1897
entered the active practice of law. Ran that year for state attorney, but was defeated by eighteen votes! In 1907 removed
to Cleveland and took up insurance, as assistant actuary of the
Cleveland Life. Leaving them in about three years he vibrated
between Greenville and Troy, Ohio (which he gave as his permanent address), describing himself as ''field counsel—insurance
law and field technique.'' In 1913 he became field counsel for
the Union Central Life, with the Dayton, Ohio, management.
Here he remained until 1922, when his connections were severed,
and he returned to Troy. Here he is still supposed to be living,
though he does not reply to recent notices.

HARRISON PICKERING NOWELL

Born at Portsmouth, New Hampshire, 20 December 1869, of Thomas
  Shepard Nowell (capitalist) and Lydia Ham.
Fitted with Dr. E. R. Humphreys.
Class Status: Regular.
Degree: A.B. 1893.

Nowell is reported to be deceased, but the Secretary has been
unable to obtain any details. When last heard from (November 11, 1920) he was connected with the Government Army
Store at San Francisco as Acting Branch Manager, but expected
to leave that position shortly. His brother George Manning
Nowell was in the Law School as late as 1906, but cannot now
be located.

CHARLES READ NUTTER

Born at Boston, 8 November 1871, of Thomas Franklin Nutter (lawyer)
    and Adelaide Julia Read.
Fitted at Browne and Nichols.
Class Status: Regular.
Degree: A.B. 1893.
Married Medora Cheatham Addison at Stamford, Connecticut, 31 October
    1911. Children:
  Thayer ⎫ twins, born 29 August 1912.
  Morris ⎭
Now in business at Boston.

Cornered at last by the Indefatigable One, informed that
"to-morrow" is positively the last call, realizing that "to-
morrow" creeps on apace (a fast pace), I, too, must attend
the confessional and reveal in "three hundred words" to him
who runs (if he can be held long enough) a life of dire events
and blood-curdling incidents. On second thoughts—all crimi-
nals are permitted second thoughts—I will refer the running
reader to the last report (from the preparation of which I
scarce have recovered) for the direness and bloody curdles. Let
them fade into the stained oblivion which all discovered crimi-
nals pray for. (Observe "on your left" the first one hundred
mile post). These years of crime were passed, first in teaching
in Groton School and in Harvard, then in publishing in New
York and later in Boston, then, during the war, in the New
England Division of the Red Cross. When the so-called peace
came along, I became Manager of The Bureau of Foreign Trade
of the Boston Chamber of Commerce. I note "the following
topics suggested" by the Indefatigable One. First: "Business or profession." Well, I'm caught at a critical and, so to
say, untangled moment. For I'm trying to take over, with
another criminal, what is alluringly called a "going" business;
but, as the tangle of procedure is still tangled, I can say no
more, but must leave the curiosity of the running reader un-
satiated—perhaps forever, if this class report is, as claimed,
the "last in the quinquennial series of class reports." (This
handling of the R. R.'s curiosity has been done in equally good
novels). Second, says the I. O. "Sports and pastimes." To
the young man these terms seem similar in meaning; but for
detailed information let the R. R. observe the life of any other
average young man among us. And so, joyfully (for I passed

the second mile-stone some way back), to the other topics.
"Public position and offices." So far, thank Heaven, none.
"Degrees and distinctions." Degreeless and without distinction. "Publications and speeches." Class reports and addresses to the I. O. "Societies and clubs." Too exclusive
for the public eye. Now, if the **R. R.** thinks I have, like Sam
Weller at Mr. Pickwick's trial, said "just as little respecting
[myself] as might be," details can be furnished on request.
For other and unspecified topics—I can say I am enjoying
life, good health, a tolerably bearable family, infernal winters,
the shrunk dollar, and frequent chats with the I. O. Perhaps
I have overrun the limit of words, but I suspect the **R. R.**
withdrew some ways back.

THOMAS EDWARD OLIVER

Born at Salem, Massachusetts, 16 December 1871, of Samuel Cook Oliver
     [H. C. 1849] (Civil War invalid) and Mary Elizabeth Andrews.
Fitted at Salem High.
Class Status: Regular.
Degrees: A.B. 1893; Ph.D. (Heidelberg) 1899.
Married Elisabeth Reinhardt at Cleveland, 9 June 1904. Children:
     Elisabeth Andrews, born 12 May 1905.
     Martha Reinhardt, 3 September 1907.
     Sarah Chever, 23 March 1913.
     John Lee, 2 January 1911 (adopted 30 November 1921).
Now Professor of Romance Languages at the University of Illinois.

After nearly a year (1893-1894) in the Harvard Medical
School I was obliged to leave because of ill-health and bad eyes.
A final operation for cataract gave me what vision I have since
had after which I decided to abandon medicine and take up the
study of modern languages which had been my main interest in
college. Accordingly I went to Europe in November, 1894, and
studied at Leipsig, Heidelberg, and Paris, securing my Ph.D.
at Heidelberg in March, 1899. I travelled extensively in Northern Europe during vacations, mostly by bicycle. One of these
trips, in the summer of 1896, was with Friedman, '93, in England and Scotland. Returning to America I served one year
(1899-1900) at the University of Michigan as instructor in
French, then at Western Reserve University College for
Women for three years, coming finally as Professor of Romance
Languages to the University of Illinois in September, 1903. I

am now rounding out my twentieth year of service at Illinois, and find myself among the veterans of this faculty, on the first page of the list of instructors. This long service has been twice interrupted. In 1910-1911 I was off for my first sabbatical, dividing the time between Finland, Germany, France, England, and Switzerland. My wife and children were along also, and we visited relatives in Finland and Germany. In 1915-1916 I served in Belgium and Northern France with the Commission for Relief in Belgium. This was a trying but most interesting experience; interesting because I was behind the German lines, a witness to a military despotism in Belgium, and trying because I was for several months unable to get word from my family.

We have a little summer home on the shores of Lake Hamlin, near Ludington, Michigan, and have been going up there the past eleven years. My chief avocations are amateur acting with the Players' Club, a faculty organization, attendance at the monthly meetings of our local Harvard Club, and the many duties of a trustee of the Urbana Unitarian Church. Otherwise my life is the quiet one of a teacher, full of pleasant contacts with colleagues and with the never-ending stream of college youth. I do not feel a bit older as the years pass, and ascribe this in largest measure to the spirit of youth all about me. Can life be much fairer than this?

Gilbert Francis Ordway

See Report VI, Page 217, and Supplement, Page 129.

LOUIS ERNEST OSBORN

Born at Boston, 4 April 1871, of Edward Field Osborn (railroads) and Helen Frances Watson.
Fitted at Franklin School, Cincinnati, Ohio.
Class Status: With class four years.
Degree: A.B. 1894, as of 1893.
Married Josephine Newman at Louisville, Kentucky, 12 August 1922.
Now railroad treasurer at Cincinnati, Ohio.

At last I can report that something worth while has happened in my life—"Mirabile dictu"—I am now a benedict. This fact so surmounts everything that has happened to me before or since that I feel that this statement alone is ample and sufficient to make this report a satisfactory one, although brief.

However, I must add that another pleasant event has been experienced by me recently, and that was the dinner given by our New York Classmates, on February 2nd, 1923, to which I was invited and enjoyed thoroughly. Kindly permit me to take this opportunity to thank them all for the wonderful time I had, due to their courteous hospitality.

GEORGE ALFRED PAGE

Born at London, England, 30 May 1872, of Charles Albert Page [Columbian Univ.] (lawyer) and Grace Darling Coues.
Fitted at Brookline High.
Class Status: Regular.
Degree: A.B. 1893.
Married Mabel Hurd at Brookline, Massachusetts, 15 June 1898. Children:
> Charles Albert, born 13 March 1899.
> Helen Bruce, 18 January 1902.
> George Alfred, Jr., 11 December 1907.
Now in publishing business at Boston.

I have very little news since the last class report as I am pursuing the even tenor of my way with few interruptions. I am in the publishing business and am still interested in gardening. In fact, three years ago I purchased a farm of about one hundred acres so that I would have room to dig in the dirt to my heart's content. The farm is situated in Sherborn, only twenty miles from Boston, so that I spend my summers there and motor to and from my office. My family is growing up rapidly and they are beginning to think of me as more or less of a dignified old man. One son graduated from Harvard in 1921 and has started to make his way in the world. The other son is at Middlesex where "Rick" Winsor is teaching him to be a good student, a good sport and a good Harvard-man-to-be.

JOHN HARLESTON PARKER

Born at Boston, 27 November 1872, of Harleston Parker [Harvard 1843] and Adeline Ellen Reynolds.
Fitted at G. W. C. Noble's.
Class Status: Regular.
Degree: A.B. 1893

Married Edith Value Stackpole at Nahant, Massachusetts, 12 September 1904. Children:
Edith Harleston, born 28 June 1905.
John Harleston, Jr., 12 July 1907.
James, 6 January 1909.
Margaret Stackpole, 23 November 1918.
Now practising architecture at Boston.

Entered the Massachusetts Institute of Technology the autumn of 1893 as a special student in architecture and remained two years. Studied in Italy in 1896-1897 and entered the Ecole des Beaux Arts where I remained till 1900, when I returned and formed the firm of Parker and Thomas. The firm became Parker, Thomas and Rice in 1907, and has remained so ever since. During the war we built one large housing project for the government and large munition plants in Baltimore, Rochester and Chicago, as well as a number of smaller buildings for camps, Army and Navy Clubs, etc. My life has been entirely devoted to my profession in which I am tremendously interested. I expect to keep actively at work in it as long as I am able to.

VERNON LOUIS PARRINGTON

Born at Aurora, Illinois, 3 August 1871, of John William Parrington [Colby 1855] (lawyer) and Louise McClellan.
Entered from Emporia College.
Class Status: Entered Junior.
Degrees: A.B. (Emporia) 1892; A.B. 1893; A.M. (Emporia) 1895.
Married Julia Rochester Williams at Seattle, Washington, 31 July 1901. Children:
Elizabeth, born 27 April 1902.
Louise Wrathal, 29 April 1907.
Vernon Louis, Jr., 28 April 1913.
Now Professor of English at the University of Washington.

Taught in the College of Emporia, 1893-97; in Oklahoma University, 1897-1908; in the University of Washington, 1908-1923. Summer Session, University of California, 1922. Fourteen months in Europe, 1903-1904. Will be in Columbia Summer Session, 1923, and hope to visit Harvard for the first time since leaving Cambridge in July, 1893.

Only an inconsequential note to the foregoing. Very little happens to a teacher after he has achieved his professorship, beyond the routine of his studies and the drama of seeing his children through college. He is certain of lean fare when he retires, years hence, but he generously permits his wife to do whatever worrying needs to be done on that score, while he takes refuge in the doctrine of compensations. He has not made much stir in the world, but he likes to think of himself as more or less a philosophical spectator of the curious ways of men, and discovers satisfaction in an assumed intellectual superiority. Thank God, at any rate, we teachers are not as the Philistines, who believe whatever the newspapers would have them believe. It may be only a defense mechanism against professorial salaries, but I prefer to regard it as a pedagogic form of that romance which the ingenious Mr. Cabell would have us believe is so necessary to human happiness. I often wonder what becomes of the fine young men and women who annually make their cheerful plunge into the outside scramble. Some of them turn out Babbitts, I suppose, in spite of our warnings; but not all I am sure. There is far more intellectual ferment among the better undergraduates today than there was in our provincial time, and a goodly number of keen, well-trained minds now go out to help leaven the American lump. I never fail to point out to my Yale colleagues that of the younger American intellectuals who are heckling the self-righteous today, more have come out of Harvard than from all the other universities; and I take pleasure in rubbing the fact in. Ninety-three has contributed somewhat conspicuously to the great game through Villard and *The Nation*. He is the only member of our class whom I really envy. What a gorgeous time he must have, laying on at every smug and shoddy respectability that crosses his path! And I get my fun out of it rooting from the bleachers.

WILLIAM EDWIN PARSONS

Born at Kennebunkport, Maine, 25 August 1865, of John Parsons [Brown 1842] (clergyman) and Sarah Ayer Chase.
Fitted at Chauncy Hall.
Class Status: 1888-90, with '92. 1891-93, with '93.
Degree: A.B. 1893.
Now Insurance agent at Boston.

[Not heard from.]

GEORGE EVERETT PARTRIDGE

Born at Worcester, Massachusetts, 31 May 1870, of George Partridge (real estate) and Sarah Boyden Capron.
Fitted at Worcester High.
Class Status: Freshman year only.
Degree: Ph.D. (Clark Univ.) 1899.
Married Emelyn Smythe Newcomb at New York City, 31 August 1898.
    Children:
        Elaine Newcomb, born 19 February 1900 (died 14 August 1901).
        Miriam Newcomb, 6 June 1902.
        Philip Newcomb, 31 July 1909.
Now in psychological practice at Boston, Massachusetts.

My record from college to the Sixth Report may be summarized in a very few words. I lived the life of a student under limitations imposed by a persisting condition of imperfect health. The significant events were those set down chronologically above. There was little more to write about in the quarter of-a-century. Clarke University gave me the degree of Doctor of Philosophy in 1899; I taught three years in the West; returned to Clark as lecturer (1904-1906); and wrote a few books.

Despite all secretarial encouragement, the five years just past must be entered as "the same continued." The publication of "The Psychology of Nations," in 1919 is the only evidence of activity recently. I have been collaborating with another man in writing a book that is not yet finished; and what I still regard as my "contribution" to philosophy lies in manuscript. Publishers say they would like to put their imprint on it, etc., but up to present writing, for certain business reasons, they decline the honor. The only item to be added is that I have moved to Boston, and there (with my wife) have entered the field of psychological practice.

Horace Wilbur Patterson

See Report VI, Page 222.

George Eckhard Paul

See Report VI, Page 223, and Supplement, Page 129.

HENRY GREENLEAF PEARSON

Born at Portland, Maine, 26 December 1870, of George Henry Pearson
(nautical instrument repairer) and Mary Frances Hitchcock.
Fitted at Portland High.
Class Status: Regular.
Degree: A.B. 1893
Married Elizabeth Ware Winsor at Weston, Massachusetts, 6 September
1898. Children:
Anne Winsor, born 13 November 1899 (died 11 August 1901).
Theodore, 7 July 1903.
Mary, 31 January 1906 (died 30 October 1906).
Robert Winsor, 18 February 1910.
Henry Greenleaf, Jr. 10 November 1912.
Now Head of the Department of English and History at Technology.

Immediately after graduation I began to teach in the Department of English and History at the Massachusetts Institute of Technology. I have been there ever since; from 1915 I have been head of the Department. Since 1918 the work has been especially absorbing on account of the greatly increased registration at the Institute and the necessity of combining with English instruction in History.

My avocation is the writing of biography. My fifth work of this sort, "A Business Man in Uniform," is just complete. It is a life of Colonel Raynal Bolling (Harvard 1900) who, having advocated preparedness for two years, was sent abroad at the beginning of the war as head of the Bolling Aeronautical Mission, and after distinguished service in organizing a post of the Air Service of the A. E. F., was killed at the time of the German drive. I am glad to have had the chance to interpret for others the story of his heroic labors and sacrifices. My other books are "Life of John A. Andrew," "An American Railroad Builder," "Wadsworth of Geneseo," and "Life of William Howe McElwain."

Occupations of this sort are a source of happiness that may well be mentioned here. So are the friends of '93· Greetings to them all!

WALTER ALBERT PEASE

Born at New York City, 14 December 1871, of Walter Albert Pease
(stockbroker) and Mary Louise Hollister.
Fitted at Halsey's Collegiate School.
Class Status: Left Junior year.
Married Martha Chambers Rodgers at Pittsburgh, Pennsylvania, 8 June
1899. Children:

Calbraith Perry Rodgers, born 15 July 1901 (died 15 February 1902).
Perry Rodgers, 9 March 1904.
Martha Carroll, 5 May 1905.
Now in real estate business at New York City.

About five years ago I decided to retire from the Corporation of Pease and Elliman of which I had been President, as I wanted to get away from the small real estate business. I opened an office at 50 East Forty-second Street, under my own name and am still active in real estate, but confine myself mostly to large sales, appraisals and expert testimony work. I was recently made President of a new mortgage company, The Empire Bond and Mortgage Corporation, of which I hope you will hear more in the future, as it promises to be very successful.

I suppose I'm growing older, but I don't feel so. I now have a boy who is a Freshman at Harvard and a daughter almost grown up.

Charles Cushman Peirce

See Report VI, Page 225.

Richard Francis Perkins

See Report VI, Page 226.

ROLAND EDWARD PHILLIPS

Born at Cleveland, Ohio, 30 May 1872, of William A. Phillips [Phys. and Surg. N. Y.] (physician) and Marion E. Nickerson.
Entered from Adelbert College.
Class Status: Entered Senior.
Degree: A.B. 1893.
Married Mrs. Gertrude Mary (Shepard) Hunter, at London, 16 April 1894, with one son, Malcolm. Children:
Marion, born 16 January 1897.
Roland, Jr., 12 September 1898. (Killed in action near Chateau-Thiery, 28 July 1918.)
Gordon, 18 November 1901.
Now literary adviser to various publications, New York City.

After leaving college, I went to Johns Hopkins for graduate work in modern languages. Then and later, spent considerable time abroad in France, Germany, England, Italy and so on, most of the time in study at the leading universities there. My father was anxious that I should be a professor—particularly a professor at Harvard. But the preparation was a good one, too, for journalism, which was my choice. I took up this profession and earned my first money as a reporter on the *Figaro* in Paris.

Returning home, I engaged for a short time in newspaper work in New York City. Then became Managing Editor of Harper's Weekly at the time Colonel George Harvey was the Editor. I then went with Walter Page as Managing Editor of Everybody's Magazine and, in a short time, as contributing Editor of the World's Work which was then being started. I then became Editor of Cosmopolitan Magazine.

When the war came, I gave up my work and went abroad, first as Lieutenant and later as Major in the Red Cross. My chief work there was to visit each Division of the A. E. F. in turn and to assist in carrying out a plan I suggested which insured the coöperation of the Army with the Red Cross in sending home news about the "boys." The plan was suggested by the fact that my own son, Roland, Jr., was killed in action there and we could get no official news of him. It was—and is —a great source of gratification that with the assistance of the Army whose organization, with the approval of General Pershing and Adjutant-General Davis. was used for the purpose, we were enabled to send home several hundred thousand letters and cables to the fathers and mothers at home.

After the war I returned for a short time to the Cosmopolitan; but after about a year I gave up the routine work and at the present time am amusing myself—and earning a little money for my family—by "free-lancing" and "literary advising."

And at present moment I am a "grand-pop." My daughter Marion did it—a fine boy. Now what do you think of that?

CARL HORTON PIERCE

Born at Boston, 24 January 1870, of Charles Fletcher Pierce (manufacturer) and Jennie Morse.
Fitted at Harvard School, Chicago.
Class Status: With class four years.
Degree:A.B. 1894, as of 1893.
Married (1) Edythe Gross at Brooklyn, New York, 4 June 1900. Children:
Charles Wilder, born 11 December 1901.
Doris, 28 October 1903.
David Warren, 26 June 1908 (died 5 February 1914).
Married (2) Florence MacCulloch at Hoboken, N. J., 15 October 1919.
Now in real estate business at New York.

I started in business the day I got back to Chicago, at the Libby Glass Works at the Chicago World's Fair. After gaining a fair insight into the glass business and finding that it was on the wane, I went into the telephone business, serving the Chicago Telephone Company from the bottom of the ladder to manager.

Circumstances brought my family to New York just before the Spanish War, and I came East also and went into the newspaper business, starting on the Sunday New York World, and occupying positions on the Journal, the Herald, the Mail and Express, ranging from reporter to news editor, etc. This work lasted for about five years.

Then came a demand for a story of New Harlem—the town. At first it was designed simply as a newspaper story. Later it grew somewhat in size, finally launching itself into a fairly good sized book of perhaps 30,000 words, entitled "New Harlem, Past and Present."

With the newspaper work and the writing came the thought of teaching young men how to prepare for newspaper work. This was undertaken at the 23rd Street Y. M. C. A. in New York City in 1904 with some success. Following the newspaper teaching came the demand for teaching of salesmen, and this work took root with surprising rapidity. Brooklyn, Newark, and other places, as well as New York, engaged the course. It called for a text book and this was written, entitled "Scientific Salesmanship," which had a considerable sale, and I became president of an institution entitled "The Scientific Salesmanship School of New York, Inc." In addition I was New York salesmanager for Canfield Brothers, eastern agents of the Standard Adding Machine Company.

After several years of teaching, I entered the motion picture field as executive manager, and was in it for eight years, with Bosworth, Inc., Oliver Morosco Company, Photoplay and Pallas Pictures, and later with the Paramount Pictures Corporation, and Famous Players Lasky Corporation, being manager of the service department and special representative. I have now entered the real estate field as general manager of a company handling the largest surburban real estate development around Greater New York, with headquarters at 247 West 34th Street, New York City.

GEORGE BURGESS PIERCE

Born at Milton, Massachusetts, 21 January 1872, of Edward Lillie Pierce
 [Brown 1850, Harvard Law 1852] (lawyer) and Elizabeth Helen
 Kingsbury.
Fitted at Phillips Exeter.
Class Status: Regular.
Degrees: A.B. 1893; M.D. 1898.
Married Marion Stone Douglass at Orange, New Jersey, 28 June 1919
 (died 16 April 1921).
Now living in Llewellyn Park, West Orange, New Jersey.

Surgical house officer, Massachusetts General Hospital. Appointed assistant in anatomy at Harvard Medical School, but resigned. Alternate delegate at McKinley-Roosevelt convention. Defeated for Congress in 1900 and for State Senate in 1901. Harvard Law School 1900-1901. President of Republican City Committee of Boston in 1902-1903. Became treasurer and part owner Monadnock Paper Mills. Sold out in January, 1912, and took Mediterranean trip. Same trip in 1913. In 1914 same trip, but went up the Nile as far as Assouan, seeing Luxor and Thebes. Met many British officers, now dead. Stood by Kitchner one night. Crossed to Marseilles with the famous gambler, the earl of Rosslyn, as travelling companion. Played tennis in Nice tournaments with varying success all three years. In 1915 was surgeon of the French Red Cross, an interesting experience. In 1916 failed at last moment to go with Belgian Relief. A man speaking French was desired, but my ''activities with the French Red Cross'' were a bar. Fished in Jamaica and the Chagres River, Panama, for tarpon. Was in Costa Rica's capitol when the president was ousted by arms. Climbed Mt. Irazu.

In 1918 the Armistice kept me from going to Europe as a member of the United States Military Police. January 15, 1919, went to Florida to fish in the Gulf Stream and was at Palm Beach. June 28, 1919, was married at Llewellyn Park, Orange, New Jersey (my present home) and travelled much until my wife's death, April 16, 1921. In Canada in July, 1919; in Florida, New Orleans and Richmond in spring of 1920. Salmon fishing in the Grand Cascapedia, Quebec, in June, 1920-1921. Went to England, the devastated regions, France and Italy in July to November, 1920. January, 1922 went to Florida (where my father-in-law died) returning in April.

July 7, 1922, I broke my patellar ligament at tennis. After operation, six months ago, I am getting a good leg.

Clubs: Harvard of New York, New Jersey, and Boston, Norfolk Hunt Club, Union Club of Boston, Essex County Country Club, University of New York.

CHARLES BURRALL PIKE

Born at Chicago, 29 June 1871, of Eugene Samuel Pike [Antioch] (capitalist) and Mary Rockwell.
.Fitted at Harvard School, Chicago.
Class Status: Regular.
Degrees: A.B. 1893; LL.B. 1896.
Married Frances Aura Alger at Washington, D. C., 18 May 1898.
'Now in real estate business at Chicago.

Since my father's death in 1916, I have been the managing trustee of the Eugene S. Pike Estate Land Trust. In 1920, Mrs. Pike and I toured France and Spain. In 1922, we took a Mediterranean cruise, stopping at Madeira, Gibraltar, Monaco, Naples, Athens, Alexandria and Cairo. We went up the Nile by Dahabeah as far as Assuan—a wonderful experience,—returning by way of Italy, France and England. Sports and pastimes: Duck shooting, racquets and golf.

In December, 1922, I was elected President of the Military Training Camps Association of the United States, the headquarters of which were moved to Chicago the first of the year. In order to more effectively coöperate with the War Department, the plan submitted by me to the Secretary of War, creating Civilian Aides—one for each Corps Area and one for each State—was adopted. As President of the Military Training Camps Association I have been appointed Chief Civilian Aide to the Secretary of War and as such, I have nominated to the Secretary of War Civilian Aides for each Corps Area and State in the United States.

In 1920 I was elected a Trustee of the American Field Service for French Universities. I have been a Director and Trustee of the Chicago Historical Society since 1918, and this year one of the Vice-Presidents. In January of this year I was elected President of the Racquet Club of Chicago, now organizing.

Publications: The "Annuals" in connection with the Citizens' Military Training Camps—one for each Camp held in the

Central Department of the Military Training Camps Association: For Camp Knox, "The Mess Kit"; Fort Snelling, "The Barracks Bag"; Camp Custer, "Preparedness"; Camp Des Moines, "Citizen"; Jefferson Barracks, "Jeffersonian".

Club and societies: Chicago Club, University Club, Onwentsia Club, Racquet and Tennis Club of Chicago, Old Elm, Shore-acres, Sanganois, Mid Day Club, Saddle and Cycle, Racquet and Tennis Club of New York, Harvard Club of New York, Yondo-tega Club of Detroit.

J[AMES] MONROE TAYLOR POPE

Born at Syracuse, New York, 10 August 1870, of Charles Clarus Pope
  (chemical manufacturer) and Laura Maria Allen Taylor.
Fitted at Wilson and Kellogg's.
Class Status: Left during Sophomore year.
Married Frances Cythera Twombly at New York City, 4 April 1894
  (divorced). Child:
    Donald Twombly, born 3 February 1896.
Now retired from insurance business, in Indianapolis.

In the fall of 1891 entered the J. Monroe Taylor Chemical Company at New York City, and remained there for about ten years. After an interval of "no occupation," took up the insurance business about 1906, attending to all insurance matters in the large real estate office of J. P. Day, New York City. Here remained till 1920, when again retired from business and removed to Indianapolis, where is residing at present.

JOHN REED POST

Born at New York City, 15 July 1872, of Jotham William Post (banker)
  and Eliza Chapman.
Fitted at Brookline High.
Class Status: Left after Sophomore year.
Married Mabel Davis at Boston, 5 June 1902. Children:
    Mary Lincoln, born 3 November 1903.
    Madeline Blaau, 3 November 1907.
Now in cotton brokerage at Boston.

Since leaving college, I first went into an insurance office in Boston for a short time, then took a job in the Water Department under Judge Robert Grant. In 1894 decided to go into the cotton business and set sail for Galveston, Texas, which marked the beginning of nine years in the South, in Texas, Mississippi and Alabama, which was interesting, but Bostonians.

are not good colonists and I was glad to get a job in a cotton office in 1903 (especially as I married in 1902), and settle down here for the rest of my days. Boston is good enough for anybody, I think. I became a partner in the firm of Ellerton L. Dorr and Company a few years after my return to Boston and when Mr. Dorr, senior, died in 1913, his son and I formed a partnership under the name of Dorr and Post, and that is our firm today. The last five years have been quite uneventful. When we went into the war, I joined the home branch of the First Corps of Cadets in Boston, called the First Motor Corps, the other branch being the 101st Engineers, which went to the front. When the police strike came in Boston in 1919, the First Motor Corps was called out and we had several days and nights of guard duty in South Boston, and afterward for a number of weeks served as traffic police in the Boston streets. I am interested in the Family Welfare Society of Boston, serving as a director and attending the weekly conferences in one of the districts. In the sport line I go in for golf and bridge.

Warwick Potter

See Report VI, 230.

EDWARD PEARSON PRESSEY

Born at Salem, New Hampshire, 28 June 1869, of John Pressey (merchant) and Mary Ellen Colby.
Fitted at Pinkerton Academy.
Class Status: With class four years.
Degree: A.B. 1894; as of 1893.
Married (1) Grace Harriet Gibson at Londonderry, New Hampshire, 22 June 1897 (died 2 December 1907). Children:
Dorothea, born 13 July 1898.
Elizabeth, 3 March 1903.
John Emanuel, 5 November 1905.
Married (2) Grace deWolf Gamwell at Westfield, Massachusetts, 22 May 1909. Children by adoption:
Naomi deWolf, born 19 July 1901.
Philip Moseley, 5 April 1906.
Now with Schenectady Gazette, Schenectady, N. Y.

I was in the Divinity School of the University two years after graduation. Held pastorates in Derby, Connecticut, Rowe and Montague, Massachusetts, for the next ten years. While in Montague my wife and I devised an application or social settlement work for enlivement of some of the torpid conditions incident to the continuous drain of the energies and capital to the larger centers of population. The "New Clairvaux" movement went into history for whatever it was worth after fourteen years of existence. The record is told in eleven printed volumes of "Country Time and Tide" and an 8vo volume "The Vision," now in many of the principal libraries of the United States. In 1915 I moved to Woodstock, Vermont, and took up a two hundred and ten acre tract of mountain farm and forest. There in seclusion of wholly private life during three years I thought out the next philosophical thing to do.

Five years ago I went to Manchester, New Hampshire, near my native place, and plunged into journalism and war work as a four-minute man in volunteer government publicity work. Four years ago I took a permanent position with the leading daily of this "Dorp." As a side line I am doing research work on the evolution of democracy which I hope in about two years to publish. It will be my apology for a Harvard education.

CHESTER WELLS PURINGTON

Born at Boston, 27 October 1871, of Joseph Albert Purington (merchant) and Lydia Jane Chase Morrill.
Fitted at Boston Latin.
Class Status: Regular.
Degree: A.B. 1893.
Married Charlotte Calhoun Wells at Amesbury, Massachusetts, 6 April 1905. Child:
> Frank Calhoun, born 29 April 1913.
Now mining engineer at Yokohama, Japan.

Since last report mostly engaged in gradual acquisition for a British Company of gold-bearing property at and about Okhotsk on the Pacific Coast of Siberia. As the district has been constantly in a zone of revolution and civil war, many difficulties have been experienced, but we appear to be over the worst of them. Have made several journeys between London and Yokahama, including three trips through the Suez Canal, and two via America. During 1920 was stranded on Cape Patience, Sakhaline Island, in Japanese fishing schooner. Same year visited Okhotsk and the Kuktui River, North Siberia. In 1922 made a second journey to Okhotsk, for an inspection of the gold properties. In Japan have inspected several gold dis-

tricts, the Taio Mine, near Kurumé, Island of Kyushu, the Toi
Mine on Izu Peninsula, Sado Gold Mine on Sado Island, off the
west coast of main Island.   Last summer visited the Usatonai
district of North Hokkaido, in the Ainu country, and the gold
and platinum placers of the Uriu district, in Central Hokkaido.

Since 1918, mining engineers who attempt to deal, as I do,
with the sources of non-ferrous metals, feel that they have been
living in a rather purposeless backwater, and several have
adopted other occupations quite unrelated to mining.   Today
there seems a slight improvement in the demand for metals and
some reduction in the cost of mining.

The profession which I adopted thirty years ago, first that of
geologist and finally that of appraising engineer of mines, has
been enjoyable and profitable in the best sense.   There has been
no financial success worth mentioning, nor desire for such.
Possibly it is not a "gainful" occupation as card-indexed.
That does not worry me.   To be a spectator at the pageant of
humanity, to observe the marts and peoples of the world, to be
sufficiently in touch with affairs to avoid becoming the theoretical dryasdust, and to have enough of earth-science to read with
keen enjoyment the parched desert or the snowy sierra, these
are the privileges of the engineer who elects to take the world
for his oyster, and to open it.

One can recommend this profession.   (Incidentally one's
weight appears to remain the same as in college).   But the slight
lifting of the veil on the hidden mysteries of the vast continent
of Asia is like the cup of Tantalus.   Truly can one say with
Ulysses: . . .

> "All experience is an arch, wherethrough
> Gleams that untravelled world, whose margin fades
> For ever and for ever when I move."

Frank Howard Ransom, Jr.

Born at Buffalo, New York, 25 March 1871, of Frank Howard Ransom
 [Union] (manufacturer) and Isabelle Clara Jones.
Fitted at Browne and Nichols.
Class Status: 1889-91, with '93· 1892-94, with '94· 1894-95, I Medical.
 1895-96, with '96·
Degrees: A.B. 1896; M.D. (Buffalo) 1900.
Married Annette Scott Rychen at Buffalo, New York, 16 June 1898.
Died of acute dilatation of the heart, 2 April 1919, at Buffalo, New York.

Frank Howard Ransom, Jr., died at Buffalo after an illness of five years, resulting from over-work, April 2, 1919. He was born there March 25, 1871, the son of Frank Howard and Isabelle Clara (Jones) Ransom. His father was a student at the Law School in 1865-66, but later took up manufacturing. Frank entered Harvard from Browne & Nichols School, Cambridge, in 1889, but left in sophmore year. He later returned to college and in 1892-94 was a member of '94, was a first year medical student in 1894-95, and took his A.B. in 1896. Always having been interested in medicine, he studied at the University of Buffalo and took his M.D. there in 1900. For a year he was resident physician at the German Deaconess's Hospital in that city, and then studied abroad for two years. On coming back to Buffalo he entered active practice, specializing in obstetrics. In this he held a number of important staff positions, including the Deaconess's Hospital, St.Mary's Maternity Hospital, and progressing in 1908 to "the most advanced hospital in western New York," the Buffalo General. Deeply absorbed in his subject he overworked himself mercilessly, and in 1914, just as he was realizing his ambition to become a recognized expert, he was attacked with acute dilation of the heart, which steadily increased and forced him to give up everything. To the last he was hopeful, patient and full of interest and sympathy for all around him. When unable to serve longer, he was honored with the appointment of "Consulting Obstetrician" to the Buffalo General Hospital. In avocations he was fond of reading and literary work, and was surgeon to the Buffalo Naval Brigade in 1908. On June 16, 1898, at Buffalo, he married Annette Scott Rychen, who survives him.

CHAUNCEY OTIS RAWALT

Born at Canton, Illinois, 14 January 1870, of Milton Rawalt [Urbana Univ.] (farmer) and Alice Bartels.
Entered from Knox College.
Class Status: Entered Senior. Grad. Sch. 1894-96.
Degrees: A.B. (Knox) 1892; A.B. 1893.
Married Jennie Irene Mayo at Providence, Rhode Island, 3 November 1897. Children:
      Doris Anita, 25 August 1898 (deceased.)
      Chauncey Otis, Jr., 7 April 1904.
Now with American Telephone and Telegraph Co., at New York City.

My story of thirty years can be told in a few words. Two more years under the old elms, then twenty-eight years with the American Telephone and Telegraph Company in various capacities. During much of this time I have been in New York directing the designing of the Long Distance toll system of transcontinental lines. This occupation in pursuit of the Bell Company's purpose of "Universal Service" has been extremely fascinating because of rapid business growth and advances in the art. Constant toil has been required to keep ahead of the game, but don't get the idea that it has been all grind. I have had plenty of fun and still have it. Just now I am having more than ever, watching my son get his bearings as a freshman at Columbia.

THOMAS FRANCIS RAY

Born at Boston, 18 November 1869, of Thomas Ray (merchant) and
    Margaret Ryan.
Fitted at Boston Latin.
Class Status: Regular.
Degree: A.B. 1893.
Married Jennie Lee at Seattle, Washington, 30 June 1910. Children:
    Margaret Isabel, born 17 October 1914.
    Thomas Lee, 18 December 1920.
Now practising law at Tacoma, Washington.

Practised law in Boston 1897 to 1903. Visited Lower California for several months, 1903-1904, and finally came to Seattle, Washington. In May, 1905, settled in Tacoma. Connected with legal side of street car company here and later with Judge W. P. Reynolds. In 1908 formed a partnership with J. Charles Dennis, Harvard 1897, who is now City Attorney of Tacoma, under the firm name of Ray & Dennis and practised law together until January, 1919. At that time joined the staff of the Prosecuting Attorney of Pierce County, and have been since thereto attached, and we have just been elected for the next four years.

Married as you know in June, 1910, and wife and daughter, Margaret Isabel, eight years old and son, Thomas Lee, two years old, are the pride of my whole career. Tommy, Jr., Harvard 1941, sends greetings.

Motte Alston Read

Born at Augusta, Georgia, 20 June 1872, of William Melvin Read (cotton merchant) and Jane Ladson Alston.
Fitted at Germantown Academy.
Class Status: Special Scientific, 1889-93.
Degree: S.B. 1902 as of 1893.
Died at Charleston, South Carolina, 12 July 1920.

Motte Alston Read died at Charleston, South Carolina, July 12, 1920, from weakening of the heart superinduced by many years' acute suffering from arthritis. He was born at Augusta, Georgia, June 20, 1872, of William Melvin and Jane Ladson (Alston) Read. On both sides he came from old Southern stock. The Reads were from Charlotte County, Virginia; his father served with Lee in the Civil War and later became a famous cotton merchant, receiving the very unusual honor of election to the Liverpool Cotton Exchange. His mother was the daughter of Jacob Motte Alston, of Charleston, of the family which included the painter, Washington Alston (H. C. 1800). Motte's health was always delicate, and he was sent North to school at Germantown Academy, near Philadelphia. Thence he entered Harvard in 1889 as a special student in the Lawrence Scientific School, taking courses in geology until 1893. On leaving Cambridge his health compelled him to spend three years on a Texas cattle ranch, which he managed himself—an experience which he always rated as equal in value to his college course. He then went to Europe and till 1901 was engaged in further study at Munich and in geological excursions throughout the Continent, his chief publication being "Gastropods of the Volcanic Tuff of the Seisser Alp." For the next two years he was instructor in geology at Harvard, taking his degree of S.B. in 1902 as of 1893. He was also appointed instructor in physiography at the Massachusetts Institute of Technology. His painful disease had already fastened upon him, however, and now forced him to return to out-of-door life in Texas. But his devotion to scientific research never wavered, and later he removed to Washington, where he had full facilities for it. In 1909 he took up permanent residence in Charleston and was elected to the chair of biology and geology in the College of Charleston, a position his increasing infirmity never allowed him to fill. Confined to his own library—although his productiveness became daily more limited by pain and loss of physical powers—he continued his work in physiography and palæontology, taking also a deep interest in heredity, especially as shown in the development of the old families of Virginia and the Carolinas. He left some four hundred note books filled with the results of his studies along this line, which he hoped to put together as a history of the Colonial families of South Carolina. His inherited taste in art was highly developed. He had great skill with his pencil, and his college note books are full of exquisite drawings of specimens. He made a fine collection of Japanese color prints.

Read's mind was always alert and active. He was vivacious, enthusiastic, optimistic, and through his long years of suffering and disappointments as to his health, which forced him to give up one opportunity after another, he kept up his spirits and worked at intellectual pursuits whenever it was physically possible for him to do so. He made a delightful companion and guest. With his infectious enthusiasm, ready laugh and well stocked memory he was a capital story-teller, and his graphic descriptions of ranch life, student days in Munich, and travel, are a vivid recollection of his many friends and pupils. He never married, but the devoted care of his mother did all that could be done to make his life happy. Her death occurred only a short time before his own. His loyalty to his friends, and his fortitude under suffering, make a memory of a tragic life nobly borne.

WILLIAM MAXWELL REED

Born at Bath, Maine, 12 January 1871, of Edwin Reed [Bowdoin 1861] (ship builder) and Emily Putnam Fellows.
Fitted at Browne and Nichols.
Class Status: Left during Junior year.
Married Jannetta Gordon Studdiford at Montclair, New Jersey, 15 April 1913.
Now in telephone work at New York City.

After leaving college in my junior year I worked at the Astronomical Observatory. I was in charge of the West Equatorial Telescope and was engaged in researches in photometry. Part of my time was spent in teaching astronomy in the College and in the Summer School. Later I was for several years Assistant Professor of Practical Astronomy at Princeton. From Princeton I entered the steel mills of John A. Roebling's

Sons Company, where I organized and managed the cost department. I have been engaged in manufacturing ever since until two years ago when I joined the Commercial Engineer's Office of the American Telephone and Telegraph Company.

During the war I was plant manager of the American Wringer Company at Woonsocket, Rhode Isand. I tried a very modified form of industrial democracy which gave excellent results. For the mill was one of the very few in the neighborhood that went through that period without a strike. We doubled our production with fifty per cent. increase in the number of employees.

I am now engaged in research work in methods of doing business. In many respects the American Telephone and Telegraph Company is the general staff for the Bell System. The company therefore investigates business methods and establishes standard practices as well as improves the engineering features of voice transmission.

HARRISON GARFIELD RHODES

Born at Cleveland, 2 June 1871, of James Harrison Rhodes [Williams] (lawyer) and Adelaide Maria Robbins.
Entered from Adelbert College.
Class Status: Entered Sophomore.
Degree: A.B. 1893.
Now in literary and dramatic work at New York City and elsewhere.

Since last report (I possibly lap over, as I have no last report here) I have published: "American Towns and People," "High Life," "A Gift Book for My Mother," also various magazine articles and stories. Also plays, "The Willow Tree," "Her Friend the King." In 1921 I had a cerebral hemorrhage, from which I am gradually and slowly recovering.

JOHN WOLCOTT RICHARDS

Born at Providence, Rhode Island, 15 March 1871, of Charles Augustus Lewis Richards [Yale 1849] (clergyman) and Mary White Wiltbank.
Fitted at University Grammar School, Providence, Rhode Island.
Class Status: Special, 1889-92.
Married Grace O'Hara at Huntington, Long Island, 9 July 1912.
Now in paper business at New York City.

It is true that there is "nothing new" except that I have been ill for the last five months and out of business entirely and in a hospital for the last six weeks. There is no change in my

business except that we have moved from Seventh Avenue to
323 West 16th Street. My home address remains 39 West 67th
Street.

NATHANIEL THAYER ROBB

Born at New York City, 5 July 1870, of James Hampden Robb [H. C.
    1866 Sci.] (banker) and Cornelia Van Rensselaer Thayer.
Fitted at Groton.
Class Status: Regular.
Degree: A.B. 1893.
Married Frances Beatrix Henderson at New York City, 26 November
    1895. Children:
        Janet Henderson, born 7 September 1896.
        James Hampden, 22 December 1898.
        Cornelia Van Rensselaer, 5 March 1904.
Now Director and Manager British International Corporation H. G. M.
    B. H. Cologne, Germany.

After leaving college was employed in the Manhattan Trust
Company until 1898 when I went into the 12th New York Infantry, National Guard of New York, as a Second Lieutenant.
Went, after the Spanish War, into Henderson and Company
and had a seat on the New York Stock Exchange. Was with
them three years when I became a partner in the firm of
Francke, Thompson and Robb, where I remained until 1909,
when I went to Europe and became a director of R. Hoe
and Company in London. Was with them until the outbreak
of the Great War, when I went into the English Army with
rank of Captain, serving in the Intelligence branch and in the
field until 1918, when I was made a First Lieutenant, Infantry,
U. S. A. Was at Chaumont on General Nolen's division and
was made Captain in 1918. Port Officer and Intelligence Officer
in Liverpool until June, 1919. Was Assistant Military Attaché,
London, until September, 1919, when I was mustered out. Have
been in Germany at Cologne ever since as Director and Manager
of the German Branch of the British International Corporation. I am still in the army reserve. I have travelled a lot in
Europe during the last years and do not agree with the French
occupation, I having been here ever since the fall of 1919. I
belong to the Harvard Club of New York, and Brook Club of
New York.

LEWIS NILES ROBERTS .

Born at Boston, 10 May 1870, of Lewis Augustus Roberts (publisher) and Alice Niles.
Fitted with W. N. Eayrs.
Class Status: Regular.
Degree: A.B. 1893.
Married Gina Vittoria Panecaldo of Rome, at London, England, 18 July 1908.
Now living in Paris, France.

Lived until 1899 in Milton, engaged in literary work, though "with much interruption from illness, deaths, and travel." Spent the winter of 1899-1900 at the Law School, when went abroad for a year. Returned to Boston until 1904. Then spent twelve years abroad, most of the time at Paris· and Fontainbleau, but after 1913 at "St. Margaret's" on the south coast of England near Dover, suffering a good deal from ill health. In 1915 came back to Boston and soon became very actively interested in war relief work for Italy. In 1917 wrote "The Story of Nedda," which produced large contributions for this object. He served as chairman of the publicity committee of the Italian War Relief Fund of America, at Boston, and then went to New York and organized the Immediate Relief to Italy Fund. He was aided by his wife, a native of Rome, who subsequently received a gold medal from the Italian Government. In about eighteen months he raised nearly $170,000 for the work. After the Armistice he organized the American-European Supply Company at Boston, and was its president. In June of 1919 he sailed for France to take charge of its Paris branch. He is still abroad, and has not recently been heard from.

WILLIAM HENRY ROBEY

Born at Boston, 3 July 1870, of William Henry Robey (merchant) and Mary Virginia Smith.
Fitted at Boston English High.
Class Status: Scientific, 1889-91. Medical, 1891-94.
Degree: M.D. 1895.
Married Isabelle Torrens Alexander at New York City, 22 April 1897.
Child:
Andrew Alexander, born 16 February 1898.
Now Assistant Professor of Medicine, Harvard.

Retired from active duty, Medical Corps, United States Army, March 21, 1919, with the rank of Lieutenant Colonel, having served in France during my entire time as consultant in medicine on the staff of General W. S. Thayer. My original assignment comprised eighteen base, evacuation and camp hospitals in the advance section. Now a Colonel in the Medical Reserve Corps, United States Army.

Since 1914 I have had charge of the course in Physical Diagnosis at the Harvard Medical School with nine assistants. In 1919 appointed Assistant Professor of Medicine at Harvard. I have been a public lecturer at Harvard three times and the lecture of last year has been published by the Harvard University Press, with the title, "The Causes of Heart Failure". Have contributed numerous articles to scientific journals principally on diseases of the chest, and lectured before various state societies.

Visiting physician to the Boston City Hospital; chairman of the Committee on the Examination of House Officers; secretary of the Senior Staff; chief of the Heart Service. Chairman of the Boston Association for the Relief and Control of Heart Disease. In private practice: limited to internal medicine. The "Jr." after my name has been discontinued.

EDWARD HARTWELL ROGERS

Born at Lexington, Massachusetts, 19 May 1870, of George Marcus Rogers (real estate) and Mary Ann Hartwell.
Fitted at Cambridge Latin.
Class Status: Regular.
Degrees: A.B. 1893; LL.B. 1896.
Married Caroline Elizabeth Heizer at Corning, Iowa, 4 April 1900.
Children:
John, born 3 January 1901.
George Edward, 25 February 1903.
Edgar Heizer, 10 September 1905 (died 24 March 1907).
Alfred Peet, 30 January 1908.
David Frederick, 17 May 1910.
Edward Hartwell, Jr., 20 April 1914.
Now a trustee at Cambridge, Massachusetts.

Ever since graduation, I have been a resident of Cambridge, although I have not always lived in the same house. I have seen Cambridge developed into a large manufacturing center, and noted the great changes that have taken place during these thirty years. All the time, however, has been occupied in the management of a trust estate in this city, and I have not cared for public office. Yet I have managed to take a couple of trips. across the country to see if I could find a better place than New England, but I have returned more satisfied than ever with home scenery.

On the side, I have an apple farm in the country which in blossom-time I think, will compare with the famous cherry blooms of Japan, and certainly as a true New Englander I believe that its home grown apples cannot be beaten. I have also tried to do a little foresting with white pine, but fires and other casualties have rendered my efforts useless.

Thompson Lamar Ross

.Born at Macon, Georgia, 28 July 1870, of John Bennett Ross (merchant)
    and Mary Ann Lamar.
Entered from University of Mississippi.
Class Status: Entered Senior.
Degrees: Ph.B. (Univ. Miss.) 1890; A.B. 1893, LL.B. (Univ. Miss.) 1896..
Married Juanita Josephine Brinker at Washington, District of Columbia,.
    7 June 1899. Child:
        Lucius Lamar, born 16 July 1902.
.Died of accidental gun shot, 3 January 1920, at Grenada, Mississippi.

Thompson Lamar Ross, born July 28 1870, at Macon, Georgia, was descended from old North Carolina stock. His parents. were John Bennett and Mary Ann (Lamar) Ross. He died January 3, 1920, at Grenada, Mississippi, from the effects of an accidental pistol wound.

In 1879 the family removed to Mississippi, where his youth. was spent. He graduated from the University of that State with the degree of Ph.B. in 1890. For the next two years he was employed in a bank at Grenada, Mississippi. In 1892 he entered Harvard, where he received the degree of A.B. in 1893. The next year he worked at banking. He then studied law in 1894-1895 at the Harvard Law School, and the following year at the University of Mississippi Law School, from which he graduated with the degree of LL.B in 1896. He began the practice of law in New Orleans in 1896. Due to ill health he withdrew after a few months and devoted himself to recuperation. In 1897 he entered business, in which he continued for twelve years. He first engaged in shoe manufacturing for a brief time.

at Louisville; then in banking for four years at Kansas City, and for seven years in New York City. In 1909 he resumed the practice of law at Jackson, Mississippi, in which he was active for three years. In 1912, owing to failing eyesight, he abandoned professional life and retired to his plantation at Tie Plant, Mississippi, where he had his home until his death.

He was hampered by ill health while in college and subsequently at recurring periods throughout his career. Though this compelled change of occupations, his fine character and intellectual equipment brought him a large measure of success in whatever he undertook. He was particularly gifted as a public speaker. He was awarded one of the two first Boylston Prizes for elocution. He also carried off the honors in the Yale-Harvard debate of his year. During the World War he made numerous addresses in support of the activities of the Government. He was held in highest esteem by fellow lawyers and business associates wherever he located. Modest and highly endowed by nature, he possessed a personal charm which endeared him to all who enjoyed his friendship.

F. G. C. '91·

Benjamin Hill Rounsaville
See Report VI, Page 240.

WALTER LINCOLN SANBORN

Born at Newton Centre, Massachusetts, 28 March 1871, of John Hayes
    Sanborn (merchant) and Agnes Elizabeth McJannet.
Fitted at Newton High.
Class Status: Regular.
Degree: A.B. 1893.
Married Fannie Fisher at Ashmont, Massachusetts, 17 April 1907 (died
    20 February 1920). Child:
        Dorothy, born 3 November 1911.
Now with the Press Syndicate of New York, at Boston.

Upon graduation, I entered the employ of Silver, Burdett and Company, school book publishers, with whom I remained for three or four years. Since that time I have been generally engaged in the investment or brokerage business for the most part, although during the war I accepted temporarily an executive position with a manufacturing corporation which was making war material. More recently I have also found time to

Dibblee   Cary Falk   Stevens   Ellsworth   Pierce

'93 FOOTBALL TEAM—CLASS CHAMPIONS

do some very interesting work for the Press Syndicate of New York, whose business is "Publicity."

In 1896 I made my second trip to Europe, the first having been in the summer of 1892. In 1899 several weeks of the winter were spent in the South, principally in the Bahamas. Have also made several trips to the western part of this country. In 1895 I enlisted as a charter member of the reorganized Battery A, Field Artillery, of the Massachusetts Volunteer Militia, as did several of my classmates, and continued in active military service till May, 1913, having in the meantime attained the grade of Lieutenant Colonel, with assignment as Brigade Adjutant of the First Brigade.

For a number of years I enjoyed active participation in political work. though never with a view to, nor desire for, holding political office. As to recreation, I am still struggling to solve the secrets of golf, but find them as elusive as they were many years ago.

LOUIS PECK SANDERS

Born at Helena, Montana, 23 October 1869, of Wilbur Fisk Sanders
(lawyer and U. S. Senator) and Harriet Peck Fenn.
Fitted at Phillips Exeter.
Class Status: Regular.
Degree: A.B. 1893.
Married (1) Helen Fitzgerald at San Francisco, 18 April 1900. Children:
A daughter, born 9 June 1902 (died in infancy).
Louis Fitzgerald, 12 June 1903 (died 17 February 1904).
Helen Fitzgerald, 12 June 1904.
Wilbur Fisk, 15 December 1905.
Alice Francis, 8 February 1908 (died in infancy).
Louise Merris, 30 June 1909.
Jean Geraldine, 12 May 1911.
Marion, 22 May 1914.
Married (2) Natalie Rood Brown, 16 September 1920, at Butte.
Now practising law at Butte, Montana.

A plea for a sketch of three hundred words from and about a man who can tell it in as few words as are usually employed in a standard epitaph on a tombstone, fills me with grave misgivings as to whether or not my wind will last until I write the final syllable.

But here goes! From 1893 to 1897 I studied law in the office of my father then residing in Helena, Montana. Immediately after my admission to practice my profession I entered the Na-

tional Guard of my state, and, almost overnight, found myself
as a Battalion Adjutant in the First Montana Infantry, U. S.
V., on my way to the Philippine Islands to do my bit in the
Spanish-American War. There I served in many capacities
from a dog-robbing Regimental Commissary to Aide to Brigadier General H. G. Otis, later as Aide to Major General Elwell
S. Otis, and still later as Captain of Company B of my regiment with which I returned home in the winter of 1899. In
January, 1900, I removed to Butte, Montana, where I have since
resided and without interruption or digression have practised
the profession of law. In 1907 I associated myself with Mr.
J. Bruce Kremer and his brother, Mr. Alf C. Kremer, young
lawyers from Louisville, Kentucky; and with them I have continued to plug away at the same old game. Our firm, quite naturally, has drifted into the practise of mining law and we look
after the interests of all the mining corporations in Butte, except the Anaconda Copper Mining Company and the concerns
owned by Senator W. A. Clark.

In 1910 I ran for District Judge on the Republican ticket
and was defeated. In 1918 I ran for State Senator on the Republican ticket and was defeated. In 1922 I ran for State Senator on the Republican ticket and was defeated. There are
some indications that as a politician I am not a glittering success.

Philip Henry Savage

See Report VI, Page 242.

Huntington Saville

Born at Boston, 9 November 1870, of Henry Martyn Saville [Amherst
1853] (physician) and Antoinette Hale Carruth.
Fitted at J. P. Hopkinson's.
Class Status: Regular.
Degrees: A.B. 1893; LL.B. 1896.
Married Anne Pierce Whittier at Boston, 22 May 1900.
Died of acute bulbar paralysis, 27 July 1918, at Cambridge.

Huntington Saville was born in Boston, November 9, 1870.
His father was Henry Martyn Saville, a physician and a graduate of Amherst in the class of 1853. His mother's maiden
name was Antoinette Hale Carruth. He went to St. Paul's, but
entered Harvard College in the class of '93 from Hopkinson's

School. After graduation with his class at Harvard he entered the Law School and received his LL.B. in 1896. Upon graduating from the Law School he immediately became associated with the firm of Shattuck and Monroe, of Boston, where he stayed until the dissolution of that firm on acount of the death of the senior members in 1905. In partnership with Albert M. Chandler, Harvard 1900, Huntington Saville took charge of most of the legal work that had occupied the old firm. And the supervision of many large estates that had been handled by Shattuck and Monroe became his personal .work. This partnership was maintained until just prior to his death. On May 22, 1900, he married Anne Pierce Whittier, who survives him.

To an unusual degree Huntington Saville was interested in increasing the happiness of his fellow men. Nearly all his leisure time was devoted to public work of one kind or another. Immediately after leaving Law School he took an active part in Cambridge politics. He was an enthusiastic supporter of the party that advocated good government. His devotion to his religious organization and to many forms of church work was not from fanatical zeal nor for personal reasons, but was because he believed that the country and the world would be happier when the ideals that his church organization was trying to achieve were realized. His very efficient support of the National Guard, which won him the rank of Captain (Company M. 12th Regiment, M. V. M.) was not primarily because he was interested in fighting, but because he wished to do his share on the side that he believed to stand for human progress in the great struggle that was convulsing the world at that time. Those who knew him well realized that fighting from the mere joy of combat played a very small part in his character. Even in his legal profession he preferred the care of estates—conservation of property—to a career devoted primarily to litigation.

To all these activities he gave his whole strength, both physical and mental, which was perhaps a contributing cause of his untimely death. The amount of time and energy that Huntington Saville gave to his church organization is well illustrated by the following list of positions that he held: Secretary and later President of the Episcopalian Club of Massachusetts;

member of the Diocesan Convention; treasurer of the Boston
City Mission; delegate to the General Convention; and member of the Board of Directors of *The Churchman*.   In addition
to these regular duties he was exceedingly successful as an
organizer of many financial campaigns for the Y. M. C. A. and
for church purposes.   Too many times such strict devotion to
a cause is accompanied by fanatical characteristics.   But it
was Huntington's tolerance that won for him the affection of
intimate friends who held views that were at variance with
those principles that he considered were of fundamental importance.

W. M. R.

FRANK CHARLES SCHRADER

Born at Sterling, Illinois, 6 October 1860, of Christian Schrader (farmer)
    and Angeline Marie Piepo.
Entered from University of Kansas.
Class Status: Entered Senior.
Degrees: S.B., S.M. (Univ. Kansas) 1891; A.B. 1893; A.M. 1894.
Married Kathrine Batwell at New York City, 19 October 1919.
Now government geologist at Washington, District of Columbia.

The first three years after leaving college, or graduation, I
devoted to graduate study in geology and helping teach geology
at Harvard.   In 1896 I entered the service of the United States
Geological Survey, specializing in mining geology, in which
professional work I have since travelled widely, visiting nearly
all parts of Alaska, the United States and portions of Canada,
the North Territory and Mexico.   The next six years, 1896-
1902, I devoted to making reconnaissance surveys and explora-
tory examinations of the geology and ore deposits or mineral
resources in nearly all parts of Alaska, including the Arctic
Coast, the first expedition being made with Spurr, '93, as head
and Goodrich, '92.   The remaining twenty-one years, 1902-
1923, I devoted nearly all to mining geology and allied work,
mainly in the mountainous portion of the western United
States, including nearly all States lying between Mexico and
Canada.   The last fifteen years includes also extensive examination of mines and properties in connection with Government
land classification work for various departments of the Government, including the Forest Service, the General Land Office,
the Post Office, the Indian Office, and the Department of Jus-

tice. In this work I have been chief examiner and chief witness in giving testimony on the same in the Federal Courts in many leading cities of the United States, including New York, Chicago, Spokane, Durango, Denver, Washington, Cleveland, and Santa Fe. I also testified on mineral lands in Alaska and the adjacent Northwest Territory, and recommended methods for examining certain remotely situated frontier lands on the headwaters of the Amazon in South America. During the Great World War my entire attention was given to the investigation of ore deposits of much-needed war metals, notably manganese, pyrites, and quicksilver, mostly in the South and Southwest, and since the war I have prepared reports on them. Since the war or during the last five years my chief task has been the prosecution of field and office work on numerous mining camps in Nevada, on two of which a report entitled, "The Jarbidge Mining District" is now in press. In this period I also prepared current reports on the mineral resources of the United States, my specialty being antimony.

Life fellow Geological Society of America; member American Institute Mining and Metallurgical Engineers; National Geographic Society; American Forestry Association; Washington Academy of Sciences; American Association for Advancement of Science; Mining and Metallurgical Society of America; Society of Economic Geologists; Geological Society of Washington; Mineralogical Society of Washington; Pick and Hammer Club; Petrologists Club; Cosmos Club; Midriver Club (president now for four years).

CARL LINCOLN SCHURZ

Born at Washington, District of Columbia, 28 February 1871, of Carl Schurz (transportation) and Margaret Meyer.
Fitted with Dr. J. Sachs.
Class Status: Regular.
Degrees: A.B. 1893; LL.B. (N. Y. Law School) 1895.
Married (1) Harriet Tiedemann at Munsey, New York, 20 October 1897 (divorced, July 1920).
Married (2) Mrs. Marie Hart at New York City, 2 August 1922.
Now practising law at New York City.

I can add very little of interest to the meagre items of the sixth report. The most important events in my life since 1918 were the dissolution of my first marriage (Mrs. Schurz having obtained a decree in Reno in July, 1920) and my subsequent

marriage to Mrs. Marie Hart in New York on August 2, 1922.
In other respects my life has been uneventful. I have continued
to devote my time to the practice of my profession (the law),
and have been fairly successful. I have served on various charity committees and societies. but have taken no active part in
politics and have held no political office.

Edgar Scott

Born at Philadelphia, 17 October 1871, of Thomas Alexander Scott (rail-
roads) and Anna Dike Riddle.
Fitted at Groton.
Class Status: Freshman 1889-90.   Sophomore 1891-92.
Married Mary Howard Sturgis at Philadelphia, 28 February 1898. Chil-
dren:
    Edgar, Jr., born 11 January 1899.
    Warwick Potter, 16 April 1901.
    Anna Dike, 5 June 1907.
    Susan Brimmer Sturgis, 22 November 1908.
Died suddenly, 20 October 1918, at Chaumont, France.

Edgar Scott was born at Philadelphia October 17, 1871, the
son of Anna Dike Riddle and Thomas Alexander Scott, for
many years president of the Pennsylvania Railroad. He was
educated at Farnboro', England, and at Groton School, where
he was editor of the school paper and played on the football
team. He came to Harvard with our class in the autumn of
1889, leaving college in his junior year. In 1893, with his
nephew Hugh and his friends Sherrard Billings and Warwick
Potter, he travelled around the world, and on his return settled
down to the study of law at the University of Pennsylvania.
For two years, from 1897 to 1899, he served as second secretary
of the American Embassy in Paris.

Scott was married in 1898 to Mary Howard Sturgis, daughter of Robert S. Sturgis of Boston, and they had four children,
Edgar, Warwick Potter, Anna Dike and Susan Brimmer Sturgis. During the years that followed. he lived mainly at Lans-
downe, near Philadelphia, passing his summers in Bar Harbor, yacht racing, riding, and playing tennis, entering into
all these games with great zest and enjoyment.

When our country began to prepare for war in 1915, he was
among the first to volunteer for the military training camp at
Plattsburg. Into this work he threw himself with a fine energy,
setting a notable example of steadiness and perseverance, and

showing, as all of us who were there with him well remember, an unusual aptitude for soldiering. So it followed quite naturally that in the spring of 1917 when the United States had finally joined the allies in the great war, Scott and his elder son Edgar, between whom there was a rare understanding and affection, went to France as members of one of the American Ambulance units. He was later transferred to the Norton-Harjes Ambulance Corps and served very efficiently in an executive capacity at the Paris office until the ambulance service was taken over by the army. After this he was for a short period a liaison officer of the Red Cross. During all his ambulance and Red Cross work, his ambition to be in the army had been very keen, and it was a great happiness to him when in February of the next year he was commissioned first lieutenant and appointed aide to Major General Andre Brewster, inspector-general of the American Expeditionary Force, with headquarters at Chaumont.

From the first his service was of a high order; his knowledge of the French language, his accuracy and thoroughness, his initiative and keen enthusiasm all combined to make him a valuable staff-officer. so much so that in August, 1918, he was taken into the inspector-general's department and given the rank of major. His work was extremely varied, and covered the expediting of the transportation of men and supplies, the application to newly arrived divisions of the successful results achieved in earlier ones, and the investigation of complaints from all sources. It meant long nerve-racking days with great responsibility, and here again Scott distinguished himself signally, as two very touching letters from his superior officers show. General Brewster writes of his hard and unselfish work and of the impossibility of ever filling his place, while Brigadier General Malin Craig, Chief of Staff of the First Corps, emphasizes his effectiveness and his utter disregard of himself while there was work to do. But unceasing work, with insufficient sleep during nights passed in damp, unhealthy billets combined to cause a severe strain, under which his health finally broke down, and which ultimately caused his death at Chaumont on the 20th of October. Here he was buried in the American cemetery with full military honours.

Edgar Scott gave his life for his country, and we who are

his classmates and who knew him are glad that he found such a
happy fulfillment of his life; and we shall ever be proud of the
example that he left behind him of patriotic service and un-
swerving devotion to duty.

C. K. C.

WALTER [JUDD] SCOTT

Born at Byron, Michigan, 4 September 1865, of Marvin Judd Scott (clergy-
man) and Loretta Crawford.
Entered from Albion College.
Class Status: Special 1889-90.
Now with *The Daily Silver Belt* at Miami, Arizona.

I have retired as editor of the Daily Silver Belt and expect
to leave in the near future for Mexico. Please put in merely
the address—care of the Daily Silver Belt, and let it go until
next time.

Harry Edward Sears

Born at Boston, 11 April 1870, of Edward Shailer Sears (journalist)
and Belle Wagner.
Fitted at Boston Latin.
Class Status: Regular.
Degrees: A.B. 1893; M.D. 1896.
Married Myrtle Belle Walker at Beverly, Massachusetts, 28 October 1902.
Children:
Norman Walker, born 12 November 1903.
Harry Edward, Jr., 22 August 1906.
Died at Beverly, 20 October 1920.

Harry Edward Sears died suddenly at Beverly, Oct. 20, 1920.
He was born at Boston, April 11, 1870, the son of Edward
Shailer Sears and Belle Wagner. He came of an old family of .
Cape Codders, descended from Richard Sears, of the Plymouth
Colony. He entered Harvard in 1889 from the Boston Latin
School. He was a brilliant scholar, and completed the necessary
eighteen courses in three years, but preferred to take his degree in 1893, so spent the fourth year in beginning work at the
Medical School, having always wished to be a doctor. He was
thus able to take him M.D. in 1896, *cum laude*. For the next
eighteen months he was a house surgeon at the Boston City Hospital. He then entered practice at Dorchester, but almost immediately relinquished it to enlist for the Spanish War as acting assistant surgeon, stationed first at Montauk Point and then

at San Juan, Porto Rico. After recovering from an attack of army typhoid he opened an office at Beverly, which thenceforward became his home. Besides attending to a large general practice he was secretary of the Essex (South District) Medical. Society, surgeon at the Beverly Hospital, associate medical examiner for the Seventh Essex District, censor and councilor in the Massachusetts Medical Society, and examiner for several life insurance companies. Among his avocations he was an expert shot, and in 1912 was a member of the United States Revolver Team at the Olympiad in Stockholm, winning a gold medal and wreath. When this country entered the Great War he obtained a commission (July 16, 1917) as Captain in the Medical Corps, and enlisted and organized Field Hospital No. 30, of which he was made commanding officer early in 1918. In June he sailed with his outfit (practically all from Norwood and Beverly) for France, and was present at the opening of the St. Mihiel Drive. In September he was promoted to Major, and in October was assigned to Evacuation Hospital No. 1, at Toul, close behind the American lines. In May, 1919, he was promoted Lieutenant-Colonel and ordered home. Unfortunately he had contracted stomach trouble, which necessitated an operation the following May, and which finally affected his mind. He will be remembered as an able and devoted physician, a cheery and welcome friend, a loyal classmate, and a patriotic citizen. October 28, 1902, he married Myrtle Belle Walker, of Beverly, who with two sons survives him.

Langley Sears

Born at Boston, 11 July 1870, of William Barnas Sears (insurance) and Emily Adaline Faunce.
Fitted at Brookline High.
Class Status: Regular.
Degrees: A.B. 1893; Grad. Rochester Theol. Sem. 1896.
Married Maybelle Tillinghast at Providence, Rhode Island, 16 June 1897.
Child:
Harold Tillinghast, born 5 June 1898.
Died of pneumonia, 2 December 1918, at Monson, Massachusetts.

Langley Sears was descended from good New England stock. His grandfather, Barnas Sears, was a former president of Brown University, and an honorary S. T. D. of Harvard. He was related on his mother's side to Prof. Samuel P. Langley, former Secretary of the Smithsonian Institute, and after him he was named. He passed his boyhood at the foot of Corey Hill, which was named for his great grandfather.

He fitted for college at the Brookline High School. In college he was an earnest and conscientious student. Early in his college course he decided to make the Christian ministry his life work. Accordingly, on leaving college he entered the Rochester Theological Seminary, where he graduated in 1896. The next year he married Maybelle Tillinghast of Providence, R. I. His married life was a very happy one. His wife entered into the spirit of his work with fine helpfulness. His son, Harold, of whom he was justly proud, entered the army, while already a student at Harvard.

His pastorates include churches at Rockford, Ill., Groton, Conn., Charlestown, Mass., South Deerfield, Mass. and Monson, Mass. At about the middle of his career as a preacher he passed through the mental conflict of a change of denominational affiliation, leaving the Baptist for the Congregational ministry. It took great courage to make this change, but to his honor it must be said that he did this with an unwavering devotion to the highest ideals of his chosen life work. In all his pastorates he won the devotion and love of his parishioners to a very marked degree. In the midst of service in a happy pastorate at Monson he fell a victim to the prevailing epidemic of bronchial pneumonia.

Sears was a genial fellow and a good comrade. He was most loyal to his class and to Harvard. He had the highest ideals of fine, clean, strong manhood. The whole record of his life was that of unselfish devotion to duty and to the truth as he saw it. He was a man who loved his fellow man and proved his love by service. [The middle name of Barnas was added when he was about fourteen; he discontinued it a few years before his death.]

F. M. S.

HAROLD INGALLS SEWALL

Born at Boston, 25 February 1871, of William Bull Sewall (merchant)
    and Lena French Ingalls.
Fitted at G. W. C. Noble's.
Class Status: Regular.
Degree: A.B. 1893.

Married Virginia Simms Evans at Tokyo, Japan, 29 April 1903. (Divorced October 1913). Children:
Robley Evans, born 26 March 1904 (died 3 May 1908).
Dorothy Neville, 2 May 1905.
Now living in Porto Rico.

Real estate in Boston, 1894 to 1901. Prospecting for sugar lands in Porto Rico and Cuba. Travelled to the East, 1902-1903. Invested in sugar in Porto Rico 1904 and became actively and officially interested in manufacturing company, taking up my winter residence in the island. In 1911 sold out company and turned to the agricultural end of the business, operating sugar properties and raising cane. Retired from sugar raising in 1921 and leased my properties. At present time am growing a little fruit on my home property but can not truthfully call it an especially gainful occupation; investments in sugar properties probable cause of my continued residence down here—though chilblains, chapped hands and cold feet are contributary causes for my avoidance of New England during the winter season.

Have suffered for fifty years from repression of unquenchable artistic nature which I have now unleashed and find myself absorbed in breeding peacocks, growing night blooming water-lilies, studying music, and writing outdoor sketches of tropical life for a small but appreciative public. Have spent some time and labor in developing my home place down here, introducing foreign tropical trees and shrubs and practising landscape gardening in a small way. The belief that no other spot in the world within four days travel of New York can equal this island in charm of climate and scenery will probably keep me here for many winters to come.

In looking back over the years I am impressed with the fact that fifty years aboard this planet leaves one in a more contemplative and philosophical attitude toward life than our early feverishness would lead one to expect. I find myself far less concerned about fortune and fame and more interested in quiet and comfort—or is this only *Tropicalitis* biting in, as my friends in the North insist? Perhaps! but anyway, here in the West Indies is the ideal place for such a life and I can not do better than to urge restless classmates to come down and visit me; it may be that they will be tempted to agree with me and stay on.

CHARLES GRANT SHAFFER

Born at Lewisburg, Pennsylvania, 6 November 1869, of Abraham Shaf-
fer and Elizabeth Diefenderfer.
Entered from Bucknell University.
Class Status: Senior year only.
Degrees: A.B. (Bucknell) 1892; A.B. 1893; A.M. (Bucknell) 1894.
Married Dora Valesca Becker at New York City, 29 June 1899.
Now Principal of Eliot and Summer Place Schools, Newark, New Jer-
sey.

Have been in educational work since leaving college. Seven
years in the south and the last twenty-three years in Newark,
New Jersey. Have made four trips abroad, 1902, 1906, 1909,
1913. Have been President of the University Club, the School-
men's Club, the Principals' Club, and Secretary and Treasurer
of the Harvard Club of New Jersey. Member of Executive
Committee of American Red Cross. Chairman of Junior Red
Cross. Member of the Board of Examiners. Assistant Supervisor of Summer Schools. Avocation, Organist and Choir-Mas-
ter, last nine years at St. Mark's Protestant Episcopal Church.
Contemplate a trip around the world in 1925.

THOMAS HALL SHASTID

Born at Pittsfield, Illinois, 19 July 1866, of Thomas Wesley Shastid
[Missouri Med. 1856] (physician) and Louisa Minerva Hall.
Entered from University of Vermont.
Class Status: Entered Junior.
Degrees: M.D. (Univ. Vt.) 1888; A.B. 1893; A.M. (Univ Mich) 1901;
LL.B. (Univ. Mich.) 1902; F.A.C.S. (1914); Sc.D. (Hon. Univ. Wis.)
1922; F.A.C.P. 1923.
Married Fannie Fidelia English at Pittsfield, Illinois, 16 May 1897.
Child:
        Louisa Minerva, born 16 February 1901 (deceased).
Now medical opthalmologist at Superior, Wisconsin.

Behold me as described in "Who's Who in America," 1922-
1923:
"Shastid, Thomas Hall, opthalmologist. Began practice
Pittsfield, ·1889; professor history of medicine, American Medical College, St. Louis, 1907-1912, later honorary professor; resided Superior, Wisconsin, since 1914. Consulting ophalmolo-
gist, St. Mary's Hospital, Superior. Member Douglas County,

Wisconsin, Medical Society; honorary member of Interurban (Duluth-Superior) Academy of Medicine; fellow American College Surgeons; member American Medical Academy, American Academy Opthalmology and Oto-Laryngology, International Congress of Opthalmology; honorary life member Société Acad émique d'Histoire Internationale (with gold medal), and of Académie Latine des Sciences, Arts et Belles-Lettres (with gold cross). Republican, Presbyterian, Mason. Author: A Country Doctor, 1898; The Forensic Relations of Opthalmic Surgery, 1911; Medical Jurisprudence in America, 1912; Opthalmic Jurisprudence, 1915; Simon of Cyrene, Dimarchaerus Splendens (novel). Translator: Hemholtz's Description of an Opthalmoscope, 1916. Collaborator with Dr. Howard A. Kelly in Cyclo. of American Medicine. Biography and Dictionary of American Medical Biography; with Dr. James Moores Ball on Modern Opthalmology, third and fourth editions; and with Dr. Casey A. Wood on numerous volumes. Late editorial secretary of Opthalmic Record; late associate editor Michigan Law Review; Collaborator American Journal of Opthalmology and "Revista Cubana de Oftalmologia." Contributor to scientific and other Journals, also more than three thousand articles to American Encyclopedia of Opthalmology. Home: 1920 John Avenue, Superior, Wisconsin. Office: Lyceum Building, Duluth, Minnesota."

EDGAR DWIGHT SHAW

Born at Leominster, Massachusetts, 22 August 1871, of Francis Henry Shaw and Isabella Rhoda Warfield.
Fitted at Phillips Exeter.
Class Status: Regular.
Degree: A.B. 1893.
Married (1) Anna Jane Hill at Brooklyn, New York, 14 January 1897.
Children:
Tiny }
Dorothy } twins, born 8 May 1904. (Tiny died in infancy).
Married (2) Gertrude May Stevenson at New York City, 12 May 1921.
Now publisher of the Boston Advertiser and on general management of Hearst publications.

Thirty years at one game and still getting a kick out of it would seem something of a testimonial to newspaper work as a profession—a span of years when the interest and variety have never diminished. Perhaps, too, the opportunity for association with the giants of the newspaper world—Frank A. Munsey, Arthur Brisbane and William Randolph Hearst—have had much to do with making life and work full of enduring interest and stimulation. The happy circumstance of having experienced every branch of the work—reporter, city editor, managing editor and publisher—ultimately brought about the opportunity to have executive charge of all departments of various newspapers and, in the last five years to have both the responsibility and fun of remaking newspapers in four cities—Washington, Detroit, Milwaukee and Chicago—followed by the starting and installing from the ground up of new papers in two other cities, Rochester and Syracuse.   Circumstances required record breaking installation in these two cities and the resources of the organization made it possible to achieve a record for newspaper installation of 21 days in Rochester, speedily followed and broken by 18 days in Syracuse.

If today I were to have my choice of occupations I should undoubtedly elect newspaper work, since with a lot of grind and a little luck, it offers the two chief requisites of a life job—work which in itself gives satisfaction and provides proceeds which are more than ample for the practical needs of life.

Obviously this program is inconsistent with settled living, but at least it prevents one from getting mouldy and does keep one in touch with a number of things, a number of places and an increasing number of people. Mrs. Shaw, who was Miss Gertrude Stevenson of Boston until May of 1921, and I have a home in New York occupied about two months in two years and in that time have experienced much of the hollowness of hotel pretensions in four cities. Only a wife such as she and one who because she makes writing her own profession has a sympathetic understanding of the waywardness of newspaper work could serenely accept such a fate.

At the present time, I am a member of the board of general management of the Hearst publications with executive offices at 119 West 40th street, and at the moment headed for Boston to publish the *Boston Advertiser*, grateful to a job sufficiently obliging to return me to Boston for the thirtieth reunion and anticipating the prospect of a long deferred vacation in Europe when the Leviathian sails July 4th.

HUBERT GROVER SHAW

Born åt Fall River, Massachusetts, 29 August 1867, of Orlando Hamilton Shaw (carpenter) and Ursula Gwynneth.
Fitted at Fall River High.
Class Status: with class four years.
Degrees: A.B. 1894, as of 1893; Ph.D. (Ohio Univ.) 1894.
Married Elizabeth Ann de Quedville at Cambridge, Massachusetts, 29 June 1893. Child:
    Charles Bunsen, born 5 June 1894.
Now teaching at Asheville University.

After graduation I taught school for several years—working as a civil engineer during the summer vacations. From 1897 to 1901 was science master at the Melrose High, then to the Murdock School, Winchendon. In 1905 became principal of the high school at Wethersfield, Connecticut, where I raised the enrollment from seven to sixty. Four years later became submaster at Torrington, Connecticut, where I had one of the finest chemical laboratories in the State. In 1918 became member of Shaw and Gwynneth, chemical engineers, of Torrington. My health was poor a few years ago and I became interested in outdoor life in Florida, to the extent that I bought a little land and have brought a grove of grapefruit trees up to the bearing stage. It is at Lake Gem, Florida, and is called Gwynneth Grove.

I have recently been professor of chemistry at the Georgia School of Technology, Atlanta, Georgia, but shall teach next year at Ashville University. I am rapidly gaining in strength, so do not have me on your lists as a sick man. I am going to live thirty years more, and attend the Sexigennial Reunion.

My public positions and offices have been limited to just one—library trustee in Winchendon. My publications and speeches are nothing at all; I am just as silent as I used to be when I was a Freshman. I joined the Masons a few years after graduation, and have had the honor of being a past master, past high priest, and past illustrious master. A brief summary of my uneventful career would be "Hard at Work Ever Since."

Oliver Wadsworth Shead

See Report VI, Page 252.

GEORGE LAWSON SHELDON

Born at Nehawka, Nebraska, 31 May 1870, of Lawson Sheldon (farmer)
     and Julia Pollard.
Entered from University of Nebraska.
Class Status: I. Graduate School, 1892-93.
Degrees: Litt.B. (Univ. Nebraska) 1892; A.B. 1893; LL.D. (Hastings)
     1908.
Married Rose Higgins at Roseville, Illinois, 4 September 1895. Children:
     George Lawson, Jr., born 19 May 1897.
     Mary, 7 August 1900.
     Julia Pollard, 9 October 1903.
     Anson Hoisington, 5 June 1905.
Now farming at Wayside, Mississippi.

Sheldon apparently gets all his class mail, but doesn't care to
reply. Some years ago Mrs. S. came all the way from Mississippi
to call on the secretary (and other classmates) and express her
interest and admiration for '93· It's a pity she can't transfuse
some of her enthusiasm into our only living ex-governor.

HOWARD COCKS SHERWOOD

Born at San Francisco, 21 November 1870, of Benjamin Franklin Sher-
     wood (banker) and Almira Theresa Dickinson.
Fitted at Phillips Exeter.
Class Status: Regular.
Degrees: A.B. 1893; LL.B. 1896.
Now practising law at New York City.

As a brief summary of my doings since leaving the Law
School, I would say that, after short periods spent successively
with the law firms of Carter and Ledyard, and Olney and Com-
stock, I entered the office of Miller, Peckham and Dixon, where
I spent four years as managing clerk. I then (1902) started
into practice on my own account, which I have continued uninterruptedly ever since, except for the period of war work (October, 1917, to May, 1919) which were spent with the War
Trade Board. My practice has had to do chiefly with wills and
estates and I am trustee of several trusts, which occupy a considerable amount of my time.

FRANK PALMER SIBLEY

Born at Chelsea, Massachusetts, 15 September 1871, of Arthur Sibley
     [Harvard 1862] (manufacturer) and Sarah Ann Timmerman.
Fitted at Chelsea High.
Class Status: Special, 1889-91.

Married Louie Florence Maria Lyndon at Boston, 18 July 1894 (died 18 May 1922).
Child:
   Helen, born 22 February 1896.
Now reporter on the *Boston Globe.*

Began newspaper work in 1891 on the *Transcript.* Have worked on thirteen papers in seven cities of the United States, and edited one magazine. Since 1902 on the staff of the *Boston Globe.* Still a reporter, twenty-one years later, and glad of it.

Assigned to the Mexican Border in 1916 as correspondent, was consequently sent to France in like position in September, 1917. Stayed with the 26th Division till date of sailing for home in March, 1919. Since then straight newspaper work; only one assignment of great interest, the Sacco-Vanzetti murder trial. Last summer sent to France to go over again the ground covered during the war. First grand-daughter, Patricia Paulsen, born March 31, 1920.

George Frederick Sibley

See Report VI, Page 255.

BURNETT NEWELL SIMPSON

Born at Lawrence, Kansas, 13 July 1869, of Samuel Newell Simpson (real estate) and Katherine Lion Burnett.
Fitted at G. W. C. Noble's.
Class Status: Regular. Law School, 1894-95.
Degree: A.B. 1893.
Married Caroline Coalter Gamble of Richmond, Virginia, at Kansas City, 9 December 1903.
Now practising law at Kansas City.

Two weeks after my law course at Harvard ended, I entered the law office of a firm in Kansas City, whose junior partner ten years later became my partner. Since the dissolution of our partnership five years later I have practised law unassociated. Do not practise in court, but specialize in real property law and handling estates. I was one of the founders of our University Club, and as Chairman of the Scholarship Committee of the Harvard Club of Kansas City, take keen delight in aiding men to go to Harvard. During the war was on the Draft Board and aided in other war activities. I was in Paris when the war started, and delighted to have Harvard men as companions amid discomforts, on the ship coming home.. Cannot attend the thirtieth Reunion of '93, but hope to see some of my classmates at this year's meeting of Associated Harvard Clubs, in Kansas City.

FRANCIS HINCKLEY SISSON

Born at Galesburg, Illinois, 14 June 1871, of William Pardon Sisson
 (manufacturer) and Harriet Hinckley .
Entered from Knox College.
Class Status: Senior year only.
Degrees: A.B. (Knox) 1892; A.B. 1893; LL.D. (Knox) 1921.
Married Grace Emma Lass at Galesburg, Illinois, 16 June 1897.
Now Vice-President, Guaranty Trust Company of New York.

Immediately after leaving college I entered newspaper work in Chicago, later becoming editor and part owner of the Evening Mail, of Galesburg, Illinois, and the Transcript, of Peoria, Illinois. In 1904 I came to New York as a member of the staff of McClure's Magazine and was engaged in various publishing and advertising activities as Vice-President of the H. E. Lesan Advertising Agency of New York. In 1915 I was made Assistant Chairman of the Standing Committee of the Railway Executives Association, and in 1917 was elected a Vice-President of the Guaranty Trust Company, which position I still hold. During this period I have been writing and speaking on business and financial matters, discussing economic topics generally. During the war I was active in Liberty Loan and Red Cross work. I received the decoration of Chevalier of the Order of the Crown from the King of Belgium in recognition of work for that country. In 1921 I received the degree of LL.D. from Knox College. In presenting the degree, the President of the college made the following characterization:

"The task of a twentieth century banker differs widely from that of yesterday. The financial leader of today must interpret conditions to the business men of the country, must be a leader in matters of public finance, and must be able to command large public confidence. In this service you have gained well merited distinction. As vice-president of one of the greatest banking institutions in the country, you have won praise for your business ability. You have rendered large service through public speech and through leadership in the science of finance."

I am a member of the American Economic Association, Council on Foreign Relations, Academy of Political Science, Merchants' Association, and the Chamber of Commerce of the State of New York, and of the following clubs: City, Harvard, Lawyers, Metropolitan, Economic, Advertising, Bankers, Beta Theta Pi, National Press, Press, University Club of Washington, Hudson River Country Club, Sleepy Hollow Country Club.

CONRAD HENSLER SLADE

Born at Chestnut Hill, Massachusetts, 4 March 1871, of Daniel Denison Slade [Harvard 1844] (physician) and Mina Louise Hensler.
Fitted at W. Nichols'.
Class Status: Regular.
Degree: A.B. 1893.
Married ———— (a niece of the painter Renoir).
    Child:
        John Louis, born 9 December 1920.
Now painting at Nice and Paris, France.

In 1918 passed the summer at Aix-les-Bains, where I got in touch with many of our men sent for a few days for recreation there. Took to playing tennis (have kept it up since), and made some good friends by making portrait drawings of some of the men, which they sent to their mothers at home. Have since passed winters at Nice and Cagnes, and summers in Paris or vicinity, painting. At Cagnes got to know Renoir—saw and talked with him a few minutes two days before he died; and was much touched to have him say he was glad to see me again. My son, John Louis Slade, was born at Cagnes, December 9, 1920. Since then I am much absorbed by paternal duties, taken no doubt the more seriously that they have come so late in my life.

HERBERT BRUSH SMITH

Born at Muncy, Pennsylvania, 16 April 1870, of Lewis Schuyler Smith (merchant) and Mary Rose Crouse.
Fitted at Tilton Grammar School.
Class Status: Special 1889-93.
Degree: LL.B. (N. Y. Univ.) 1895.
Now practising law at New York City.

I am still practising law at the old stand, and still unmarried, with prospects of changing latter condition diminishing. It is a fact that I hear a good deal of music and attend the concerts of the Symphony Orchestras, where I often see brother Collamore. Books and "things about books" also take up probably

too much of my time and attention. Snaring the electro-mag-
netic wave has been one of my hobbies (I have a number) for
several years past; this interest manifesting itself rather in ex-
perimentation and the fabrication of wireless apparatus than
listening-in to Jazz and the weather reports. I have found that
hand labor, with a judicious admixture of brains,—not too
much, fortunately—is conducive to a happy and contented state
of mind. I enjoy living as much, if not more, than ever. James
Anthony Froude on his fiftieth birthday (I think it was) said:
"I feel just as young as when I was twenty-five, only I can't
jump as high." At the time our last class report was prepared
I was able, after a few trials, to vault over the back of my
horse; at the present writing I am lucky to land on top. Otherwise I feel as young as ever.

My record is a little slim, I am afraid, on the side of accomplishments which might be said to benefit mankind in general
or advance the race in its evolutionary processes; at least I can't
think of anything to record at this time.

HOWARD CASWELL SMITH

Born at New York City, 19 February 1871, of Charles Stewart Smith
    (Près. N. Y. Chamber of Commerce) and Henrietta Haight Caswell.
Fitted with Dr. Callisen.
Class Status: Regular.
Degree: A.B. 1893.
Married (1) Katherine Lyall Moen at New York City, 26 October 1898.
    Children:
        Caswell Moen, born 10 July 1899
        Howard Caswell, Jr., 2 March 1901.
        René Moen, 15 August 1904.
        St. Clair Moen, 18 September 1908.
Married (2) Anna Barry Phelps of Washington, D.C., 6 December 1919.
    Child:
        Barry Phelps, born 1 November 1920.
Now in commercial paper at New York City.

Shortly after graduating I entered the employ of Charles
Hathaway and Company to which firm I was admitted January
1, 1897. My present firm is its successor.

I was in Squadron A, Cavalry, N. G. N. Y., from 1894 to
1900 and did strike duty twice but did not get into the Spanish
War. I entered the Depot Unit during the Mexican Border
troubles and served as First Lieutenant and Adjutant. During
the World War I served New York State in various duties;

principally as Inspector General. I continued my work in the
New York Guard until January 1, 1919, being retired to the
reserve list on that date with rank of Colonel from December,
1918. After January 1, 1919, I retired from the State service
and returned to my own business where I have since remained.

The course of my business took me into several financial re-
organizations from time to time and later I was honored by a
number of directorates shown elsewhere. Since 1894 I have
served on one or another hospital board but have now retired
from this activity.

On December 6, 1919, I married Miss Anna Barry Phelps,
of Washington, D. C., and on November 1, 1920, my fifth son,
Barry Phelps Smith, was born in New York City. January,
1919, also ended my term as Commodore of the Seawanhaka-
Corinthian Yacht Club and since then I have returned to the
ranks of ordinary yachtsman and have gloried in racing a
"Class S" sloop. My adventures since last report have been
few and plain hard work has been my lot.

I adventured for a brief period as President of a College and
for two years conferred degrees on the graduates of the New
York Homoeopathic Medical College and Flower Hospital, but
this duty proved too heavy for my simple mind and I released
the honor to another. Aside from this, I have continued my
activities as a director as before and have also kept active in
the Chamber of Commerce of New York. In all other respects
I am at the same old stands; my office at 45 Wall Street and my
home at Oyster Bay, where all visiting yachtsmen and especially those from Boston flying a Harvard flag at their mastheads
are always welcome. Some "cheer" still remains.

ROBERT KEATING SMITH

Born at Brooklyn, New York, 2 August 1865, of George Robert Keating
Smith (manufacturer) and Anna Amelia Gooch.
Entered from Stevens Institute of Technology.
Class Status: Entered Junior.
Degrees: M.E. (Stevens Inst.) 1889; A.B. 1893; S.T.B. (Episc. Theol.
School, Camb.) 1895.
Married Bertha Helena Wiles at Albany, New York, 17 June 1896.
Children:
Mabel Wiles, born 8 December 1898.
Helen Lord, 1 January 1902.
Now in Episcopal ministry at Westfield, Massachusetts.

1893 to 1895 in Cambridge Episcopal Theological School as student. 1896-1901, Rector St. Paul's Episcopal Church, Kansas City, Missouri. 1901-1906, Assistant Grace Episcopal Church, Newton, Massachusetts. 1906 to present time, Rector of Episcopal Church of the Atonement, Westfield, Massachusetts.

During the past five years I have been working steadily on my study of the religious history of Central Europe, with the purpose of writing a book. I have been very active in the Boy Scouts of America, being a member of the National Council, as well as Scoutmaster of Troop I in my own town. I have the honor of having trained a group of Boy Scouts called the "Otter Patrol," recognized as an almost perfect type and nationally famous. In July, 1920, I was Assistant Chaplain of the International Jamboree Boy Scout Camp at Richmond, London, and for ten consecutive days worked from 6 A. M. until 1 the next A. M., looking after the welfare of six thousand boys from all parts of the world, who were in the camp. During the past year, I took a year's leave of absence from my regular pastoral work and have been studying boys' work in the Episcopal Church, especially the Boy Scouts' program, spending a good part of my time in the West Side and East Side of New York City.

During August and September, 1920, I paid a special visit to Czechoslovakia for the purpose of studying religious conditions there, being sent officially by the Presiding Bishop and Council of the Episcopal Church. I made contact there with the leaders of the newly organizing "Czechoslovak Church." I met President Masaryk and a number of the Cabinet Ministers, some of the professors of Prague University, many business men, working men, and peasants in Eastern Slovakia in the Carpathian Mountains. In December of this year I accompanied the Bishop of Moravia, of the Czechoslovak Church, in his visit to the United States, and I worked as the intermediary between him and the Presiding Bishop and Council of the Episcopal Church in the establishment of a Covenant between the two Churches, and finally succeeded in bringing about an official Covenant.

The first of February I made a trip to Czechoslovakia on a twofold errand; I am interested in the religious reformation going on there, and have much to do with its leaders in several

Denominations, so I visited with them in Bohemia and Moravia. In Slovakia, eastward toward Russia, there is a little village in the Carpathian Mountains whose inhabitants for many years have emigrated back and forth between their home village and Westfield. In Westfield they are my parishioners, so I visited them at this village. My sympathies are so identified with Czechoslovakia that I have introduced a new form of unifying the antagonistic sentiment of the East and West, namely, by getting the Boy Scouts of the two sections in correspondence with one another. This was the second purpose of my errand.

I found the little Republic (it is just about the area of New England, with twice its population) most prosperous, and its people very happy. They are great manufacturers, and many articles of common use in our own country will be found to be stamped "Made in Czechoslovakia,"—pencils, crayons, glassware, etc. They have installed some great electric power plants in England, equipped the Egyptian Railway with a "De Luxe" train, supplied Roumania with locomotives and Russia with tractors, and their great steel plants and other factories are running day and night. Their public school system is very efficient, and they have erected 3,000 new public schools since the War. The University of Prague, founded in 1348, has now 16,000 students, co-educational. Several thousand are from Russia and from Siberia, many of whom have walked a thousand miles to get there and are without any money whatever. There is an organization of college workers, American and Czechoslovak, which is doing a wonderful piece of service in reaching these needy students.

I have now, after my year's leave of absence, gone back to my work in Westfield as pastor of a congregation mostly of working people and farmers. I have been appointed a Special National Field Commissioner of the Boy Scouts of America to promote the Scout program in the Episcopal Church throughout the country. It is very pleasant, in this .work among the Boy Scouts, to run side by side with Jim Wilder from time to time. I am in charge, under the National Council of the Episcopal Church, of the coöperative work with the American branch of the Czechoslovak National Episcopal Church which has six organized congregations here. I am going on with my natural history work for the "R. K. Smith and W. F. Clapp Collection of New England Shells'' in the Agassiz Museum and am establishing a small conchological laboratory in my acre island on the Rhode Island seashore for some original investigations. I have at last got together my material for a history of the Christian Church in Central Europe which I expect to offer as part of my work for the degree of Doctor of Divinity, and have started at it with much enthusiasm. It all seems a very happy prospect up to our fortieth, with the pleasures of snowshoeing in the winter, trout fishing in the spring, with my family at the shore in the summer, and hiking alone, or with Boy Scouts, and camping here and there in the Berkshires during the autumn. I live right next to the cemetery here, but I don't believe I want to think of being planted there yet; say after our fiftieth or sixtieth!

WAYNE PRESCOTT SMITH

Born at Latrobe, Pennsylvania, 3 November 1866, of George Washington
    Smith (railroad employee) and Mary Hullenbaugh.
Entered from University of Wooster.
Class Status: I. Graduate School, 1892-93.
Degrees: A.B. (Univ. Wooster) 1891; A.M. (Univ. Wooster) 1892;
    A.B. 1893; Ph.D. (Univ. Wooster) 1893.
Married Ivy Josephine Girvin at Honolulu, 26 May 1909.
Now educational administration and writer.

Since the last report my occupation has been chiefly educational, partly editorial in text book publishing organizations, partly in the field of authorship, having successfully completed a text-book of importance (though it may not so have impressed the kindly world), and partly, for somewhat more than two years, in the Rehabilitation Division of the Federal Board for Vocational Education and the larger, later United States Veterans' Bureau. In this service my efforts have been territorially diversified, for a while in District No. 1, headquarters at Boston, later in District No. 8, headquarters at Chicago, and for two years in District No. 11, headquarters at Denver. Have organized several vocational or trade schools, the last being at Salt Lake City, Utah, where I labored for about one and one-half years. Recently the District Manager invited me to assume the responsibilities of supervision of the vocational schools of the District. Have been on this job for several months.

As for the work, it is about the most interesting and difficult that I have had the pleasure of undertaking. It confronts one with almost every sort of problem in human nature. It is about the most dominating, all-inclusive job I know anything about—consuming every possible atom of energy and time discoverable. It leaves no leisure for aught else; but it certainly gives one experience that will be most valuable in the work which I hope to complete, after this work—so far as I am concerned—is finished. The wealth of experience which this labor brings is capital that can hardly be equalled in quality or variety in any other field of activity with which I am acquainted.

Publications: "Introduction to the Study of Science," The Macmillan Company, 1918. (A first-year science book for high schools). Several other items published, but of no mentionable importance. Sports: Hunting and fishing (for the speckled beauties whenever and wherever opportunity offers, occasionally for bass, and even still less occasionally for certain of the fishy tribes of the ocean); travelling in some of the scenic parts of the United States, as Western Wyoming (Jackson Hole), Northern Utah, and almost any section of Colorado. Have acquired something like "real" knowledge of these parts of the best country on earth.

TOWNSEND HODGES SOREN

Born at Dorchester, Massachusetts, 28 November 1868, of Jonathan Wales Soren (accountant) and Harriet Amanda Brown.
Fitted at Boston Latin.
Class Status: Regular.
Degree: A.B. 1893.
Married Gara Mabel Parker at Dorchester, Massachusetts, 5 June 1901. Children:
      Parker, born 14 March 1902.
      Garafelia Tucker, 26 December 1905.
Now Vice-president of Hartford Electric Light Company.

Since the date of last report, have been vice-president of the Hartford Electric Light Company, which position I now hold. In 1922 was elected vice-president of the Connecticut Power Company, which is intimately associated with the Hartford Electric Light Company to distribute its power through the western part of the State. The principal work of interest is the designing and construction of a modern power station for this company, which has attracted some little attention, as the economy is far ahead of any station of its size, and compares favorably with some of the largest and most economical stations in the country.

FRANK ENOS SOULE

Born at Freeport, Maine, 14 January 1869, of Enos Corydon Soule (shipping) and Helen Louisa Gore.
Fitted at Phillips Exeter.
Class Status: Special, 1888-91. I. Law, 1891-92.
Married Bessie Mae Pace at Boston, 21 June 1912.
Now Assistant Local Manager, Pittsburgh Plate Glass Company, Boston.

My principal doings for the first five years out of college were to work at the plate glass business with a few vacations. Beginning 1898 I went on a fishing trip to Nova Scotia the first Friday in May, and kept this up for fourteen years. We caught square tail trout on a fly. There is early fishing there because the water is not deep and Weymouth, Nova Scotia, is almost as far south as Portland, Maine. All of our fishing was from canoes.

In about 1901 I went to Jamaica, and 1913 Mrs. Soule and I went to Bermuda. These are the extent of my travels excepting a few fishing trips to Northern Maine and some vacations in Casco Bay near Portland. My summer vacations during the last seven years were at Cape Cod or Compton, New Hampshire. I was married in 1912 and lived at Englewood Avenue until 1915, then moved to Chestnut Hill Avenue until June, 1921. Purchased a house at 15 Maple Terrace, Auburndale, where we still live. My official duties are now to call on six sash and blind houses every morning (which takes about one hour and a half), answer correspondence, and keep our glass stock up. I suppose Sam will give me an E on this paper because I fall short of his required three hundred words. I am not enclosing a return postal for early information as to my mark.

HORACE CLAFLIN SOUTHWICK

Born at Brooklyn, New York, 28 June 1871, of John Claflin Southwick (merchant) and Ella Mather Clapp.
Fitted with E. Phillips.
Class Status: Regular.
Degree: A.B. 1893.
Now residing in New York City.

Was two years in School of Mines, Columbia College. Then spent five years in Paris studying architecture. Returned to New York and practised architecture for a number of years, sharing an office for several years with the late Charles P. Huntington, '93· Two years ago, while visiting my sister in Newport, had a severe attack of inflammatory rheumatism, which laid me up in the Newport Hospital for three months. Have not entirely recovered at this date. Prohibition is expensive and demoralizing as well.

FRED MAURICE SPALDING

Born at Pawtucket, Rhode Island, 31 May 1870, of Charles Hubbard
    Spalding [Brown 1865] (clergyman) and Annie Eliza Carpenter.
Fitted at Berkeley School, Boston.
Class Status: Regular.
Degrees: A.B. 1893; M.D. 1897.
Married (1) Adelaide Frances Lecompte at Boston, 11 October 1905
    (died 30 October 1906). Child:
        Francis Lecompte, born 30 October 1906.
Married (2) Elise Alice Jecko at Cambridge, Massachusetts, 9 March
    1909. Children:
        Fred Maurice, Jr., born 24 October 1910.
        Elise Jecko, 2 January 1915.
Now practising medicine at Boston.

After graduating from the Harvard Medical School in 1897, and spending three years in hospital work, I began the practice of medicine, limiting my work to the eye. After my house service at the Massachusetts Charitable Eye and Ear Infirmary I was appointed a clinical assistant and passed through the various grades, serving as eye surgeon for about ten years. My private practice demands now so much of my time that I have had to curtail my hospital work. I am still connected with the staff of the Infirmary, but my work is more supervisory, my title being Chief of Service. I am consulting eye surgeon to the Massachusetts General Hospital, New England Baptist Hospital, and New England Deaconess Hospital. During the war I tried to do my bit by doing extra hospital work. My work has kept me from travelling very much.. I hope that the time is not far distant when I shall be able to see something of the world. My chief pastimes are amateur farming at my place at Squam Lake, and golf. I am a member of the Charles River Country Club and the Laconia Country Club. In Boston I belong to the Union Club and the St. Botolph Club. I am a member of the Vestry of All Saints Church, Brookline. I belong to several medical societies, the most important of which is the American Ophthalmological Society. I was president of the New England Ophthalmological Society for the year 1921.

HARTWELL BALLOU SPAULDING

Born at Milford, Massachusetts, 11 October 1870, of Benjamin Hartwell
  Spaulding (manufacturer) and Elvira Daniels Ballou.
Fitted at Milford High.
Class Status: Special, 1889-91.
Married Anna Thwing Whitney at Milford, Massachusetts, 6 December
  1894. Child:
    Almon Whitney, born 30 September 1895.
Now with Collins & Fairbanks Co., at Boston.

Began as superintendent and salesman for Nelson and La Dow, at Upton, Mass. In July, 1899, this concern failed. Was then for a year with the R. I. Sherman Manufacturing Company at Boston. For next two years with the Hills Company at Amherst, having charge of their fine goods department. 1902-1903, superintendent of the straw goods plant of George B. Burnett and Son. Since September, 1903, salesman for Collins and Fairbanks Company at Boston. Lived for many years in Dorchester, but in 1916 sold house and purchased a bungalow at Newton Highlands, 15 Brewster Road. Son Almon Whitney graduated from Massachusetts Agricultural College in 1917, enlisted in the Amherst College Unit of the Ambulance Corps, and served in France. No special changes during last five years.

JOHN FRANCIS CYRIL SPENCER-TURNER

Born at Brooklyn, 5 November 1869, of John Spencer Turner (cotton
  merchant) and Cornelia Jane Eddy.
Fitted at G. W. Dickerman's and St. Paul's.
Class Status: Freshman year only.
Now living in Rome, Italy.

Name originally John Spencer Turner, Jr. Left college after freshman year to study for the Episcopal ministry at the General Theological Seminary, New York City. Was ordained in November, 1893. Served as assistant minister in the House of Prayer, Newark, New Jersey, and in Holy Cross Church, New York City; then became rector of the Church of the Good Shepherd at Rochester, New York. Had always been an extreme ritualist, and finding himself unable to carry out his ideas, was received into the Roman Catholic Church in July, 1898, making his submission at the Passionists' Church of St. Joseph in Paris, and being rebaptized John Francis Cyril Spencer-Turner. He did not, however, take orders. Has resided ever since in Rome, occupied somewhat with social-religious work among the poor, and greatly interested in political affairs—of course espousing the papal party. He was made a marquis in the papal nobility by Leo XIII, July 1, 1902; given the Commenda of the pontifical order of St. Gregory the Great by Pius X, December 9, 1905; and created a Knight of Malta (the only American ever received into the order) by Prince Grand Master Galeazzo January 22, 1907. His father, a prominent citizen of Brooklyn, died in 1905, leaving him a considerable property. At that time the New York papers described him as "a gentleman in waiting to the cardinals connected with the Vatican"—a description which he subsequently disclaimed as "too absurd." In 1906 he reported himself as "thoroughly Italianized! Still without a better half, and trying consequently to do one of the hardest things in the world—keep up a bachelor's establishment." He is said to have married in London about 1910, his wife dying soon afterwards; but no new information has been received from him since 1909, his recent reports merely repeating his formal data, titles, etc. He now gives his permanent address as care of Sebasti & Co., 20 Piazza di Spagna, Rome.

JOSIAH EDWARD SPURR

Born at Gloucester, Massachusetts, 1 October 1870, of Alfred Sears
    Spurr (mariner) and Oratia Eliza Snow.
Fitted at Gloucester High.
Class Status: Joined class Junior year from '92.
Degrees: A.B. 1893; A.M. 1894.
Married Sophie Clara Burchard at Washington, District of Columbia,
    18 January 1899. Children:
        Edward Burchard, born 2 February 1900.
        John Constantine, 5 July 1901.
        William Alfred, 24 December 1905.
        Robert Anton, 23 March 1913.
        Stephen Hopkins, 14 February 1918.
Now Editor of *Engineering and Mining Journal-Press*, New York City.

On leaving college in 1893, I secured a job as assistant on the Minnesota Natural History and Geological Survey, and made the first geological map of the Mesabi Iron Range. The next spring I joined the United States Geological Survey as assistant

geologist, working in the mining camps of Leadville, Aspen, and .
Mercur. In 1896 I was selected to head the first expedition of
the United States Geological Survey into the interior of Alaska.
With Goodrich, of '92, and Schrader, of '93, I went over the
Chilkoot Pass and through the Yukon country, examining the
placer gold diggings. In 1897 I travelled and studied in
Europe; in 1898 explored in Alaska in the Susitna-Kuskokwim
region; in 1899 traversed the deserts of Nevada and California,
assisting at the completion of a geologic map of the United
States. In 1900 I went to Turkey as consulting geologist and
mining engineer to the Sultan of Turkey; after being in Turkey for some time I was appointed by the Sultan on a commission, together with the Minister of Mines and the Grand Vizier.
I returned to the United States Geological Survey in 1901, and
made various studies including the ore-deposits of Tonopah,
Nevada. In 1905 I became chief geologist for allied New York
interests, including the American Smelting and Refining Company, etc. In 1908 I organized the firm of Spurr and Cox, Incorporated, composed of mining engineers who were eminently
qualified specialists in different branches of the mining profession. This firm was most successful, with offices in New York,
Denver, El Paso, and Mexico City. In 1911 the firm was discontinued, and I organized the firm of Spurr and Company,
for the same purpose. In 1912 I became vice-president in
charge of mining, and advising engineer, to the Tonopah Mining
Company of Nevada, with offices at Philadelphia.

When we entered the war I went to the United States Shipping Board, at one dollar per annum, to make studies, recom-
mendations, decisions, and adjustments in the matter of ore
importations, and the consequent saving of ships. I resigned
from the committee on Mineral Imports to become Executive,
War Minerals Investigations, Bureau of Mines; later became
Chief Engineer, War Mineral Relief, together with many other
war activities connected with mineral supplies. In 1920 became
Editor-in-Chief of *Engineering and Mining Journal,* of New
York, and in 1922 of *Engineering and Mining Journal-Press,* by
combination with the Mining and Scientific Press of San Francisco. In 1921, President of the Mining and Metallurgical Society of America; in 1923 President of the Society of Economic
Geologists.

Member of Cosmos Club, Washington, D. C., Harvard and Engineers' Clubs, New York; Society of Economic Geologists; Mining and Metallurgical Society of America; American Institute of Mining and Metallurgical Engineers; Society of Mayflower Descendants; Society of Colonial Governors.

FRANCIS UPHAM STEARNS

Born at Haverhill, Massachusetts, 12 January 1871, of Charles Augustus.
    Stearns (electrician) and Mary Elizabeth Burnham.
Fitted at Boston Latin.
Class Status: Regular.
Degree: A.B. 1893.
Married Lucie Kirtland Macdonald at New York City, 6 November 1901.
    Children:
        Francis Upham, Jr., born 27 May 1904.
        Ranald Macdonald, 27 November 1906.
        Charles Burnham, 30 May 1908.
Now in dry goods commission business at New York City.

In September, 1893, I entered the employ of J. H. Lane and Company, Boston, in the dry goods commission business. Moved to New York in May, 1897, for the same firm. In September, 1898, I entered the employ of A. D. Juillard and Company, New York, dry goods commission merchants, and in 1905 I became associated with Converse and Company, New York. Here I remained until January, 1911. when I organized F. U. Stearns and Company, dry goods commission merchants. Since November of 1905 I have also been Treasurer of the Renfrew Manufacturing Company of Adams, Massachusetts. I live in Adams four or five months in the summertime, and in New York during the winter. In New York I give practically my whole time to the business of F. U. Stearns and Company, with the exception of regular exercise. In Adams I ride horseback, play golf, and try to prevent a small farm from using up all my surplus. I have served as Vice-President of the First District of the Republican Club of Massachusetts. During the war I was on the Exemption Board for Division 2 of Massachusetts throughout the war. Since last October I have been on the sick list, and since January have been at Hot Springs, Virginia, but I am gaining steadily and hope to be with the crowd (escorting Mrs. Stearns) at the Thirtieth Anniversary Celebrations in June.

WALLACE NELSON STEARNS

Born at Chagrin Falls, Ohio, 26 August 1866, of Horatio Nelson Stearns (clergyman) and Adeline Munn.
Entered from Ohio Wesleyan University.
Class Status: Entered Senior.
Degrees: A.B. (Ohio Wesleyan) 1891; A.B. 1893; S.T.B. 1896; A.M, 1897; Ph.D. (Boston Univ.) 1899.
Married Addie McClain at Urbana, Illinois, 31 December 1913.
Now Professor of Biblical Literature at McKendree College, Lebanon, Illinois. (After September 1, Illinois Woman's College.)

Returned to Ohio Wesleyan as instructor in Greek, Assistant Professor. Also set to organize the gymnasium work with one hundred and eighty men to look after. On duty thirty-five hours a week! Professor of Latin and New Testament Greek in Baldwin University, Berea, Ohio; also spoke every Sunday in interests of the college; attendance nearly doubled. Financial Secretary of Religious Education Association, 1903-1904. First month we took in $150.00; eighth month we received $2,000.00. Became Private Secretary to President James of Northwestern University and, later, a university examiner in the medical school (for admission). Followed President James to the University of Illinois. Began work on question of religious education in State Universities, 1904. Prepared three reports (two published) on the subject; wrote sixteen papers, appeared in six national conventions, secured adoption of resolution in University section of National Education Association, projected and helped organization of first national conference on subject (Urbana, 1904) and edited the proceedings. Helped to organize Wesley College (at State University) of North Dakota, and was first Professor of Biblical Literature. Helped in organization of University Extension in North Dakota, and was first field secretary. Organized Sunday School teacher training in North Dakota, and had over thirty-five hundred studying. Professor Biblical Literature in Fargo College, organizing the department, also taught history, 1912-1918. Assistant Editor Quarterly Journal, University of North Dakota, 1908-1912.

Y. M. C. A. Area Educational Secretary in England and France, 1918-1919. Army Educational Corps, 1919. Located in South England and Western France (Camp Pontenazen, etc.). Professor of Biblical Literature in McKendree College, 1919——; organized a department unique in many ways.

Winsor   Dallinger   Fridenberg

Pearson   Howerth   Muzzey   [Mack]

Have studied summers in Chicago, 1901; Oxford, 1911; Berlin, 1912. Toured Egypt, Palestine, Greece, Italy; visited Damascus, Smyrna, Constantinople, 1922 (summer).

Belong to several societies: "Archaeological Institute of America"; "Palestine Exploration Fund" (State Secretary); "Egypt Exploration Fund" (one of American vice-presidents); "Society of Biblical Literature"; "American Geographical Society of New York" (fellow); overseas member of "Author's Club" (London); S. A. R.; Mason; Methodist; Republican; still an optimist. Chief sports: camping and fishing.

J[OSEPH] HENRY STEINHART

Born at New York City, 19 July 1872, of Israel Steinhart (merchant) and Emilie Schubart.
Fitted with Dr. Julius Sachs.
Class Status: Freshman only.
Married Cecil Lopez Duffin at New York City, 13 November 1919.
Now dealing in contractors' supplies at Havana, Cuba. .

Still doing business at the old stand, importing iron and steel products, sugar mill supplies, etc., for consumption in this little Republic. Am operating as a company, of which I am president and treasurer. Also president of the Cuban Vitrolite Company, an allied company to the Vitrolite Company, Chicago, Illinois. Am a director of the American Chamber of Commerce of Cuba, chairman of its Publicity Committee, and editor of its Monthly Bulletin.

My wife lets me off occasionally and I put in a day at golf, at which I am a first-class "dub." Also get in a day or so of hunting and a bit of fishing now and then. If you and your friends in Washington will leave the poor sugar planters alone for a year or two, I hope to be able to quit work and make a trip back to Cambridge, Bowdoin Square, Riverside, and a few other places that I don't care to give the names of in this report.

Belong to all the Clubs here and make my headquarters at the Harvard Club in New York, where "Cully" helps to liven up things for me.

FRANK ELIOT STETSON

Born at New Bedford, Massachusetts, 10 May 1869, of Thomas Meriam Stetson [Harvard 1849] (lawyer) and Caroline Dawes Eliot.
Fitted at Friends' Academy.
Class Status: Regular.
Degrees: A.B. 1893; M.D. 1897.

Married Sigrid Möller at Cambridge, Massachusetts, 9 February 1905.
Children:
> Frederick Meriam, born 26 May 1907.
> David Forbes, 3 March 1912.
> Karin, 23 September 1914.

Now practising medicine at South Dartmouth, Massachusetts.

For a year and a half served in United States Army as Captain in Medical Corps at Camp Sevier in South Carolina and at Camp Hancock in Georgia. Since then have lived and practised in South Dartmouth, Massachusetts.

RALPH LESLIE STEVENS

Born at Cambridge, Massachusetts, 10 November 1870, of Abraham Walter Stevens [Meadville Theol.] (clergyman) and Elizabeth Ellen Whitney.
Fitted at Cambridge Latin.
Class Status: Regular.
Degree: A.B. 1893.
Married Maria Cary Clarke at Lexington, Massachusetts, 3 October 1900.
Children:
> Ruth, born 8 November 1902.
> Alexander Clarke, 17 February 1904.
> Barrett Whitney, 21 May 1907.

Now in cotton yarn business at New York.

In the fall of 1893 went with the Boston Book Company, Law Book Publishers in Boston. On May 1st, 1895, went with Harding, Whitman Company, dry goods commission merchants in Boston, later William Whitman Company, Inc. Remained with them twenty years, leaving May 1st, 1915. In July, 1915, organized with my two brothers the company C. H. and R. L. Stevens, Inc., with offices in Boston and Philadelphia, to deal in cotton yarns. This business was in December, 1915, merged as a "department" with J. Spencer Turner Company, 86 Worth Street, New York City.

On February 1st, 1919, organized, again with my two brothers, the Stevens Yarn Company, Inc., to deal in cotton yarns; with main office at 1 Thomas Street, New York City, and branch offices in Boston, Philadelphia and Charlotte, North Carolina. On January 1st, 1923, we reopened a branch office in Boston, having moved our Boston office to Providence, Rhode Island in 1919, which we still continue.

On March 1st, 1923, we moved our New York office to 86 and 88 Worth Street, so returning to the location where I first started my New York business experience in 1915. In this manner the circle seems to have been completed and everything indicates that I have forsaken Boston and become a permanent resident of New York.

My older boy whom I had hoped to send to Harvard next year, preferred to go into business. He is now with Minot, Hooper and Company, dry goods commission merchants, New York. My younger boy will graduate from Ridgefield School in June, 1924, and enter Harvard in the class of 1928. He will thereby wear the orange and black of '93·

HENRY HARDING STICKNEY

Born at Chelsea, Massachusetts, 20 May 1870, of Joseph Wingate Stickney (paints) and Harriet Harding.
Fitted at Chelsea High.
Class Status: Regular.
Degree: A.B. 1893.
Married Mrs. Harriet Lounsbery (Boynton) Howard of Cambridge, 26 August 1918, with child, Marcia Harriet Howard. Children:
Anne Caroline, born 30 March 1920.
Rebecca Barrett, 9 November 1921.
Now manufacturing paints, etc., at Boston.

After college days, I spent till 1900 as assistant editor of "The Congregationalist," Boston, when an opening in business with my father was attractive, and I have continued therein, as a manufacturer, to the present time. In 1918 I married, taking a wife and her daughter for the start of a family. Two other little girls have been added to our list. We are settled in Belmont, Massachusetts.

ARTHUR PARKER STONE

Born at Groton, Massachusetts, 16 January 1870, of Valancourt Stone and Ellen Anna Mason.
Fitted at Cambridge Latin.
Class Status: Regular.
Degrees: A.B. 1893; LL.B. 1895.
Married Alice Holman Stratton at Cambridge, Massachusetts, 26 September 1899. Children:
Ruth Sybil, born 15 December 1900.
Sybil Alice, 17 March 1904.
Anne Frances, 4 March 1908.
Ellen Drusilla, 10 December 1912.
Now practising law in Boston, and Justice Third District Court of Eastern Middlesex.

I am still practising law in Boston, in partnership with my nephew, Mason H. Stone, '07, and associated, as I have been for many years, with Joseph Wiggin, '93. Upon retirement of Judge Charles Almy, '72, I was appointed Justice of the District Court at Cambridge where I had been a Special Justice for a number of years. The longer I hold that office the more impressed I am with the fact that it offers immense opportunity for service, and by the feeling that I am meeting those opportunities on the whole rather inadequately. Under the Massachusetts law I was appointed for life, or during good behavior. As the years go on I am becoming convinced that the Governor made a mistake.

With regard to my amusements I can say but little. I used to play golf but, as I mentioned in the last report, I gave that up for gardening. I still maintain a garden but I find that I enjoy it most when the work is done by proxy. Some day when my income catches up with my expenditures I intend to take up croquet or some other equally beneficial exercise for old gentlemen. Socially my life is uneventful. I will not play bridge and I cannot afford to play poker. Up to a year ago I was somewhat active in the Masonic Fraternity and was Master of Belmont Lodge in the year 1922. I am now retired from my Masonic labors and am enjoying a rest which was earned if not deserved.

Philip Deland Stone
See Report VI, Page 270.

Richmond Stone
See Report VI, Page 270.

WILLIS WHITTEMORE STOVER
Born at Charlestown, Massachusetts, 19 March 1870, of Augustus Whittemore Stover (bank treasurer) and Elizabeth Maria Rugg.
Fitted at Boston Latin.
Class Status: Special, 1889-90.
Degree: LL.B. (Boston Univ.) 1896.
Married Alice Beswick at Charlestown, Massachusetts, 9 October 1901.
Now practising law at Boston.

After leaving college I worked for two years as a reporter and "desk man" on the Boston Traveler. Entered Boston Unisity School of Law in 1893, graduating in 1896. Admitted to the bar in October, 1896, I began active practice of law in the office of William A Morse, remaining with this office until the outbreak of the war with Spain in 1898. Served in the War with Spain as Captain of Company A, 5th Massachusetts Volunteer Infantry. Mustered out on March 31, 1899, I formed a law partnership with E. Leroy Sweetser, a brother officer in the Army, and our firm still continues to do business, having been reinforced by the admission of Willard P. Lombard as a partner in 1916.

In 1913 was appointed Special Justice of the Charlestown Municipal Court. Otherwise my business career has been uneventful, though profoundly disturbed by my absence in the War with Spain, and the very serious set-back to our office due to the absence of my partner, General Sweetser, and myself for more than two years in the World War. Have no complaints, however. The game was worth all it cost.

In 1916, I served on the Mexican Border, in command of the 5th Massachusetts Infantry. This regiment was mobilized in July, 1917, and although it was greatly depleted by drafts of enlisted men and junior officers to fill the ranks of the 26th Division, enough was left me to form the nucleus of a very fine regiment. In February, 1918, the designation of the regiment was changed to the 3d Pioneer Infantry, and it served abroad under that name.

After my overseas leave in June, 1918, which made it possible for me to attend the 25th reunion of our Class, we were sent abroad. The regiment was immediately sent to the American front, and served through the latter part of the St. Mihiel offensive, and through the whole of the Meuse-Argonne campaign. After the Armistice, which found us in the line, we were left on the battle ground to destroy the German ammunition, mines, etc., and spent the winter in the sector around Verdun. From April till July the regiment served as the railroad police of the A. E. F., being scattered over France and Germany, with smaller detachments in Holland and Belgium. My job was to administer and direct this scattered outfit, and in doing it I had an opportunity to see Europe at the expense of the Government that has come to few Americans.

My record in the war was not conspicuous, but there are two highly satisfactory facts about it. First, I took my regiment overseas, commanded it there, and brought it back to the States,.

without being relieved, suspended, or in any way being disturbed. Very few Colonels had that record. Second, when my
regiment was mustered out, the enlisted men asked me to hold a
reception, and each shook hands with me. These two evidences
that my service was satisfactory both to my superior officers and
to the men under my command console me for the lack of decorations which seemed to be flying around pretty thickly but which
some how or other missed me.

I don't like to brag, but the best military service I have ever
rendered was in the establishment and development of the
Massachusetts Military Training School for the training of candidates for commissions in the National Guard. I was the first
commandant of this school, which was established in 1913, quite
largely as a result of my efforts to get the Commonwealth to try
it out. It was a conspicuous success, and Professor Johnston,
of Harvard, now deceased, said that it was the first great step
toward the training of citizen soldiers that had been undertaken
since the adoption of the Constitution. The Plattsburg schools
were copied from it, and its policies were adopted by the candidates' school at Langres. It is gratifying to me to believe that
thirty years of study on my part was reflected in its influence.

JESSE ISIDOR STRAUS

Born at New York City, 25 June 1872, of Isidor Straus (merchant) and
  Ida Blun.
Fitted with Dr. J. Sachs.
Class Status: Regular.
Degree: A.B. 1893.
Married Irma Sally Nathan at New York City, 20 November 1895. Chil-
  dren:
      Beatrice Nathan, born 27 September 1897.
      Isidor, 2d, 13 January 1900.
      Robert Kenneth, 22 October 1905.
Now President of R. H. Macy and Company, at New York City.

If my days were crowded with outstanding events, I might
have something of interest to report; but, being engaged as a
merchant, in a highly competitive industry, which of necessity
occupies most of my time, I do not have opportunity to enter
into other fields where public honors are to be found. I have,
therefore, received none, and while I have not sought any, I
have never had to decline.

I am still engaged in business in New York as President of

R. H. Macy and Company, Inc. I do, however, find occasional opportunity to interest myself in public affairs, political and philanthropic, and in the general activities of my craft. I have just retired as President of the National Retail Dry Goods Association. I make an occasional address quasi-financial or pseudo-economic. I manage to travel to Europe occasionally.

Of course my interest in Harvard is as active and keen as ever. My older son, Isidor Straus, 2nd, Class of '21, is now with me in business; my younger son, Robert Kenneth, is now at St. George's School, and expects to enter Harvard in the autumn. I am in good health, and feel that I am holding my own, with age not yet the master, even though I was recently presented with a grandchild.

Member of Harvard Club of New York, Harvard Club of Boston, and the usual variety of associations, political, commercial and philanthropic.

LIONEL ALEXANDER BURNET STREET

Born at Mahone Bay, Nova Scotia, 29 September 1869, of Jerome Charles
 Street (physician) and Frances Margaret Lane.
Fitted at Victoria Collegiate Commercial School, Douglas, Isle of Man,
 and with tutors.
Class Status: Special, 1889-90.
Degree: M.D. (Tufts) 1898.
Married Mrs. Emily Monteaux (Hildreth) Shields at Campobello, New
 Brunswick, 24 August 1897, with son, William E. Shields.
Now practising medicine at Los Angeles, California.

In 1918 gave up a lucrative practice in Shanghai, China, to go overseas, where subsequently I was commissioned a Major and appointed Surgeon-in-Chief of a Red Cross Medical Unit. This service took me to the Balkans, and on my return to Paris was ordered to Poland as Epidemiologist and Trachoma Expert. The travel involved carried me in various directions through the devastated countries of Europe, and the memory of it all (in my case as in that of others similarly occupied) will never be effaced. November, 1919, I returned to Shanghai, but was unable to reconcile myself to remaining longer in the Orient, so sold out my interests and returned to Europe in 1920, and later spent five months in London in special studies. Came to California in the fall of 1921 and deciding that I liked the climate, reëntered the practice of my profession in the city of Los

Angeles. My future activities will be limited to practice as an
internist. At present I hold an appointment with the United
States Veterans' Bureau as cardio-vascular and lung specialist,
and am ·in private practice. No special social activities. Am
a charter member of the Los Angeles Masonic Club, and am
much interested in promoting the China Club of Southern California.

WILLIAM JAMES HENRY STRONG

Born at Council Bluffs, Iowa, 16 October 1869, of William Barstow Strong
and Abby Jane Moore.
Fitted at Boston Latin.
Class Status: Regular.
Degrees: A.B. 1893; A.M. (Univ. Wooster) 1900.
Married Martha Almira Leavitt at Beloit, Wisconsin, 26 June 1901. Chil-
dren:
> Abby Rutha, born 16 October 1902.
> William Leavitt, 24 November 1907.
> John Kendrick, 19 February 1911.
> Robert Campbell, 29 September 1915.
> James Ashley, 11 April 1918.
Now manufacturing non-electric fans in Chicago.

After graduating, continued Y. M. C. A. work (of which I
was vice-president in college) by attending Moody's Bible Institute at Chicago, 1893-1894. The next year was a student at
Emerson College of Oratory, Boston. Then studied at Eastman
National Business College, Poughkeepsie, New York, and in 1896
was made "Master of Accounts" thereat. After travelling extensively abroad in 1897 on account of ill-health, returned to
Emerson College, completed full four years' course, and taught
there in 1899-1900. Was then called to be Professor of Expression at the University of Wooster, Ohio, where I remained for
two years, receiving the A.M. degree.

Life then changed, and I went into manufacturing, as president of the American Company, Incorporated, of Rockford, Illinois, removing in 1906 to Momence, Illinois, where I manu-
factured hardware specialties. Three years later I removed to
Des Moines, Iowa, and continued business, also going into investment work. About 1915 organized Strong Engineering
Company at Chicago, developing steam power plants, inventing
special apparatus, etc. Became consulting engineer in mechan-
ics, especially aeronautics. At present, president of Chicago

Helicopters, Limited, for design, manufacture, and sale of those devices. Also statistician, writer and lecturer on allied topics. Have filed a claim (uninflated) against Germany, for business losses occasioned by the Great War, of about $200,000. Member of American Historical Association, New England Geneological Society, numerous patriotic societies of "descendants," Masons, Aviation Club of Chicago, Chicago Air Board, American Association of Engineers (past president of Chicago Chapter), etc.

FRANK RAYMOND STUBBS

Born at Cambridge, Massachusetts, 6 February 1872, of Joseph Andrew Stubbs (merchant) and Mary Smith Wiley.
Fitted at Cambridge Latin.
Class Status: Regular.
Degrees: A.B. 1893; M.D. 1897.
Married Ethel May Dow at Cambridge, Massachusetts, 19 July 1898.
Children:
Joseph, born 28 April 1899.
Eleanor Dow, 20 December 1902.
Frank Raymond, Jr., 12 July 1909.
Now practising medicine at Newton, Massachusetts.

I still enjoy the practice of medicine. Having reached the age of fifty, as I slide down my last half-century stretch, next to the joy of service to my patients, I find the greatest pleasure in the contemplation of my children, of whom I have three. The oldest, Joseph, graduated from Harvard in 1920; my daughter, Eleanor, is completing her sophomore year at Smith College; my youngest, my namesake, is already conning the Harvard requirements, in order to enter Harvard in four years more, "Harvard, 1931." One can hardly write of the last five years without a thought of the ravages of the war in the families of the men in our class of '93. Never, shall I forget the anxious hours, the horror of the daily telegrams, from the War Department, when my son Joseph was stricken with double pneumonia at Camp Lee. He was, however, by some miracle, spared, and came back to us at last. I am extremely proud of all my children, and feel confident that they will carry out all the hopes and ideals that their dad of '93 has for them.

Charles Russell Sturgis

See Report VI, Page 276.

Walter Dana Swan

See Report VI, Page 277.

THOMAS HENRY SYLVESTER, JR.

Born at Chelsea, 13 April 1870, of Thomas Henry Sylvester (manu-
facturer) and Elmira Hamlin Foster.
Entered from Boston University.
Class Status: Entered Junior.
Degree: A.B. 1893.
Married (1) Marie Dudley Ryder at Boston, 28 March 1895 (divorced).
Children:
      Hamlin Ryder, born 16 October 1896.
      Elaine, 5 March 1901 (died 10 March 1908).
Married (2) Theresa Baker at Brooklyn, New York, 5 February 1919.
Now special agent for New York State Hospital Commission at New
York City.

For four years after graduating I was engaged in patent
brokerage business in Boston and New York. Then took up
Christian Science and practised at Worcester, being also First
Reader to the Church of Christ, Scientist, there. About 1912
removed to New York City and a year or two later to San
Diego, California. The years 1913-1918 contain so many un-
fortunate occurrences that I like to forget them. After the
crash was all over, and I had picked myself up, I found that
I could still smile. The opportunity then presented itself to
enter into the State Hospital Service of New York. A conscientious and exhaustive study at close range was made of
these State institutions; Social Service, including after-care
of patients when paroled, was taken up (my help coming
mostly from Dr. Cabot of Boston, a Harvard Graduate); also
occupational therapy, with its daily exemplification by, and
in behalf of, patients as an aid in the overcoming of many
types of mental diseases. In addition, it has been my privilege to assist in securing, through legislative measures, increased pay for the employees of the State hospitals, and the
betterment of a number of conditions which heretofore had
been very trying. Another bill is now pending, and I hope
to see its passage before the Legislature adjourns.

Through the Metropolitan office of the State Hospital
Commission where I am now assigned to duty, 5,500 new com-

mitments were handled last year, and the receipts to the State as the result of this work amounted to $750,000. We hustle, for there are only three of us to handle this work. The work is intensely interesting, for we stand as intermediaries between the Commission and the public, to educate the latter as to what the Commission is endeavoring to accomplish in behalf of those unfortunates legally committed to its care.

FREDERICK JOSEPH TAUSSIG

Born at Brooklyn, New York, 26 October 1872, of Joseph Seligman Taussig (banker) and Mary Louise Cuno.
Fitted at Smith Academy.
Class Status: Regular.
Degrees: A.B. 1893; M.D. (Washington, Mo.) 1898.
Married Florence Gottschalk at St. Louis, 4 May 1907. Children:
Mary, born 21 February 1911.
Frederick, 9 November 1913.
Now practising medicine at St. Louis.

Were it not for the "mess" in Europe for which we by our selfish indifference are largely responsible, life would have been an unmixed joy in the last five years. Having specialized in gynecology and obstetrics for the past twenty years since graduation from Medical School, I did not actively participate in the war but remained at home to care for the wives and mothers.

Outside of practice my greatest interest has been in the control of cancer. Having taken an active part in the organization of the American Society for the Control of Cancer, I am still devoting considerable time to the educational campaign each year, emphasizing the importance of early recognition in this disease. The treatment with radium has greatly interested me. We should all be proud of the work of our class-mate, Dr. Duane, in this important field.

Have also been interested in the care of expectant mothers, and public health work to improve conditions for maternity cases. As I look back on college days, I feel that the inspiration to do this work, outside of the humdrum of practice and money-making, came from the ideals of my Harvard associations. That, to my mind, is the most valuable asset of a college education.

JOHN CLARENCE TAUSSIG

Born at St. Louis, Missouri, 5 February 1872, of John J. Taussig (bank-
er) and Leonore Taussig.
Entered from Washington University.
Class Status: Special, 1889-90. Joined class Sophomore year.
Degrees: A.B. 1893; LL.B. (Washington Univ.) 1895.
Now practising law at St. Louis, Missouri.

Lawyer in St. Louis, Missouri, since September 19, 1895;
also, during last two years active in business as director and
treasurer of a financial corporation. A glorious summer abroad
with our classmate Philip Becker Goetz. Play at golf. As my
golfing clothes are respectable and my clubs are very good I
make a fairly decent appearance on the links—until I begin
playing. City father for two years. Had a good time. Made a
lot of speeches—but none that will go down to posterity. Member, two years, Public Recreation Commission of St. Louis.
Perennial Secretary of a Unitarian church; a job out of which
I get great satisfaction. Not inconsistently, I believe, member executive committee of Missouri branch, Association Op-
posed to Prohibition. Almost violent on that subject. Very
well, thank you. Still unmarried.

WILLIAM OSGOOD TAYLOR

Born at Nashua, New Hampshire, 8 January 1871, of Charles Henry
    Taylor (newspaper publisher) and Georgianna Olivia Davis.
Fitted with J. W. H. Walden and Boston Latin.
Class Status: Regular.
Degree: A.B. 1893.
Married Mary Moseley at Boston, 28 March 1894. Children:
    Moseley, born 30 January 1895.
    Eunice, 20 December 1897.
    Margaret, 3 September 1900 (died 10 May 1914).
    Elizabeth, 24 March 1906.
    William Davis, 2 April 1908.
Now President of the Globe Newspaper Co. at Boston.

Since the day after Commencement in 1893, I have been connected with the Boston Globe, and since July, 1921, have been
president of the Globe Newspaper Company. I am also a trustee
of several estates. My oldest daughter, Eunice, married, in November, 1917, Lieutenant Daniel W. Armstrong, U. S. N., and I
now have two granddaughters. I play golf whenever I get an
opportunity and also still do some yachting. Every fall I try to

get a vacation, in the woods, which I consider one of the most healthful forms of relaxation. Since graduation, I have attended the class reunions whenever possible, and I consider the dinners given by the New York members of our class most entertaining and enjoyable.

MOSELEY TAYLOR—THE CLASS BABY

Prepared for college at Noble and Greenough's and Andover. At Noble and Greenough's he received his letters two years running, in track, football, and crew, and in the spring of 1913 he was captain of the crew. In the year 1913-1914, he was at Andover, where he received his letters in football, wrestling, hockey, and track. In the fall of 1914 he entered Harvard College, and rowed No. 6 on the Freshman Crew. In the fall of his Sophomore year he received his varsity letter in football and in the spring of 1916 rowed No. 6 in the Harvard Varsity crew at New London. As for scholarship, at the end of his Junior year he was credited with fifteen full courses towards his degree. After the hour-exams. in April, 1917, he left college and enlisted in the Navy for the war as second class seaman and was assigned to the study of aviation at Newport News. In October he received his commission as Ensign in the United States Naval Reserve Flying Corps, and in November he was ordered overseas. On arriving in France he was made a Lieutenant and attached to the British Night Bombing Squadron, in which service he remained until he was mustered out in December, 1918. He married on March 8, 1919, Emily Pope of San Francisco. Their home is in Brookline. After leaving the service he joined the Boston Globe, where he has been ever since, being now assistant treasurer of the Globe Newspaper Company.

HARRY LORENZO TEETZEL

Born at Milwaukee, Wisconsin, 18 June 1870, of Lorenzo Harry Teetzel (salesman) and Frances Grant.
Fitted at Milwaukee Academy.
Class Status: Regular.
Degree: A.B. 1893
Now Musician and Painter.

After leaving college I settled down as teacher of piano and voice and have not missed a lesson, so far as I remember, in twenty-five years. In 1915, my business being reduced to next

to nothing on account of the war, I took up water color work as
another occupation for my spare time. I am making a fine success out of it, artistically, and enough to live on, financially,
with promise of very good things to come a little later when society at large begins to take more interest in the arts. Every
day and every night I have kept up my regular study and work
along the lines which it has pleased God to lay down for me, and
in the work I have been blessed. I always loved the woods and
waters, so I have specialized along this line of pure landscape—
no figures nor architecture. My pleasures are my work and out-
door pastimes like swimming, fishing and especially bicycling.
I have no social distractions whatever, as I consider such things
a waste of time—for me.

There is not a blooming, blessed thing more that I can add to
this excepting that I hope we beat Yale every year for ever.

(DERRICK) ANTHONY TE PASKE

Born at Greenleafton, Minnesota, 15 October 1868 of Henry John Te
Paske (farmer) and Gezina Tammel.
Entered from Iowa College.
Class Status: Entered Senior.
Degrees: A.B. (Iowa College) 1892; A.B. 1893.
Married Agnes Dykstra at Sioux Center, Iowa, 2 July 1903. Children:
Amy Ruth, adopted 1 March 1913 (born 12 May 1908).
Maurice Anthony, born 5 January 1916.
Adelphos Herman, 28 November 1917.
Now practising law at Sioux Center, Iowa.

Upon leaving the sacred shrines of Cambridge and her en-
virons I seem to have taken the spade with me back to the old
heaths of my boyhood days, and Sioux Center, Iowa, has been
my home for about thirty years since, as it was for almost twenty years before (since 1874 to be exact). From 1893 to 1897
I taught English and Greek at the Northwestern Classical
Academy at Orange City, Iowa. Meanwhile I continued to read
law, which I had begun at Harvard; and was admitted to practice by the Iowa Supreme Court in 1897. In the law practice
at Orange City for a little over a year, and since 1898 in the law
practice at Sioux Center. Was County Attorney from January 1, 1901, to January 1, 1905, and again from November,
1914, to January 1, 1923, when I voluntarily withdrew. All the
time I have also had a general practice, the probate branch of

the practice being the best. I have served as Mayor of the town for eight years; for a while as member of the local school board; for years as member of the Northwestern Classical Academy Board of Trustees; and since 1910 as first vice-president of the First National Bank of Sioux Center, Iowa. Was Government Appeal Agent for Sioux County during the War.

July 2, 1903, married Agnes Dykstra, a school teacher almost ten years my junior. She was admitted to the Iowa Bar in 1909. In 1913 we adopted a girl (Amy Ruth), then five years old. On January 5, 1916, came a real boy (Maurice Anthony), in the ordinary way, in the scant habiliments of father Adam. And his brother (Adelphos Herman) on November 28, 1917. Two years ago I happened to be prosecuting a number of people for stealing goods from merchandise cars (though Iowa juries do not seem to regard stealing from a railroad as a punishable crime). Well, my two sons had overheard something I had said, and had gotten the drift of the story pretty well. After dinner their mother overheard their observations:

Adelphos—''Our papa wouldn't steal would he?''

Maurice—''No; he's a lawyer—he just takes things.''

LOUIS BARTLETT THACHER

Born at Yarmouth, Massachusetts, 12 May 1867, of Henry Charles Thacher (merchant) and Martha Bray.
Fitted at J. P. Hopkinson's.
Class Status: Special, 1889-92. With '95, 1892-93.
Degree: A.B. 1894, as of 1893.
Married Delia Aimee Tudor at Boston, 8 October 1907 (died 21 July 1921). Children:
    Elizabeth Tudor, born 4 March 1909.
    Henry Charles, 6 April 1910.
    Louis Bartlett, Jr., 23 November 1911.
Now President Thacher and Co., Inc., Shoe Manufacturers, Boston.

The middle of July, 1893, I was on the steamer Saale with Sam Davis, bound for a walking trip of two months through Tyrol and Switzerland. On my return, after ten days at the Chicago World Exposition, I started in business as a clerk with H. C. Thacher and Company, wool merchants. The years 1894-1896 I was with Wilbur H. Davis and Company, shoe manufacturers, at Haverhill, Mass. In 1896 became member of H. C. Thacher and Company, then doing a banking and agent business; the same year director of Davis Boot and Shoe Company.

In 1900 became active trustee of H. C. Thacher Estate and
President Davis Boot and Shoe Company. In 1909 Thacher
and Company took over business of Davis Boot and Shoe Company, and I became member of the firm. When Thacher and
Company was incorporated in 1916 was elected its President,
with factory at East Boston. The last five years my business
activities have been much the same except that I have given
more time to my duties as Trustee, and to the affairs of H. C.
Thacher and Company.

My life has nothing. striking to report. Even during the
stirring days of the Great War my part seemed to be to sub-
scribe to Liberty Bond issues and War Relief drives and to plod
away at my desk; and outside of business hours, owing to the
poor health of my wife, to devote my time to the wants and demands of three young children. A most serious change, however, has come to my personal life, for in July, 1921, my wife
died at Santa Monica, California. She had gone west with the
children in October, 1919, hoping to regain her failing health.
Left with two boys and a girl of ages from nine to twelve, I became more than ever a family man.

I have travelled more or less in these thirty years in Europe,
Egypt, and the United States. Belonged to social, political and
charitable and civic organizations. However, most of this
sounds rather trivial, so Classmates you need not read my report if it bores you.

RUFUS KEMBLE THOMAS

Born at Boston, 30 August 1870, of Alexander Thomas [Harvard 1822]
    (physician) and Margaret Atwood Williams.
Fitted at J. P. Hopkinson's.
Class Status: Freshman year only.
Now with the United Fruit Company in Guatemala.

1895-1898 in cotton brokerage business at Jackson, Mississippi,
when I enlisted with Roosevelt's Rough Riders and spent three
months at Tampa, Florida. Returned to Boston and took up
stock brokerage until 1908. Took a position with the United
Fruit Company in Costa Rica. Remained there for several years,
then shifted to Guatemala, and later to Honduras, still with the
same concern. In 1917 returned to Cambridge to enter the
Quartermaster Course at the Harvard R. O. T. C.; but receiv-

ing an offer to go to France with the Red Cross, accepted and sailed July 9. Was appointed Red Cross representative with the 26th Division and remained with it until April, 1919, when it returned. Immediately went back to old position, and have been continuously in the service of the United Fruit Company since that date, in Honduras, Colombia, and at present in Guatemala, where I have been for a little over a year. Mail addressed to the Somerset Club, Boston, will always reach me.

WILLIAM LELAND THOMPSON

Born at Troy, New York, 4 April 1871, of William Augustus Thompson
   [Rensselaer Polytechnic] (merchant) and Harriette Clarkson Crosby.
Fitted at Hatch and Hinckley's and at Albany Academy.
Class Status: Special, 1889-90. With '94, 1890-91. Joined class Junior
   year.
Degree: A.B. 1893.
Married Martha Groome at Philadelphia, 6 January 1909. Children:
       William Leland, Jr., born 4 December 1909.
       John Groome, 11 March 1912 (died 10 May 1914.)
       Martha Evans, 14 December 1913.
       Peter Schuyler, 8 December 1917.
Now in wholesale drug business at Troy, New York.

After leaving college in the fall of 1893 I entered the wholesale drug business of my father, following in his footsteps and those of my grandfather in a business that was established in 1797 and consequently today is 125 years old. Since the day I took up the pestle to grind drugs in the old mortar I have never let it be very long from my hand and during the thirty years have passed from a junior clerk to President of the Company. For the first ten years my life was uneventful until the death of my father, when I practically took control of the business and succeeded to his many business activities. I am now a director of the United National Bank, Troy Savings Bank, Troy Gas Company, Troy Public Library, Troy Chamber of Commerce, Emma Willard School and Russell Sage College, and Secretary of both these educational institutions. I have been for eighteen years on the Board of Education of Troy and for sixteen years its President. I have also been for two terms President of the New York State Association of School Boards and have held these last educational positions despite the fact that English A proved to be a Waterloo. For many years I have been a director of the Y. M. C. A., and am now Senior Warden in St.

John's Episcopal Church and am a member of the standing committee of the diocese of Albany. All these various avoca. tions have made the time since leaving college pass happily— though too rapidly when I realize that the men. who were cele. brating their thirtieth anniversary when we graduated were Civil War Veterans.

For over fifteen years I was in the National. Guard and went away with the Second New York Volunteer Infantry to the Spanish War, and later served as aide on the staff of Brig. adier General Charles F. Roe. Unfortunately I was prevent-ed from doing my bit as a military man and going overseas in the World War, although I was able to do something in my position on the School Board in organizing a vocational school for enlisted men.

I have been able to travel quite considerably during these past years which has been most refreshing and stimulating. My summers are spent on a farm that I own near Troy which I am endeavoring to turn into a successful business proposition, but I fear my experience may be the same as many another gentle- man farmer. However, it keeps me interested and is excellent for the children.

My greatest regret as I look back upon the past thirty years is that during that time I have seen so very little of the men of '93, for a finer lot of men never graduated from the dear old place.

FREDERICK CHARLES THWAITS

Born at Milwaukee, Wisconsin, 24 May 1871, of William Thwaits and
    Fannie Elizabeth Tasker.
Entered from University of Wisconsin.
Class Status: Sophomore, 1891-92. Senior, 1892-93.
Degrees: A.B. 1893; LL.B. 1896.
Now in real estate at Milwaukee.

1908-1911: Regent of the University of Wisconsin. 1912- 1913: President of the American Whist League. 1915: Member of Plattsburg Training Camp. 1916-1917: Member of the Com- mission for Relief in Belgium. Remained in Belgium from July, 1916, until April 2nd, 1917, first as Assistant Delegate for Brussels, then as Assistant Delegate for Antwerp, and then as Chief of the Department of Inspection and Control for all of

Belgium. April, 1917, to September, 1917: Hoover representative in Italy. December, 1917, to January, 1919: Delegate of the American Red Cross for the Venito outside of Venice and the adjacent islands. Headquarters at Padua. February, 1919, to November, 1919, American Red Cross Commissioner for Bosnia and Herzegovina, and representative of American Relief Administration for child feeding work. Headquarters at Sarajevo, Bosnia. . December, 1919, to May, 1920, in Paris on leave of absence. Decorations: (1) Cavaliere del Ordine della Corona d'Italia. (2) Chevalier de la Couronne de la Belgique. Grade: Deputy Commissioner of the American Red Cross with assimilated rank of Major in the Army of the United States. Am now back in Milwaukee looking after my real estate and investment interests.

ARCHIBALD READ TISDALE

Born at Walpole, Massachusetts, 12 August 1870, of Francis Atrides Tisdale (farmer) and Katharine Jane Barrett.
Fitted at St. Mark's.
Class Status: Left after Sophomore year. Law School, 1891-93.
Degree: LL.B. 1895, as of 1894.
Now practising law at Boston.

My connection with the Boston and Maine Railroad, begun incidentally, in the office of Sigourney Butler, Esq., in 1893, has continued, directly, ever since his death in 1898. The work consists of attention to the legal aspects of various matters with which a railroad corporation is concerned and involves office routine as well as appearance before courts and commissions.

I have no voyages or travels to record. A poor player, I brave ridicule in a few score games of tennis when summer vacation comes, but no longer course about a hand-ball or squash racquet court. As a pastime I have watched many an audience squirm in amateur theatricals.

No public position or office has ever been strained from its fair use by my incumbency. No distinctions or degrees have descended upon me from on high. No publications or speeches can be pointed at as mine, to turn and rend me, unless one should so classify briefs submitted to judges, who are paid to read them.

Member of St. Botolph; Papyrus Club; The Footlight Club;

Union Boat Club, Boston; Pokonoket Club, Dover, Mass.; Players Club, New York.   Harvard Musical Association; Waltham Association, 101st Engineers; American Folk Lore Society; Bar Association of the City of Boston; Massachusetts Bar Association; American Bar Association.

HOWE TOTTEN

Born at Washington, District of Columbia, 11 March 1870, of Enoch Totten [Univ. Wooster, Ohio] (lawyer) and Mary Eliza Howe.
Fitted at Phillips Exeter.
Class Status: Regular.
Degrees: A.B. 1893; LL.B. (Georgetown) 1895; LL.M. (Georgetown) 1896.
Married Priscilla Stearns at Washington, District of Columbia, 16 May 1906. Children:
    Elinor Alice, born 17 May 1908.
    Enoch Howe, 1 June 1909.
    Priscilla Stearns, 29 May 1911.
    Ann, 5 December 1914.
Now farming and raising Great Danes at Baldwin, Maryland.

Since last report I have had to live in Washington for the school days on account of the children but spent all week ends and holidays at the farm.   Farming has become a secondary occupation and I have become a very successful operator for my own account solely, in Washington realty.   But the BIG DOGS are still my principal avocation.

EDWARD SANDS TOWNSEND

Born at Chelsea, Massachusetts, 12 December 1869, of True Whitmore Townsend (real estate) and Susan Elizabeth Colby.
Fitted at Somerville High.
Class Status: "Four years in three."
Degrees: A.B. 1892; LL.B. 1895.
Married (1) Georgie Dunlap Sanborn at Somerville, Massachusetts, 17 February 1897. Children:
    Charles Edward Sanborn, born 7 May 1898.
    Newell Colby, 27 January 1902.
    Clara Gary, 22 February 1905.
    Edith Helen, 25 November 1907.
Married (2) Karey Newell Lee Iselin of Louisville, Kentucky, 11 October 1919. Child:
    Edward Iselin, born 6 February 1921.
Now practising law at Boston.

I moved to Rhode Island, October, 1919, having married a second time. I lived at Cranston. Rhode Island, till August 9, 1922, when I moved to Needham, Mass., where I am now living. A boy was born February 6, 1921, at Cranston, Rhode Island. Am a confirmed family man and very happy in my family life. My present wife is the grand-daughter of a Confederate veteran and was formerly from Louisville, Kentucky, the daughter of J. Templeton Iselin and Sybil Lee (Newell) Iselin.

FREDERICK TOWNSEND

Born at Albany, New York, 28 October 1871, of Frederick Townsend [Union 1843] and Sarah Rathbone.
Fitted at Albany Academy.
Class Status: Regular.
Degrees: A.B. 1893; LL.B. 1897.
Married Harriet Davis Fellowes at New York City, 17 April 1911.
    Children:
        Sarah Rathbone, born 13 July 1912.
        Frederick, Jr., 2 January 1918.
Now President of Savings Bank at Albany, New York.

1893-1894: Went around the world with H. J. Coolidge, '92. 1894-1897: Harvard Law School. 1897-1920: Practised law in Albany with same firm, finally known as Tracy, Cooper and Townsend (now Tracy, Cooper and Savage). 1920 to date: President of Albany Savings Bank which, except for the Bank for Savings in New York City, is the oldest savings bank in the State (chartered 1820). Residence, Town's End, Loudonville, New York.

WILLIS MERRICK TOWNSEND

Born at Peterboro, New Hampshire, 30 January 1870, of Charles Horace Townsend (apothecary) and Josephine Carolilla Fairbanks.
Fitted at Murdock School, Winchendon, Massachusetts.
Class Status: Special, 1889-90.
Degree: M.D. (Boston Univ.) 1893.
Married Harriette Ellen Stone at Melrose Highlands, Massachusetts, 7 October 1897. Children:
        Frances Elizabeth, born 10 May 1899 (died 11 May 1899).
        Miriam 2 November 1901.
        Felicia, 26 May 1912.
Now practising medicine at Melrose Highlands, Massachusetts.

The history of the last thirty years has been in a way uneventful, or at least lacking in lurid details. I have not written a book. I have not had my name in the front page of the newspapers. I have not found a new reason for our living or dying. So much for the negative. I have accomplished something perhaps. I have tried to make people happier. I have helped nature to get them well. I have tried to make them learn to take better care of themselves. I still live in the same city that received me when I graduated from the Medical School. We have made many civic improvements with the most of which I have been identified and actively interested.

My club life has been largely confined to the various state and national Medical Societies and the International Tuberculosis Society. Electrical therapeutics has also been of much interest to me the last few years. I am a member of the various Masonic bodies—Blue Lodge, Commandery, Consistory and Shrine. The Melrose Hospital, my pet hobby, invited me to become a member of its staff twenty years ago and for the last twelve years I have been a member of its governing board. The Bellevue Golf Club is helping me to keep away from arterio-sclerosis. My distinctions: To have my elder daughter, Miriam, in this year's graduating class at Vassar, and my younger daughter entered and on her way to the same college. During the war I was a member of the Medical Service Corps—but saw no service. My discharge makes good reading but my expert rifleman's button means more to me. With Mrs. Townsend I have made many interesting trips. To Seattle by way of Yellowstone Park, down the Pacific Coast to Southern California, and back by way of the Southern Pacific, with a head-on collision at the foot of the Rockies when two transcontinental expresses tried to pass each other on a single track. At another time, a three months' stay in Bermuda while convalescing from my only severe illness. We have wandered through the French Quarter in New Orleans, have gone among the bayous and the old plantations along the Mississippi, have travelled over the battle grounds of the Civil War, have journeyed into Canada and visited the large cities and the rural towns with their numerous wayside shrines. Have fished for pike and muscalongue in the St. Lawrence River, for trout in the various lakes of Maine, have hunted deer with the rifle and in later years with the camera and taken canoe trips into the wilderness for a month or more with our guides as our sole companions. In the summer of 1922 we had the best trip of our lives: Went on a cruise to Iceland, as fascinating as it was out of the way. With its native population looking us over as if we were strangers from another world which we really were for no ship from this country had been there for the last six or eight years. There we had our first experience of a nightless day with a football game at 10.30 P. M., and a glorious sunset at midnight and sunrise at 3 A. M. Then above the arctic circle to Hammerfest and the great promontory of the North Cape when we looked across the Arctic Ocean and thought it is only a short jump to the North Pole. And then the wondrous midnight sun—never below the horizon during the twenty-four hours, and thence down the coast of Norway and into its fascinating fjords with perpendicular sides three to four thousand feet high where the farmers miles apart ran their hay on wires down the mountain side to their barns it was so steep, and where the nanny goat reigned supreme and the scraggy little ponies drew us in the wheeled "stalljerries" without springs till we ached and rode no more. Bergen and Christiania, Copenhagen and down to Zeebrugge with its parapets and dismantled guns to just remind us what had so recently happened. And so on to Ostend, Bruges and Brussels and then across devastated France to Paris for two delightful weeks and across to London by air in a Handley Page plane and then home after two more weeks in England.

BERNARD WALTON TRAFFORD

Born at Westport, Massachusetts, 2 July 1871, of William Bradford Trafford (cotton manufacturer) and Rachel Mott Davis.
Fitted at Fall River High School and Phillips Exeter.
Class Status: Regular.
Degree: A.B. 1893.
Married Leonora Brooks Borden at Fall River, Massachusetts, 5 June 1901. Children:
　　Leonora, born 14 June 1902.
　　Rachel, 17 July 1903.
　　Bernard Walton, Jr., 30 April 1905.
　　Annette, 9 October 1909.
　　Ada Brooks, 24 November 1913.
Now banker at Boston.

Since graduation, my business life has been divided into two periods—twenty years of telephone work with the American Telephone & Telegraph Company and its affiliated companies—

followed by ten years of banking at Boston as Vice President of
The First National Bank of Boston.

Beginning telephone work at Boston on the engineering side,
which necessitated about four years of travelling in the United
States, I entered the operating field, managing a number of Bell
Companies, which required my living successively in New York,
Philadelphia, Washington, Detroit, and finally Chicago. At the
latter point, I was vice-president in charge of operations of the
group of Bell Companies in the Middle West competitive field,
made up of the Chicago, Wisconsin, Michigan, Cleveland and
Central Union(Ohio, Indiana, Illinois) Companies. I maintain my association with the telephone as a director and member of the Executive Committee of the New England Telephone
and Telegraph Company.

My present occupation is general banking. As the bank of
which I am vice-president is engaged in foreign as well as domestic financing, the business is very interesting, involving
contact with other countries. One trip abroad and one to South
America have resulted, with more in prospect. As a director
of the Westport Manufacturing Company and president of the
Sterling Ring Traveler Company, I am interested in a small
way with the cotton manufacturing business, to which my
father devoted his life work. Am director of the Eastern Massachusetts Street Railway Company and of the Stollwerck Choc-
olate Company.

Made one visit to the Coast in 1909, two trips to Europe in
1907 and 1913, and a delightful excursion, 1918-1919, to South
America. Small boat sailing, in which my wife and five children join me, is my hobby. I still spend a vast amount of time on
the tennis courts in summer (doubles only), play formless golf
in spring and fall, and do considerable one-legged skating in
winter. Spent one session at Officers' Training Camp at Fort
Oglethorpe, Georgia, in 1916, and conducted during the war,
as New England Chairman, two of the Red Cross Drives, one
for membership and one for funds. Have served on the War-
rant Committee and as Park Commissioner of Milton. Clubs
are Union, Country, Exchange, Harvard and Hoosic-Whisick,
in or near Boston; Bankers and Harvard Club, New York.

LYMAN TREMAIN

Born at Albany, New York, 14 March 1871, of Grenville Tremain [Union 1865] (lawyer) and Eliza Martin.
Fitted at Groton.
Class Status: Left after Sophomore year.
Married Mabel Vance at Santa Ana, California, 10 October 1912.
Now growing oranges in Santa Ana Canyon, California.

In Pennsylvania Railroad, 1891-1903, in various positions from clerk to contracting agent in traffic department. March, 1903, appointed traffic manager of New York Glucose Company, and upon that company acquiring the Corn Products Company, its chief competitor, I was made traffic manager of the Consolidated Company, Corn Products Refining Company. Reorganized and constructed most of the traffic department for all the factories, had two offices, one at 26 Broadway, New York City, and the other in Heyworth Building, Chicago, and spent every ten days on the road between my two offices.

In August, 1907, my health broke down, and for the next two years spent all my time in sanatoriums. Came to California in April, 1909, and from June, 1909, to August, 1910, worked for Santa Fe Railway as claim adjuster in Los Angeles; then ranching with my cousin at Harper, California, and (after my marriage) on my own account in the Santa Ana Canyon, growing oranges.

PHILIP EDMUND TRIPP

Born at Fall River, Massachusetts, 22 March 1870, of Azariah Shove Tripp and Elizabeth Rebecca Griffin.
Fitted at Phillips Exeter.
Class Status: Special, 1889-90. Scientific, 1890-92. Joined Class Senior year.
Degree: A.B. 1894 as of 1893.
Married Anne Borden Chase at Fall River, Massachusetts, 28 June 1904.
Children:
Borden Chase, born 19 April 1905.
Judith, 12 July 1907.
Mary Elizabeth, 13 April 1917.
Now manufacturing cotton at Fall River, Massachusetts.

The Secretary greatly regrets that Tripp has not replied to repeated calls. He continues to live in Fall River, interested in cotton mills there, and in farming and lobstering at Westport Harbor, fifteen miles away.

JOSHUA DAMON UPTON

Born at North Reading, Massachusetts, 17 June 1870, of John Killam
    Upton (farmer) and Elizabeth Damon.
Fitted at Phillips Andover.
Class Status: Regular.
Degrees: A.B. 1893; LL.B. 1896.
Married Edith Balch at Brookline, Massachusetts, 23 October 1901. Chil-
    dren:
        John Balch, born 8 February 1903.
        Eleanor, 8 March 1905.
        Joshua Damon, Jr., 12 May 1911.
.Now practising law at Boston.

I believe I have in previous reports recounted fully the con-
summate achievements of my life during the first twenty-five
years since graduation, but in order that my classmates may be
saved from vain searching I will, as requested, briefly sum-
marize, to wit.

1893-1918.   Nothing.

After very careful, painstaking preparation, I submit the account of the last five years, the minutest details, of which are
here given.

1919.   Nothing.   Note.   I have acquired the facility of expres-
1920.   Nothing.   sion so plainly noticeable in the description of
1921.   Nothing.   these details, partly from making out my in-
1922.   Nothing.   come tax returns, and partly from deep medi-
1923.   Nothing.   tation since prohibition broke out in U. S. A.

I am now writing my first poem, the basis of which—and indeed also the stimulus and inspiration—has its roots deep in
thirty years of rich experience. Its title, "On the run, or a
couple of jumps ahead," is all I have as yet settled upon, but
I have a lot of material, and I feel sure I will have it ready for
publication in our last class report or the one next subsequent
to it.

Davis Righter Vail

See Report VI, Page 291.

THOMAS WAYLAND VAUGHAN

.Born at Jonesville, Texas, 20 September 1870. of Samuel Floyd Vaughan
    [Louisiana Med.] (physician) and Annie Rebecca Hope.
Entered from Tulane University, Louisiana.
Class Status: Graduate School, 1892-94.
Degrees: S.B. (Tulane) 1889; A.B. 1893; A.M. 1894; Ph.D. 1903,

Married Dorothy Quincy Upham, at Washington, District of Columbia, 22 March 1909   Child:
    Caroline Ely, born 30 August 1911.
Now government geologist at Washington, District of Columbia.

Became assistant geologist, United States Geological Survey in 1894 upon leaving Harvard and subsequently was gradually promoted until in 1907 I was placed in charge of the Section of Coastal Plain Investigations; later I have had charge of the investigations of sediments and West Indian Geological Surveys. As my administrative duties had become so onerous that I could do but little personal research, in 1922 I requested that I be relieved of the Coastal Plain Investigations and for a time I was also relieved of the West Geological Surveys. Since 1903 I have been custodian (honorary) of Madreporarian corals in the United States National Museum. From 1908-1915 I was an investigator associated with the Department of Marine Biology of the Carnegie Institution of Washington.

I have done geological field work in all the coastal states from Massachusetts to Texas, inclusive; also in other states from Tennesee to California. Outside the United States I had done field work in Mexico, Panama, Cuba. Haitian and Dominican Republics, Porto Rico, many of the smaller West Indian Islands, the Bahamas, and the Hawaiian Islands.

I have published many papers, over 150, on areal geology, historical geology, ground water, fossil and living corals, coral reefs and sediments.

In 1904 I was the organizing secretary of the National Society of Fine Arts, which developed into the American Federation of Arts, and I conducted the first correspondence preparatory to the formation of the Federation. The Washington Society then became the Washington Society of the Fine Arts, of which I have been a vice-president for many years. I belong to the following societies: National Academy of Sciences; American Academy of Arts and Sciences; Philadelphia Academy (correspondent); Washington Academy (president, 1923); Geological Society of America (member of council. 1919-1922; vice-president. 1923); Paleontological Society (president, 1923); Geological Society of Washington (president, 1915); Biological Society of Washington; Association of American Geographers; American Association of Advanced Science; National Geographers Society; and others.

I am invited to attend the Second Pan-Pacific Scientific Conference in Australia in August, 1923, and have accepted the invitation. I expect to do some field work, while on the trip, in the Fijiis, New Zealand, and Australia.

Clubs: Cosmos and Washington Biologists Field Club. I have no special amusements and I don't feel the need of them, as my life normally has great variety. I have to travel and cousequently see many new scenes and meet a large variety of people. I might narrate some experiences with Mexican bandits, as evidence of variety in a geologist's life. My life in general has been a happy one—my only regret is that my energy is so limited. But I suppose I have done as much of what I should like to do as I might reasonably expect.

ENOCH HOWARD VICKERS

Born in Washington County, Maryland, 14 March 1869, of Walter William Vickers (farmer) and Jerusha Mullen.
Entered from West Virginia University.
Class Status: Entered Senior.
Degrees: A.B. (W. Va. Univ.) 1890; A.B. 1893; A.M. 1894.
Married Kiyo Nellie Nishigawa at· Tokyo, Japan, 20 December 1899.
Children:
Fannie Clay, born 23 December 1900.
Kate Alethea, 29 January 1902.
Walter William Howard, 1 August 1904.
Now Head of Department of Economics at West Virginia University.

Graduate student of Harvard University: Resident, 1893-1895; non-resident and Robert Treat Paine Fellow, Berlin, Germany,1895-1896, Paris, France, 1896-1897;. Continued studies at Paris, 1897-1898. Professor of Economics and Public Finance, Keiogijuku University, Tokyo, Japan, 1898-1910. Professor of Economics and Sociology and head of Department, West Virginia University, since January, '1911· Member of Asiatic Society of Japan (honorary life), formerly Secretary and Vice-President successively; Harvard Club of Japan, formerly President; Tokyo Club; American Economic Association; American Association for Labor Legislation; American Association of University Professors; Phi Kappa Psi; Phi Beta Kappa. Decorated by Emperor of Japan (Meiji) Order of Rising Sun.

During the last five years, I have had only four experiences which might be worthy of note in the class chronicle. I served as Advisor to the Japanese Imperial Labor Commission during the International Labor Conference held at Washington, October and December, 1919; served as special expert in the Department of State during the Conference on Limitation of Armaments, Washington, 1921; was listed in Who's Who in America for 1922-1923; and became a proud grandfather, July 1, 1922.

OSWALD GARRISON VILLARD

Born at Wiesbaden, Germany, 13 March 1872, of Henry Villard [Munich; Wurzburg] (railroads) and Fanny Garrison.
Fitted with J. H. Morse.
Class Status: Regular.
Degrees: A.B. 1893; A.M. 1896; Litt.D. (Washington and Lee) 1906; LL.D. (Lafayette) 1915.
Married Julia Breckinridge Sandford at Athens, Georgia, 18 February 1903. Children:
  Dorothea Marshall, born 21 September 1907.
  Henry Hilgard, 18 January 1911.
  Oswald Garrison, Jr., 17 September 1916.
Now Editor *The Nation,* New York.

Since my sale of the New York Evening Post to T. W. Lamont, '92, in July, 1918, I have continued my editorial work as editor of the Nation, New York, and owner of the Nautical Gazette. I have also been active in business as head of an iron-mining company and in other directions. As a journalist I attended the Versailles Peace Conference, the Washington Conference for the Limitation of Armaments, and the futile Economic Conference at Genoa in April, 1922, visiting thereafter eight different countries, including Bulgaria, Czecho-Slovakia, Jugo-Slavia, and Poland, and doing quite a little flying—from Warsaw to Strassburg in eight hours.

My life has continued remarkably interesting and varied and extremely happy. The growth of *The Nation,* in which I have the privilege of saying just what I feel on every subject with complete freedom, is a rich reward for the most strenuous labor it has demanded. I have several books under way; one on some of our dailies and their editors is to appear this year; and expect to spend the summer with my family in Scotland and England.

BERNARD WILLIAM VOGEL

Born at New York City, 30 December 1870, of William Vogel (merchant) and Hannah Scherick.
Fitted at Dr. J. Sach's.
Class Status: Freshman year only.
Married Mildred Jane Porter at New York City, 16 April 1918.
Now in warehousing at New York.

After leaving college I served in the retail business for nearly twenty years, retiring in 1912. The following year I engaged in the warehouse business and in 1920 again retired. During the deflation of 1920, 1921 and 1922, I was called upon by some of the banks and big merchants to help liquidate some of the mercantile concerns which found themselves in trouble. I was a sort of Business Doctor, and gave advice in my capacity as a merchant. The work was very interesting and constructive. I am now president of two companies and vice-president of another. My principal job is to look wise and try to make other fellows work so as to produce dividends.

Was married in 1918 and have been very happy ever since. Sorry to report no sons and no daughters. I take a great interest in charity. Am a trustee of the Technical School for Girls, also secretary of the Board. Around election time I become active in local politics, but am not seeking office. I have travelled extensively—this country, Europe, West Indies, and part of South America. Physically am fine and fit for an old '93 man.

Henry Ingersoll Waite

Born at Boston, 27 September 1868, of Henry Edward Waite (treasurer) and Ellen Ingersoll Broughton.
Fitted at Allen's.
Class Status: Freshman year only.
Died 30 September 1920, at Westboro, Massachusetts.

Henry Ingersoll Waite died September 30, 1920, in the Westboro Asylum. He was born at Boston, September 27, 1868, son of Henry Edward Waite (treasurer) and Ellen Ingersoll Broughton, the family having been long associated with North Brookfield. He entered in 1889 from the Allen School of West Newton, but after freshman year was overcome by nervous prostration and forced to leave college. For many years he lived as an invalid at West Newton, and in 1912 became hopelessly insane.

GEORGE WALCOTT

Born at Cambridge, Massachusetts, 26 January 1871, of Henry Pickering
    Walcott [Harvard 1858] (physician) and Charlotte Elizabeth Rich-
    ards.
Fitted at Browne and Nichols.
Class Status: Regular.
Degree: A.B. 1893.
Married Lilla Evelyn Nickerson at Brooklyn, 5 December 1894. Children:
        Henry Richards, born 6 May 1896 (H. C. 1918).
        Roger Conant, 6 October 1900 (H.C. 1922).
        Charlotte Elizabeth, 3 July 1904.
Now in dry goods commission business at New York City.

I have been in the dry goods commission business in New
York ever since 1894; for the last ten years I have been interested in southern cotton mills and the selling of their products.
Our company sells for some sixty mills from North Carolina to
Texas, and has branch offices throughout this country and
South America. Business takes up most of my time, my family
the rest. I have the usual vices but nevertheless am quite hale
and hearty, even though a grandfather. My home address is
850 Park Avenue, New York City.

JULIAN CONSTANTINE WALKER

Born at Hockessin, Delaware, 6 November 1866, of William Hicks Walker
    (farmer) and Anna Phebe Shortlidge.
Fitted at Shortlidge's Media Academy.
Class Status: Freshman year only.
Degree: LL.B. (Dickinson Coll.) 1897.
Married Lucy Eastburn at Hockessin, Delaware, 26 June 1906. Children:
        Sarah Eastburn, born 4 September 1907.
        Anna Phebe, 27 October 1908.
        John Shortlidge, 12 April 1910.
Now supposed to be practising law at Wilmington, Delaware.

Walker is another splendid specimen of *Homo Ossificatus*, or
petrified man, resisting with magnificent immobility every form
of stimulus known to science. Of course there have to be some
of this genus in every class, or the secretary would have nothing
to do but draw his pay.

ALFRED WALLERSTEIN

Born at Philadelphia, 23 August 1870, of Edward Wallerstein (manu-
    facturer) and Caroline Simons.
Fitted with F. Babbitt.
Class Status: "Four years in three," from '94.
Degree: A.B. 1893.

Married Wilhelmina Rachel Jastrow at Philadelphia, 25 November 1895.
Child:
Bertha, born 25 May 1899.
Now in advertising business at New York City.

Really nothing of general interest to report. Continue in the advertising business in which I reported myself last time. Am now president of the Wallerstein-Sharton Company, Incorporated, an advertising agency at 70 West 40th Street, New York City. Living at 33 West 49th Street.

HENRY WARE

Born at Brookline, Massachusetts, 26 December 1871, of Charles Pickard
Ware [Harvard 1862] (teacher) and Elizabeth Lawrence Appleton.
Fitted at Roxbury Latin.
Class Status: Regular.
Degrees: A.B. 1893; A.M. 1894; LL.B. 1896.
Married Louisa Fuller Wilson at Brookline, Massachusetts, 9 June 1898.
Children:
Caroline Farrar, born 14 August 1899.
Henry, 8 June 1905.
Now practising law at Boston.

The previous reports have all the information to 1918. Since then I have been continuing to practise law, particularly the examination of the legality of municipal bonds. Since 1919 I have been a member of the school committee of the town of Brookline.

A trip abroad with my family in the summer of 1921 was made all the more pleasant by our taking tea with Lapsley in his rooms at Trinity College, Cambridge. For the past year or more Harwood and I have been making a practice of starting early and getting in nine holes of golf before going to business. We recommend it,—but say nothing about the quality of the golf.

EDGAR HAGA WARNER

Born at Tuscarawas, Ohio, 22 September 1868, of Jonas Warner (farmer)
and Catharine Lister.
Entered from Baldwin University, Ohio.
Class Status: Entered Senior.
Degrees: A.B. (Baldwin) 1892; A.B. 1893.
Married Mary Louisa Sperry at Axtel, Ohio, 1 May 1895. Children:
Edgar Gordon, born 20 February 1907.
Lilan Ruth, 6 July 1911.
Now in Methodist Episcopal ministry at Cadiz, Ohio.

Schurz   W. C. Nichols   Hand   Converse   Wilder   French   Ware   Winsor

Since the last report I have been pastor at Tiffin, Ohio, and am now pastor at Cadiz, Ohio. I left Barberton in 1918 and was in Tiffin 1918-1922. In 1922 I moved to Cadiz.

The only thing of any special interest would come under the head of travels. In 1920 Mrs. Warner and I made a trip to Cambridge, Harvard, Boston, Lexington, Concord, Salem, Gloucester, Quincy, Plymouth, and New York.

OSCAR LEON WATKINS

Born at Fultonham, Ohio, 27 September 1861, of John Watkins [Univ. of Md.] (physician) and Sarah Jane Southard.
Entered from Denison University.
Class Status: Senior year only.
Degree: A.B. 1893.
Married Rosa Mills, at Chillicothe, Ohio, 29 April 1896. Children:
  Osric Mills, born 6 February 1897 (died at Bar-le-Duc, 23 October 1918, Lieutenant in U. S. A. A. S.)
  Maida, 27 May 1900 (married to Goodwin S. Elkin, 30 September 1920).
  Dorothy Wordsworth, 26 February 1904.
Now agent for Ginn & Co., publishers, at Indianapolis, Indiana.

Naturally my business has taken large toll of my time. But I have never become so steeped in it as to lose my soul. To save one's soul—that is the great aim and result of an effective university education. I have traveled little since the Great War, studied much and lectured very frequently. The Indianapolis Literary Club helps to keep alive the literary trend of my mind. The Sons of the Revolution (of which I am a State officer) feeds my patriotism and the Beta Theta Pi Club my fraternal feelings. The memory of Harvard is ever dear.

My family life has been simple and happy. My daughter Maida graduated at Wellesley, married, and is now the mother of a boy and a girl. My daughter Dorothy is to enter Wellesley this year. Into my life has come one tremendously fateful experience, the loss of my only begotten son Osric. He was a Lieutenant in the U. S. Army Air Service. He died at the front at Bar-le-Duc, France, October 23, 1918. Harvard graduated him with the Class of 1919. He was a member of the Pi Eta and "Dicky" clubs. He was one of the finest spirits I have ever known. A man hopes to find his immortality on earth in his son. For me it is not to be. Yet for the true immortality I am not hopeless. My face is to the west, but the sun shines bright and beyond it lies the land of our hopes and dreams where I shall meet him and you, my class-mates of '93· Good-bye.

FRANK MILTON WATTERS

Born at Fall River, Massachusetts, 12 November 1870, of Joseph Watters (manufacturer) and Mary Whitehead.
.Fitted at Phillips Exeter.
Class Status: Special, 1889-91.
Married Elizabeth Anne Hunt at Montclair, New Jersey, 27 June 1904.
Child:
Elizabeth Frances, born 18 July 1916.
Now manufacturing fire-extinguishers at Utica, New York.

Still in the fire apparatus business. Through consolidations in 1922 company is now known as the Foamite-Childs Corpora-tion. We are engineers and manufacturers. A large part of our business is the protection of oil tank farms, refineries, and oil-burning vessels against fires. My position is that of vice-president and general manager.

No voyages or travels except business trips. Living in the snow-belt, am interested in winter sports—curling, snow-shoe-ing, etc. Am a golf enthusiast in season, but a very ordinary player. My personal appearance has undergone quite some change in the last year. About mid-year in 1921 my weight was 215 pounds; it is now 175. Not due to illness. All class "overweights" apply!!! Keep in line, please!

No public positions, no distinctions, no publications. Clubs: Nothing distinguished. Member of three local golf clubs, local curling club. Fort Schuyler Club, Utica (social). Engineers also Harvard Club of New York City.

LORENZO WEBBER

Born at Watkins, New York, 22 July 1869, of John Almer Webber (banker) and Mary Ellen Mason.
.Fitted at Phillips Andover.
Class Status: Left after Sophomore year.
Married Dora Alice Stone at Portland, Michigan, 27 September 1899.
Children:
Charlotte Elizabeth, born 31 January 1902.
John Almer, 7 November 1903.
Christine, 19 January 1906.
Constance, 22 October 1911.
Now in banking at Portland, Michigan.

Left college at end of Sophomore year (1891) to go into private bank with my father. He died in 1905. In 1908 the bank was incorporated as a State bank of which I was made cashier and my mother president. At my mother's death in February, 1921, I was made president of the bank. We call such a bank as ours a country bank. In 1918 a charter commission of five men was elected to make a new charter for the Village of Portland with a commission form of government. I was one of the five men and after the charter was adopted I was elected as one of the three commissioners and president for six years. I have been too free, perhaps, in taking part in matters outside of the banking business, for instance, at times I have been member of School Board, delegate to County and State Conventions, Chairman of the County Y. M. C. A., leader in Sunday School orchestra, Church Trustee, District Superintendent in County S. S.. Director in local Chamber of Commerce. My wife is now moderator of the School Board. Of our children, Charlotte and John are attending Oberlin College, Christine goes to Milwaukee Downer next year and Constance, eleven years, is in the grades. Each plays some musical instrument and we have good times together. Church and Grange dinners, Community dances, with plenty of good books to read, furnish most of our amusements.

JOSEPH ROWE WEBSTER

Born at Lynn, Massachusetts, 30 August 1871, of Joseph Rowe Webster [Harvard 1854] (physician) and Priscilla Hayden Hollis.
Fitted at Roxbury Latin.
Class Status: Regular.
Degree: A.B. 1893.
Married Ethel Kate Brittain at Montreal, Quebec, 15 April 1903. Children:
John Rowe, born 25 December 1904.
Anne Rowe, 10 September 1906 (died 25 December 1906).
Brittain, 25 November 1907.
Isabel Brittain, 30 March 1909.
Penelope Rowe, 22 December 1911.
Now tutoring at Cambridge, Massachusetts.

My life since leaving college has been a very narrow and a very personal affair. It has been directed by two purposes: (1) to earn enough money to keep the pot boiling; (2) to find my balance in what to me was an incomprehensible and maddening world. In regard to the first object, I have not yet achieved my aim: I do not begin to do as much as I should like to do in the way of fulfilling my immediate responsibilities. But I see every reason to hope for an increase of efficiency and for an increase in welfare.

In regard to the second object after what has been for me a bitter and discouraging struggle, I have been helped to win much ground. Balance—health—ability—with me depends upon loyalty to (1) daily morning exercises designed to keep all the viscera on the job; (2) work; (3) play; (4) my friends and my non-friends; (5) Jesus Christ. Not the wishy-washy, namby-pamby, perfumed minion of the sentimentalists; not the sickly degenerate of many of the painters; not the imperial ruler sitting on the far-away throne of the hymns; but the Christ who is working for every man harder than any man is working for Him.

I wish with all my heart that Harvard University and her sons would be consistent—would either rip out the words *Christo et Ecclesiae* from her official seal or else have them recut in bolder type as an assertion that the life of *Veritas* is to be found only in them.

Just a few qualifications. I do not think that any human institution is conterminous with Christianity; and I have absolutely no sympathy with any form of churchmanship which does not tend to make a man of more service to his fellows little by little as the days roll on.

KENNETH GRANT TREMAYNE WEBSTER

Born at Yarmouth, Nova Scotia, 10 June 1871, of John Lindsay Ross Webster [Coll. Phys. and Surg., N. Y.] (physician) and Helen Ogilvie Gordon Geddes.
Entered from Dalhousie College.
Class Status: Entered Senior.
Degrees: A.B. (Dalhousie) 1892; A.B. 1893; A.M. 1894; Ph.D. 1902.
Married Edith Forbes at Naushon, Massachusetts, 15 August 1903. Children:
Edith Emerson, born 24 November 1909.
Frederic Augustus, 3 April 1912.
Now Asssistant Professor of English at Harvard.

Since I left the swivel-chair in Washington in the spring of 1919 its been the same old life, varied only by a summer spent *solus* in France trotting from one ruined castle to another. I resigned my position as director of the Harvard Summer School in 1918, and the Summer School, in spite of that disaster, has increased greatly, and become one of the few "paying" parts of the University. Even students are beginning to feel that it is not absolutely necessary to loaf the whole summer. I am still chairman of the Academic Board at Radcliffe—a distinguished college that has not received its mead from Harvard men interested in the education of women. Its relations to Harvard are interesting. I keep up my connection with Nova Scotia by owning a deserted farm there and spending part of each summer in that cool and forgotten spot. It's a privilege to teach in Harvard College, to be irrigated by such a stream of youth as comes through it, and to be fertilized by contact with its great scholars. But after all this life is like my study table, where the pile of books to be read, and the list of articles to be written and of chores to be done increases each day through the term, only to be swept away unfinished at Commencement to await the resurrection next year.

EDWARD MOTLEY WELD

Born at Dedham, Massachusetts, 4 September 1872, of Stephen Minot Weld [Harvard 1860] (merchant) and Eloise Rodman.
Fitted with E. D. Marsh.
Class Status: Regular.
Degree: A.B. 1893.
Married Sarah Lothrop King at Boston, 22 April 1897. Children:
    Lothrop Motley, born 16 February 1898.
    Edward Motley, Jr., 24 May 1906.
    Anne King, 4 April 1910.
Now in cotton business at New York City.

Since leaving college, I have been associated with my father's firm of Stephen M. Weld and Company, cotton merchants, for the first two years as office boy at $5 per week, and since September, 1895, as a partner. Up to 1900 my headquarters were with the Boston office; but in that year I removed to New York where I have since lived. My avocations have consisted chiefly of polo, shooting, salmon fishing, racing and golf.

David Dwight Wells

See Report VI, Page 304.

LEONARD ABEL WHEELER

Born at Troy, Ohio, 23 October 1868, of Thomas Bemis Wheeler (miller)
    and Mary Richmond Smith.
Fitted at Troy High.
Class Status: Special, 1889-90.
Married Charlotte Agatha Thompson at Saginaw, Michigan, 1 November
    1898. Children:
        Thomas Bemis, 2d, 21 June 1904.
        Margarite Thompson, 31 May 1906.
        Mary Richmond, 21 February 1909.
        Charlotte Thompson, 4 September 1910.
Now in tobacco business at Troy, Ohio.

For the past twenty-five years I have been buying, handling,
and selling cigar leaf tobacco. It has been a very interesting life and at fifty-four am in good health—thanks to quite a
bit of travel and a month or more each summer at a camp on
Higgins Lake, Michigan, with the family. Just now, am very
much interested in schools and colleges. My son Tom, graduates from the Hill School this June and plans to go to Dartmouth in the fall, preferring a small college where he gets nearer to the instructors and there are less outside attractions. A
very interesting subject is whether or not to send the girls to
college. I don't enthuse very much over the College girls these
days. I think the good, old-fashioned finishing school is better.

GEORGE ALBERT WHIPPLE

Born at Worcester, Massachusetts, 15 October 1871, of William Henry
    Whipple (merchant) and Jemima Aurilla Hill.
Fitted at Somerville High.
Class Status: Regular.
Degree: A.B. 1893.
Married Edna Bigelow Foote at Somerville, Massachusetts, 29 June 1911.
    Children:
        Louise Bigelow, born 8 August 1913.
        Charles Foote, 23 February 1915.
Now teaching at Evanston, Illinois.

I continue to find my work very enjoyable. Ground was
broken January 2nd on our fifty-five acre lot for our new High
School, and in 1925 we shall have a splendid structure on as
extensive grounds as any in the country. Vacations have been
spent on the shores of Buzzards Bay or of Lake Superior.
Golf has been my recreation. Our home is delightfully located
near Lake Michigan and is kept merry by a pair of lively children.

HERBERT HILL WHITE

Born at Rye, New York, 29 June 1869, of Henry White and Henrietta
Lavinia Hill. .
Fitted at Montclair High.·
Class Status: Special, 1889-90. Joined Class Junior year.
Degrees: A.B. 1913, as of 1893; (Hon.) A.M. 1919.
Married Clarissa Watts Lewis at Brookline, Massachusetts, 3 October
1895.
Now Treasurer of University Press at Cambridge.

Commanded auxiliary ketch "Ajax," Marblehead (December 7, 1919) to Honolulu (February 22, 1920), an exciting trip
which I described and pictured to classmates at the dinner at
the Boston Yacht Club two years ago. For the rest, I. am trustee of various estates, director or other officer in various companies, and treasurer of the University Press at Cambridge.

EDWARD DWIGHT WHITFORD

Born at Waltham, Massachusetts, 27 September 1868, of George Henry
Whitford and Martha Ann Stickney.
Fitted at Bridgewater Normal School.
Class Status: Special Scientific, 1889-91; with '92, 1891-92.
Degrees: A.B. 1892; LL.B. 1896.
Married Edith May Loring at Newton, Massachusetts, 19 June 1900 (died
19 October 1922). Child:
Ethel, born 3 July 1906.
Now vice-president Harvard Trust Company at Cambridge.

1896-1901: Practiced law. 1901-1915: Treasurer John P.
Squire and Company of Boston. 1915-1919 Joint managing director, Swift Beef Company, London, England. 1921 to date:
Vice-president Harvard Trust Company, Cambridge, Massachusetts.

JAMES RAYNOR WHITING

Born at New York City, 17 October 1872, of James Raynor Whiting
[Williams 1857] (lawyer and manufacturer) and Gertrude Ingersoll
Allen.
Entered from Williams College.
Class Status: Entered Junior.
Degrees: A.B. 1893; M.D. (Columbia) 1896.
Married Mildred Eveleigh Taylor at Poughkeepsie, New York, 7 May
1904. Children:
James Raynor, Jr., born 21 April 1905.
Frank Taylor, 9 October 1907.
Now naval surgeon at Submarine Base, New London, Connecticut.

Upon leaving college I entered the College of Physicians and Surgeons, Columbia University, and graduated in 1896, with the degree of M.D. Was interne at New York Hospital from January 1st, 1897, to June, 1898, when I entered the United States Navy as Assistant Surgeon, and served until August, 1901. This was a very interesting three years; for we cruised over 52,000 miles, visiting the Mediterranean, the east coasts of Africa, and South America, and the West Indies.

After my resignation from the Navy in 1901 I practised medicine at New York until April, 1917. During this time I was connected with Columbia University as Instructor and Chief of Clinic at Vanderbilt Clinic; with Bellevue Hospital as Assistant Surgeon; with New York Hospital as Chief of Clinic, Out Patient Department; and with the House of Relief as Chief of Clinic.

At the outbreak of the war in 1917 I went into the United States Naval Reserve Force as an Assistant Surgeon, doing recruiting duty at New York from March 19th, until July 5th, when I was ordered to the U. S. S. *Lydonia.* We were ordered to the Mediterranean, where we did patrol and escort duty. In May, 1918, I was ordered to the Base at Gibraltar where I acted as Medical Officer at the Barracks, and later as Executive Officer at the Hospital. Was promoted through the various grades until I became Lieutenant Commander in the Fleet Naval Reserve on September 22, 1918.

I was ordered home in the end of December, 1918, and then to the U. S. S. *Agamemnon,* then engaged in transporting the troops home. After eight months of this duty I was ordered to the United States Naval Hospital at Charleston, South Carolina, where I remained about nineteen months. I was then sent to the Naval Hospital at Chelsea, Massachusetts, and reëntered the Regular Navy Service in July, 1921, as Passed Assistant Surgeon with the rank of Lieutenant. After remaining at Chelsea until July, 1922, I was ordered to the Submarine Base at New London, Connecticut, where I am still serving.

This not much of a story, but mine is a quiet life. Now and then come bright spots, one of the brightest of which was the '93 dinner at Boston in 1921. I belong to the University Club, New York; to the Army and Navy Club of America, and to the Dutchess Golf and Country Club.

CHARLES EDWARD WHITMORE

.Born at Quincy, Illinois, 12 December 1870, of Charles Edward Whitmore
[Washington Univ.] (broker) and Ada Jane Holmes.
.Fitted at Cutler's School, Newton.
Class Status: Entered Sophomore.
.Degrees: A.B. 1893; LL.B. 1897.
.Now Membership Secretary of the City Club, New York.

Dearest Lottie,

Who should I bump into, yesterday but our old friend.
"Ted" Whitmore! He was very communicative—oh, very
communicative indeed—so of course I just let him commune.
Sometimes it comes in handy. He tells me that in 1893-1894
he was in the Law School, then studying English and German in the Graduate School for a year, then back to the Law
School 1895-1897. Not satisfied with taking his LL.B. in the
latter year, he stayed on as a graduate student of law (my
dear, how learned!) for another year. But then, says you,
what did he do next? Went into the fire-extinguisher business in Boston! However, from 1902 to 1905 he did practise
law there, but then turned stock broker. After that, what
does this versatile baby do but begin teaching at Dr. Tal-
bot's School in Washington, and in 1909 goes to Roland Mulford's "Ridgefield School" in Connecticut, where he was secretary for two years. But like all really wise birds he can't
keep away from little old N. Y., where he promoted pineapple
orchards and played squash (quite a vegetable existence!)
till 1915, when he blossomed into membership secretary of
the City Club. Here he still smiles and extends the glad
flipper. During the war he did wonderful work, organizing
the City Club Ambulance Unit and going over to visit them
at Verdun in October of 1917. Also he has been supervisor of
the State Census for the 27th Assembly District, and oh, so·
many other things! More when I see you—much more.

Yours till the freeze-over,

MAE.

Oliver Whyte, Jr.

See Report VI, Page 308, and Supplement, Page 131..

Walter Herriman Wickes

See Report VI, Page 309.

JOSEPH WIGGIN

Born at Exeter, New Hampshire, 7 March 1871, of Joseph Furnald Wiggin [Harv. Law School] (lawyer) and Ruth Hurd Hollis.
Fitted at Malden High.
Class Status: Regular.
Degrees: A.B. 1893; LL.B. 1896.
Married Grace Parker Corbett at Malden, Massachusetts, 2 January 1901. Children:
> Dorothy, born 3 July 1902.
> Katharine, 17 July 1904.
> Barbara, 4 July 1905.
> Ruth, 9 September 1906.
> Grace, 25 October 1908.

Now practising law at Boston.

I began at the law with my father (Law School, '59-60) and continued as his partner until his death in 1906. Have had no partners since. Have shared offices with several Harvard men, including Dallinger and A. P. Stone. Stone and I are now in offices together for our twenty-first year. I have always stuck closely to the law and its "by-products," make long days, frequently work evenings and holidays, and content myself with a short vacation in the summer. Put in my spare time with the family and the young friends of my children. The youngsters permit it and so help keep me young. I can report no travels, no publications, degrees or distinctions. I try few cases and so am not much in the "press" and have no legal triumphs to report. Belong to the usual bar associations and happen just now to be on the governing board of two of them.

Have devoted considerable time and energy to (mostly unpaid) semi-public and public affairs in Malden, keeping out of political office. Have been City Solicitor, on School Board, Planning Board, and am now serving about my fifteenth year as Public Library Trustee. Am Trustee for a "Home" and President of a scholarship corporation that sends three or four youngsters to college each year. Was chairman of the four Liberty Loan Committees and am Trustee and Director in three local banking institutions and President of a national bank. Am Treasurer and Director of an endowed school in New Hampshire that serves as a high school for some ten towns unable to afford a high school of their own.

My health is good and my enthusiasm and interest in life

seem unabated. Have two girls in college and three preparing. Any family man (or his wife) can tell just what Mr. and Mrs. J. W. (D. V.) will be busy upon for the next ten years.

JAMES AUSTIN WILDER

Born at Puunui, Hawaiian Islands, 27 May 1868, of Samuel Gardner Wilder (shipping) and Elizabeth Kinau Judd.
Fitted at Belmont School, California.
Class Status: With Class four years.
Degree: A.B. 1894, as of 1893.
Married Sarah Harnden at Alameda, California, 12 September 1899.
　Children:
　　James Harnden, born 5 December 1900.
　　Kinau, 28 November 1902.
Now Chief Sea Scout, Boy Scouts of America, at New York City.

1895: After two aimless years at the Law School left the '95 Glee Club at Chicago and went westward to mix up in the Hawaiian Revolution, and was in time to be properly thrilled by these, for all of us, stirring events. Following my dead father's hopes I entered the firm of Wilder's Steamship Company, and suffered the agonies of one whose whole existence seemed blighted in the bud. One day "The Stud" and a Milwaukee pal showed up, bound for the Orient. They seemed to ooze money and ideas, and I resigned from the firm to entertain them. I awoke from this dream in Yokohama, sub-editor of a funny paper. I had asked a cousin of mine to be my steward and my solicitor. His letters, until 1898, were gloomed by the reiterated statement, "No dividends." I resigned the paper to join the Furness-Hiller Expedition to Borneo, on a salary and all expenses paid. Blissful year of wild adventures! We went into the very bowels of the Head-hunting Country, and I became the blood-brother of a Borneo "prince," now King of the Baram. (I am booked to visit my brother next year). Bill Furness found me for myself. . . . And I have been happy ever since. He told me I was not "funny" at all . . . never had been. Said I was a poet and an artist . . . and built up my conceit on totally new lines. These have persisted, with occasional lapses, till now. After Borneo, Japan again and back to the paper. Then, at her long sad calling, back to Home and Mother for awhile. Crafty old dear! . . . the house in Honolulu, Eskbank (see "The Wrecker" by **R. L. S.**, Chapter I), was full of unbelievably beautiful girls . . . among them the

Divine Sarah, of a tribe friendly for four generations back "Nuf sed" . . . back to Japan to complete my ambition to speak and write this terrible language.

1898: Terribly bored. Began to yearn for Elysian Fields . . . you get me? Seeking surcease of sorrow I sailed in the copra schooner *Esmeralda* to Guam, then a Spanish "Cranford," quaint, fast asleep, adorable. I was marooned here by the wreck of our beautiful vessel. Dismasted off Yap by a squall. Left me in Guam without a bean, picking me up on April 29th, the skipper whispering the secret that war was on with Spain! While here, broke, I started doing portraits for $1.00 MEX. Made about ten bones a week and was the wealthiest fellow in Agana. Learned Spanish with a Guam accent and Guamese with a Spanish accent. Owned and fought the justly-celebrated ash-colored rooster "Don Heime" (or rather "Jamie") and cleaned out the town four times. Got away at midnight leaving everything but the clothes I had on, and hurtled homeward. Being refused enlistment on account of eyesight, I beat it for Paris to study ART *chez* Julian, under Benjamin Constant and old Jean-Paul Laurens. Had with me a boy from Guam, given me by his mother. Left him in the Latin Quarter guarding my belongings while I went back to marry the Divine. ((1899). She and I now circled the globe . . annexation having feathered my nest . . . our nest, excuse me! Lived in Paris among a galaxy of artists, architects, musicians, and just plain sports until 1906. Begat two entertaining children, Jimmy Junior and Kinau, named for my mother, who was the namesake and pet of Kinau-kuhina-nui, Queen Regent in the thirties. We left Paris for home on the beach at Waikiki. Kindergarten, croup, and measles. First automobile—a Cadillac. Known favorably as "Wobbling Winnie." Taught my wife to leave Hawaii. Kept open house. Twice president of the Harvard Club. Won the Christmas pig 1909 with a golf score of 89 and 91, smearing all comers . . . handicap 16. Camping, climbing, a five-hundred-mile ride with the Territorial Secretary on the big island, and then to Samoa, Fiji, Tonga, and the seldom-visited Oneata and Lakemba. Left wee wifey home to mind the babes. On the steamer coming back was an Englishman who was hipped on Boy Scouts.

Here beginneth my real work. All to now was piffle! We went

to Europe (1910-1911)—sugar 4.30 and steady. Our Packard was called the A-ke-ahi (Fresh Fires are Alight), and I delved deep in my new departure . . . scouting. We travelled eight months in that machine . . . from John O'Groats to Lands End. . . . getting lost was the most fun . . . and Sally and I knew our England you bet! Then Germany, then France, and then Paris . . . where I painted for a spell, just to keep my hand in. In London I was scouting about . . . meeting Baden Powell and General Byng . . . the type of men who go in for scouting over there. (Alas! when are our ''great men'' going to get busy as scoutmasters? You'll all be sorry some day. Jump in!).

Home again! (Chicken-pox and whooping-cough period of home-building). Second Reader. Dancing School. Swimming. Spanking. 1915. All hands to New York. Winter in Washington . . . (Connecticut.) . . . where the maternal side of my house first settled. Seth Hastings, my great-great-grandfather, and the Parmelees. Then to New York and the National Boy Scout Headquarters, where I was put in charge of the defunct Sea-scouting. Jimmy to Pomfret. Kinau to Spence's.

1916, 17, 18, 19, 20, 21 in New York, where I became an habitué of the New York Yacht Club, Harvard, Players, Amateur Comedy Club, and Coffee House. We had our old Paris friends, Boston pals, and now and then Yokahama and Honolulu folk to play with. But I began to be ''featured'' as a Scout Spieler, travelling all over the States, meeting thousands of boys and men. They call me ''Pine Tree Jim,'' and I tell stories, sing, and when I've got the gang, I let 'em have it straight! Deliver the goods! No hypocrisy! Play ball!

My war work was hard and hurt. I was due at the Navy Yard at 8 A. M., and had to get up at 6 to make it . . . day after day. You bet I was glad when one of my yeomanettes danced into the room and acted so queerly that . . . well, four days later came the Armistice. I was a year on the job. We now began to push the Sea-scouts. The Navy were so pleased at our work . . . chasing up next-of-kin mostly . . . that it has backed us to the limit. All we want now is the leadership. A sea-scout-master has to be a gentleman, a genius and a scholar-small-boat-navigator. He also has to be rich, imaginative, practical, and patient. I once told my Aunt Augusta that MY wife would know how to dress, cook, sing, dance, and play the harpsichord

... and she said "You won't find her here. Heaven is your home!" But we get scout-masters slowly, and are founding Seamanship Schools east and west. I am booked as Chief Sea-scout, and am to travel around every year for four months, bucking them up ... until I get too old to move. Between times we will live in Honolulu, London, and Paris.

My son is a senior this year ... and plans to take a year at Cambridge, England. My daughter is just now at San Moritz, Switzerland, learning to waltz on skates. She can learn cooking later. My wife is an amateur potter and turns out lapis lazuli and turquoise blues, some of which have been seen in the Metropolitan Museum. Oh, I don't know! What? My Sarah! I have just painted the Prince Delegate for the Old Throne Room, and have three more orders before I pull out to gather my family together in Boston, June 1st, 1923. Come to Sunday breakfast, 9 to 10 A. M. On me this time!

Henry Francis Willard

See Report VI, Page 311.

CHARLES EDWIN WILLIAMS

Born at Mechanicsburg, Ohio, 11 June 1867, of Charles William Williams
    (merchant) and Rebecca Ann Guy.
Entered from Ohio Wesleyan University.
Class Status: Entered Junior.
Degrees: A.B. (Ohio Wesleyan) 1892; A.B. 1893.
Married Ethel Howlett of Syracuse, New York, at London, England,
    16 June 1913. Children:
        Jean, born 31 May 1914.
        Frank Howlett, 10 July 1916.
        Phillis, 24 October 1921.
Now real estate broker at New York City.

Two years devoted to tutoring and European travel. Since 1895 in real estate business in New York City. Principally interested in sales and leases of property in the center at Forty-second Street and Fifth Avenue. Married in 1913 Miss Howlett of Syracuse, N. Y.

Have three children, one of whom is a boy who is being groomed for the famous class of 1935. I have not gone in for sports very much and have spent much time on a farm I own near by.

Best part of my leisure time in the last two years has been devoted to cussing out Henry Cabot Lodge and his ilk on their attitude toward the League of Nations.

Franklin James Williams

See Report VI, Page 313, and Supplement, Page 131.

GEORGE PERRY WILSON

Born at Pittsburgh, 8 June 1870, of John Aaron Wilson [U. of P.] (law-
yer) and Belle Jane Wilson.
Fitted at Central High, Pittsburgh.
Class Status: Regular.
Degree: A.B. 1893.
Now American Vice Consul at Catania, Italy.

After leaving college I studied law in my father's office in Pittsburgh. There I remained practising law till July, 1918, when I went to Milan as American Vice-Consul. After a little more than a year there came a transfer to the Consulate in Genoa, and in just a little less than a year later another trans-fer to Catania, Italy, where I have been ever since.

Life has been very quiet for me, always a single man, and I have never been before the public in books or papers. From having visé'd so many passports I should not be surprised if I were better known among the Italians of Mulberry street, New York, than elsewhere. Sicily is backward and the life is that of some time in the middle of the XIX century, but there may be one or two '93 men yet left who would like to sit in one of the little restaurants here, where the grape juice is still obtain-able—fermented, of course. This is classic land and nearby are the huge stones Polyphemus hurled at Odysseus, the smok-ing Aetna, the ruins of Siracusa and Calypso's isle, but not even a Greek professor would recognize them now.

GEORGE PARKER WINSHIP

Born at Bridgewater, Massachusetts, 29 July 1871, of Albert Edward Win-
ship [Andover Theol.] (editor) and Ella Rebecca Parker.
Fitted at Somerville High.
Class Status: Regular.

Degrees: A.B. 1893; A.M. 1894; Litt.D. (Michigan) 1917.
Married Claire Bliven at Westerly, Rhode Island, 23 June 1912　Children:
　　　George Parker, Jr., born 17 March 1914.
　　　Ann, 27 December 1917.
　　　Stephen, 24 January 1921.
Now librarian, Harry Elkins Widener Collection, Harvard Library.

I staid on at Cambridge for two years after graduation to postpone taking up the newspaper job that I supposed was to be my business for the rest of my life. Quite unexpectedly, I was picked by the owner of a large private library to take care of his books, with the result that taking care of books, which is a very different thing from being a "librarian" as that term is ordinarily understood, has been my principal occupation ever since.

After the aforesaid owner, John Nicholas Brown of Providence, died in 1900, his library and librarian were transferred to Brown University, and for the next fifteen years I tried to work out the problem of establishing a place for the private library in the public institution, keeping the advantages of private ownership and attempting (not very successfully as things have turned out) to erect barriers against the casualties incidental to institutional control.

In 1915 I was selected to have charge of the library of Harry Elkins Widener, which was given to Harvard in fulfillment of his wishes. This involved me in problems similar to those in Providence, with what is on the whole an added difficulty, that of maintaining the individuality of a collection of books housed inside a much larger collection. Up to date, the incidental complications have been quite sufficient to keep me interested in my job.

Inevitably, an unusual kind of occupation results in curious by-products. For three years I was largely preoccupied in compiling a list of books owned in America, which were printed before 1501—known technically as "Incunabula." This was printed in 1919 and seems to be very well thought of especially by the European bookish—"bibliographical"—crowd. Since then, I have just finished a longish account of French newspapers printed in the United States before 1800; and before getting involved in that subject I did a dreary account of 13 different editions of a facsimile of a New England Primer of

1777, wherein there is one bright spot that discusses our ancestors' interest in "Uriah's wife unadorned."

The really important event of my recent years was the purchase of a dozen acres on the Charles River, near the railway station of that name, in the town of Dover. There, thanks to the Boston tunnel, I was only about twice as far (in time) from the library as when we lived in Cambridge, until railway time-tables ceased to have any relation to facts. On the whole, the family seems to have no more troubles than the neighbors we left in the city, and we have no intention of returning. If I get caught on coal, I can keep the furnace going with wood off the place, and the cow and hens will keep us alive until it is time to kill the pig.

When I'm not farming it, I amuse myself with types, having set up a press and a picture of a beautiful dragon known as "The Sign of The George." The press that goes by that name already has to its credit "first editions" of Stevenson, Kipling, Henry James, and G. P. W., Jr.

CHARLES GIBSON WINSLOW

Born at Boston, 4 February 1871, of George Scott Winslow (merchant) and Sarah Train.
Fitted at Repton School, Derbyshire, England.
Class Status: Special, 1889-91. Law School, 1891-95.
Degree: LL.B. 1895.
Married Rosamond Gibson at Boston, 11 October 1916. Child: Warren, born 25 June 1918.
Now in real estate business at Boston.

1896-8 I was with the N. C. Pittsburgh Gulf R. R. (now N. C. Southern) with headquarters in Kansas City, Mo. 1899 Planters Compress Co., which "busted." Then about ten years with J. Murray Howe and since by myself, both latter in Boston.

I went abroad about every other year, several times fox hunting in England with Sam Chew and once with him to Egypt. I play a lot of court-tennis and golf now; formerly went in entirely for racquets and squash. No public positions, distinctions or speeches. Clubs; Somerset and Tennis and Racquet.

Nothing worth while to report in last five years except the constant companionship of my wife and son. I spend the summers at Cohasset, winters at 310 Marlboro Street. Health and thirst good.

FREDERICK WINSOR

Born at Winchester, Massachusetts, 29 March 1872, of Frederick Winsor
[Harvard 1851] (physician) and Anne Bent Ware.
Fitted at Roxbury Latin.
Class Status: Regular.
Degree: A.B. 1893.
Married Mary Anna Lee Paine at Weston, Massachusetts, 18 June 1894.
Children:
Charles Paine, born 19 June 1895. (A.B. Harvard 1917).
Dorothy, 27 August 1896, (married Aug. 10, 1922, to Elliot W:
Bisbee).
Frederick, Jr., 15 October 1900. (M. I. T.)
John Bryant, 28 April 1903 (died June 8, 1919).
Theresa, 7 June 1904.
Now Head Master Middlesex School, Concord, Massachusetts.

Just about this time, the spring of 1918, I became a civilian
employee of the Air Service, as an adviser to the ''Ground
Schools Branch'' of the ''Training Section.'' I continued doing that work till August, 1918, when I was commissioned Captain and put in charge of ''Ground Instruction'' at all flying
fields where cadets were under instruction in flying. I was discharged in December, 1918. I then returned to my work at
Middlesex School.

A trip abroad in the summer of 1920, when I spent several
weeks in motoring over the Western battle lines, is the only
noteworthy departure from a life of unexciting routine. My
chief ''gainful occupation'' is really beating Fiske at golf, and
I never made very much money out of that.

SAMUEL LEE WOLFF

Born at Baltimore, 15 January 1874, of Leopold Wolff (coffee merchant)
and Amelia Meyer.
Fitted with Dr. J. Sachs.
Class Status: ''Four years in three.''
Degrees: A.B. 1892; A.M. (Columbia) 1895; LL.B. (Columbia) 1897;
Ph.D. (Columbia) 1911.
Married Mathilde Abraham at New York City, 20 May 1914. Children:
Robert Lee, born 22 December 1915.
James Lawrence, 6 October 1919.
Now Assistant Professor of English, Columbia University.

1893-1896 studied at Columbia Law School and at office
of Parsons, Shepard and Ogden; 1896-1902 (about) practised law in New York; 1900 began graduate study at Columbia, in Comparative Literature and in English, chiefly under

G. E. Woodberry; 1903-1911 taught English in New York City High Schools, at the University of Tennessee, and at the University of Michigan; 1911 to date, taught English at Columbia.

During the summers of 1910, 1912, and 1914 I was abroad, travelling in the beaten path and also in Greece and Asia Minor. Publications: "Robert Greene and the Italian Renaissance," in *Englische Studien xxxvii*, 321-374; "A Source of *Euphues, The Anatomy of Wyt*," in *Modern Philology vii*, 577-585; "The Jacobean Boccaccio," in *The Nation* (New York), vol. 89, p. 14; "Laurence Stere," *Ibid.*, vol. 89, p. 346; "The Greek Gift to Civilization," *Ibid.*, vol. 90, p. 339; and a number of unsigned reviews in *Nation* and *Dial*. "The Greek Romances in Elizabethan Prose Fiction," New York, Columbia University Press, 1911. Two chapters in *The Cambridge History of American Literature* "Divines and Moralists, 1783-1860," vol. ii, pp. 196-223 (1918); "Scholars," vol iv, pp. 444-491 (1921). "The Humanist as Man of Letters: John Lyly" in *The Sewanee Review*, January, 1923.

Clubs: Authors Club, New York; Andiron Club, New York; Faculty Club, Columbia University.

ARTHUR MAYER WOLFSON

Born at Chicago, 10 April 1873, of Rudolph Wolfson (merchant) and Nancy Mayer.
Fitted at Kansas City High.
Class Status: "Four years in three" from '94.
Degrees: A.B. 1893; A.M. 1896; Ph.D. 1898.
Married Mildred Hartmann at Chicago, 17 July 1910. Children:
  Jean Elizabeth, born 16 November 1911.
  Alan Hartmann, 17 September 1915.
  Anne Hartmann, 21 May 1917.
Now Secretary, Hartmann Trunk Co., Racine, Wisconsin.

The first twenty years were devoted to teaching history and political science; the next seven to organizing and directing two of the largest high schools in New York City. In 1920, I resigned my position as principal of the High School of Commerce, in part because I was out of sympathy with the educational ideals of the state and the city, in part because business offered financial opportunities which my family said I ought not to despise. At present, I am a member of the Board of Directors and secretary of the Hartmann Trunk Co. Thank you, I am doing very well.

Albert Bowman Wood

See Report VI, Page 318.

ERNEST HENRY WOOD

Born at Uxbridge, Massachusetts, 29 January 1870, of Cyrus Grout Wood (manufacturer) and Mary Farnum Southwick.
Fitted with G. E. Gardner.
Class Status: Regular.
Degree: A.B. 1893.
Married Adelaide Richards Wyman at Worcester, Massachusetts, 9 November 1898. Children:
    Cyrus Wyman, born 31 January 1900.
    Austen, 25 May 1903.
    Daniel, 20 September 1904.
    Louisa, 27 October 1905.
Now President and Treasurer Worcester Storage Company.

The most important result of the past five years is that I have three sons at college at the same time—one of the class of 1923, and two of the class of 1926. Can any other classmate beat it, or perhaps equal it?

RALPH WOODWORTH

Born at Tomales, California, 7 May 1871, of Abijah Woodworth (farmer) and Abby Hall.
Entered from University of California.
Class Status: ''Four years in three'' from '94.
Degrees: A.B. 1893; LL.B. 1895.
Married Mabel Caroline Goodwin at Boston, 4 December 1897. Children:
    Marion,
    Laura,
    James,
    Janet,
    Ralph.
Now practising law in Boston.

The practice of law at Boston has held my nose to the grindstone without a break (in either) for nearly thirty years. But gosh! What's Law? A mental handicraft more and more discredited. During that period, Medicine, Engineering, Chemistry, even Dentistry have advanced by leaps and bounds, and won more and more appreciation and admiration —while Law has merely stuck in the mud and sunk deeper and deeper in popular estimation. While a surgeon is now little less than a demi-god, a lawyer is little more than a second-story man. Forget it! My real work out here in Wayland is the scientific education of the hen. For the past thirteen years I have been studying the pesky critters. The most serious problem I have had to deal with is what I may term "housewives' preference." There are those who will have only brown eggs, and those who will have only white eggs (they say their husbands prefer 'em that way). The difficulty of getting brown eggs to "brown" customers, and white eggs to "white" customers is amazing, and requires the most intense application. But for interesting problems, give me an egg in preference to the law, any day in the week.

ARTHUR RUFUS TREGO WYLIE

Born at Condit, Ohio, 5 November 1871, of Robert Wylie [Marietta] (clergyman) and Sarah Adelia Jadden.
Entered from Wooster University.
Class Status: Entered Senior.
Degrees: A.B. (Univ. Wooster) 1892; A.B. 1893; M.D. (Univ. Minn.) 1906.
Married Eugenia Heaton Radcliffe at St. Paul, Minnesota, 8 June 1899.
Now Superintendent, Institution for the Feeble Minded at Grafton, North Dakota.

Being interested in psychology, on leaving college I became psychologist at the Minnesota School for Feeble Minded. So was a pioneer in the psychology of mental deficiency. From this slight stimulus, the work was developed later by Goddard and others along the lines of mental testing into the large field it now occupies in the courts, schools, army, etc.

In 1906, I graduated in medicine and became assistant physician at the Minnesota School. In 1910 I was appointed Superintendent of the Institution for Feeble Minded, Grafton, North Dakota, and still retain the position. My work here is the supervision, care and training of those under my immediate charge, as well as to try to educate the people of our state to the meaning of mental deficiency and the care that should be given these children.

CHARLES LOWELL YOUNG

Born at Somerville, Massachusetts, 12 July 1865, of Benjamin Franklin
　　Young (merchant) . and Justina Louise Lowell.
Fitted at Somerville High and Tufts College.
Class Status: Regular.
Degree: A.B. 1893.
Now Professor of English Literature at Wellesley.

With the exception of three lines in the Fourth Report, has
never contributed any information further than the above.
He writes, under date of March 11, 1918: "So far as I have
any power or rights, legal or moral, to control what goes into
the report about me, I forbid that anything not sent by me
expressly for that purpose be published about me in the class
report, or elsewhere printed."

The Secretary bitterly regrets that he is therefore unable to
add to the above.

FRANK LESTER YOUNG

Born at Hustisford, Wisconsin, 28 November 1865, of George Samuel
　　Young (farmer) and Abbie Ann Bartlett.
Fitted at State Normal School, Illinois.
Class Status: Special, 1889-90.　Joined Class Sophomore year.
Degrees: A.B. 1893; LL.B. 1896.
Married Estelle May Roberts at Boston, Massachusetts, 29 January 1908.
Now in real estate business at Boston.

Attended Harvard Law School the next 3 years after graduation; then practiced law in Boston; but during the last five
years I have been principally engaged in business, buying and
selling real estate, taking care of the real estate which I keep
as an investment, and collecting the rents.

An English View of Class Day, 1893

From *Harvard College by an Oxonian,* by George Birkbeck
Hill, D.C.L. (New York and London, 1894.)

The weather, which I am told almost always favours Class
Day, this year showed it no indulgence. I have heard Americans
on our side of the Atlantic complain of the changeableness of tne
climate, not only of England, but of Europe. It was a disappointment to me to find how uncertain a New England June can
be. There was a variety in it that was worthy of Cumberland
or Devonshire. On the afternoon of the seventh of the month
the thermometer in my room in Cambridge stood at 91, though
the Venetian shutters had been kept closed. On the thirteenth,
at a little village on the sea-coast we were all sitting round a
blazing log fire. On the seventeenth fires were kept burning all
day. On the twenty-fourth, calling at two houses in Cambridge,
in both I found my friends sitting round the fire. In the southern parts of England I had never seen a fire so late in the summer, and yet Boston is in the same latitude as Rome. If the
summer is late in coming and is uncertain even when it has
come, in the clearness of the air and the blueness of the sea,
on fine days, it displays the charms of the Mediterranean
shore. Hawthorne was disappointed by the Italian skies. They
were, he said, what he had been used to all his life in New England. In the exaggerated expectations which he had formed of
them, he had been misled by the English poets, who had
judged them by the quiet colours of cloudy England. It was
with no Italian sky, but with cold and heavy rain that Class
Day set in. The break in the weather that we anxiously looked
for never came, and I was kept a prisoner to the house the whole
day. The following description of all that went on I quote from
a letter written by my wife:—

"Class Day this year broke wet and stormy, much to our
disappointment. Great trouble had been taken to secure for us
tickets for everything worth seeing. Without these tickets
no one can gain admission. The Graduating Students are the
hosts, and issue them to all as their guests. At ten we had to
be in our places in Sanders Theatre. The whole place looked

very much like the Sheldonian at Commemoration, crowded
with mothers and sisters and cousins in gay summer dresses,
a good many of the Professors and a fair sprinkling of young
men. We missed, however, the gowns, Professors looking only
like ordinary mortals; and there was no Undergraduates' Gallery and no noise such as we are used to at home. Imagine, if
you can, a Commemoration at which all was done 'decently and
in order,' no uproar, no foolish jokes; but that is a flight beyond the imagination of any one who has seen and heard Oxford men on such an occasion.

"The body of the Hall was reserved for those students who
were to receive their degree, and at eleven they marched in,
two and two, in cap and gown. The Bishop-elect followed with
the students who are the office-bearers of the year; they took
their seats on the dais on chairs placed in front of palms and
flowering shrubs, with a gigantic **'93** in flowers fastened to the
gallery over their heads. In this gallery was an excellent string
band which played between the various exercises. The meeting began with prayer, the Bishop praying in the name of the
Class of 1893; and then the Senior Marshal called upon the
Orator to begin his Oration. The Orator, who was a member
of the graduating Class chosen for the office by his classmates,
stepped to the front of the dais and began. He had learned
his oration carefully by heart, and had been trained in the
method of delivery; he spoke it well; matter and style were
good, but they lacked fire and spontaneity. He was followed
in turn by the Poet, the Ivy Orator (whose business it is to
make a comic speech full of allusions to what has lately been
happening in the University), and the Odist, who repeated a
short ode of his own composition. It was then sung by every
one to the tune of *Fair Harvard, i.e.* 'My lodging is on the
cold ground,' which may be called the national air of Harvard.
After this we were dismissed by the Bishop-elect with his bless-
ing.

"The one distinguishing feature of the gathering was its completely democratic nature. The President of the University
sat there with his wife in the central seat of the Auditorium;
but he was nothing more than one of the many spectators. The
Dons, as Dons, were non-existent. The men of '93 were every-

thing. They had chosen the spokesmen of the day; orations, poem, and ode were all addressed to them; every arrangement had been made by them, and was carried out by them as supreme. Even in what was said and sung there was not the slightest reference to any other authority. Harvard took form in one's mind as a large democracy, the students governing themselves in all things.

"Our next duty was to attend one of the 'Spreads.' *Spread* is the name given to a meal provided by the students, and means lunch or supper, or still more often one that goes on a great part of the day. It is of the nature of a ball supper; salads, sandwiches, and ice-creams, with many varieties of cake, being what is usually provided. Strawberries and cream are usually added during the summer. One of the largest and gayest of the Spreads on Friday was held in the great Gymnasium. Here the large hall had been adorned with a profusion of flowers and evergreens, and with garlands hung from side to side of the high roof. Again a great '93 in flowers was conspicuous in front of the gallery. When we arrived there about half-past three o'clock, dancing was going on vigorously. The Class of '93 looked very droll dancing in cap and gown. Many of the girls had pretty dresses and pretty faces, too, the exercise giving them just that touch of colour which American girls so often lack. The chaperones sat round the room, and the long refreshment-table was down one side; the band in the gallery above. The expense of the whole was borne by a small party of young men of the Graduating Class.

"By half-past four the ball was over, the Gymnasium deserted, and we were once more plodding through the rain and mire, in goloshes and waterproofs, to the quadrangle in which were to take place the Tree Exercises, the thing I was especially anxious to see. This part of Harvard Class Day is always considered the most important, as well as the prettiest sight for visitors to see. The tree, a tall and stately American elm, stands in the centre of a wide lawn with College buildings on three sides. For Class Day the lawn is enclosed by tiers of wooden raised seats, and the tree is garlanded by a long wreath of flowers wound many times closely round the trunk about ten or twelve feet above the ground; while the date of the

year in crimson and white flowers is placed some eight feet
higher still. Above this again the branches spring, the bark
below being quite unbroken and offering a difficult task enough
to climbers. The rain continued as pitilessly as ever. The
seats had been covered with awnings, but not to much effect.
When we arrived they were all shining with water, and every
here and there a small stream descended from some hole or
drop by drop fell upon some devoted bonnet from a thin-
ner spot in the canvas. At five o'clock the Class of '94
marched in under umbrellas; followed by more of '95 and '96;
then all in turn seated themselves on carpets which had been
hurriedly spread upon the grass. A large group of Graduates
took up their position near them; when all were settled, to
the sound of a band in marched the men of '93· First came the
three marshals, then the band, and then some seventy or
eighty young fellows in football dress, stout jerseys, buff knicker-
bockers, long stockings and buff shoes, and all bareheaded.
They came in two by two; the men behind with their hands
on the shoulders of those in front, making a long, continuous
winding chain, which wound round and round the tree, and
finally formed a compact mass encircling it and the Senior
Marshall, who stood at its foot in cap and gown, those of the
class who were not to take part in the struggle, also in cap and
gown, took up their position near.

"And now began the cheering. Led by the Marshal they
gave the Harvard yell—Rah-rah-rah; Rah-rah-rah; Rah-rah-
rah; Har—vard! rising in a sort of yell and repeated over
and over again in perfect time. It was begun first by '93,
and then taken by '94, '95, '96, and the Graduates in regular
succession. They cheered the Classes; they cheered the Halls;
they cheered the President and a few favourite Professors, and
then they cheered the ladies; each body cheering alone and in
regular order. Finally all joined in cheering Harvard, and
then the whole mass standing, visitors and students together,
sang *Fair Harvard*. As we came to the last line of the song the
first marshal gave a signal to the athletes, and at once a tuss-
ling began; each one of them trying to get at the trunk of the
tree and to mount high enough on the shoulders of the man
in front to be within reach of the garland. The struggle was

tremendous, like a gigantic scrimmage at football; the mass seemed at one time all legs and arms, at another a furious combat in which some one must lose life or limb. First one and then another rose high on the backs or shoulders of those below, only to fall back and be lost in the crowd. The spectators cheered and shouted and screamed with laughter. When at last the first bunch of flowers was successfully torn away, we all cheered as if some great and glorious victory had been gained. It took about ten minutes to gain possession of the long wreath; bit by bit it was clutched away, and flung among the men below. But there still remained the crimson '93 high above, and I dare say another ten minutes were spent before the frantic efforts to reach it were crowned with success. Only two or three men were brave enough to attempt the feat; the famous gymnast of the year was the one finally to achieve it. Again and again he was dragged down; again and again we saw him engaged in a free fight with obstinate opponents from the vantage ground of the shoulders of his supporters; his jersey was torn, his body must been covered with bruises and his nails all in pieces; but in the end the rosy '93 fell amid the shouts of everybody, and the fun was over.

"But only for a time. The crowd dispersed to rest and eat, and dress for the various balls and receptions which closed this busy day. Those students who were lucky enough to have rooms looking on the College Yard had had them thronged with guests by eight in the evening. From wide-open windows every one was looking down on the coloured lamps hung from the fine trees and listening to the Harvard Glee Club, who, in spite of the heavy rain, sang manfully under their umbrellas the songs that have been sung for so many years. But we were too wet and too tired to go out again, and we feel that we shall have to come back some day to Cambridge to see Class Day under a blue sky and learn what it really is."

Commencement Parts

SPEAKERS

Latin Oration
DAVID SAVILLE MUZZEY

Disquisition
IRA WOODS HOWERTH
"Political Optimism"

Dissertations
SOLOMON LEWIS FRIDENBERG
"Fin de Siècle"

HENRY GREENLEAF PEARSON
"The Greeks Again"

Oration .
FREDERICK WILLIAM DALLINGER
"A Word About the Caucus"

Law School Part
EDWIN SOLOMON MACK
"Bankruptcy Legislation"

ORATIONS

(Summa cum laude.)

Edward Angus Burt	George Daniel Hammond
Frederick William Dallinger	Billings Learned Hand
Robert Gray Dodge	David Saville Muzzey

DISSERTATIONS
(*Magna cum laude.*)

Ernest Hamlin Abbott
John Alden
Fred Howes Anderson
Percy Lee Atherton
Sidney Miller Ballou
Gordon Knox Bell
Francis Gano Benedict
Henry Newhall Berry
Edgar Francis Billings
Augustus Jesse Bowie
Ernest Gisborne Burke
Patrick Thomas Campbell
Joseph William Carr
Edward Russell Coffin
Howard Hamblet Cook
James Ambrose Cotter
Walter Howard Cushing
Albert James Dibblee
Walter Cazenove Douglas
Horace Ainsworth Eaton
Frank Edgar Farley
William Oliver Farnsworth
Alfred Julius Freiberg
Solomon Louis Fridenburg
Lee Max Friedman
Philip Becker Goetz
Thomas Hall
John Goddard Hart

John Henry Harwood
Oscar Brown Hawes
Ernest Osgood Hiler
Robert William Hunter
Charles Edward Hutchison
Frederick Gibbs Jackson
Gaillard Thomas Lapsley
Ralph Clinton Larrabee
Walton Brooks McDaniel
Stephen Andrew McIntire
Henry Orlando Marcy
Arthur Allen Marsters
William Vaughn Stoy Moody
Howard Pervear Nash
Thomas Edward Oliver
Gilbert Francis Ordway
George Alfred Page
Henry Greenleaf Pearson
Edward Hartwell Rogers
Josiah Edward Spurr
Frederick Joseph Taussig
Frederick Townsend
Henry Ware
George Albert Whipple
Joseph Wiggin
Arthur Mayer Wolfson
Ralph Woodworth
Frank Lester Young

DISQUISITIONS
(*Cum laude.*)

William Henry Allison
Charles Russell Bardeen

Ralph Hartt Bowles
John Ira Cochrane

Gilman Collamore
John Lawrence Sarsfield Connolly
Ambrose Collyer Dearborn
Joseph Phillips Dimmick
George Richmond Fearing
Oliver Bridges Henshaw
Joseph Clark Hoppin
Tracy Hoppin
Ira Woods Howerth
Chauncey Giles Hubbell
Harold Hutchinson
Walter Augustus Lecompte
Charles Henry Lincoln
Harry Chamberlain Low
George Grant McCurdy
Frederick Chase McLaughlin
Frederick Roy Martin
Albion Leroy Millan
Ralph Gifford Miller
Fred Wadsworth Moore
Charles Henry Fiske
Frank Bernard Gallivan

Charles Merrick Gay
Louis Whitmore Gilbert
Arthur Hale Gordon
Andrew Hahn
Albert Hale
Samuel Prescott Hall
Frederick Grantham Henderson.
William Julian Henderson
Howard Gardner Nichols
Chester Wells Purington
Harrison Garfield Rhodes
Benjamin Hill Rounsaville
Walter Lincoln Sanborn
Philip Henry Savage
Thomas Hall Shastid
George Frederick Sibley
Henry Harding Stickney
William James Henry Strong
Frank Raymond Stubbs
Frederick Charles Thwaits
George Walcott
George Parker Winship
Charles Lowell Young

HONORARY DEGREES
LL.D.

Winfield Scott Chaplin
John Joseph Keane
Robert Todd Lincoln

Thomas Raynesford Lounsbury
Frederick Law Olmstead
Richard Olney

Magnus Gustaf Retzius.

D.D.
William Lawrence.

A.M.

George Alonzo Bartlett
Frank Bolles

Daniel Hudson Burnham
Andrew McFarland Davis.

Hollis Horatio Hunnewell.

'93 Phi Beta Kappa

Gordon Knox Bell
Henry Newhall Berry
Augustus Jesse Bowie
Ernest Gisborne Burke
Frederick Shepherd Converse
Howard Hamblett Cook
Frederick William Dallinger
Albert James Dibblee
Robert Gray Dodge
Walter Cazenove Douglas
Horace Ainsworth Eaton
Philip Becker Goetz
Billings Learned Hand
John Goddard Hart

John Henry Harwood
Frederick Gibbs Jackson
Frederick Palmer Kidder
Gaillard Thomas Lapsley
Ralph Clinton Larrabee
Walton Brooks McDaniel
Henry Orlando Marcy
William Vaughn Moody
David Saville Muzzey
Thomas Edward Oliver
Henry Greenleaf Pearson
Frederick Townsend
Henry Ware
Joseph Wiggin

PHI BETA KAPPA, 1893

'93 "H" Men

From *The "H" Book of Harvard Athletics* 1923
By J. A. Blanchard, '91

William Francis Baker	Track, 1893
Charles Russell Bardeen	Track, 1892, 1893
*Harold Munro Battelle	Crew (cox.), 1890, 1891
Charles Arthur Blake	Track, 1893
*George Ebenezer Burgess	Crew, 1893
Gilman Collamore	Track, 1892, 1893
Charles Kimball Cummings	Crew, 1891, 1892, 1893
Philip Whitney Davis	Track, 1891, 1892, 1893
Samuel Craft Davis	Crew 1892
George Richmond Fearing	Football, 1889. Track, 1890, 1891, 1892, 1893. Crew, 1893
Louis Adams Frothingham	Baseball, 1890, 1891, 1892, 1893
Frank Walton Hallowell	Football, 1889, 1890, 1891, 1892. Baseball, 1891, 1892, 1893.
Oscar Brown Hawes	Track, 1891
*John Ashley Highlands	Baseball, 1892, 1893.
Everett Chase Howe	Baseball, 1890, 1891
Chauncey Giles Hubbell	Track, 1893
George Howard Kelton	Crew, 1890, 1891, 1892
Ralph Gifford Miller	Crew, 1893
Fred Wadsworth Moore	Football, 1891, 1892
*Edward Stanton Mullins	Track, 1891
*Oliver Wadsworth Shead	Track, 1892, 1893
Conrad Hensler Slade	Crew, 1892
Frank Enos Soule	Baseball, 1890, 1891, 1892
Arthur Parker Stone	Baseball, 1892
William Leland Thompson	Track, 1891, 1892, 1893
Bernard Walton Trafford	Football, 1889, 1890, 1891, 1892. Baseball, 1890, 1891, 1892, 1893.
Joshua Damon Upton	Football, 1889, 1890, 1892. Baseball, 1890, 1891, 1892, 1893.
*Davis Righter Vail	Crew, 1891, 1893.
Joseph Wiggin	Baseball, 1891, 1892, 1893, 1894.

'93 Men in "Who's Who"

(Edition of 1922-23)

Ernest Hamlin Abbott, Editor.
George Henry Alden, Educator.
William Henry Allison, University Professor.
Percy Lee Atherton, Composer.
Sidney Miller Ballou, Lawyer.
Edgar James Banks, Archaeologist.
Charles Russell Bardeen, Anatomist, University Dean
Murray Bartlett, University President.
Francis Gano Benedict, Chemist.
Ralph Wilhelm Bergengren, Author.
Rudolph Michael Binder, Professor of Sociology.
James Abercrombie Burden, Iron Manufacturer.
Edward Angus Burt, Botanist.
William Horace Davis, Statistician.
Frederick Shepherd Converse, Composer.
George Cram Cook, Author.
Louis Craig Cornish, Clergyman.
Frederick William Dallinger, Congressman.
Bradley Moore Davis, Botanist.
William Ernest Castle, Zoölogist.
Jasper Newton Deahl, University Professor.
William Duane, Physicist.
Frank Edgar Farley, College Professor.
Lee Max Friedman, Lawyer.
Louis Adams Frothingham, Lawyer.
James Waterman Glover, College Professor.
Philip Becker Goetz, College Professor.
Learned Hand, Judge.
Joseph Clark Hoppin, Archaeologist.
Elwin Lincoln House, Clergyman—Lecturer.
Ira Woods Howerth, College Professor.
John Homer Huddilston, University Professor.
George Hoadly Ingalls, Railroad Official.
Thomas Augustus Jaggar, Geologist.

Theodore Wesley Koch, Librarian
Arthur Gordner Leacock, Academy Professor.
George Grant MacCurdy, Anthropologist.
Walton Brooks McDaniel, College Professor.
Frederick Roy Martin, Journalist.
James Andrew Merrill, Geologist.
Roland Jessup Mulford, Head Master.
Louis Christian Mullgardt, Architect.
David Saville Muzzey, Author.
Herbert Vincent Neal, Biologist.
Thomas Edward Oliver, College Professor.
George Everett Partridge, Author.
Harrison Garfield Rhodes, Author.
Louis Peck Sanders, Lawyer.
Frank Charles Schrader, Geologist.
Carl Lincoln Schurz, Lawyer.
Thomas Hall Shastid, Ophthalmologist.
George Lawson Sheldon, Ex-Governor.
Francis Hinckley Sisson, Banker.
Howard Caswell Smith, Commercial Paper.
Robert Keating Smith, Clergyman.
Josiah Edward Spurr, Geologist.
Wallace Nelson Stearns, University Professor.
Frederick Joseph Taussig, Gynecologist.
Thomas Wayland Vaughan, Geologist.
Enoch Howard Vickers, Professor of Economics.
Oswald Garrison Villard, Journalist.
George Parker Winship, Librarian.
Frederick Winsor, Educator.

Oldest and Youngest Men

1852
*Silas Dinsmoor—Sept. 30

1859
E. A. Burt
J. N. Deahl

1860
I. W. Howerth
H. Lyon
F. C. Schrader

1861
E. L. House
G. H. Kelton
J. A. Merrill
O. L. Watkins

1862
H. L. Coar
J. F. Crosby
*B. H. Rounsaville

1863
J. Heiss
G. G. MacCurdy

1864
*D. Blaustein
H. F. Butler
*G. D. Hammond
J. F. Jones
L. J. Malone
W. C. Moore

1865
H. B. Bacon
R. M. Binder
*G. S. Callender

J. H. Fennessy
A. B. Frizell
*F. P. Gulliver
*W. H. Isely
C. E. Moody
W. E. Parsons
W. J. Scott
R. K. Smith
C. L. Young
F. L. Young

1866
G. H. Alden
E. J. Banks
C. W. Collier
H. Dodson
C. W. Downing
T. A. Gifford
L. Hutchinson
L. C. Mullgardt
T. H. Shastid
W. P. Smith
W. N. Stearns
J. C. Walker

1867
A. T. Browne
C. B. Burger
W. E. Castle
A. C. Fay
E. H. Frantz
G. L. McElroy
H. G. Shaw
L. B. Thacher
C. E. Williams

1868
(19 men)

1869
(46 men)

1870
(133 men)

1871
(134 men)

1872
(47 men)

1873
*E. R. Coffin
G. C. Cook
*A. C. Dearborn
A. J. Freiberg
F. G. Henderson
*P. D. Stone
A. M. Wolfson

1874
S. L. Wolff—Jan. 15

Bachelors of '93

Percy Lee Atherton
Willis Adams Bailey
Charles Lowell Barlow
Lewis Bass
Samuel Francis Batchelder
Edward Mellen Bennett
Augustus Jessie Bowie, Jr.
Philip Turner Brown
Percy Fletcher Burrows
Walter Cary
Clifford Hoffman Chase
Gilman Collamore
Howard Hamblet Cook
Philip Whitney Davis
Charles Lunt DeNormandie
Louis Eugene Desbecker
Divie Bethune Duffield
Wiliam Oliver Farnsworth
Lovat Fraser
Frederick Aaron Freeark
Lee Max Friedman
Leonard Alden Frink
Arthur Bowes Frizell
Thomas Ashley Gifford
Andrew Hahn

William Carter Heywood
Ernest Osgood Hiler
Lincoln Hutchinson
James Francis Jones
Gaillard Thomas Lapsley
George Leary McElroy
Stephen Andrew McIntire
Samuel Hubbard Mansfield
Selden Erastus Marvin, Jr.
Maxwell Norman
William Edwin Parsons
Harrison Garfield Rhodes
Walter Judd Scott
Howard Cocks Sherwood
Herbert Brush Smith
Horace Claflin Southwick
John Clarence Taussig
Harry Lorenzo Teetzel
Rufus Kemble Thomas
Frederick Charles Thwaits
Archibald Read Tisdale
Charles Edward Whitmore
George Perry Wilson
Charles Lowell Young

Occupation List

(This classification, based on the United States Census, has been prepared in collaboration with Professor Edmund E. Day of the School of Business Administration. It is given in full, although, in this Class, there are no entries under some of its divisions. Since it is an attempt to systematize a subject now in much confusion, constructive criticism will be welcomed.)

BUSINESS

Advertising or Publicity:
C. E. Cook, Hubbell, Wallerstein.

Banking, Brokerage, Bonds, Commercial Paper:
Bacon, Barney, G. B. Bennett, Blagden, Brewer, Carr, Emerson, Ewer, Frantz, Hale, Manning, Marvin, Sanborn, Sisson, H. C. Smith, F. Townsend, Trafford, Webber, Whitford.

Building Trades and Supplies:
Steinhart.

Farming (including Fruit, Dairy, Conservatories), Ranching, or Stock Raising:
Crosby, Curtis, Dennett, Emmet, O. D. Fisk, F. G. Henderson, Kelton, Kent, Kittredge, Manchester, Sewall, Sheldon, Thomas, Totten, Tremain.

Fisheries and Marine Interests (except Shipping):

Forestry:

Hotel, Club, Camp, or Athletic Work:
A. S. G. Clarke, F. W. Moore, Whitmore, Wilder.

Insurance:
C. A. Blake, A. T. Browne, Collamore, Cullinan, Hume, North, Parsons, Pope.

Manufacturing:
Ayer, Bailey, Currier, Holland, Brookfield, R. B. Brown, Burden, Cary, Dole, Dunn, Falk, Fennessy, Gould, Grigor, J.

H. Hall, Harwood, W. J. Henderson, Hildreth, P. T. Jackson, Nutter, G. B. Pierce, Stevens, Stickney, Strong, Thacher, Thompson, Tripp, Watters, White, Wolfson.

Mining (including Smelting, Quarrying, Oil or Gas Wells):
Brabrook, A. L. Cochrane, Fraser.

Public Defense, Health, or Safety (Army, Navy, Police, Fire, Hospital-Service, etc.):
Sylvester, Wylie.

Public Office or Government Administration (including Judiciary and Law Officers)
Clagstone, Dallinger, Frothingham, Gade, S. P. Hall, Hand, Kline, Ray, Stone, Wilson.

Publishing (Book or Newspaper)
Page, E. D. Shaw, Taylor, Villard, Watkins.

Real Estate:
Beal, Burrows, W. A. Clark, Maynard, Pease, C. H. Pierce, Williams, Winslow, F. L. Young.

Stenography (Public):

Telegraph, Telephone, Postal Operation, Electric (or Gas) Light and Power:
Baker, Moody, Rawalt, Reed, Soren.

Trade (Wholesale or Retail), Commission Business, Salesmen, Collections, etc.:
Earle, A. C. Fay, Furber, Hallowell, Luce, Mansfield. Post, H. B. Spaulding, Soule, F. U. Stearns, Richards, Robb, Walcott, Weld, Wheeler, Farwell.

Transportation (including Aviation and Expressing):
Dimmick, Ingalls, Osborn.

Trustee and Investor (for Self or Others):
F. S. Blake, S. C. Davis, Dows, Fearing, Goodrich. Hathaway, Malone, Norman, Pike, Rogers, Thwaits.

Warehousing or Storage:
Vogel, Wood.

PROFESSIONS

Accounting (public) or auditing:
Gifford.

Architecture (including Landscape):
Cummings, Farquhar, Flint, Gay, McElroy, Mullgardt, Parker, Southwick.

Chemistry:
Booth, Macallister.

Dentistry:

Education:
Alden. Allison, Bardeen, Bartlett, Binder, Burger, Burt, Campbell, Castle, Coar, B. M. Davis, Deahl, Dodson, Duane, H. A. Eaton, Farley, Farnsworth, H. G. Fay, Frizell, Glover, Goetz, Hart, Heiss, J. C. Hoppin, Howerth, Huddilston, Humphreys, L. Hutchinson, F. G. Jackson, Kenney, Lapsley, Latham, Leacock, MacCurdy, McDaniel, Manley, Merrill, W. C. Moore, Mulford, Muzzey, Neal, Oliver, Parrington, Pearson, Shaffer, Shaw, W. P. Smith, W. N. Stearns, Vickers, J. R. Webster, K. G. T. Webster, Whipple, Winsor, Wolff, C. L. Young.

Engineering:
Bowie, P. W. Davis, Fletcher, Purington, Spurr.

Journalism or Editorial Work (other than Publishing):
Abbott, DeWolf, Eichinger, Martin, Newlin, Phillips, Pressy, Scott, Sibley.

Law (except Judiciary and Public Law Officers):
Apsey, Ballou, Barlow, Bass, Batchelder, Bell, E. M. Bennett, Berry, H. F. Blake, H. F. Butler, Connolly, Cotter, DeNormandie, Dent, Desbecker, Dibblee, Dodge, Douglas, Duffield, J. E. Eaton, Elmore, C. H. Fiske, Freeark, Fridenberg, Friedman, Frink, Gans, Heywood, Hickey, Hiler, Howe, Hughes, Kendricken, McIntire, McLaughlin, Millan, Miller, Nash, Sanders, Schurz, Sherwood, Simpson, H. B. Smith, Stover, J. C. Taussig, TePaske, Tisdale, E. S. Townsend, Upton, Walker, Ware, Wiggin, Woodworth.

Library Work:
Koch, Lincoln, Winship.

Literature and Lecturing:
Bergengren, Chase, J. I. Cochrane, House, Jones, Kennedy,
Kimball, Rhodes.

Medicine (except Dental):
Allen, Broughton, C. S. Butler, Conro, Ellsworth, Hunt,
Johnson, Larrabee, Low, Partridge, Shastid, F. M. Spalding,
Stetson, Street, Stubbs, F. J. Taussig, W. M. Townsend, Whit-
ing, Robey.

Ministry or Social Service:
Carson, Collier, Cornish, Gordon, Grant, Hahn, Hawes, C. E.
Hutchison, Kennedy, Lindh, R. K. Smith, Spencer-Turner,
Warner.

Music (Composer, Teacher, or Performer):
Atherton, Converse, Teetzel.

Painting or Sculpture:
T. Hoppin, Slade.

Science (except Chemistry), Applied or Research:
Benedict, Jaggar, Lyon, Schrader, Vaughan.

Statistics:
W. H. Davis.

Theatrical or Public Entertainment Work:
Banks, G. C. Cook.

Unclassified or Unknown:
G. B. Blake, P. T. Brown, Livingston, Roberts, H. H. Cook,
Dow.

Geographical Distribution

(These are mailing addresses, and do not always correspond with a man's present location.)

ALABAMA

Montgomery. Dimmick.

ARIZONA

Miami. Scott.

CALIFORNIA

Anaheim. Tremain.
Lakeside. Curtis.
Los Angeles. Farquhar, Fraser, Johnson, Miller, Street.
Sacramento. Fletcher.
San Francisco. Ballou, Bowie, Clagstone, Dibblee, Mullgardt.
Santa Barbara. Carson.

COLORADO

Boulder. Burger.
Greeley. Howerth.

CONNECTICUT

Hartford. Soren.
Middletown. Farley.
New Haven. MacCurdy.
Norwich. J. H. Hall.
Washington. A. S. G. Clarke.

DELAWARE

Wilmington. Walker.

DISTRICT OF COLUMBIA

Washington. Dallinger, W. H. Davis, Kline, Schrader, Totten, Vaughan.

FLORIDA

Eustis. Banks.
Winter Haven. Manchester.

ILLINOIS

Chicago. A. T. Browne, Dent, Dunn, Freeark, Pike.
Evanston. Farnsworth, Koch, Whipple.
Lebanon. W. N. Stearns.
Urbana. Oliver.

INDIANA

Indianapolis. Cotter, Hume, Pope, Watkins.
Lafayette. Heiss.

IOWA

Ames. Eichinger.
Sioux Centre. TePaske.

LOUISIANA

New Orleans. Newlin.

MAINE

Orono. Huddilston.
Wells. Malone.

MASSACHUSETTS

Adams. F. U. Stearns.
Attleboro. Conro.
Belmont. Castle, Stickney, Stone.
Boston. Allen, Apsey, Atherton, Barlow, Batchelder, Benedict,
    E. M. Bennett, Berry, C. A. Blake, F. S. Blake, Brabrook,
    Broughton, C. S. Butler, H. F Butler, Campbell, A. L.
    Cochrane, Cornish, Cummings, DeNormandie, Dodge, Dow,
    Duane, Fearing, C. H. Fiske, Friedman, Furber, Hale,
    Harwood, Hathaway, Hildreth, Hiler, J. C. Hoppin, Howe,
    Hughes, P. T. Jackson, Kendricken, Larrabee, Low, Millan,
    Neal, Norman, Parker, Partridge, Post, Robey, Sibley, Soule,

F. M. Spaldin'g, H. B. Spaulding, Stover, Taylor, Thacher, Thomas, Tisdale, E. S. Townsend, Trafford, Upton, Wiggin, Winslow, F. L. Young, E. D. Shaw.

Brookline. Manning, Parsons, Purington, Sanborn, Ware.

Cambridge. P. W. Davis, Earle, Frizell, Hart, F. W. Moore, Rogers, J. R. Webster, K. G. T. Webster, White, Whitford.

Charles River. Winship.

Chestnut Hill. Hallowell, Page.

Concord. Nutter, Winsor.

Dorchester Centre. F. G. Jackson.

Fall River. Tripp.

Gloucester. Mansfield.

Hubbardston. Kelton.

Hyde Park. W. J. Henderson.

Lawrence. Dole.

Lenox. G. B. Blake.

Leominster. Kenney.

Lexington. Collier, Hubbell.

Lynn. Barney, Currier.

Melrose Highlands. W. M. Townsend.

Natick. Grigor.

Newburyport. W. C. Moore.

Newton. Hahn, Stubbs.

Newton Centre. Pearson.

Newton Highlands. Chase.

North Easton. Frothingham.

Petersham. O. D. Fisk.

Quincy. Bass, Ellsworth, Lindh.

Roxbury. Frink.

Scituate. Bergengren.

Somerville. Connolly.

South Dartmouth. Stetson.

Waban. Elmore

Waltham. Emerson.

Warren. Grant.

Wellesley. C. L. Young.

Westfield. R. K. Smith.

West Medway. F. G. Henderson.

West Roxbury. J. E. Eaton.

Weston. Woodworth.

Westwood. Converse.
Worcester. Lincoln, Wood.

MICHIGAN

Ann Arbor. B. M. Davis, Glover.
Detroit. Duffield.
Portland. Webber.

MINNESOTA

Owatonna. G. B. Bennett.

MISSISSIPPI

Wayside. Sheldon.

MISSOURI

Kansas City. Simpson.
St. Louis. Burt, S. C. Davis, Dodson, F. J. Taussig, J. C. Taussig.

MONTANA

Butte. Sanders.

NEW HAMPSHIRE

Bristol. Bacon.
East Alstead. Dennett.
Exeter. Leacock.

NEW JERSEY

East Orange. Binder, Hutchison.
Gloucester. Lyon.
Montclair. Reed.
Newark. Gould, Shaffer.
Princeton. Mulford.
Ridgewood. Williams.
Summit. Hawes.
West Orange. G. B. Pierce.

NEW YORK

Albany, F. Townsend.
Arcade. Crosby.
Binghamton. Kent.
Brooklyn. Frantz, Nash, Sylvester.
Buffalo. Desbecker, Gordon.
Flushing. Phillips.
Geneva. Bartlett.
Hamilton. Allison.
Manitou. Livingston.
New Rochelle. Burrows. Spurr.
New York City. Abbott, Baker, Beal, Bell, Blagden, Brewer, Brookfield, P. T. Brown, Cary, W. A. Clark, Collamore, C. E. Cook, G. C. Cook, H. H. Cook, Cullinan, Ewer, Farwell, A. C .Fay, H. G. Fay, Fennessy, Gans, Gay, Gifford, Goodrich, Hand, Heywood, Hickey, Holland, Hunt, Ingalls, McElroy, McIntire, McLaughlin, Martin, Marvin, Maynard, Moody, Pease, C. H. Pierce, Rawalt, Richards, Schurz, Sherwood, H. B. Smith, H. C. Smith, Southwick, Stevens, Straus, Villard, Vogel. Walcott, Wallerstein, Weld, Whitmore, Wilder, Wolff, Jones.
North Evans. Goetz.
Poughkeepsie. Whiting.
Rhinebeck. Dows.
Schenectady. Pressy.
Syracuse. Booth, H. A. Eaton.
Troy. R. B. Brown, Burden, Thompson.
Utica. Watters.
Yonkers. Muzzey, Sisson.

NORTH CAROLINA

Asheville. H. G. Shaw.

NORTH DAKOTA

Grafton. Wylie.

OHIO

Cadiz. Warner.
Cincinnati. Kittredge, Osborn.
Cleveland. Flint, Rhodes.

Columbus. S. P. Hall.
Marietta. Coar, Manley.
Troy. Wheeler.
Zanesville. Bailey.

OREGON

Hood River. House.
Salem. Alden.

PENNSYLVANIA

New Hope. T. Hoppin.
Philadelphia. Douglas, Fridenberg, McDaniel.

RHODE ISLAND

Bristol. DeWolf.

TEXAS

Canyan. Humphreys.
Sherman. Luce.

VERMONT

East Dorset. J. I. Cochrane.

WASHINGTON

Seattle. H. F. Blake, Parrington.
Tacoma. Ray.

WEST VIRGINIA

Morgantown. Deahl, Vickers.

WISCONSIN

Beloit. Strong.
Hudson. Carr.
Madison. Ayer, Bardeen.
Milwaukee. Falk, Teetzel, Thwaits.
Racine. Wolfson.
Superior. Merrill, Shastid.

BRAZIL

Rio de Janeiro. Gade.

CANADA
Montreal. Latham.
Port Colborne. MacAllister.

CUBA

Havana. Steinhart.

ENGLAND

Cambridge. Lapsley.
London. Hutchinson Kimball, Robb.
Warwick. Emmet.

FRANCE

Paris. Roberts, Slade.

ITALY
Catania. Wilson.
Rome. Spencer-Turner.

PORTO RICO
Naguabo. Sewall.

TERRITORY OF HAWAII
Volcano House P. O. Jaggar.

Addresses

Ernest Hamlin Abbott,
    Care The Outlook, 381 Fourth Ave., New York, N. Y.

George Henry Alden,
    326 N. Liberty St., Salem, Ore.

Freeman Allen,
    200 Beacon Street, Boston.

William Henry Allison,
    Hamilton, New York.

Albert Stokes Apsey,
    15 State Street, Boston.

Percy Lee Atherton,
    St. Botolph Club, 4 Newbury Street, Boston.

Walter Ayer,
    Care of The Fuller & Johnson Mfg. Co., Madison, Wis.

Henry Berthier Bacon,
    Bristol, N. H.

Willis Adams Bailey,
    31 North Fourth St., Zanesville, O.

William Francis Baker,
    American Telephone and Telegraph Company,
    195 Broadway, New York City.

Sidney Miller Ballou,
    Matson Building, San Francisco, Cal.

Edgar James Banks,
    Alpine, N. J. (summers).
    Eustis, Fla. (winters).

Charles Russell Bardeen,
    23 Mendota Ct., Madison, Wis.

Charles Lowell Barlow,
    11 Pemberton Square, Boston.

Edward Mitchell Barney,
>   21 Baltimore St., Lynn, Mass.

Murray Bartlett,
>   Hobart College, Geneva, N. Y.

Lewis Bass,
>   Quincy, Mass.

Samuel Francis Batchelder,
>   720 Tremont Building, Boston.

William Fields Beal,
>   130 West Forty-fourth St., New York City.

Gordon Knox Bell,
>   22 Exchange Place, New York City.

Francis Gano Benedict,
>   29 Vila St., Boston, Mass.

Edward Mellen Bennett,
>   Wayland, Mass.

Guy Brown Bennett,
>   101 North Cedar St., Owatonna, Minn.

Ralph William Bergengren,
>   Scituate, Mass.

Henry Newhall Berry,
>   85 Devonshire St., Boston, Mass.

Rudolph Michael Binder,
>   190 Prospect St., East Orange, N. J.

Dexter Blagden,
>   111 Broadway, New York City.

Charles Arthur Blake,
>   50 Kilby St., Boston, Mass.

Francis Stanton Blake,
>   Care of Blake Brothers and Co.. 111 Devonshire St., Boston, Mass.

George Baty Blake,
    Lenox, Mass.

Henry Fordyce Blake,
    1416 Boylston Ave., Seattle, Wash.

William Miller Booth,
    1801 James St., Syracuse, N. Y.

Augustus Jesse Bowie, Jr.,
    Nevada Bank Bldg., San Francisco, Cal.

George Hale Brabrook,
    Tennis and Racquet Club, Boston, Mass.

Calvert Brewer,
    55 Cedar St., New York City.

Henry Morgan Brookfield,
    132 East 78th St., New York City.

Arthur Nicholson Broughton,
    46 Eliot St., Jamaica Plain, Boston, Mass.

Philip Turner Brown,
    Racquet and Tennis Club, New York City.

Royal Benton Brown,
    193 First St., Troy, N. Y. (forwarding).

Arthur Taber Browne,
    11 South La Salle St., Chicago, Ill.

James Abercrombie Burden,
    Troy, N. Y.

Charles Roland Burger,
    R. 2, Box 209, Boulder, Col.

Percy Fletcher Burrows,
    501 Pelham Rd., New Rochelle, N. Y.

Edward Angus Burt,
    Missouri Botanical Garden, St. Louis, Mo.

Charles Shorey Butler,
    257 Newbury St., Boston, Mass.

Howard Fulton Butler,
    18 Tremont St., Room 541, Boston, Mass.

Patrick Thomas Campbell,
    111 Fenwood Rd., Boston, Mass.

Frederick Jay Carr,
    Hudson, Wisconsin.

Lewis Clinton Carson,
    17 East Micheltorena St., Santa Barbara, Cal.

Walter Cary,
    383 Park Ave., New York, N. Y.

William Ernest Castle,
    186 Payson Road, Belmont 78, Mass.

Clifford Hoffman Chase,
    340 Lake Ave., Newton Highlands, Mass.

Paul Clagstone,
    634 Merchants Exchange Building, San Francisco, Cal.

William Anthony Clark,
    27 West 44th St., New York City.

Albert Sidney Gregg Clarke,
    Washington, Conn.

Henry Livingston Coar,
    Box 341, Marietta, Ohio.

Alexander Lynde Cochrane,
    Somerset Club, Boston, Mass.

John Ira Cochrane, M.D.,
    East Dorset, Vermont.

Gilman Collamore,
    Room 809, 346 Broadway, New York City.

Christopher Walter Collier,
    595 Massachusetts Avenue, Lexington, Mass.

John Lawrence Sarsfield Connolly,
    34 Union Square, Somerville, Mass.

Arthur Clifton Conro,
    223 Bronson Building, Attleboro, Mass.

Frederick Shepherd Converse,
    Westwood, Mass.

Charles Emerson Cook,
    110 East 42d St., New York City.

George Cram Cook,
    133 MacDougal St., New York City.

Howard Hamblett Cook,
    504 Barrett Building, 40 Rector St., New York City.

Louis Craig Cornish,
    25 Beacon St., Boston, Mass.

James Coppinger Cotter,
    P. O. Lock Box 300. Indianapolis, Ind.

John Fergus Crosby,
    Arcade, New York.

Edward Conway Cullinan,
    27 West 44th St., New York City.

Charles Kimball Cummings,
    8 Beacon St., Boston, Mass. (permanent.)

Frank Josslyn Currier,
    Care of Birney C. Parsons, 19 Congress St., Boston.

George DeClyver Curtis,
    Lakeside, California.

Frederick William Dallinger,
    124 House Office Building, Washington, D. C.

Bradley Moore Davis,
    Botanical Laboratory, University of Michigan, Ann Arbor, Mich.

Philip Whitney Davis,
    104 Irving St., Cambridge, Mass.

Samuel Craft Davis,
    220 Security Building, St. Louis.

William Horace Davis,
> 5314 41st St., Chevy Chase, Washington, D. C.

Jasper Newton Deahl,
> 414 Park St., Morgantown, W. Va.

Hartley Dennett,
> East Alstead, New Hampshire.

Charles Lunt De Normandie,
> 53 State St., Boston, Mass.

Louis Lee Dent,
> 549 The Rookery, Chicago, Ill.

Louis Eugene Desbecker,
> Morgan Building, Buffalo, New York.

Bradford Colt de Wolf,
> 35 Union St., Bristol, R. I.

Albert James Dibblee,
> 642 Mills Building, San Francisco, Cal.

Joseph Phillips Dimmick,
> 419 Bell Building, Montgomery, Ala.

Robert Gray Dodge,
> 82 Bay State Road, Boston, Mass.

Hugh Dodson,
> Dodson School of Private Tutoring, 3534 Lindell Blvd.,
> St. Louis, Mo.

Charles Thurston Dole,
> Care of Champion-International Co., Lawrence, Mass.

Walter Cazenove Douglas, Jr.,
> 5960 Drexel Road, Overbrook, Philadelphia, Pa.

Henry Abijah Thompson Dow,
> Room 216, 236 Huntington Ave, Boston 17, Mass.

Tracy Dows,
> Rhinebeck, New York.

William Duane,
      Bio-Physical Laboratories, 695 Huntington Ave., Boston.

Divie Bethune Duffield,
      714 Union Trust Building, Detroit, Mich.

Morrill Dunn,
      Peoples Gas Building, Chicago, Ill.

Daniel Osborne Earle,
      17 Bates St., Cambridge, Mass.

Horace Ainsworth Eaton,
      332 Ostrom Ave., Syracuse, N. Y.

John Edgar Eaton,
      12 Whittemore St., West Roxbury, Mass.

John Waldo Eichinger,
      Ames, Iowa

Samuel Walker Ellsworth,
      180 Munroe Road, Quincy, Mass.

Samuel Dean Elmore,
      196 Windsor Road, Waban, Mass.

Guy Thorp Emerson,
      487 Main St., Waltham, Mass.

Robert Emmet,
      Moreton Paddox, Warwick, England.

Maurice Henry Ewer,
      214 Broadway, New York City.

Clarence Rudolph Falk,
      The Falk Corporation, Milwaukee, Wis.

Frank Edgar Farley,
      145 Mt. Vernon St., Middletown, Conn.

William Oliver Farnsworth,
      Northwestern University, Evanston, Ill.

Robert David Farquhar,
      California Club, Los Angeles, Cal.

Sidney Emerson Farwell,
    Care of Lord & Taylor, Fifth Ave. and 38th St., New
    York City.

Alfred Chase Fay,
    229 West 64th St., New York City.

Harrison Gilbert Fay,
    22 West 72d St., New York City.

George Richmond Fearing,
    Jackson & Curtis, 19 Congress St., Boston, Mass.

James Henry Fennessy,
    42 Broadway, New York City.

Otis Daniell Fisk,
    Petersham, Mass.

Charles Henry Fiske,
    26 Central St., Boston, Mass.

Austin Bradstreet Fletcher,
    2100 G St., Sacramento, Cal.

Herbert Lincoln Flint,
    Care of A. D. Taylor, 4614 Prospect Ave., Cleveland, O.

Elmer Hollinger Frantz,
    Care of Marion B. Frantz, 495 Sixth St., Brooklyn, N. Y.

Lovat Fraser,
    426 Metropolitan Building, Los Angeles, Cal.

Frederick Aaron Freeark,
    First National Bank Building, Chicago, Ill.

Solomon Louis Fridenberg,
    1218 Real Estate Trust Building, Philadelphia, Pa.

Lee Max Friedman,
    53 State St., Boston, Mass.

Leonard Alden Frink,
    14 Mayfair St., Roxbury, Mass.

Arthur Bowes Frizell,
    361 Harvard St., Cambridge, Mass.

Louis Adams Frothingham,
    North Easton, Mass.

William Harry Furber,
    53 State St., Boston, Mass.

F. Herman Gade,
    Norwegian Legation, Rio de Janeiro, Brazil.

Howard Schiffer Gans,
    1 Wall St., New York City.

Charles Merrick Gay,
    173 East 80th St., New York City.

Thomas Ashley Gifford,
    27 West 44th St., New York City.

James Waterman Glover,
    620 Oxford Road, Ann Arbor, Mich.

Philip Becker Goetz,
    North Evans New York.

Charles Cross Goodrich,
    17 East 42d St., New York City.

Arthur Hale Gordon,
    965 Delaware Ave., Buffalo, N. Y.

Clifford Allen Gould,
    115 Lafayette St., Newark, N. J.

Frederick Louis Grant,
    Warren, Mass.

Harry Edward Grigor,
    Box 96, Natick, Mass.

Andrew Hahn,
    Nonantum Place, Newton, Mass.

Albert Hale,
    35 Congress St., Boston, Mass.

Joseph Henry Hall,
    P. O. Box 337, Norwich, Conn.

Samuel Prescott Hall,
    1700 Oak St., Columbus, Ohio.

Frank Walton Hallowell,
    Suffolk Road, Chestnut Hill, Mass.

Learned Hand,
    United States Court House, New York City.

John Goddard Hart,
    7 Waterhouse St., Cambridge, Mass.

John Henry Harwood,
    703 Exchange Building, 53 State St., Boston, Mass.

Horatio Hathaway,
    53 State St., Boston, Mass.

Oscar Brown Hawes,
    4 Waldron Ave., Summit, N. J.

John Heiss,
    403 University St., Lafayette, Ind.

Frederick Grantham Henderson,
    West Medway, Mass.

William Julian Henderson,
    6 Dell Terrace, Hyde Park, Mass.

William Carter Heywood,
    44 Wall St., New York City.

James Henry Hickey,
    43 Exchange Place, New York City.

Henry Arthur Hildreth,
    320 Beacon St., Boston, Mass.

Ernest Osgood Hiler,
    35 Congress St., Boston, Mass.

James Edwin Holland,
    Harvard Club, 27 West 44th St., New York City.

Joseph Clark Hoppin,
    310 Sears Building, Boston, Mass.

Tracy Hoppin,
New Hope, Pa.

Rev. Elwin Lincoln House,
Hood River, Oregon.

William De Lancey Howe,
53 State St., Boston, Mass.

Ira Woods Howerth,
State Teachers' College, Greeley, Colorado.

Chauncey Giles Hubbell,
32 Muzzey St., Lexington, Mass.

John Homer Huddilston,
Orono, Maine.

John Thomas Hughes,
53 State St., Boston, Mass.

George Edgar Hume,
214 Hume Mansur Building, Indianapolis, Ind.

John Strother Humphreys,
Canyan, Texas.

Edward Livingston Hunt,
41 East 63d St., New York City.

Lincoln Hutchinson,
· American Relief Administration 67 Eaton Square, Lon--
don S. W., England.

Charles Edward Hutchison,
14 Prospect Terrace, East Orange, N. J.

George Hoadly Ingalls,
466 Lexington Ave., New York City.

Frederick Gibbs Jackson,
High School, Dorchester Center, Mass.

Patrick Tracy Jackson,
55 Congress St., Boston, Mass.

Thomas Augustus Jaggar,
>   Volcano House, Hawaii.

, Philip Van Kuren Johnson,
>   1120 Brockman Building, Los Angeles, Cal.

James Francis Jones,
>   64 West 9th St., New York City.

George Howard Kelton,
>   Hubbardston, Mass.

John Martin Kendricken,
>   68 Devonshire St., Boston, Mass.

Richard Hunter Kennedy,
>   Unknown.

William Howland Kenney,
>   60 Vine St., Leominster, Mass.

William Edward Kent,
>   8 Murray St., Binghamton, N. Y.

David Kimball,
>   Care of Brown, Shipley & Co., London, England.

William Gholson Kittredge,
>   250 Greendale Ave., Cincinnati, Ohio.

Robert Everett Kline,
>   5624 37th St. N. W., Washington, D. C.

Theodore Wesley Koch,
>   Evanston, Ill.

Gaillard Lapsley,
>   Trinity College, Cambridge, England.

Ralph Clinton Larrabee,
>   912 Beacon St., Boston, Mass.

George Warrington Latham,
>   McGill University, Montreal, Canada.

Arthur Gordner Leacock,
>   Exeter, New Hampshire.

Charles Henry Lincoln,
>   22 Dean St., Worcester, Mass.

Eric Isidore Lindh,
   118 President's Lane, Quincy, Mass.

Edward Livingston,
   Manitou, Putnam Co., N. Y.

Harry Chamberlain Low,
   139 Beacon St., Boston, Mass.

William Luce,
   1223 East King St., Sherman, Texas.

Howard Lyon,
   218 Brown St., Gloucester, N. J.

Richard Macallister,
   260 Kent St., Port Colborne, Ont., Canada.

George Grant MacCurdy,
   Yale University Museum, New Haven, Conn.

Walton Brooks McDaniel,
   264 South 44th St., West Philadelphia, Pa.

George Leary McElroy,
   19 East 52d St., New York City.

Stephen Andrew McIntire
   • 297 Fourth Ave., New York City.

Frederick Chase McLaughlin,
   25 West Forty-third St., New York City.

Llewellyn John Malone,
   Wells, Maine.

Percival Manchester,
   Winter Haven, Florida.

Joseph Manley,
   Marietta, Ohio.

Ernest Lincoln Manning,
   58 Marshal St., Brookline, Mass.

Samuel Hubbard Mansfield,
   25 Granite St., Gloucester, Mass.

Frederick Roy Martin,
    The Associated Press, 51 Chambers St., New York City.

Selden Erastus Marvin, Jr.
    Harvard Club, 27 West Forty-fourth St., New York City.

Walter Effingham Maynard,
    501 Fifth Ave., New York City.

James Andrew Merrill,
    1624 Hughitt Ave., Superior, Wis.

Albion Leroy Millan,
    53 State St., Boston, Mass.

Ralph Gifford Miller,
    Suite 804, 706 South Hill St., Los Angeles, Cal.

Charles Edward Moody,
    195 Broadway, New York City.

Fred Wadsworth Moore,
    Care of Harvard Athletic Association, Cambridge, Mass.

William Charles Moore,
    12 Holly St., Salem, Mass.

Roland Jessup Mulford,
    12 Stockton St., Princeton, N. J.

Louis Christian Mullgardt,
    Bohemian Club, Post and Taylor, San Francisco, Cal.

David Saville Muzzey,
    492 Van Cortlandt Park Ave., Yonkers, N. Y.

Howard Pervear Nash,
    44 Court St., Brooklyn, N. Y.

Herbert Vincent Neal,
    Tufts College 57, Mass.

Albert Woodward Newlin,
    2125 State St., New Orleans, La.

Maxwell Norman,
    Care of F. L. Perry, 113 Parker House, Boston, Mass.

Allen Alvin North,
Troy, Ohio.

Charles Read Nutter,
Concord, Mass.

Thomas Edward Oliver,
1004 West California Ave., Urbana, Ill.

Louis Ernest Osborn,
732 South Crescent Ave., Avondale, Cincinnati, O.

George Alfred Page,
1117 Boylston St., Chestnut Hill, Mass.

John Harleston Parker,
177 State St., Boston, Mass.

Vernon Louis Parrington,
The University of Washington, Seattle, Wash.

William Edwin Parsons,
21 Vernon St., Brookline, Mass.

George Everett Partridge,
238 Hemenway St., Boston, Mass.

Henry Greenleaf Pearson,
140 Dudley Road, Newton Center, Mass.

Walter Albert Pease, Jr.,
50 East Forty-second St., New York City.

Roland Edward Phillips,
210 South Parsons Ave., Flushing, N. Y.

Carl Horton Pierce,
110 West Thirty-ninth St., New York City.

George Burgess Pierce,
Llewellyn Park, West Orange, N. J.

Charles Burrall Pike,
39 South State St., Chicago, Ill.

J. Monroe Taylor Pope,
616 East Washington St., Indianapolis, Ind.

John Reed Post,
    53 State St., Boston, Mass.

Edward Pearson Pressey,
    The Gazette, Schenectady, N. Y.

Chester Wells Purington,
    Care of Mrs. J. A. Purington, 410 Harvard St., Brook-
    line, Mass.

Chauncey Otis Rawalt,
    195 Broadway, New York City.

Thomas Francis Ray,
    2924 North Twenty-first St., Tacoma, Wash.

William Maxwell Reed,
    48 South Willow St., Montclair, N. J.

Harrison Garfield Rhodes,
    Union Trust Co., Cleveland, O.

John Wolcott Richards,
    Care of The Seymour Co. 323-329 West Sixteenth St.,
    New York City.

Nathaniel Thayer Robb,
    Care of Brown, Shipley & Co., 133 Pall Mall, London,
    England.

Lewis Niles Roberts,
    38 Rue de Provence, Paris, France.

William Henry Robey,
    202 Commonwealth Ave., Boston, Mass.

Edward Hartwell Rogers,
    559 Main St., Cambridge 39, Mass.

Walter Lincoln Sanborn,
    14 Strathmore Road, Brookline, Mass.

Louis Peck Sanders,
    Butte, Mont.

Frank Charles Schrader,
    United States Geological Survey, Washington, D. C.

Carl Lincoln Schurz,
    15 Park Row, New York City.

Walter Judd Scott,
    Care of Daily Silver Belt, Miami, Ariz.

Harold Ingalls Sewall,
    Naguabo, Porto Rico.

Charles Grant Shaffer,
    Eliot School, Newark, N. J.

Thomas Hall Shastid,
    1920 John Ave., Superior, Wis.

Edgar Dwight Shaw,
    Care of The Boston Advertiser, Boston, Mass.

Hubert Grover Shaw,
    Chemical Laboratory, Asheville University, Asheville,
    N. C.

George Lawson Sheldon,
    Wayside, Miss.

Howard Cocks Sherwood,
    34 Pine St., New York, N. Y.

Frank Palmer Sibley,
    Boston Globe, Boston, Mass.

Burnett Newell Simpson,
    414 R. A. Long Building, Kansas City, Mo.

Francis Hinckley Sisson,
    70 Undercliff St., Yonkers, N. Y.

Conrad Hensler Slade,
    159 bis Boulevard Montparnasse, Paris, France.

Herbert Brush Smith,
    337 West Thirty-fourth St., New York City.

Howard Caswell Smith,
    45 Wall St., New York City.

Robert Keating Smith,
    Tekoa Terrace, Westfield, Mass.

Wayne Prescott Smith,
    1016 United States National Bank Building, United
    States Veterans' Bureau, Denver, Colo. (temporary).

Townsend Hodges Soren,
    Post Office Box 1329, Hartford, Conn.

Frank Enos Soule,
    99 Portland St., Boston, Mass.

Horace Claflin Southwick,
    Harvard Club, New York City.

Fred Maurice Spalding,
    128 Newbury St., Boston, Mass.

Hartwell Ballou Spaulding,
    383 Washington St., Boston, Mass.

John Francis Cyril Spencer-Turner.
    Care of Sebasti & Co., bankers, 20 Piazza da Spagna,
    Rome, Italy.

Josiah Edward Spurr,
    7 Edgewood Park, New Rochelle, N. Y.

Francis Upham Stearns,
    Care of Renfrew Manufacturing Co., Adams, Mass.

Wallace Nelson Stearns,
    Jacksonville, Ill.

Joseph Henry Steinhart,
    Post Office Box 1070, Havana, Cuba.

Francis Eliot Stetson,
    South Dartmouth, Mass.

Ralph Leslie Stevens,
    86 Worth St., New York City.

Henry Harding Stickney,
    19 Fairmont St., Belmont, Mass.

Arthur Parker Stone,
> 613 Pleasant St., Belmont, Mass.

Willis Whittemore Stover,
> Room 548, 18 Tremont St., Boston, Mass.

Jesse Isidor Straus,
> Care of R. H. Macy & Co., Inc., Herald Square, New York City.

Lionel Alexander Burnet Street,
> Pacific Mutual Building, Suite 1023, Los Angeles, Cal.

William James Henry Strong,
> 641 Church St., Beloit, Wis.

Frank Raymond Stubbs,
> 510 Centre St., Newton, Mass.

Thomas Henry Sylvester,
> Care of State Hospital Commission, Flatiron Building, 18th floor, Broadway, Twenty-third St., and Fifth Ave., New York City.

Frederick Joseph Taussig,
> 4506 Maryland Ave., St. Louis, Mo.

John Clarence Taussig,
> 4 N. Kingshighway, St. Louis, Mo.

William Osgood Taylor,
> 242 Washington St., Boston, Mass.

Harry Lorenzo Teetzel,
> 1718 Cedar St., Milwaukee, Wis.

Derrick Anthony TePaske,
> Sioux Center, Iowa.

Louis Bartlett Thacher,
> 131 State St., Boston, Mass.

Rufus Kemble Thomas,
> Care of Somerset Club, Beacon St., Boston, Mass.

William Leland Thompson,
> 161 River St., Troy, N. Y.

Frederick Charles Thwaits,
    405 Iron Block, Milwaukee, Wis.

Archibald Read Tisdale,
    100 Chestnut St., Boston, Mass.

Howe Totten,
    700 9th St. N. W., Washington, D. C.

Edward Sands Townsend,
    2 Park Sq., Boston.

Frederick Townsend,
    Care of Albany Savings Bank, Albany, N. Y.

Willis Merrick Townsend, M. D.,
    556 Franklin St., Melrose Highlands, Mass.

Bernard Walton Trafford,
    Care of First National Bank, 70 Federal St., Boston.

Lyman Tremain,
    R. F. D. No. 3, Anaheim, California.

Philip Edmund Tripp,
    10 Fenner St., Fall River, Mass.

Joshua Damon Upton,
    53 State St., Boston, Mass.

Thomas Wayland Vaughan,
    U. S. Geological Survey, Washington, D. C.

Enoch Howard Vickers,
    748 University Terrace, Morgantown, West Va.

Oswald Garrison Villard,
    20 Vesey St., New York.

Bernard William Vogel,
    39 5th Ave., New York City.

George Walcott,
    58 Worth St., New York, N. Y.

Julian Constantine Walker,
    Wilmington, Del.

Alfred Wallerstein,
    70 W. 40th St., New York City.

Henry Ware,
    82 High St., Brookline, Mass.

Edgar Haga Warner,
    301 Lincoln Ave., Cadiz, Ohio.

Oscar Leon Watkins,
    2415 North Pennsylvania St., Indianapolis, Ind.

Frank Milton Watters,
    Foamite-Childs Co., Utica. N. Y.

Lorenzo Webber,
    Portland, Mich.

Joseph Rowe Webster,
    1352 Massachusetts Ave., Cambridge, Mass.

Kenneth Grant Tremayne Webster,
    Gerry's Landing, Cambridge, Mass.

Edward Motley Weld,
    82 Beaver St., New York City.

Leonard Abel Wheeler,
    Troy, Ohio.

George Albert Whipple,
    2020 Orrington Ave., Evanston, Illinois.

Herbert Hill White,
    University Press, Cambridge 38, Mass.

Edward Dwight Whitford,
    Harvard Trust Company, Cambridge, Mass.

James Raynor Whiting,
    66 Garden St., Poughkeepsie, New York.

Charles Edward Whitmore,
    55 West 44th St., New York City.

Joseph Wiggin,
    27 State St., Boston, Mass.

James Austin Wilder,
New York Yacht Club, New York City.

Charles Edwin Williams,
11 Crest Rd., Ridgewood, New Jersey.

George Perry Wilson,
Catania, Italy.   Care of American Consulate.

George Parker Winship,
Charles River, Mass.

Charles Gibson Winslow,
310 Marlboro St., Boston.

Frederick Winsor,
Middlesex School, Concord, Mass.

Samuel Lee Wolff,
90 Morningside Drive, New York City.

Arthur Mayer Wolfson,
Hartmann Trunk Co., Racine, Wis.

Ernest Henry Wood,
88 Pleasant St., Worcester, Mass.

Ralph Woodworth,
Weston, Massachusetts.

Arthur Rufus Trego Wylie,
Grafton, North Dakota.

Charles Lowell Young,
Wellesley College, Wellesley, Mass.

Frank Lester Young,
110 State St., Boston, Mass.

Lightning Source UK Ltd.
Milton Keynes UK
UKHW020754081118
331957UK00010B/1183/P